FY-96

1/24/016
124/014

270
DEI

Deissmann, Adolf
Bible studies

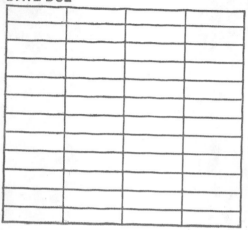

124014

DEMCO

D0926718

BIBLE STUDIES

BIBLE STUDIES

CONTRIBUTIONS
CHIEFLY FROM PAPYRI AND INSCRIPTIONS
TO THE HISTORY OF
THE LANGUAGE, THE LITERATURE, AND THE RELIGION
OF HELLENISTIC JUDAISM AND PRIMITIVE CHRISTIANITY

BY

Dr. G. ADOLF DEISSMANN

TRANSLATED BY

ALEXANDER GRIEVE, M.A., D. Phil.

PEABODY, MASSACHUSETTS 01961-3473

BIBLE STUDIES

Hendrickson Publishers, Inc. edition

ISBN: 0-943575-08-7

reprinted from the edition
originally published by T. & T. Clark, Edinburgh, 1901

First printing — November 1988

Printed in the United States of America

CONTENTS.

AUTHOR'S PREFACE TO THE ENGLISH EDITION.

Having been honoured by a request to sanction an English translation of my *Bibelstudien* and *Neue Bibelstudien*, I have felt it my duty to accede to the proposal. It seems to me that investigations based upon Papyri and Inscriptions are specially calculated to be received with interest by English readers.

For one thing, the richest treasures from the domain of Papyri and Inscriptions are deposited in English museums and libraries ; for another, English investigators take premier rank among the discoverers and editors of Inscriptions, but particularly of Papyri ; while, again, it was English scholarship which took the lead in utilising the Inscriptions in the sphere of biblical research. Further, in regard to the Greek Old Testament in particular, for the investigation of which the Inscriptions and Papyri yield valuable material (of which only the most inconsiderable part has been utilised in the following pages), English theologians have of late done exceedingly valuable and memorable work. In confirmation of all this I need only recall the names of F. Field, B. P. Grenfell, E. Hatch, E. L. Hicks, A. S. Hunt, F. G. Kenyon, J. P. Mahaffy, W. R. Paton, W. M. Ramsay, H. A. Redpath, H. B. Swete, and others hardly less notable.

Since the years 1895 and 1897, in which respec-

tively the German *Bibelstudien* and *Neue Bibelstudien*
were published, there has been a vast increase of
available material, which, again, has been much more
accessible to me as a Professor in the University
of Heidelberg than it was during my residence at
Herborn. I have so far availed myself of portions
of the more recent discoveries in this English edition;
but what remains for scholars interested in such
investigations is hardly less than enormous, and is
being augmented year by year. I shall be greatly
pleased if yet more students set themselves seriously
to labour in this field of biblical research.

In the English edition not a few additional
changes have been made; I must, however, reserve
further items for future *Studies.* With regard to the
entries κυριακός (p. 217 ff.), and especially ἱλαστήριον
(p. 124 ff.), I should like to make express reference
to the articles *Lord's Day* and *Mercy Seat* to be
contributed by me to the *Encyclopœdia Biblica.*

Finally, I must record my heartiest thanks to
my translator, Rev. Alexander Grieve, M.A., D. Phil.,
Forfar, for his work. With his name I gratefully
associate the words which once on a time the translator of the *Wisdom of Jesus Sirach* applied with
ingenuous complacency to himself: πολλὴν ἀγρυπνίαν
καὶ ἐπιστήμην προσενεγκάμενος.

ADOLF DEISSMANN.

HEIDELBERG,
27*th December,* 1900.

FROM THE PREFACE TO THE GERMAN EDITION.

Bible Studies is the name I have chosen for the following investigations, since all of them are more or less concerned with the historical questions which the Bible, and specially the Greek version, raises for scientific treatment. I am not, of course, of the opinion that there is a special biblical science. Science is method : the special sciences are distinguished from each other as methods. What is designated " Biblical Science " were more fitly named " Biblical Research ". The science in question here is the same whether it is engaged with Plato, or with the Seventy Interpreters and the Gospels. Thus much should be self-evident.

A well-disposed friend who understands something of literary matters tells me that it is hardly fitting that a younger man should publish a volume of " Studies " : that is rather the part of the experienced scholar in the sunny autumn of life. To this advice I have given serious consideration, but I am still of the opinion that the hewing of stones is very properly the work of the journeyman. And in the department where I have laboured, many a block must yet be trimmed before the erection of the edifice can be thought of. But how much still remains to do, before the language of the Septuagint, the relation

to it of the so-called New Testament Greek, the
history of the religious and ethical conceptions of
Hellenic Judaism, have become clear even in outline
only; or before it has been made manifest that the
religious movement by which we date our era originated and was developed in history—that is, in connection with, or, it may be, in opposition to, an already-
existent high state of culture! If the following pages
speak much about the Septuagint, let it be remembered that in general that book is elsewhere much
too little spoken of, certainly much less than was the
case a hundred years ago. We inveigh against the
Rationalists—often in a manner that raises the suspicion that we have a mistrust of Reason. Yet these
men, inveighed against as they are, in many respects
set wider bounds to their work than do their critics.
During my three years' work in the *Seminarium
Philippinum* at Marburg, I have often enough been
forced to think of the plan of study in accordance
with which the bursars used to work about the
middle of last century. Listen to a report of the
matter such as the following :—[1]

" With regard to Greek the legislator has laid
particular stress upon the relation in which this
language stands to a true understanding of the N.T.
How reasonable, therefore, will those who can judge
find the recommendation that the Septuagint (which,

---

[1] *Cf.* the programme (of the superintendent) Dr. Carl Wilhelm Robert:
. . . announces that the Literary Association . . . shall be duly opened . . .
on the 27th inst. . . . [Marburg] Müller's Erben und Weldige, 1772, p. 13.
That the superintendent had still an eye for the requirements of practical
life is shown by his remarks elsewhere. For example, on page 7 f., he good-
naturedly asserts that he has carried out "in the most conscientious manner"
the order that "the bursars shall be supplied with sufficient well-prepared
food and wholesome and unadulterated beer". The programme affords a fine
glimpse into the academic life of the Marburg of a past time.

on the authority of an Ernesti and a Michaelis, is of the first importance as a means towards the proper understanding of the N.T.), has been fixed upon as a manual upon which these lectures must be given! And how much is it to be wished that the bursars, during the year of their study of this book, should go through such a considerable part of the same as may be necessary to realise the purposes of the legislator ! "

I am not bold enough to specify the time when academical lectures and exercises upon the Septuagint will again be given in Germany.[1]   But the coming century is long, and the mechanical conception of science is but the humour of a day ! . . .

I wrote the book, not as a clergyman, but as a Privatdocent at Marburg, but I rejoice that I am able, as a clergyman, to publish it.

G. ADOLF DEISSMANN.

HERBORN : DEPARTMENT OF WIESBADEN,
    7th March, 1895.

[1] 1. Additional note, 1899: Professor Dr. Johannes Weiss of Marburg has announced a course upon the Greek Psalter for the Summer Session, 1899 ; the author lectured on the Language of the Greek Bible in Heidelberg in the Winter Session of 1897-98.

TRANSLATOR'S NOTE.

In addition to the supplementary matter specially contributed to the present edition by the Author, the translation shows considerable alterations in other respects. Not only has the smaller and later volume, *Neue Bibelstudien*, 1897, found a place in the body of the book, but the order of the Articles has been all but completely changed. It has not been thought necessary to furnish the translation with an index of Papyri, etc., more especially as the larger *Bibelstudien* had none; but there has been added an index of Scripture texts, which seemed on the whole more likely to be of service to English readers in general. The translator has inserted a very few notes, mainly concerned with matters of translation.

For the convenience of those who may wish to consult the original on any point, the paging of the German edition has been given in square brackets, the page-numbers of the *Neue Bibelstudien* being distinguished by an N. In explanation of the fact that some of the works cited are more fully described towards the end of the book, and more briefly in the earlier pages, it should perhaps be said that a large portion of the translation was in type, and had been revised, before the alteration in the order of the Articles had been decided upon.

The translator would take this opportunity of

expressing his most cordial thanks to Professor Deissmann, who has taken the most active interest in the preparation of the translation, and whose painstaking revision of the proofs has been of the highest service. A word of thanks is also due to the printers, The Aberdeen University Press Limited, for the remarkable accuracy and skill which they have uniformly shown in the manipulation of what was often complicated and intricate material.

ALEXANDER GRIEVE.

FORFAR,
21st January, 1901.

THE PRINCIPAL ABBREVIATIONS.

AAB. = Abhandlungen der Königlichen Akademie der Wissenschaften zu Berlin.

Benndorf u. Niemann, see p. 157, note 1.

BU. = Aegyptische Urkunden aus den Koeniglichen Museen zu Berlin, Berlin, 1892 ff.

CIA. = Corpus Inscriptionum Atticarum.

CIG. = Corpus Inscriptionum Graecarum.

CIL. = Corpus Inscriptionum Latinarum.

Clavis[3], see p. 88, note 5.

Cremer, see p. 290, note 2.

DAW. = Denkschriften der K. K. Akademie der Wissenschaften zu Wien.

Dieterich (A.), see p. 322, note 8.

Dittenberger, see p. 93, note 2.

DLZ. = Deutsche Literaturzeitung.

Fick-Bechtel, see p. 310, note 4.

Field, see p. 284, note 2.

Fleck. *Jbb.* = Fleckeisen's Jahrbücher.

Fränkel, see p. 84, note 2.

GGA. = Göttingische gelehrte Anzeigen.

HApAT. = Kurzgefasstes exegetisches Handbuch zu den Apocryphen des A.T., 6 Bde., Leipzig, 1851-60.

Hamburger, see p. 271, note.

HC. = Hand-Commentar zum N.T.

Hercher, see p. 4, note 1.

Humann u. Puchstein, see p. 309, note 1.

IGrSI., see p. 200, note 1.

IMAe., see p. 178, note 5.

Kennedy, see p. 213, note 1.

Kenyon, see p. 323, note 1.

Lebas, see Waddington.

Leemans, see p. 322, note 6.

Letronne, Recherches, see p. 98, note 3.

— Recueil, see p. 101, note 6.

Lumbroso, Recherches, see p. 98, note 2.

Mahaffy, see p. 336, note 1.

Meisterhans, see p. 124, note 1.

Meyer = H. A. W. Meyer, Kritisch exegetischer Kommentar über das N.T.

Notices, xviii. 2, see p. 283, note 3.

Parthey, see p. 322, note 5.

Paton and Hicks, see p. 131, note 1.

PER., see p. 179, note 2.

Perg., see p. 178, note 4.

Peyron (A.), see p. 88, note 1.

R-E[2] = Real-Encyclopädie für protest. Theologie und Kirche von Herzog, 2. Aufl., Leipzig, 1877 ff.

Schleusner = J. F., Novus Thesaurus philologico-criticus sive lexicon in LXX et reliquos interpretes graecos ac scriptores apocryphos V. T., 5 voll., Lipsiae, 1820-21.

Schmid (W.), see p. 64, note 2.

Schmidt (Guil.), see p. 291, note 1.

Schürer, see p. 335, note 2.

Swete = The Old Testament in Greek according to the Septuagint, edited by H. B. Swete, 3 voll., Cambridge, 1887-94.

Thesaurus = H. Stephanus, Thesaurus Graecae Linguae, edd. Hase, etc., Paris, 1831-65.

Thayer, see p. 176, note 3.

ThLZ. = Theologische Literaturzeitung.

Tromm. = Abrahami Trommii concordantiae graecae versionis vulgo dictae LXX interpretum . . ., 2 tomi, Amstelodami et Trajecti ad Rhenum, 1718.

TU. = Texte und Untersuchungen zur Geschichte der altchristlichen Literatur.

Waddington, see p. 93, note 1.

Wessely, see p. 322, note 7.

Wetstein, see p. 350, note 1.

Winer[7], or Winer-Lünemann = G. B. Winer, Grammatik des neutestamentlichen Sprachidioms, 7 Aufl. von G. Lünemann, Leipzig, 1867. [9th English edition, by W. F. Moulton, Edinburgh, 1882 = 6th German edition.]

Winer-Schmiedel = the same work, 8th Aufl. neu bearbeitet von P. W. Schmiedel, Göttingen, 1894 ff.

ZAW. = Zeitschrift für die alttestamentliche Wissenschaft.

ZKG. = Zeitschrift für Kirchengeschichte.

I.

PROLEGOMENA TO THE BIBLICAL LETTERS
AND EPISTLES.

γίνεσϑε δόκιμοι τραπεζῖται.

PROLEGOMENA TO THE BIBLICAL LETTERS AND EPISTLES.

I.

1. Men have written letters ever since they could write at all. Who the first letter-writer was we know not.[1] But this is quite as it should be: the writer of a letter accommodates himself to the need of the moment; his aim is a personal one and concerns none but himself,—least of all the curiosity of posterity. We fortunately know quite as little who was the first to experience repentance or to offer prayer. The writer of a letter does not sit in the market-place. A letter is a secret and the writer wishes his secret to be preserved; under cover and seal he entrusts it to the reticence of the messenger. The letter, in its essential idea, does not differ in any way from a private conversation; like the latter, it is a personal and intimate communication, and the more faithfully it catches the tone of the private conversation, the more of a letter, that is, the better a letter, it is. The only difference is the means of communication. We avail ourselves of far-travelling handwriting, because

---

[1] It appears sufficiently naïve that Tatian (*Or. ad Graec.*, p. 1 ʟɪ *t.*, Schwartz) and Clement of Alexandria (*Strom.* i. 16, p. 364, Potter) should say, following the historian Hellanikos, that the Persian queen Atossa (6th-5th cent. B.C.) was the discoverer of *letter-writing*. For it is in this sense that we should understand the expression that occurs in both, *viz.*, ἐπιστολὰς συντάσσειν, and not as *collecting letters together and publishing them*, which R. Bentley (Dr. Rich. Bentley's *Dissertation on the Epistles of Phalaris*, London, 1699, p. 535 f., German edition by W. Ribbeck, Leipzig, 1857, p. 532) considers to be also possible; *cf.* M. Kremmer, *De catalogis heurematum*, Leipzig, 1890, p. 15.

our voice cannot carry to our friend: the pen is employed because the separation by distance does not permit a *tête-à-tête*.[1] A letter is destined for the receiver only, not for the public eye, and even when it is intended for more than one, yet with the public it will have nothing to do: letters to parents and brothers and sisters, to comrades in joy or sorrow or sentiment—these, too, are private letters, true letters. As little as the words of the dying father to his children are a *speech*—should they be a *speech* it would be better for the dying to keep silent—just as little is the letter of a sage to his confidential pupils an *essay*, a literary production; and, if the pupils have learned wisdom, they will not place it among their books, but lay it devoutly beside the picture and the other treasured relics of their master. The form and external appearance of the letter are matters of indifference in the determination of its essential character. Whether it be written on stone or clay, on papyrus or parchment, on wax or palm-leaf, on rose paper or a foreign postcard, is quite as immaterial[2] as whether it clothes itself in the set phrases of the age; whether it be written skilfully or unskilfully, by a prophet or by a beggar, does not alter its special characteristics in the least. Nor do the particular contents belong to the essence of it. What is alone essential is the purpose which it serves: confidential personal conversation between persons separated by distance. The one wishes to ask something of the other, wishes to praise or warn or wound the other, to thank him or assure him of sympathy in joy—it is ever something personal that forces the pen into the hand of the letter-writer.[3] He who writes a letter under the impression that

---

[1] [Pseudo-] Diogenes, *ep.* 3 (*Epistolographi Graeci, rec.* R. Hercher, *Parisiis*, 1873, p. 235).—Demetr., *de elocut.*, 223 f. (Hercher, p. 13).—[Pseudo-] Proclus, *de forma epistolari* (Hercher, p. 6).

[2] *Cf.* Th. Birt, *Das antike Buchwesen in seinem Verhältniss zur Litteratur*, Berlin, 1882, top of p. 2.—It is most singular that Pliny (*Hist. Nat.*, xiii. 13), and, after him, Bentley (p. 538 f.; German edition by Ribbeck, p. 532 f.), deny that the letters on wax-tablets mentioned by Homer are *letters*.

[3] Demetr., *de elocut.*, 231 (Hercher, p. 14).

his lines may be read by strangers, will either coquet with
this possibility, or be frightened by it; in the former case
he will be vain, in the latter, reserved;[1] in both cases unnatural—no true letter-writer.   With the personal aim of
the letter there must necessarily be joined the naturalness
of the writer's mood; one owes it not only to himself
and to the other, but still more to the letter as such,
that he yield himself freely to it.   So must the letter,
even the shortest and the poorest, present a fragment

---

[1] Cic., *Fam.* 15,21 4, *aliter enim scribimus quod eos solos quibus mittimus,
aliter quod multos lecturos putamus.* Cic., *Phil.* 2,7, *quam multa ioca solent
esse in epistulis quae prolata si sint inepta videantur ! quam multa seria neque
tamen ullo modo divolganda !*—Johann Kepler wrote a letter to Reimarus
Ursus, of which the latter then made a great parade in a manner painful
to Kepler and Tycho Brahe.   Having got a warning by this, Kepler determined that for the future: "scribam caute, retinebo exemplaria".
(*Joannis Kepleri astronomi opera omnia,* ed. Ch. Frisch, i. [Frankfurt and
Erlangen, 1858], p. 284; *cf.* C. Anschütz, *Ungedruckte wissenschaftliche Correspondenz zwischen Johann Kepler und Herwart von Hohenburg,* 1599,
Prague, 1886, p. 91 f.—The Palatinate physician-in-ordinary Helisäus Rös-
linus († 1616) says about one of his letters which had been printed without
his knowledge : "I wrote it the day immediately following that on which I
first beheld with astonishment the new star—on the evening of Tuesday, the
2/12 October ; I communicated the same at once in haste to a good friend in
Strassburg. . . . . This letter (6 *paginarum*) was subsequently printed without
my knowledge or desire, which in itself did not concern me—only had I
known beforehand, I should have arranged it somewhat better and expressed myself more distinctly than I did while engaged in the writing of
it " (*Joannis Kepleri opp. omn.,* i., p. 666).   Moltke to his wife, 3rd July,
1864 : " I have in the above given you a portrayal of the seizure of Alsen,
which embodies no official report, but simply the observations of an eye-
witness, which always add freshness to description.   If you think it would
be of interest to others as well, I have no objection to copies being taken
of it in which certain personal matters will be left out, and myself not
mentioned : Auer will put the matter right for you " (*Gesammelte Schriften
und Denkwürdigkeiten des General-Feldmarschalls Grafen Helmuth von
Moltke,* vi. [Berlin, 1892], p. 408 f.).   One notices, however, in this "letter,"
that it was written under the impression that copies of it might be
made.   Compare also the similar sentiment (in the matter of diary-notes,
which are essentially akin to letters) of K. von Hase, of the year 1877:
" It may be that my knowledge that these soliloquies will soon fall into
other hands detracts from their naturalness.   Still they will be the
hands of kind and cherished persons, and so may the thought of it
be but a quickly passing shadow ! " (*Annalen meines Lebens,* Leipzig, 1891,
p. 271).

of human naïvete—beautiful or trivial, but, in any case, true.[1]

2. The letter is older than literature. As conversation between two persons is older than the dialogue, the song older than the poem, so also does the history of the letter reach back to that Golden Age when there was neither author nor publisher, nor any reviewer. Literature is that species of writing which is designed for publicity: the maker of literature desires that others will take heed to his work. He desires to be read. He does not appeal to his friend, nor does he write to his mother; he entrusts his sheets to the winds, and knows not whither they will be borne; he only knows that they will be picked up and examined by some one or other unknown to him and unabashed before him. Literature, in the truest essence of it, differs in no way from a public speech; equally with the latter it falls short in the matter of intimacy, and the more it attains to the character of universality, the more literary, that is to say, the more interesting it is. All the difference between them is in the mode of delivery. Should one desire to address, not the assembled clan or congregation, but the great foolish public, then he takes care that what he has to say may be carried home in writing by any one who wishes to have it so: the *book* is substituted for oral communication. And even if the *book* be dedicated to a friend or friends, still its dedication does not divest it of its literary character,—it does not thereby become a private piece of writing. The form and external appearance of the *book* are immaterial for the true understanding of its special character as a *book*: even its contents, whatever they be, do not matter. Whether the author sends forth poems, tragedies or histories, sermons or wearisome scientific lucubrations, political matter or anything else in the world; whether his *book* is multiplied by the slaves of an Alexandrian bookseller, by patient monk or impatient compositor; whether it is preserved in libraries as sheet, or roll, or folio: all these are as

[1] Demetr., *de elocut.*, 227 (Hercher, p. 13). Greg. Naz., *ad Nicobulum* (Hercher, p. 16).

much matter of indifference as whether it is good or bad, or whether it finds purchasers or not. *Book, literature,* in the widest sense, is every written work designed by its author for the public.[1]

3. The *book* is younger than the letter. Even were the oldest letters that have come down to us younger than the earliest extant works of literature, that statement would still be true. For it is one which does not need the confirmation of historical facts—nay, it would be foolish to attempt to give such. The letter is perishable—in its very nature necessarily so; it is perishable, like the hand that wrote it, like the eyes that were to read it. The letter-writer works as little for posterity as for the public of his own time;[2] just as the true letter cannot be written over again, it exists in but a single copy. It is only the *book* that is multiplied and thus rendered accessible to the public, accessible, possibly, to posterity. Fortunately we possess letters that are old, extremely old, but we shall never gain a sight of the oldest of them all; it was a letter, and was able to guard itself and its secret. Among all nations, before the age of literature, there were the days when people wrote, indeed, but did not yet write *books.*[3] In the same way people prayed, of course, and probably prayed better, long before there were any service-books; and they had come near to God before they wrote down the proofs of His existence. The letter, should we ask about the essential character of it, carries us into the sacred solitude of simple, unaffected humanity; when we ask about its history, it directs us to the childhood's years of the pre-literary man, when there was no *book* to trouble him.

---

[1] Birt, *Buchwesen,* p. 2: "Similarly the point of separation between a private writing and a literary work was the moment when [in antiquity] an author delivered his manuscript to his own slaves or to those of a contractor in order that copies of it might be produced".

[2] A. Stahr, *Aristotelia,* i., Halle, 1830, p. 192 f.

[3] Wellhausen, *Israelitische und Jüdische Geschichte,* p. 58: "Already in early times writing was practised, but in documents and contracts only; also letters when the contents of the message were not for the light of day or when, for other reasons, they required to be kept secret". Hebrew literature blossomed forth only later.

4. When the friend has for ever parted from his comrades, the master from his disciples, then the bereaved bethink themselves, with sorrowful reverence, of all that the departed one was to them. The old pages, which the beloved one delivered to them in some blessed hour, speak to them with a more than persuasive force ; they are read and re-read, they are exchanged one for another, copies are taken of letters in the possession of friends, the precious fragments are collected : perhaps it is decided that the collection be multiplied—among the great unknown public there may be some unknown one who is longing for the same stimulus which the bereaved themselves have received. And thus it happens now and then that, from motives of reverent love, the letters of the great are divested of their confidential character: they are *formed* into literature, the *letters* subsequently become a *book*. When, by the Euphrates or the Nile, preserved in the ruins of some fallen civilisation, we find letters the age of which can only be computed by centuries and millenniums, the science of our fortunate day rejoices ; she hands over the venerable relics to a grateful public in a new garb, and so, in our own books and in our own languages, we read the reports which the Palestinian vassals had to make to Pharaoh upon their tablets of clay, long before there was any Old Testament or any People of Israel; we learn the sufferings and the longings of Egyptian monks from shreds of papyrus which are as old as the book of the Seventy Interpreters. Thus it is the science of to-day that has stripped these private communications of a hoary past of their most peculiar characteristic, and which has at length transformed letters, true letters, into literature. As little, however, as some unknown man, living in the times of Imperial Rome, put the toy into the grave of his child in order that it should sometime be discovered and placed in a museum, just as little are the private letters which have at length been transformed into literature by publication, to be, on that account, thought of as literature. Letters remain letters whether oblivion hides them with its protecting veil, or whether now

reverence, now science, or, again, reverence and science in friendly conspiracy, think it well to withhold the secret no longer from the reverent or the eager seeker after truth. What the editor, in publishing such letters, takes from them, the readers, if they can do anything more than spell, must restore by recognising, in true historical perspective, their simple and unaffected beauty.

5. When for the first time a *book* was compiled from letters,—it would be reverential love, rather than science, that made the beginning here—the age of literature had, of course, dawned long ago, and had long ago constructed the various literary forms with which it worked. That book, the first to be compiled from real letters, added another to the already existent forms. One would, of course, hardly venture to say that it forthwith added the literary letter, the *epistle*,[1] to the forms of published literature; the said book only gave, against its will, so to speak, the impetus to the development of this new literary *eidos*.[2] The present writer cannot imagine that the composition and publication of literary treatises in the form of letters was anterior to the compilation of a book from actual letters. So soon, however, as such a book existed, the charming novelty of it invited to imitation. Had the invitation been rightly understood, the only inducement that should have been felt was to publish the letters of other venerable men, and, in point of fact, the invitation was not seldom understood in this its true sense. From almost every age we have received such collections of " genuine," "real" letters—priceless jewels for the historian of the human spirit. But the literary man is frequently more of a literary machine than a true man, and thus, when the

---

[1] In the following pages the literary letter [*Litteraturbrief*] will continue to be so named: the author considers that the borrowed word appropriately expresses the technical sense.

[2] F. Susemihl, *Geschichte der griechischen Litteratur in der Alexandrinerzeit*, ii., Leipzig, 1892, p. 579: "It may well be that the first impulse to this branch of authorship was given by the early collecting together, in the individual schools of philosophy, such as the Epicurean, of the genuine correspondence of their founders and oldest members ".

first collection of letters appeared, it was the literary, rather
than the human, interest of it which impressed him; the
accidental and external, rather than the inscrutably strange
inmost essence of it. Instead of rejoicing that his pur-
blind eye might here catch a glimpse of a great human
soul, he resolved to write a volume of letters on his own
part. He knew not what he did, and had no feeling that
he was attempting anything unusual;[1] he did not see that,
by his *literary* purpose, he was himself destroying the very
possibility of its realisation; for letters are experiences,
and experiences cannot be manufactured. The father of
the epistle was no great pioneer spirit, but a mere para-
graphist, a mere mechanic. But perhaps he had once
heard a pastoral song among the hills, and afterwards at
home set himself down to make another of the same: the
wondering applause of his crowd of admirers confirmed him
in the idea that he had succeeded. If then he had achieved
his aim in the matter of a song, why should he not do the
same with letters? And so he set himself down and made
them. But the prototype, thus degraded to a mere pattern,
mistrustfully refused to show its true face, not to speak of
its heart, to this pale and suspicious-looking companion,
and the result was that the epistle could learn no more
from the letter than a little of its external form. If the
true letter might be compared to a prayer, the epistle which
mimicked it was only a babbling; if there beamed forth
in the letter the wondrous face of a child, the epistle grinned
stiffly and stupidly, like a puppet.

But the puppet pleased; its makers knew how to bring
it to perfection, and to give it more of a human appearance.
Indeed, it happened now and then that a real artist occupied
an idle hour in the fashioning of such an object. This, of
course, turned out better than most others of a similar kind,

---

[1] *Cf.* von Wilamowitz-Moellendorff, *Aristoteles und Athen,* ii., Berlin,
1893, p. 392: "He [Isocrates] did not understand that the letter, as a confidential and spontaneous utterance, is well written only when it is written
for reading, not hearing, when it is distinguished from the set oration κατ
εἶδος ". This judgment applies also to real, genuine letters by Isocrates.

and was more pleasant to look at than an ugly child for
instance; in any case it could not disturb one by its noise.
A good epistle, in fact, gives one more pleasure than a
worthless letter, and in no literature is there any lack of
good epistles.   They often resemble letters so much that a
reader permits himself for the moment to be willingly deceived
as to their actual character.   But letters they are not, and
the more strenuously they try to be letters, the more vividly
do they reveal that they are not.[1] Even the grapes of
Zeuxis could deceive only the sparrows; one even suspects
that they were no true sparrows, but cage-birds rather, which
had lost their real nature along with their freedom and
pertness; our Rhine-land sparrows would not have left their
vineyards for anything of the kind.   Those of the epistle-
writers who were artists were themselves most fully aware
that in their epistles they worked at best artificially,
and, in fact, had to do so.   "The editor requests that the
readers of this book will not forget the title of it: it is only
a book of letters, letters merely relating to the study of
theology.   In letters one does not look for treatises, still less
for treatises in rigid uniformity and proportion of parts.
As material offers itself and varies, as conversation comes
and goes, often as personal inclinations or incidental occur-
rences determine and direct, so do the letters wind about
and flow on; and I am greatly in error if it be not this
thread of living continuity, this capriciousness of origin and
circumstances, that realises the result which we desiderate
on the written page, but which, of course, subsequently disappears in the printing.   Nor can I conceal the fact that
these letters, as now printed, are wanting just in what
is perhaps most instructive, viz., the more exact criticism of
particular works.   There was, however, no other way of
doing it, and I am still uncertain whether the following
letters, in which the materials grow always the more special,

---

[1] Von Wilamowitz-Moellendorff, *Antigonos von Karystos* (*Philologische
Untersuchungen*, iv.), Berlin, 1881, p. 151, says, "Such letters as are actually
written with a view to publication are essentially different in character from
private correspondence ".

the more important, the more personal, are fit for printing at
all. The public voice of the market-place and the confidential
one of private correspondence are, and always continue to
be, very different." Herder,[1] in these words, which are a
classical description of the true idea of a letter, claims that
his book has, in fact, the character of actual letters, but is
nevertheless quite well aware that a printed (that is, according to the context, a literary) letter is essentially different
from a letter that is actually such.

It is easy to understand how the epistle became a
favourite form of published literature in almost all literary
nations. There could hardly be a more convenient form.
The extraordinary convenience of it lay in the fact that
it was, properly speaking, so altogether "unliterary," that,
in fact, it did not deserve to be called a "form" at all.
One needed but to label an address on any piece of tittle-
tattle, and lo! one had achieved what else could have been
accomplished only by a conscientious adherence to the strict
rules of artistic form. Neither as to expression nor contents
does the epistle make any higher pretensions. The writer
could, in the matter of style, write as he pleased, and the
address on the letter became a protective mark for thoughts
that would have been too silly for a poem, and too paltry
for an essay. The epistle, if we disregard the affixed
address, need be no more than, say a *feuilleton* or a *causerie*.
The zenith of epistolography may always be looked upon as
assuredly indicating the decline of literature; literature becomes decadent—Alexandrian, so to speak—and although
epistles may have been composed and published by great
creative spirits, still the derivative character of the movement cannot be questioned: even the great will want to
gossip, to lounge, to take it easy for once. *Their* epistles
may be good, but the epistle in general, as a literary phenomenon, is light ware indeed.

6. Of collections of letters, bearing the name of well-
known poets and philosophers, we have, indeed, a great

---

[1] *Briefe, das Studium der Theologie betreffend*, Third Part, Frankfurt
and Leipzig, 1790, Preface to the first edition, pp. i.-iii.

profusion. Many of them are not "genuine"; they were composed and given to the world by others under the protection of a great name.[1] A timid ignorance, having no true notion of literary usages, inconsiderately stigmatises one and all of these with the ethical term *forgery;* it fondly imagines that everything in the world can be brought between the two poles *moral* and *immoral,* and overlooks the fact that the endless being and becoming of things is generally realised according to non-ethical laws, and needs to be judged as an ethical *adiaphoron.* He who tremulously supposes that questions of genuineness in the history of literature are, as such, problems of the struggle between truth and falsehood, ought also to have the brutal courage to describe all literature as forgery. The literary man, as compared with the non-literary, is always a person under constraint; he does not draw from the sphere of prosaic circumstance about him, but places himself under the dominion of the ideal, about which no one knows better than himself that it never was, and never will be, real. The literary man, with every stroke of his pen, removes himself farther from trivial actuality, just because he wishes to alter it, to ennoble or annihilate it, just because he can never acknowledge it as it is. As a man he feels indeed that he is sold under the domain of the wretched "object". He knows that when he writes upon the laws of the cosmos, he is naught but a foolish boy gathering shells by the shore of the ocean; he enriches the literature of his nation

---

[1] The origin of spurious collections of letters among the Greeks is traced back to "the exercises in style of the Athenian schools of rhetoric in the earlier and earliest Hellenistic period," *Susemihl,* ii., pp. 448, 579. If some callow rhetorician succeeded in performing an exercise of this kind specially well, he might feel tempted to publish it. But it is not impossible that actual forgeries were committed for purposes of gain by trading with the great libraries, *cf. Susemihl,* ii., pp. 449 f.; Bentley, p. 9 f., in Ribbeck's German edition, p. 81 ff.; A. M. Zumetikos, *De Alexandri Olympiadisque epistularum fontibus et reliquiis,* Berlin, 1894, p. 1.—As late as 1551, Joachim Camerarius ventured on the harmless jest of fabricating, " *ad institutionem puerilem,*" a correspondence in Greek between Paul and the Presbytery of Ephesus (Th. Zahn, *Geschichte des Neutestamentlichen Kanons,* ii., 2, Erlangen and Leipzig, 1892, p. 365).

by a Faust, meanwhile sighing for a revelation; or he is
driven about by the thought that something must be done
for his unbelief—yet he writes Discourses upon Religion.
And thus he realises that he is entangled in the contradiction between the Infinite and the Finite,[1] while the small
prosperous folks, whose sleepy souls reck not of his pain,
are lulled by him into the delightful dream that we only
need to build altars to truth, beauty, and eternity in order
to possess these things; when they have awaked, they can
but reproach him for having deceived them. They discover
that he is one of themselves; they whisper to each other
that the sage, the poet, the prophet, is but a man after all
—wiser, it may be, but not more clever, or better, than
others. He who might have been their guide—not indeed to his own poor hovel but to the city upon the hill,
not built by human hands—is compensated with some
polite-sounding phrase. The foolish ingrates! Literature
presents us with the unreal, just because it subserves the
truth; the literary man abandons himself, just because he
strives for the ends of humanity; he is unnatural, just because he would give to others something better than himself. What holds good of literature in general must also
be taken into account in regard to each of its characteristic
phenomena. Just as little as Plato's Socrates and Schiller's
Wallenstein are "forgeries," so little dare we so name the
whole "pseudonymous"[2] literature. We may grant at
once, indeed, that some, at least, of the writings which go
under false names were intentionally forged by the writers

[1] *Cf.* the confession made by U. von Wilamowitz-Moellendorff, *Aristoteles
und Athen,* i., Berlin, 1893, Preface, p. vi.: "The task of authorship demands
an end attained—in irreconcilable antithesis to the investigations of science.
The *Phaedrus* has taught us that the book in general is a pitiful thing as
compared with living investigation, and it is to be hoped that we are wiser in
our class-rooms than in our books. But Plato, too, wrote books; he spoke
forth freely each time what he knew as well as he knew it, assured that he
would contradict himself, and hopeful that he would correct himself, next
time he wrote."

[2] The term *pseudonymous* of itself certainly implies blame, but it has
become so much worn in the using, that it is also applied in quite an innocent sense.

of them; pseudonymity in political or ecclesiastical works
is in every case suspicious, for no one knows better how to
use sacred and sanctifying ends than does the undisciplined
instinct of monarchs and hierarchs, and the followers of
them. But there is also a pseudonymity which is innocent,
sincere, and honest,[1] and if a literary product permits of any
inferences being drawn from it respecting the character of
the writer, then, in such a case of pseudonymity, one may
not think of malice or cowardice, but rather of modesty and
natural timidity. Between the genuine [2] and the pseudonymous epistle there does not exist the same profound and
essential difference as between the epistle and the letter.
The epistle is never genuine in the sense in which the letter
is; it never can be so, because it can adopt the form of the
letter only by surrendering the essence. An epistle of
Herder, however like a letter it may look, is yet not a letter
of Herder: it was not Herder the man, but Herder the
theological thinker and author, that wrote it: it is genuine
in an ungenuine sense—like an apple-tree which, flourishing
in September, certainly has genuine apple blossoms, but
which must surely be altogether ashamed of such in the
presence of its own ripening fruits. Literary "genuineness" is not to be confounded with genuine naturalness.
Questions of genuineness in literature may cause us to rack
our brains: but what is humanly genuine is never a problem

---

[1] *Cf.* on this point specially Jülicher, *Einleitung in das N. T.*, p. 32 ff.

[2] The discussion which occupies the remainder of this paragraph is one
which may, indeed, be translated, but can hardly be transferred, into English.
It turns partly on the ambiguity of the German word *echt*, and partly on
a distinction corresponding to that which English critics have tried to
establish between the words "genuine" and "authentic"—a long-vexed
question which now practice rather than theory is beginning to settle. *Echt*
means *authentic*, as applied, for instance, to a book written by the author
whose name it bears; it also means *genuine* both as applied to a true record
of experience, whether facts or feelings, and as implying the truth (that is
the naturalness, spontaneity or reality) of the experience itself. The translator felt that, in justice to the author, he must render *echt* throughout
the passage in question by a single word, and has therefore chosen *genuine*,
as representing, more adequately than any other, the somewhat wide con-
notation of the German adjective.—Tr.

to the genuine man. From the epistle that was genuine in a mere literary sense there was but a step to the fictitious epistle; while the genuine letter could at best be mimicked, the genuine epistle was bound to be imitated, and, indeed, invited to imitation. The collections of genuine letters indirectly occasioned the writing of epistles: the collections of genuine epistles were immediately followed by the literature of the fictitious epistle.

II.

7. In the foregoing remarks on questions of principle, the author has in general tacitly presupposed the literary conditions into which we are carried by the Graeco-Roman civilisation, and by the modern, of which that is the basis.[1] These inquiries seem to him to demand that we should not summarily include all that has been handed down to us bearing the wide, indefinite name of *letter*, under the equally indefinite term *Literature of letters* (*Brieflitteratur*), but that each separate fragment of these interesting but neglected compositions be set in its proper place in the line of development, which is as follows—*real letter, letter that has subsequently become literature, epistle, fictitious epistle.* Should it be demanded that the author fill up the various stages of this development with historical references, he would be at a loss. It has been already indicated that the first member of the series, *viz.*, the *letter*, belongs to pre-literary times: it is not only impossible to give an example of this, but also unreasonable to demand one. With more plausibility one might expect that something certain ought to be procured in connection with the other stages, which belong in a manner to literary times,

---

[1] The history of the literature of "letters" among the Italian Humanists is, from the point of view of method, specially instructive. Stahr, *Aristotelia*, ii., p. 187 f., has already drawn attention to it. The best information on the subject is to be found in G. Voigt's *Die Wiederbelebung des classischen Alterthums oder das erste Jahrhundert des Humanismus*, ii.[3], Berlin, 1893, pp. 417-436.

and, as such, can be historically checked. But even if the broad field of ancient "letters" were more extensively cultivated than has hitherto been the case, still we could establish at best no more than the first known instance of a subsequent collection of real letters, of an epistle or of a fictitious epistle, but would not reach the beginnings of the literary movement itself. The line in question can only be drawn on the ground of general considerations, nor does the author see how else it could be drawn. No one will question that the real letter was the first, the fictitious epistle the last, link in the development; as little will any one doubt that the epistle must have been one of the intervening links between the two.[1] The only uncertainty is as to the origin of the epistle itself; it, of course, presupposes the real letter, being an imitation of it; but that it presupposes as well the collection of real letters, as we think probable in regard to Greek literature, cannot be established with certainty for the history of literature in general. As a matter of fact, the epistle, as a form of literature, is found among the Egyptians at a very early period, and the author does not know how it originated there. The Archduke Rainer's collection of Papyri at Vienna contains a poetical description of the town of Pi-Ramses, dating from the 12th century B.C., which is written in the form of a letter, and is in part identical with Papyrus Anastasi III. in the British Museum. This MS. "shows that in such letters we have, not private correspondence, but literary compositions, which must have enjoyed a wide circulation in ancient Egypt; it thus affords us valuable materials towards the characterisation of the literature of ancient Egypt".[2] If,

---

[1] Von Wilamowitz-Moellendorff, *Antigonos von Karystos*, p. 151: "I cannot imagine that fictitious correspondence, as a species of literature, was anterior in time to genuine".

[2] J. Karabacek, *Mittheilungen aus der Sammlung der Papyrus Erzherzog Rainer*, i., Vienna, 1887, p. 51; *cf.* J. Krall, Guide-book of the Exhibition [of the Pap. Erzh. Rainer], Vienna, 1894, p. 32.—The author doubts whether the term *literature* should really be applied to the letters in cuneiform character which were published by Fried. Delitzsch (*Beiträge zur Assyriologie*, 1893 and 1894) under the title of "Babylonisch-Assyrische Brief*littertaur*".

therefore, we can hardly say that the epistle first originated among the Greeks, yet, notwithstanding the above facts, we may assume that it might arise quite independently under the special conditions of Greek Literature, and that, in fact, it did so arise.

8. Now whatever theory one may have about the origin of the epistle among the Greeks, that question is of no great importance for the problem of the historian of literary phenomena in general, *viz.*, the analysis into their constituent parts of the writings which have been transmitted to us as a whole under the ambiguous name of "letters". What is important in this respect are the various categories to which those constituent parts must be assigned in order that they may be clearly distinguished from each other. We may, therefore, ignore the question as to the origin of these categories—like all questions about the origin of such products of the mind, it is to a large extent incapable of any final solution ; let it suffice that all these categories are represented among the "letters" that have been transmitted from the past. The usage of scientific language is, indeed, not so uniform as to render a definition of terms superfluous. The following preliminary remarks may therefore be made ; they may serve at the same time to justify the terms hitherto used in this book.

Above all, it is misleading merely to talk of *letters*, without having defined the term more particularly. The perception of this fact has influenced many to speak of the *private letter* in contradistinction to the literary letter, and this distinction may express the actual observed fact that the true letter is something private, a personal and confidential matter. But the expression is none the less inadequate, for it may mislead. Thus B. Weiss,[1] for instance, uses it as the antithesis of the *pastoral letter* (*Gemeindebrief*) ; a terminology which does not issue from the essence of the letter, but from the fact of a possible distinction among those to whom it may be addressed. We might in the same way distinguish between the private letter and the *family*

[1] Meyer, xiv.[5] (1888), p. 187.

letter, i.e., the letter which a son, for instance, might send from abroad to those at home. But it is plain that, in the circumstances, such a distinction would be meaningless, for that letter also is a private one. Or, take the case of a clergyman, acting as army chaplain in the enemy's country, who writes a letter[1] to his distant congregation at home; such would be a *congregational letter*—perhaps it is even read in church by the *locum tenens;* but it would manifestly not differ in the slightest from a private letter, provided, that is, that the writer's heart was in the right place. The more private, the more personal, the more special it is, all the better a congregational letter will it be; a right sort of congregation would not welcome paragraphs of pastoral theology— they get such things from the *locum tenens,* for he is not long from college. The mere fact that the receivers of a letter are a plurality, does not constitute a public in the literary sense, and, again, an epistle directed to a single private individual is not on that account a private letter —it is literature. It is absurd, then, to define the specific character of a piece of writing which looks like a letter merely according to whether the writer addresses the receivers in the second person singular or plural;[2] the distinguishing feature cannot be anything merely formal (formal, moreover, in a superficial sense of that word), but can only be the inner special purpose of the writer. It is thus advisable, if we are to speak scientifically, to avoid the use of such merely external categories as *congregational letter,* and also to substitute for *private letter* a more accurate expression. As such we are at once confronted by the simple designation *letter,* but this homely term, in consideration of the indefiniteness which it has acquired in the course of centuries, will hardly suffice by itself; we must find an adjunct for it.

---

[1] *Cf.* for instance the letter of K. Ninck to his congregation at Frücht, of the 1st September, 1870—from Corny; partly printed in F. Cuntz's *Karl Wilh. Theodor Ninck. Ein Lebensbild.* 2nd edn., Herborn, 1891, p. 94 ff.

[2] This difference does not, of course, hold in modern English; we can hardly imagine a letter-writer employing the singular forms *thou, thee.* But the distinction does not *necessarily* hold in German either.—Tr.

The term *true letter* is therefore used here, after the example of writers [1] who are well able to teach us what a letter is.

When a true letter becomes literature by means of its publication, we manifestly obtain no new species thereby. To the historian of literature, it still remains what it was to the original receiver of it—a true letter: even when given to the public, it makes a continual protest against its being deemed a thing of publicity. We must so far favour it as to respect its protest; were we to separate it in any way from other true letters which were fortunate enough never to have their obscurity disturbed, we should but add to the injustice already done to it by its being published.

A new species is reached only when we come to the letter published professedly as *literature*, which as such is altogether different from the first class. Here also we meet with various designations in scientific language. But the adoption of a uniform terminology is not nearly so important in regard to this class as in regard to the true letter. One may call it *literary letter*,[2] or, as has been done above for the sake of simplicity, *epistle*—no importance need be attached to the designation, provided the thing itself be clear. The subdivisions, again, which may be inferred from the conditions of origin of the epistle, are of course unessential; they are not the logical divisions of the concept *epistle*, but simply classifications of extant epistles according to their historical character, *i.e.*, we distinguish between *authentic* and *unauthentic* epistles, and again, in regard to the latter,

---

[1] E. Reuss, *Die Geschichte der h. Schriften N. T.*[6] § 74, p. 70, uses the expression *true letters, addressed to definite and particular readers.* Von Wilamowitz-Moellendorff, *Aristoteles und Athen*, ii., p. 393; *cf.* p. 394: *real letters; ibid.*, p. 392, *letters, ἐπιστολαί in the full sense of the word.* The same author in *Ein Weihgeschenk des Eratosthenes*, in Nachrichten der Kgl. Gesellschaft der Wissenschaften zu Göttingen, 1894, p. 5: *true private letter.*—Birt also uses—besides the designations *private writing* (*Buchwesen*, pp. 2, 20, 61, 277, 443) and *incidental letter* (pp. 61, 325)—the expression *true correspondence* (*wirkliche Correspondenzen*, p. 326). Similarly A. Westermann, *De epistolarum scriptoribus graecis* 8 *progrr.*, i., Leipzig, 1851, p. 13, calls them "*veras* epistolas, h. e. tales, quae ab auctoribus ad ipsos, quibus inscribuntur, homines revera datae sunt".

[2] Von Wilamowitz-Moellendorff, *Ein Weihgeschenk des Eratosthenes*, p. 3.

between innocent fabrications and forgeries with a "tendency".

Furnished with these definitions, we approach the immense quantity of written material which has been bequeathed to us by Graeco-Roman antiquity under the ambiguous term ἐπιστολαί, *epistulae*. The sheets which we have inherited from the bountiful past, and which have been brought into confusion by legacy-hunters and legal advisers, so to speak, perhaps even by the palsied but venerable hand of their aged proprietrix herself, must first of all be duly arranged before we can congratulate ourselves on their possession. In point of fact, the work of arrangement is by no means so far advanced as the value of the inheritance deserves to have it.[1] But what has already been done affords, even to the outsider, at least the superficial impression that we possess characteristic representatives, from ancient times, of all the categories of ἐπιστολαί which have been established in the foregoing pages.

III.

9. We can be said to possess *true letters* from ancient times—in the full sense of the word *possess*—only when we have the originals. And, in fact, the Papyrus discoveries of the last decade have placed us in the favourable position of being able to think of as our very own an enormous number of true letters in the original, extending from the Ptolemaic period till far on in mediæval times. The author is forced to confess that, previous to his acquaintance with ancient Papyrus letters (such as it was—only in facsimiles), he had never rightly known, or, at least, never rightly realised within his own mind, what a letter was. Comparing a Papyrus letter of the Ptolemaic period with a fragment from a tragedy, written also on Papyrus, and of

[1] Among philologists one hears often enough the complaint about the neglect of the study of ancient "letters". The classical preparatory labour of Bentley has waited long in vain for the successor of which both it and its subject were worthy. It is only recently that there appears to have sprung up a more general interest in the matter.

about the same age, no one perceives any external difference; the same written characters, the same writing material, the same place of discovery. And yet the two are as different in their essential character as are reality and art: the one, a leaf with writing on it, which has served some perfectly definite and never-to-be-repeated purpose in human intercourse; the other, the derelict leaf of a *book*, a fragment of literature.

These letters will of themselves reveal what they are, better than the author could, and in evidence of this, there follows a brief selection of letters from the Egyptian town of Oxyrhynchus, the English translation of which (from Greek) all but verbally corresponds to that given by Messrs. Grenfell and Hunt in their edition of the Oxyrhynchus Papyri.[1] The author has selected such letters as date from the century in which our Saviour walked about in the Holy Land, in which Paul wrote his letters, and the beginnings of the New Testament collection were made.[2]

I.

Letter from Chaireas to Tyrannos.[3]   A.D. 25-26.

"Chaireas to his dearest Tyrannos, many greetings. Write out immediately the list of arrears both of corn and money for the twelfth year of Tiberius Caesar Augustus, as Severus has given me instructions for demanding their payment. I have already written to you to be firm and demand payment until I come in peace. Do not therefore neglect this, but prepare the statements of corn and money from the . . . year to the eleventh for the presentation of the demands. Good-bye."

Address: " To Tyrannos, dioiketes ".

[1] *The Oxyrhynchus Papyri*, edited . . . by Bernard P. Grenfell and Arthur S. Hunt, Part I., London, 1898; Part II., London, 1899. For those who feel themselves more specially interested in the subject, a comparison with the original Greek texts will, of course, be necessary.

[2] The German edition of this work contains a Greek transcription, with annotations, of ten Papyrus letters (distinct from those given here) from Egypt, of dates varying from 255 B.C. to the 2nd-3rd centuries A.D.

[3] *The Oxyrhynchus Papyri*, No. 291, ii., p. 291. Chaireas was strategus of the Oxyrhynchite nome. Tyrannos was διοικητής.

II.

Letter of Recommendation from Theon to Tyrannos.[1]
About A.D. 25.

"Theon to his esteemed Tyrannos, many greetings. Herakleides, the bearer of this letter, is my brother. I therefore entreat you with all my power to treat him as your protégé. I have also written to your brother Hermias, asking him to communicate with you about him. You will confer upon me a very great favour if Herakleides gains your notice. Before all else you have my good wishes for unbroken health and prosperity. Good-bye."
Address : "To Tyrannos, dioiketes".

III.

Letter from Dionysios to his Sister Didyme.[2] A.D. 27.

"Dionysios to his sister Didyme, many greetings, and good wishes for continued health. You have sent me no word about the clothes either by letter or by message, and they are still waiting until you send me word. Provide the bearer of this letter, Theonas, with any assistance that he wishes for. . . . Take care of yourself and all your household. Good-bye. The 14th year of Tiberius Caesar Augustus, Athyr 18."
Address : "Deliver from Dionysios to his sister Didyme".

IV.

Letter from Thaeisus to her mother Syras.[3] About A.D. 35.

"Thaeisus to her mother Syras. I must tell you that Seleukos came here and has fled. Don't trouble to explain (?). Let Lucia wait until the year. Let me know the day. Salute Ammonas my brother and . . . and my sister . . . and my father Theonas."

V.

Letter from Ammonios to his father Ammonios.[4] A.D. 54.

"Ammonios to his father Ammonios, greeting. Kindly write me in a note the record of the sheep, how many more

---

[1] *The Oxyrhynchus Papyri*, No. 292, ii., p. 292.
[2] *Ibid.*, No. 293, ii., p. 293.   [3] *Ibid.*, No. 295, ii., p. 296.
[4] *Ibid.*, No. 297, ii., p. 298.

you have by the lambing beyond those included in the first
return. . . . Good-bye. The 14th year of Tiberius Claudius
Caesar Augustus, Epeiph 29."

Address: "To my father Ammonios".

VI.

Letter from Indike to Thaeisus.[1] Late First Century.

"Indike to Thaeisus, greeting. I sent you the bread-
basket by Taurinus the camel-man; please send me an
answer that you have received it. Salute my friend Theon
and Nikobulos and Dioskoros and Theon and Hermokles,
who have my best wishes. Longinus salutes you. Good-
bye. Month Germanikos 2."

Address: "To Theon,[2] son of Nikobulos, elaiochristes
at the Gymnasion".

VII.

Letter of Consolation from Eirene to Taonnophris and Philon.[3] Second Century.

"Eirene to Taonnophris and Philon, good cheer. I
was as much grieved and shed as many tears over Eumoiros
as I shed for Didymas, and I did everything that was fitting,
and so did my whole family,[4] Epaphrodeitos and Thermuthion
and Philion and Apollonios and Plantas. But still there is
nothing one can do in the face of such trouble. So I leave
you to comfort yourselves. Good-bye. Athyr 1."

Address: "To Taonnophris and Philon".

VIII.

Letter from Korbolon to Herakleides.[5] Second Century.

"Korbolon to Herakleides, greeting. I send you the
key by Horion, and the piece of the lock by Onnophris, the
camel-driver of Apollonios. I enclosed in the former packet
a pattern of white-violet colour. I beg you to be good
enough to match it, and buy me two drachmas' weight, and
send it to me at once by any messenger you can find, for

---

[1] *The Oxyrhynchus Papyri*, No. 300, ii., p. 301.
[2] Theon is probably the husband of Thaeisus.
[3] *The Oxyrhynchus Papyri*, No. 115, i., p. 181.
[4] πάντες οἱ ἐμοί. Grenfell and Hunt: *all my friends*.
[5] *The Oxyrhynchus Papyri*, No. 113, i., p. 178 f.

the tunic is to be woven immediately. I received everything
you told me to expect by Onnophris safely. I send you by
the same Onnophris six quarts of good apples. I thank all
the gods to think that I came upon Plution in the Oxyrhynchite nome. Do not think that I took no trouble about
the key. The reason is that the smith is a long way from
us. I wonder that you did not see your way to let me have
what I asked you to send by Korbolon, especially when I
wanted it for a festival. I beg you to buy me a silver seal,
and to send it me with all speed. Take care that Onnophris
buys me what Eirene's mother told him. I told him that
Syntrophos said that nothing more should be given to
Amarantos on my account. Let me know what you have
given him that I may settle accounts with him. Otherwise
I and my son will come for this purpose. [On the *verso*] I
had the large cheeses from Korbolon. I did not, however,
want large ones, but small. Let me know of anything that
you want, and I will gladly do it. Farewell. Payni 1st.
(P.S.) Send me an obol's worth of cake for my nephew."
    Address : " To Herakleides, son of Ammonios."

    10. But we must not think that the heritage of true
letters which we have received from the past is wholly com-
prised in the Papyrus letters which have been thus finely
preserved as autographs. In books and booklets which have
been transmitted to us as consisting of ἐπιστολαί, and in
others as well, there is contained a goodly number of true
letters, for the preservation of which we are indebted to the
circumstance that some one, at some time subsequent to
their being written, treated them as literature. Just as at
some future time posterity will be grateful to our learned
men of to-day for their having published the Papyrus letters,
i.e., treated them as literature, so we ourselves have every
cause for gratitude to those individuals, for the most part
unknown, who long ago committed the indiscretion of
making books out of letters. The great men whose letters,
fortunately for us, were overtaken by this fate, were not on
that account epistolographers ; they were letter-writers—
like the strange saints of the Serapeum and the obscure
men and women of the Fayyûm. No doubt, by reason of
their letters having been preserved as literature, they have

often been considered as epistolographers, and the misunderstanding may have been abetted by the vulgar notion that
those celebrated men had the consciousness of their cele-
brity even when they laughed and yawned, and that they
could not speak or write a single word without imagining
that amazed mankind was standing by to hear and read.   We
have not as yet, in every case, identified those whom we
have to thank for real letters.   But it will be sufficient for
our purpose if we restrict ourselves to a few likely instances.

The letters of *Aristotle* († 322 B.C.) were published at a
very early period : their publication gave the lie, in a very
effective manner, to a fictitious collection which came out
shortly after his death.[1]   These letters were "true letters,
occasioned by the requirements of private correspondence,
not products of art, *i.e.*, treatises in the form of letters ".[2]
This collection is usually considered to be the first instance
of private letters being subsequently published.[3]   It is therefore necessary to mention them here, though, indeed, it is
uncertain whether anything really authentic has been preserved among the fragments which have come down to us ; [4]
by far the greater number of these were certainly products
of the fictitious literary composition of the Alexandrian
period.[5]—The case stands more favourably with regard to
the nine letters transmitted to us under the name of *Isocrates*
(† 338 B.C.).[6]   The most recent editor [7] of them comes to
the following conclusions.   The first letter, to Dionysios, is
authentic.   The two letters of introduction, Nos. 7 and 8, to
Timotheos of Heracleia and the inhabitants of Mitylene
respectively, bear the same mark of authenticity : " so much

---

[1] Von Wilamowitz-Moellendorff, *Antigonos von Karystos*, p. 151.

[2] Stahr, *Aristotelia*, i., p. 195.

[3] Von Wilamowitz-Moellendorff, *Antigonos von Karystos*, p. 151 ; Susemihl, ii., 580.

[4] Hercher, pp. 172-174.   [5] Susemihl, ii., 580 f.

[6] Hercher, pp. 319-336.

[7] Von Wilamowitz-Moellendorff, *Aristoteles und Athen*, ii., pp. 391-399.
It is unfortunate that some of the most recent critics of Paul's Letters had
not those few pages before them.   They might then have seen, perhaps,
both what a letter is, and what method is.

detail, which, wherever we can test it, we recognise to be
historically accurate, and which, to a much greater extent,
we are not at all in a position to judge, is not found in
forgeries, unless they are meant to serve other than their
ostensible purposes. There can be no talk of that in the
case before us. In these letters some forms of expression
occur more than once (7, 11 = 8, 10), but there is nothing
extraordinary in that. If Isocrates wrote these we must
credit him with having issued many such compositions."[1]
These genuine letters of Isocrates are of interest also in
regard to their form, as they show " that Isocrates applied
his rhetorical style also to his letters. . . . Considered from
the point of view of style, they are not letters at all."[2]   The
author considers this fact to be very instructive in regard to
method ; it confirms the thesis expressed above, *viz.*, that in
answering the question as to what constitutes a *true* letter,
it is never the form which is decisive, but ultimately only
the intention of the writer ; there ought not to be, but as a
matter of fact there are, letters which read like pamphlets ;
there are epistles, again, which chatter so insinuatingly that
we forget that their daintiness is nothing but a suspicious
mask. Nor need one doubt, again, the genuineness of the
second letter—to King Philip : " its contents are most undoubtedly personal ".[3] Letter 5, to Alexander, is likewise
genuine, " truly a fine piece of Isocratic finesse : it is genuine
—just because it is more profound than it seems, and because
it covertly refers to circumstances notoriously true ".[4] The
evidence for and against the genuineness of letter 6 is
evenly balanced.[5] On the other hand, letters 3, 4 and 9 are
not genuine ; are partly, in fact, forgeries with a purpose.[6]
This general result of the criticism is, likewise of great value
in regard to method : we must abandon the mechanical idea
of a *collection of letters*, which would lead us to inquire as to
the genuineness of the- collection as a whole, instead of
inquiring as to the genuineness of its component parts. Un-
discerning tradition may quite well have joined together one

[1] P. 391 f.   [2] P. 392.   [3] P. 397.
[4] P. 399.   [5] P. 395.   [6] Pp. 393-397.

or two unauthentic letters with a dozen of genuine ones ;
and, again, a whole book of forged " letters " may be, so to
speak, the chaff in which good grains of wheat may hide
themselves from the eyes of the servants : when the son of
the house comes to the threshing-floor, he will discover them,
for he cannot suffer that anything be lost.—The letters of
the much-misunderstood *Epicurus* († 270 B.C.) were collected
with great care by the Epicureans, and joined together with
those of his most distinguished pupils, Metrodorus, Polyænus,
and Hermarchus, with additiọns from among the letters
which these had received from other friends,[1] and have in
part come down to us. The author cannot refrain from
giving here [2] the fragment of a letter of the philosopher to
his child (made known to us by the rolls of Herculaneum),
not, indeed, as being a monument of his philosophy, but because it is part of a letter which is as simple and affectionate,
as much a true letter, as that of Luther to his little son
Hans :—

　　... [ἀ]φείγμεθα εἰς Λάμψακον ὑγιαίνοντες ἐγὼ καὶ Πυθο-
κλῆς κα[ὶ "Ερμ]αρχος καὶ Κ[τή]σιππος, καὶ ἐκεῖ κατειλήφαμεν
ὑγ[ι]αίνοντας Θεμίσταν καὶ τοὺς λοιποὺς [φί]λο[υ]ς. εὖ δὲ
ποιε[ῖ]ς καὶ σὺ ε[ἰ ὑ]γιαίνεις καὶ ἡ μ[ά]μμη [σ]ου καὶ πάπᾳ
καὶ Μάτρω[ν]ι πάντα πε[ί]θη[ι, ὥσπ]ερ καὶ ἔ[μ]προσθεν. εὖ
γὰρ ἴσθι, ἡ αἰτία, ὅτι καὶ ἐγὼ καὶ ο[ἱ] λοιποὶ πάντες σε μέγα
φιλοῦμεν, ὅτι τούτοις πείθῃ πάντα. . . .

Again in Latin literature we find a considerable number of real letters.　"Letters, official [3] as well as private,
make their appearance in the literature [4] of Rome at an
early period, both by themselves and in historical works,[5]

[1] Susemihl, i., p. 96 f. ; H. Usener, *Epicurea*, Leipzig, 1887, p. liv. ff.

[2] From Usener's edition, p. 154.

[3] Of course, official letters, too, are primarily " true letters," not literature, even when they are addressed to a number of persons.—(This note and
the two following do not belong to the quotation from Teuffel-Schwabe.)

[4] Hence in themselves they are manifestly not literature.

[5] The insertion of letters in historical works was a very common literary
custom among the Greeks and Romans.　It is to be classed along with the
insertion of public papers and longer or shorter speeches in a historical report.
If it holds good that such speeches are, speaking generally, to be regarded as

and, soon thereafter, those of distinguished men in collections."[1]   We may refer to a single example—certainly a very instructive one.   Of *Cicero* († 43 B.C.) we possess four collections of letters ; in all 864, if we include the 90 addressed to him.   The earliest belongs to the year 68, the latest is of the date 28th July, 43.[2]   "Their contents are both personal and political, and they form an inexhaustible source for a knowledge of the period,[3] though partly, indeed, of such a kind that the publication of them was not to Cicero's advantage.   For the correspondence of such a man as Cicero, who was accustomed to think so quickly and feel so strongly, to whom it was a necessity that he should express his thoughts and feelings as they came, either in words or in letters to some confidential friend like Atticus, often affords a too searching, frequently even an illusory,[4] glance into his inmost soul.   Hence the accusers of Cicero gathered the greatest part of their material from these letters."[5]   The letters show a noteworthy variation of language : "in the letters to Atticus or other well known friends Cicero abandons restraint, while those to less intimate persons show marks of care and elaboration ".[6]   The history of the gathering together of Cicero's letters is of great importance for a right understand-

---

the compositions of the historian, yet, in regard to letters and public papers, the hypothesis of their authenticity should not be always summarily rejected. In regard to this question, important as it also is for the criticism of the biblical writings, see especially H. Schnorr von Carolsfeld, *Über die Reden und Briefe bei Sallust*, Leipzig, 1888, p. 1 ff., and the literature given in Schürer, i., p. 66, note 14 [Eng. Trans. I., I., p. 90]; also Teuffel-Schwabe, i., p. 84, *pos.* 8, and Westermann, i. (1851), p. 4.

[1] W. S. Teuffel's *Geschichte der römischen Literatur*, revised by L. Schwabe[5], i., Leipzig, 1890, p. 83.

[2] Teuffel-Schwabe, i., p. 356 ff.

[3] This point is also a very valuable one for the critic of the biblical "letters" in the matter of method. For an estimation of the historical importance of Cicero's letters, the author refers, further, to J. Bernays, *Edward Gibbon's Geschichtswerk* in the *Gesammelte Abhh. von J. B.*, edited by H. Usener, ii., Berlin, 1885, p. 243, and E. Ruete, *Die Correspondenz Ciceros in den Jahren 44 und 43*, Marburg, 1883, p. 1.

[4] The present writer would question this.

[5] Teuffel-Schwabe, i., p. 356 f.   [6] *Ibid.*, i., p. 357.

ing of similar literary transactions. " Cicero did not himself
collect the letters he had written, still less publish them, but
even during his lifetime his intimate friends were already
harbouring such intentions." [1]   " After Cicero's death the
collecting and publishing of his letters was zealously pro-
moted ; in the first place, undoubtedly, by Tiro, who, while
Cicero was still living, had resolved to collect his letters." [2]
Cornelius Nepos, according to a note in that part of his
biography of Atticus which was written before 34 B.C., had,
even by that date, a knowledge, from private sources, of the
letters to Atticus ; [3] " they were not as yet published, indeed,
as he expressly says, but, it would appear, already collected
with a view to publication. The first known mention of a
letter from Cicero's correspondence being published is found
at the earliest " in Seneca.[4]   The following details of the
work of collection may be taken as established.[4]   Atticus
negotiated the issue of the letters addressed to him, while
the others appear to have been published gradually by Tiro ;
both editors suppressed their own letters to Cicero.   Tiro
arranged the letters according to the individuals who had
received them, and published the special correspondence of
each in one or more volumes, according to the material he
had.   Such special materials, again, as did not suffice for a
complete volume, as also isolated letters, were bound up in
miscellanea (embracing letters to two or more individuals),
while previously published collections were supplemented in
later issues by letters which had only been written subsequently, or subsequently rendered accessible.   The majority
of these letters of Cicero are " truly confidential outpourings
of the feelings of the moment," [5] particularly those addressed
to Atticus—" confidential letters, in which the writer ex-

---

[1] Teuffel-Schwabe, i., p. 357, quotes in connection with this Cic. *ad
Attic.*, 16, 5₅ (44 B.C.) *mearum epistularum nulla est συναγωγή, sed habet Tiro
instar LXX, et quidem sunt a te quaedam sumendae ; eas ego oportet perspiciam,
corrigam ; tum denique edentur*,—and to Tiro, *Fam.*, 16, 17₁ (46 B.C.) *tuas quo-
que epistulas vis referri in volumina.*

[2] Teuffel-Schwabe, i., p. 357.   [3] *Ibid.*

[4] *Ibid.*, p. 358.   [5] *Ibid.*, p. 83.

presses himself without a particle of constraint, and which often contain allusions intelligible to the receiver alone. In some parts they read like soliloquies." [1] The authenticity of the letters to Brutus, for instance, has been disputed by many, but these assailants " have been worsted on all points, and the authenticity is now more certain than ever. The objections that have been urged against this collection, and those, in particular, which relate to the contradictions between Cicero's confidential judgments upon individuals and those he made publicly or in utterances of other times, are of but little weight." [2]

11. The fact that we know of a relatively large number of literary letters, *i.e.*, *epistles*, of ancient times, and that, further, we possess many such, is a simple consequence of their being literary productions. Literature is designed not merely for the public of the time being; it is also for the future. It has not been ascertained with certainty which was the first instance of the literary letter in Greek literature. Susemihl [3] is inclined to think that the epidictic triflings of *Lysias* († 379 B.C.) occupy this position—that is, if they be authentic—but he certainly considers it possible that they originated in the later Attic period. *Aristotle* employed the " imaginary letter " (*fictiver Brief*) for his Protreptikos. [4] We have " didactic epistles " of *Epicurus,* as also of *Dionysius of Halicarnassus,* and we may add to these such writings of Plutarch as *De Conjugalibus Praeceptis, De Tranquillitate Animi, De Animae Procreatione* [5]—literary productions to which one may well apply the words of an ancient expert in such things, [6] οὐ μὰ τὴν ἀλήθειαν ἐπιστολαὶ λέγοιντο ἄν, ἀλλὰ συγγράμματα τὸ χαίρειν ἔχοντα προσγεγραμμένον, and εἰ γάρ τις ἐν ἐπιστολῇ σοφίσματα γράφει καὶ φυσιολογίας,

---

[1] Teuffel-Schwabe, i., p. 362.

[2] *Ibid.*, p. 364. This is another point highly important in regard to method,—for the criticism of the Pauline Letters in particular.

[3] ii., p. 600.

[4] Von Wilamowitz-Moellendorff, *Aristoteles und Athen*, ii., p. 393.

[5] Westermann, i. (1851), p. 13. See Susemihl, ii., p. 601, for many other examples in Greek literature.

[6] Demetr. *de elocut.*, 228 (Hercher, p. 13), and 231 (H., p. 14).

γράφει μέν, οὐ μὴν ἐπιστολὴν γράφει.[1] Among the Romans, *M. Porcius Cato* († 149 B.C.) should probably be named as one of the first writers of epistles;[2] the best known, doubtless, are Seneca and Pliny. *L. Annaeus Seneca*[3] († 65 A.D.) began about the year 57—at a time when Paul was writing his " great " letters—to write the *Epistulae Morales* to his friend Lucilius, intending from the first that they should be published ; most probably the first three books were issued by himself. Then in the time of Trajan, *C. Plinius Caecilius Secundus*[4] († ca. 113 A.D.) wrote and published nine books of " letters " ; the issue of the collection was already complete by the time Pliny went to Bithynia. Then came his correspondence with Trajan, belonging chiefly to the period of his governorship in Bithynia (*ca.* September 111 to January 113). The letters of Pliny were likewise intended from the first for publication, " and hence are far from giving the same impression of freshness and directness as those of Cicero " ;[5] " with studied variety they enlarge upon a multitude of topics, but are mainly designed to exhibit their author in the most favourable light " ;[6] " they exhibit him as an affectionate husband, a faithful friend, a generous slaveholder, a noble-minded citizen, a liberal promoter of all good causes, an honoured orator and author " ;[7] " on the other hand, the correspondence with Trajan incidentally raises a sharp contrast between the patience and quiet prudence of the emperor and the struggling perplexity and self-importance of his vicegerent ".[8] " All possible care has likewise been bestowed upon the form of these letters." [9]

There are several other facts illustrative of the extremely

---

[1] A saying of the Rhetor Aristides (2nd cent. B.C.) shows how well an ancient epistolographer was able to estimate the literary character of his compositions. In his works we find an ἐπὶ ᾿Αλεξάνδρῳ ἐπιτάφιος dedicated τῇ βουλῇ καὶ τῷ δήμῳ τῷ Κοτυαέων, of which he himself says (i., p. 148, Dindorf), ὅπερ γε καὶ ἐν ἀρχῇ τῆς ἐπιστολῆς εἶπον ἢ ὅ τι βούλεσθε καλεῖν τὸ βιβλίον. Hence Westermann, iii. (1852), p. 4, applies to this and to another "letter" of Aristides the name *declamationes epistolarum sub specie latentes.*

[2] Teuffel-Schwabe, i., pp. 84, 197 f. 　　　[3] *Ibid.*, ii., p. 700.
[4] *Ibid.*, ii., pp. 849, 851 ff. 　　　　　　[5] *Ibid.*, ii., p. 852.
[6] *Ibid.*, ii., p. 849. 　　　　　　　　　　[7] *Ibid.*, ii., p. 852.
[8] *Ibid.*　　　　　　　　　　　　　　　　　[9] *Ibid.*

wide dissemination of the practice of epistle-writing among
the Greeks and Romans.   The epistle, having once gained a
position as a literary *eidos*, became differentiated into a
whole series of almost independent forms of composition.
We should, in the first place, recall the poetical epistle [1]
(especially of Lucilius, Horace, Ovid) ; but there were also
juristic epistles—a literary form which probably originated
in the written *responsa* to questions on legal subjects ; [2]
further, there were *epistulæ medicinales*,[3] gastronomic "letters,"[4]
etc.   In this connection it were well to direct particular
attention to the great popularity of the epistle as the special
form of magical and religious literature.   " All the Magic
Papyri are of this letter-form, and in all the ceremonial and
mystic literature—to say nothing of other kinds—it was the
customary form.   At that time the pioneers of new religions
clothed their message in this form, and even when they
furnish their writings with a stereotype title of such a kind,
and with particularly sacred names, it would yet be doing
them an injustice simply to call them forgers."[5]

12. A very brief reference to the pseudonymous epistolography of antiquity is all that is required here.   It will
be sufficient for us to realise the great vogue it enjoyed, after
the Alexandrian period, among the Greeks and subsequently
among the Romans.   It is decidedly one of the most characteristic features of post-classical literature.   We already
find a number of the last-mentioned epistles bearing the
names of pretended authors ; it is, indeed, difficult to draw
a line between the "genuine" and the fictitious epistles
when the two are set in contrast to letters really such.[6]   As
may be easily understood, pseudonymous epistolography
specially affected the celebrated names of the past, and not
least the names of those great men the real letters of whom
were extant in collections.   The literary practice of using

---

[1] Teuffel-Schwabe, i., p. 39 f.   [2] *Ibid.*, i., p. 84.
[3] *Ibid.*, i., p. 85.   [4] Susemihl, ii., p. 601.
[5] A. Dieterich, *Abraxas*, p. 161 f.   Particular references will be found
there and specially in *Fleck. Jbb. Suppl.* xvi. (1888), p. 757.
[6] *Cf.* pp. 15 and 20 above.

assumed or protective names was found highly convenient by
such obscure people as felt that they must make a contribution to literature of a page or two ; they did not place their own
names upon their books, for they had the true enough presentiment that these would be a matter of indifference to their
contemporaries and to posterity, nor did they substitute for
them some unknown *Gaius* or *Timon :* what they did was to
write "letters" of Plato or Demosthenes, of Aristotle or
his royal pupil, of Cicero, Brutus or Horace. It would be
superfluous in the meantime to go into particulars about any
specially characteristic examples, the more so as the present
position of the investigation still makes it difficult for us to
assign to each its special historical place, but at all events
the pseudonymous epistolography of antiquity stands out
quite clearly as a distinct aggregate of literary phenomena.
Suffice it only to refer further to what may be very well
gleaned from a recent work,[1] *viz.*, that the early imperial
period was the classical age of this most unclassical manu-
facturing of books.

IV.

13. The author's purpose was to write Prolegomena to
the biblical letters and epistles : it may seem now to be high
time that he came to the subject.   But he feels that he
might now break off, and still confidently believe that he has
not neglected his task.   What remains to be said is really
implied in the foregoing pages.   It was a problem in the
method of literary history which urged itself upon him; he
has solved it, for himself at least, in laying bare the roots by
which it adheres to the soil on which flourished aforetime
the spacious garden of God—Holy Scripture.

To the investigator the Bible offers a large number of
writings bearing a name which appears to be simple, but
which nevertheless conceals within itself that same problem
—a name which every child seems to understand, but upon
which, nevertheless, the learned man must ponder deeply

[1] J. F. Marcks, *Symbola critica ad Epistolographos Graecos*, Bonn, 1883.

if ever he will see into the heart of the things called by it.
"Letters"! How long did the author work with this term
without having ever once reflected on what it meant; how
long did it accompany him through his daily task in science
without his observing the enigma that was inscribed on its
work-a-day face! Others may have been more knowing:
the author's experiences were like those of a man who
plants a vineyard without being able to distinguish the
true vine-shoots from the suckers of the wild grape. That
was, of course, a sorry plight—as bad as if one were to
labour upon Attic tragedies without knowing what an Attic
tragedy is. One may, indeed, write a letter without
necessarily knowing what a letter is. The best letter-
writers have certainly not cherished any doctrinaire opinions
on the subject. The ancient Greek and Latin " guides to
letter-writing"[1] appeared long after Cicero: neither did the
Apostles, for that matter, know anything of Halieutics.
But if one is to understand those literary memorials in the
Bible which have come to us under the name of "*letters*,"
and to make them intelligible to others, the first condition
is, of course, that one must have an historical comprehen-
sion of his purpose, must have previously divested the
problematic term of its problematic character: οὐ γὰρ ἐπειδὴ
ἐπιστολὴ προσαγορεύεται ἐνικῷ ὀνόματι, ἤδη καὶ πασῶν τῶν
κατὰ τὸν βίον φερομένων ἐπιστολῶν εἶς τις ἐστι χαρακτὴρ καὶ
μία προσηγορία, ἀλλὰ διάφοροι, καθὼς ἔφην.[2] If we rightly
infer, from an investigation of ancient literature, that the
familiar term "*letter*" must be broken up—above all, into the
two chief categories *real letter* and *epistle*, then the biblical
"letters" likewise must be investigated from this point of

---

[1] *Cf.* on this Westermann, i. (1851), p. 9 f. For Greek theorists in
letter-writing, see Hercher, pp. 1-16; for the Latin, the *Rhetores Latini
minores, em.*, C. Halm, fasc. ii., Leipzig, 1863, pp. 447 f. and 589.

[2] [Pseudo-]Procl. *De Forma Epistolari* (Hercher, p. 6 f.). This quotation, it is true, refers not to the various logical divisions of the *concept*
"letter," but to the 41 [!] various sub-classes of true letters. The process of
distinguishing these various classes ([Pseudo-]Demetr. [Hercher, p. 1 ff.]
similarly enumerates 21 categories) is, in its details, sometimes very extraordinary.

view.   Just as the language of the Bible ought to be studied
in its actual historical context of contemporary language;[1]
just as its religious and ethical contents must be studied in
their actual historical context of contemporary religion and
civilisation[2]—so the biblical writings, too, in the literary investigation of them, ought not to be placed in an isolated position.   The author speaks of *the biblical writings*, not of *the biblical literature*.   To apply the designation *literature* to certain
portions of the biblical writings would be an illegitimate
procedure.   Not all that we find printed in books at the present day was literature from the first.   A comparison of the
biblical writings, in their own proper character, with the
other writings of antiquity, will show us that in each case
there is a sharp distinction between works which were
literature from the first and writings which only acquired
that character later on, or will show, at least, that we must
so distinguish them from each other.   This is nowhere more
evident than in the case under discussion.   When we make
the demand that the biblical "letters" are to be set in their
proper relation to ancient letter-writing as a whole, we
do not thereby imply that they are products of ancient
epistolography, but rather that they shall be investigated
simply with regard to the question, how far the categories
implied in the problematic term *letter* are to be employed
in the criticism of them.   We may designate our question
regarding the biblical letters and epistles as a question
regarding the literary character of the writings transmitted
by the Bible under the name *letters*,[3] but the question regarding their literary character must be so framed that the
answer will affirm the *pre*literary character, probably of
some, possibly of all.

[1] *Cf.* p. 63 ff.

[2] The author has already briefly expressed these ideas about the history
of biblical religion in the essay *Zur Methode der Biblischen Theologie des
Neuen Testamentes, Zeitschrift für Theologie und Kirche*, iii. (1893), pp. 126-139.

[3] E. P. Gould, in an article entitled "The Literary Character of St.
Paul's Letters" in *The Old and New Testament Student*, vol. xi. (1890), pp.
71 ff. and 134 ff., seems to apply the same question to some at least of the
biblical "letters," but in reality his essay has an altogether different purpose.

The latter has been maintained by F. Overbeck,[1]—at least in regard to the "letters" in the New Testament. He thinks that the Apostolic letters belong to a class of writings which we ought not to place in the province of literature at all;[2] the writer of a letter has, as such, no concern with literature whatever,—"because for every product of literature it is essential that its contents have an appropriate literary form".[3] The written words of a letter are nothing but the wholly inartificial and incidental substitute for spoken words. As the letter has a quite distinct and transitory motive, so has it also a quite distinct and restricted public—not necessarily merely *one* individual, but sometimes, according to circumstances, a smaller or larger company of persons : in any case, a circle of readers which can be readily brought before the writer's mind and distinctly located in the field of inward vision. A work of literature, on the other hand, has the widest possible publicity in view : the literary man's public is, so to speak, an imaginary one, which it is the part of the literary work to find.[4] Though Overbeck thus indicates with proper precision the fundamental difference between the letter and literature,

---

[1] *Über die Anfänge der patristischen Litteratur* in the *Historische Zeitschrift*, 48, Neue Folge 12 (1882), p. 429 ff. The present writer cannot but emphasise how much profitable stimulation in regard to method he has received from this essay, even though he differs from the essayist on important points.

[2] P. 429, and foot of p. 428.

[3] P. 429. Overbeck would seem sometimes not to be quite clear with regard to the term *form*, which he frequently uses. The author understands the word in the above quotation in the same way as in the fundamental proposition on p. 423: "In the forms of literature is found its history". Here *form* can be understood only as *Eidos*. The *forms* of literature are, *e.g.*, Epos, Tragedy, History, etc. Overbeck, in his contention that the form is essential for the contents of a literary work, is undoubtedly correct, if he is referring to the good old εἴδη of literature. No one, for example, will expect a comedy to incite φόβος καὶ ἔλεος. But the contention is not correct when it refers to such a subordinate literary *Eidos* as the epistle. The epistle may treat of all possible subjects—and some others as well. And therefore when all is said, it is literature, a literary *form*—even when only a *bad form* (*Unform*).

[4] P. 429.

yet he has overlooked the necessary task of investigating
whether the Apostolic letters—either as a whole or in part
—may not be epistles, and this oversight on his part is the
more extraordinary, since he quite clearly recognises the distinction between the letter and the epistle. He speaks, at
least, of "artificial letters," and contrasts them with "true
letters"; [1] in point of fact, he has the right feeling, [2] that
there are some of the New Testament letters, the form of
which is quite obviously not that of a letter at all, *viz.*, the
so-called Catholic Epistles: in some of these the form of
address, being so indefinite and general, does not correspond
to what we expect in a letter, and, in fact, constitutes a
hitherto unsolved problem. Hence he is inclined to class
them along with those New Testament writings "which, in
their own proper and original form, certainly belong to
literature, [3] but which, in consideration of the paucity of
their different forms, must not be thought of as qualifying
the New Testament to be ranked historically as the beginning of that literature". Easy as it would have been
to characterise the "letters," thus so aptly described, as
epistles, Overbeck has yet refrained from doing this, and
though he seems, at least, to have characterised them as
literature, yet he pointedly disputes [4] the contention that
Christian literature begins with "the New Testament,"—
that is, in possible case, with these letters,—and he expressly says that the "artificial letter" remains wholly
outside of the sphere of this discussion. [5]

14. The present writer would assert, as against this,
that "in the New Testament," and not only there, but also
in the literature of the Jews as well as of the Christians of
post-New-Testament times, the transmitted "letters" permit
of quite as marked a division into real letters and epistles, as
is the case in ancient literature generally.

14. Most investigators of the New Testament letters
seem to overlook the fact that this same profound difference

---

[1] P. 429 at the top.　　　　　　　[2] P. 431 f.
[3] Overbeck here means the Gospels, Acts of the Apostles and Revelation.
[4] P. 426 ff.　　　　　　　[5] P. 429.

already manifests itself clearly in the "letters" found
among the writings of pre-Christian Judaism. Looking
at the writings of early Christianity from the standpoint
of literary history, we perceive that Jewish literature [1] was
precisely the literary sphere from which the first Christians
could most readily borrow and adopt something in the way
of *forms*, εἴδη, of composition.[2] If, therefore, the existence of
the εἶδος of the epistle can be demonstrated in this possibly
archetypal sphere, our inquiry regarding the early Christian
"letters" manifestly gains a more definite justification.
Should the doubt be raised as to whether it is conceivable
that a line of demarcation, quite unmistakably present in
"profane" literature, should have also touched the outlying
province of the New Testament, that doubt will be stilled
when it is shown that this line had actually long intersected
the sphere of Jewish literature, which may have been the
model for the writers of the New Testament. Between the
ancient epistles and what are (possibly) the epistles of early
Christianity, there subsists a literary, a morphological connection; if it be thought necessary to establish a transition-link,
this may quite well be found in the Jewish epistles. The
way by which the epistle entered the sphere of Jewish authorship is manifest: Alexandria, the classical soil of the epistle
and the pseudo-epistle, exercised its Hellenising influence

---

[1] Not solely, of course, those writings which we *now* recognise as
canonical.

[2] The influence of a Jewish literary form can be clearly seen at its best
in the Apocalypse of John. But also the Acts of the Apostles (which, along
with the Gospels, the present writer would, *contra* Overbeck, characterise as
belonging already to Christian *literature*) has its historical prototype, in the
matter of form, in the Hellenistic writing of annals designed for the edification of the people. What in the Acts of the Apostles recalls the literary
method of "profane" historical literature (*e.g.*, insertion of speeches, letters,
and official papers), need not be accounted for by a competent knowledge of
classical authors on the part of the writer of it; it may quite well be explained by the influence of its Jewish prototypes. When the Christians
began to make literature, they adopted their literary forms, even those
which have the appearance of being Græco-Roman, from Greek Judaism, with
the single exception of the *Evangelium*—a literary form which originated
within Christianity itself.

upon Judaism in this matter as in others. We know not
who the first Jewish epistolographer may have been, but it
is, at least, highly probable that he was an Alexandrian.
The taking over of the epistolary form was facilitated for
him by the circumstance that already in the ancient and
revered writings of his nation there was frequent mention
of " letters," and that, as a matter of fact, he found a number
of " letters " actually given verbatim in the sacred text.
Any one who read the Book of the Prophet Jeremiah
with the eyes of an Alexandrian Hellenist, found, in chap.
29 (the prophet's message to the captives in Babylon),[1]
something which to his morbid literary taste seemed like an
epistle. As a matter of fact, this message is a real letter.
perhaps indeed the only genuine one we have from Old
Testament times ; a real letter, which only became literature
by its subsequent admission into the *book* of the Prophet.
As it now stands in the book, it is to be put in exactly the
same class as all other real letters which were subsequently
published. In its origin, in its purpose, Jer. 29, being a
real letter, is non-literary, and hence, of course, we must not
ask after a literary prototype for it. The wish to discover
the first Israelitic or first Christian letter-writer would be
as foolish as the inquiry regarding the beginnings of Jewish
and, later, of Christian, epistolography is profitable and
necessary ; besides, the doctrinaire inquirer would be cruelly
undeceived when the sublime simplicity of the historical
reality smiled at him from the rediscovered first Christian
letter—its pages perhaps infinitely paltry in their contents :
some forgotten cloak may have been the occasion of it—
who will say ? Jer. 29 is not, of course, a letter such as
anybody might dash off in an idle moment ; nay, lightnings
quiver between the lines, Jahweh speaks in wrath or in
blessing,—still, although a Jeremiah wrote it, although it
be a documentary fragment of the history of the people and
the religion of Israel, it is still a letter, neither less nor more.
The antithesis of it in that respect is not wanting. There

---

[1] It is, of course, possible, in these merely general observations, to avoid
touching on the question of the integrity of this message.

has been transmitted to us, among the Old Testament
Apocryphal writings, a little book bearing the name ἐπιστολὴ
Ἰερεμίου. If Jer. 29 is a letter of the prophet Jeremiah,
this is an *Epistle of " Jeremiah "*. Than the latter, we could
know no more instructive instance for the elucidation of the
distinction between letter and epistle, or for the proper
appreciation of the idea of pseudonymity in ancient literature. The Greek epistolography of the Alexandrian period
constituted the general literary impulse of the writer of the
Epistle of "Jeremiah," while the actual existence of a real
letter of Jeremiah constituted the particular impulse. He
wrote an epistle,—as did the other great men of the day : he
wrote an epistle of "Jeremiah," just as the others may have
fabricated, say, epistles of "Plato". We can distinctly see,
in yet another passage, how the motive to epistolography
could be found in the then extant sacred writings of
Judaism. The canonical Book of Esther speaks, in two
places, of royal letters, without giving their contents : a
sufficient reason for the Greek reviser to sit down and
manufacture them, just as the two prayers, only mentioned
in the original, are given by him in full ! [1]

Having once gained a footing, epistolography must
have become very popular in Greek Judaism ; we have still
a whole series of Græco-Jewish "letters," which are unquestionably epistles. The author is not now thinking of
the multitude of letters, ascribed to historical personages,
which are inserted in historical works [2] ; in so far as these
are unauthentic, they are undoubtedly of an epistolary

---

[1] The following is also instructive : It is reported at the end of the
Greek Book of Esther that the "Priest and Levite" Dositheus and his son
Ptolemaeus, had "brought hither" (*i.e.*, to Egypt) the ἐπιστολὴ τῶν Φρουραί
(*concerning the Feast of Purim*) from Esther and Mordecai (LXX Esther
9²⁹, *cf.* ²⁰), which was translated (into Greek) by Lysimachus, the son of
Ptolemaeus in Jerusalem. It would thus seem that a Greek letter concerning Purim, written by Esther and Mordecai, was known in Alexandria. It
is not improbable that the alleged bearers of the "letter" were really the
authors of it.

[2] The Books of Maccabees, Epistle of Aristeas, specially also Eupolemos
(*cf.* thereon J. Freudenthal, *Hellenistische Studien*, part i. and ii., Breslau,
1875, p. 106 ff.), Josephus.

character, but they belong less to the investigation of epistolography than to the development of historical style. We should rather call to mind books and booklets like the *Epistle of Aristeas*, the two [1] epistles at the beginning of the *2nd Book of Maccabees*, the *Epistle of "Baruch" to the nine and a half tribes in captivity*, attached to the Apocalypse of Baruch,[2] perhaps the *twenty-eighth " Letter of Diogenes,"* [3] and certain portions of the collection of " letters " which bears the name of *Heraclitus*.[4]

15. Coming, then, to the early Christian "letters " with our question, *letter or epistle?* it will be our first task to determine the character of the "letters " transmitted to us under the name of Paul. Was Paul a letter-writer or an epistolographer? The question is a sufficiently pressing one, in view of the exceedingly great popularity of epistolography in the Apostle's time. Nor can we forthwith answer it, even leaving the Pastoral epistles out of consideration, and attending in the first place only to those whose genuineness is more or less established. The difficulty is seen in its most pronounced form when we compare the letter to Philemon with that to the Romans; here we seem to have two such heterogeneous compositions that it would appear questionable whether we should persist in asking the above disjunctive question. May not Paul have written *both* letters *and* epistles? It would certainly be preposterous to assume, *a priori*, that the " letters " of Paul must be either all letters or all epistles. The inquiry must rather be directed upon each particular " letter "—a task the fulfilment of which lies outside the scope of the present

---

[1] C. Bruston (*Trois lettres des Juifs de Palestine, ZAW.* x. [1890], pp. 110-117) has recently tried to show that 2 Macc. 1^{1}-2^{18} contains not two but three letters ($1^{1-7 a}$, 1^{7b-10a}, $1^{10 b}$-2^{18}).

[2] Unless this be of Christian times, as appears probable to the present writer. In any case it is an instructive analogy for the literary criticism of the Epistle of James and the First Epistle of Peter.

[3] *Cf.* J. Bernays, *Lucian und die Kyniker*, Berlin, 1879, p. 96 ff.

[4] J. Bernays, *Die heraklitischen Briefe*, Berlin, 1869, particularly p. 61 ff.

methodological essay.[1] But, as it is, the author may here at least indicate his opinion.

It appears to him quite certain that the authentic writings of the Apostle are true letters, and that to think of them as epistles [2] is to take away what is best in them. They were, of course, collected, and treated as literature—in

[1] At some future time the author may perhaps pursue the subject further. He hopes then to treat also of so-called formal matters (form of the address, of the beginning and the end, style of letter, etc.), for which he has already gathered some materials.

[2] But seldom has this been more distinctly maintained than quite recently by A. Gercke, who designates the letters of Paul, in plain language, as "treatises in the form of letters" (*GGA.*, 1894, p. 577). But this great and widely-prevalent misconception of the matter stretches back in its beginnings to the early years of the Christian Church. Strictly speaking, it began with the first movements towards the canonisation of the letters. Canonisation was possible only when the non-literary (and altogether uncanonical) character of the messages had been forgotten; when Paul, from being an Apostle, had become a literary power and an authority of the past. Those by whom the letters were treated as elements of the developing New Testament considered the Apostle to be an epistolographer. Further, the pseudo-Pauline "letters," including the correspondence between Paul and Seneca, are evidences of the fact that the writers of them no longer understood the true nature of the genuine letters; the bringing together of the Apostle and the epistolographer Seneca is in itself a particularly significant fact. We may also mention here the connecting—whether genuine or not— of Paul with the Attic orators (in the Rhetorician Longinus: *cf.* J. L. Hug, *Einleitung in die Schriften des Neuen Testaments*, ii.[3], Stuttgart and Tübingen, 1826, p. 334 ff.; Heinrici, *Das zweite Sendschreiben des Ap. P. an die Korinthier*, p. 578). The same position is held very decidedly by A. Scultetus († 1624), according to whom the Apostle imitates the "letters" of Heraclitus (*cf.* Bernays, *Die heraklitischen Briefe*, p. 151). How well the misunderstanding still flourishes, how tightly it shackles both the criticism of the Letters and the representation of Paulinism, the author will not further discuss at present; he would refer to his conclusions regarding method at the end of this essay. In his opinion, one of the most pertinent things that have been of late written on the true character of Paul's letters is § 70 of Reuss's Introduction (*Die Geschichte der heiligen Schrr. N.T.* p. 70). Mention may also be made—reference to living writers being omitted —of A. Ritschl's *Die christl. Lehre von der Rechtfertigung und Versöhnung*, ii.[3], p. 22. Supporters of the correct view were, of course, not wanting even in earlier times. Compare the anonymous opinion in the Codex Barberinus, iii., 36 (saec. xi.): ἐπιστολαὶ Παύλου καλοῦνται, ἐπειδὴ ταύτας ὁ Παῦλος ἰδίᾳ ἐπιστέλλει καὶ δι' αὐτῶν οὓς μὲν ἤδη ἑώρακε καὶ ἐδίδαξεν ὑπομιμνήσκει καὶ ἐπιδιορθοῦται, οὓς δὲ μὴ ἑώρακε σπουδάζει κατηχεῖν καὶ διδάσκειν, in E. Klostermann's *Analecta zur Septuaginta, Hexapla und Patristik*, Leipzig, 1895, p. 95.

point of fact, as literature in the highest sense, as canonical
—at an early period. But that was nothing more than an
after-experience of the letters, for which there were many
precedents in the literary development sketched above.
But this after-experience cannot change their original character, and our first task must be to ascertain what this
character actually is. Paul had no thought of adding a
few fresh compositions to the already extant Jewish epistles,
still less of enriching the sacred literature of his nation;
no, every time he wrote, he had some perfectly definite
impulse in the diversified experiences of the young Christian
churches. He had no presentiment of the place his words
would occupy in universal history; not so much as that
they would still be in existence in the next generation, far
less that one day the people would look upon them as Holy
Scripture. We now know them as coming down from the
centuries with the literary patina and the nimbus of canoni-
city upon them; should we desire to attain a historical
estimate of their proper character, we must disregard both.
Just as we should not allow the dogmatic idea of the mass
to influence our historical consideration of the last Supper
of Jesus with His disciples, nor the liturgical notions of a
prayerbook-commission to influence our historical consideration of the Lord's Prayer, so little dare we approach the
letters of Paul with ideas about literature and notions
about the canon. Paul had better work to do than the
writing of books, and he did not flatter himself that he
could write *Scripture;* he wrote letters, real letters, as did
Aristotle and Cicero, as did the men and women of the
Fayyûm. They differ from the messages of the homely
Papyrus leaves from Egypt not as letters, but only as the
letters of *Paul.* No one will hesitate to grant that the
Letter to Philemon has the character of a letter. It must
be to a large extent a mere doctrinaire want of taste that
could make any one describe this gem, the preservation of
which we owe to some fortunate accident, as an essay, say,
"on the attitude of Christianity to slavery". It is rather a
letter, full of a charming, unconscious naïveté, full of kindly

human nature.   It is thus that Epicurus writes to his
child, and Moltke to his wife : no doubt Paul talks of other
matters than they do—no one letter, deserving the name, has
ever looked like another—but the Apostle does exactly what
is done by the Greek philosopher and the German officer.

It is also quite clear that the note of introduction
contained in *Rom.* 16 is of the nature of a true letter.
No one, it is to be hoped, will make the objection that
it is directed to a number of persons—most likely the
Church at Ephesus ; the author thinks that he has made
it probable that the number of receivers is of no account
in the determination of the nature of a letter.[1]   But
the *Letter to the Philippians* is also as real a letter as
any that was ever written.   Here a quite definite situation
of affairs forced the Apostle to take up his pen, and the
letter reflects a quite definite frame of mind, or, at least,
enables us to imagine it.   The danger of introducing into
our investigation considerations which, so far as concerns
method,[2] are irrelevant, is, of course, greater in this case.
Some reader will again be found to contend that, in contrast to the *private letter* to Philemon, we have here a
congregational letter : some one, again, who is convinced of
the valuelessness of this distinction, will bring forward the
peculiarity of the contents · the letter is of a " doctrinal "
character, and should thus be designated a *doctrinal letter.*
This peculiarity must not be denied—though, indeed, the
author has misgivings about applying the term *doctrine* to
the Apostle's messages ; the " doctrinal " sections of the
letters impress him more as being of the nature of confessions and attestations.   But what is added towards the
answering of our question *letter or epistle ?* by the expression

---

[1] *Cf.* pp. 4 and 18 f.

[2] The relative lengthiness of the letter must also be deemed an
irrelevant consideration—one not likely, as the author thinks, to be advanced.   The difference between a letter and an epistle cannot be decided
by the tape-line.   Most letters are shorter than the Letter to the Philippians, shorter still than the " great " Pauline letters.   But there are also
quite diminutive epistles : a large number of examples are to be found in the
collection of Hercher.

"*doctrinal*" *letter*—however pertinent a term? If a letter is intended to instruct the receiver, or a group of receivers, does it thereby cease to be a letter? A worthy pastor, let us say, writes some stirring words to his nephew at the university, to the effect that he should not let the "faith" be shaken by professorial wisdom; and he refutes point by point the inventions of men. Perhaps, when he himself was a student, he received some such sincere letters from his father against the new orthodoxy which was then, in its turn, beginning to be taught. Do such letters forthwith become tractates simply because they are "doctrinal"?[1] We must carefully guard against an amalgamation of the two categories *doctrinal letter* and *epistle*. If any one be so inclined, he may break up the *letter* into a multitude of subdivisions: the twenty-one or forty-one τύποι of the old theorists[2] may be increased to whatever extent one wishes.

[1] At the present day it would be difficult enough, in many cases, to determine forthwith the character of such letters. For instance, the so-called *Pastoral Letters* of bishops and general superintendents might almost always be taken as epistles, not, indeed, because they are official, but because they are designed for a public larger than the address might lead one to suppose. Further, at the present day they are usually printed from the outset. An example from the Middle Ages, the "letter" of Gregory VII. to Hermann of Metz, dated the 15th March, 1081, has been investigated in regard to its literary character by C. Mirbt, *Die Publizistik im Zeitalter Gregors VII.*, Leipzig, 1894, p. 23. *Cf.*, on p. 4 of the same work, the observations on literary publicity. The defining lines are more easily drawn in regard to antiquity. A peculiar hybrid phenomenon is found in the still extant correspondence of *Abelard and Heloise*. It is quite impossible to say exactly where the letters end and the epistles begin. Heloise writes more in the style of the letter, Abelard more in that of the epistle. There had, of course, been a time when both wrote differently: the glow of feeling which, in the nun's letters, between biblical and classical quotations, still breaks occasionally into a flame of passion, gives us an idea of how Heloise may once have written, when *it was impossible for her to act against his wish*, and when she felt herself *altogether guilty and yet totally innocent*. Neither, certainly, did Abelard, before the great sorrow of his life had deprived him of both his nature and his naturalness, write in the affected style of the convert weary of life, whose words *like deadly swords pierced the soul* of the woman who now lived upon memories. In his later "letters" he kept, though perhaps only unconsciously, a furtive eye upon the public into whose hands they might some day fall—and then he was no longer a letter-writer at all.

[2] See p. 35.

The author has no objection to any one similarly breaking up
the Pauline letters into several subdivisions, and subsuming
some of them under the species *doctrinal letter;* only one
should not fondly imagine that by means of the *doctrinal
letter* he has bridged over the great gulf between letter and
epistle.   The pre-literary character even of the doctrinal
letter must be maintained.

    This also holds good of the *other* Letters of Paul, even of
the "*great Epistles*".   They, too, are partly doctrinal; they
contain, in fact, theological discussions : but even in these, the
Apostle had no desire to make literature.   The *Letter to the
Galatians* is not a pamphlet " upon the relation of Christianity
to Judaism," but a message sent in order to bring back the
foolish Galatians to their senses.   The letter can only be
understood in the light of its special purpose as such.[1]   How
much more distinctly do the *Letters to the Corinthians* bear the
stamp of the true letter !   The second of them, in particular,
reveals its true character in every line; in the author's
opinion, it is the most letter-like of all the letters of Paul,
though that to Philemon may appear on the surface to have
a better claim to that position.   The great difficulty in the
understanding of it is due to the very fact that it is so truly
a letter, so full of allusions and familiar references, so pervaded with irony and with a depression which struggles
against itself—matters of which only the writer and the
readers of it understood the purport, but which we, for the
most part, can ascertain only approximately.   What is
doctrinal in it is not there for its own sake, but is altogether
subservient to the purpose of the letter.   The nature of the
letters which were brought to the Corinthians by the fellow-
workers of Paul, was thoroughly well understood by the
receivers themselves, else surely they would hardly have
allowed one or two of them to be lost.   They agreed, in fact,
with Paul, in thinking that the letters had served their
purpose when once they had been read.   We may most
deeply lament that they took no trouble to preserve the
letters, but it only shows lack of judgment to reproach

[1] *Cf.* the observations upon this letter in the *Spicilegium* below.

them on this account. A letter is something ephemeral, and must be so by its very nature;[1] it has as little desire to be immortal as a *tête-à-tête* has to be minuted, or an alms to be entered in a ledger. In particular, the temper of mind in which Paul and his Churches passed their days was not such as to awaken in them an interest for the centuries to come. The Lord was at hand; His advent was within the horizon of the times, and such an anticipation has nothing in common with the enjoyment of the contemplative book-collector. The one-sided religious temper of mind has never yet had any affection for such things as interest the learned. Modern Christians have become more prosaic. We institute collections of archives, and found libraries, and, when a prominent man dies, we begin to speculate upon the destination of his literary remains: all this needs a hope less bold and a faith less simple than belonged to the times of Paul. From the point of view of literature, the preservation even of two letters to the Corinthians is a secondary and accidental circumstance, perhaps owing, in part, to their comparative lengthiness, which saved them from immediate destruction.

The *Letter to the Romans* is also a real letter. No doubt there are sections in it which might also stand in an epistle; the whole tone of it, generally speaking, stamps it as different from the other Pauline letters. But nevertheless it is not a book, and the favourite saying that it is a compendium of Paulinism, that the Apostle has, in it, laid down his Dogmatics and his Ethics, certainly manifests an extreme lack of taste. No doubt Paul wanted to give instruction, and he did it, in part, with the help of contemporary theology, but he does not think of the literary public of his time, or of Christians in general, as his readers; he appeals to a little company of men, whose very existence, one may say, was unknown to the public at large, and who occupied a special position within Christianity. It is unlikely that the Apostle

---

[1] This explains why, of the extant "letters" of celebrated men who have written both letters and epistles, it is the latter that have, in general, been preserved in larger numbers than the former. Compare, for instance, the extant "letters" of Origen.

would send copies of the letter to the brethren in Ephesus, Antioch or Jerusalem; it was to Rome that he despatched it: nor did the bearer of it go to the publishers in the Imperial City,[1] but rather to some otherwise unknown brother in the Lord—just like many another passenger by the same ship of Corinth, hastening one to that house, another to this, there to deliver a message by word of mouth, here to leave a letter or something else. The fact that the Letter to the Romans is not so enlivened by personal references as the other letters of Paul is explained by the conditions under which it was written: he was addressing a Church which he did not yet personally know. Considered in the light of this fact, the infrequence of personal references in the letter lends no support to its being taken as a literary epistle; it is but the natural result of its non-literary purpose. Moreover, Paul wrote even the "doctrinal" portions in his heart's blood. The words ταλαίπωρος ἐγὼ ἄνθρωπος are no cool rhetorical expression of an objective ethical condition, but the impressive indication of a personal ethical experience: it is not theological paragraphs which Paul is writing here, but his confessions.

Certain as it seems to the author that the authentic messages of Paul are letters, he is equally sure that we have also a number of *epistles* from New Testament times. They belong, as such, to the beginnings of "Christian litera-ture". The author considers the *Letter to the Hebrews* as most unmistakably of all an epistle. It professes, in chap. 13[22], to be a λόγος τῆς παρακλήσεως, and one would have no occasion whatever to consider it anything but a literary ora-tion—hence not as an epistle[2] at all—if the ἐπέστειλα and

---

[1] It is a further proof of these "epistles" being letters that we know the bearers of some of them. The epistle as such needs no bearer, and should it name one it is only as a matter of form. It is a characteristic cir-cumstance that the writer of the epistle at the end of the Apocalypse of Baruch sends his booklet to the receivers by an eagle. Paul uses men as his messengers: he would not have entrusted a letter to eagles—they fly too high.

[2] Nor, strictly speaking, can we count the *First Epistle of John* as an epistle—on the ground, that is, that the address **must** have disappeared. It

the greetings at the close did not permit of the supposition that it had at one time opened with something of the nature of an address as well. The address has been lost; it might all the more easily fall out as it was only a later insertion. The address is, indeed, of decisive importance for the understanding of a letter, but in an epistle it is an unessential element. In the letter, the address occupies, so to speak, the all-controlling middle-ground of the picture; in the epistle it is only ornamental detail. Any given λόγος can be made an epistle by any kind of an address. The Epistle to the Hebrews stands on the same literary plane as the Fourth Book of Maccabees, which describes itself as a φιλοσοφώτατος λόγος; the fact that the latter seems to avoid the appearance of being an epistle constitutes a purely external difference between them, and one which is immaterial for the question regarding their literary character.— The author is chiefly concerned about the recognition of the " *Catholic* " *Epistles*, or, to begin with, of some of them at least, as literary epistles. With a true instinct, the ancient Church placed these *Catholic Epistles* as a special group over against the Pauline. It seems to the author that the idea of their catholicity, thus assumed, is to be understood from the form of address in the " letters," and not primarily from the special character of their contents.[1] They are composi-

is a brochure, the literary *eidos* of which cannot be determined just at once. But the special characterisation of it does not matter, if we only recognise the literary character of the booklet. That it could be placed among the "letters" (*i.e.*, in this case, epistles) of the N.T., is partly explained by the fact that it is allied to them in character: literature associated with literature. Hence the present writer cannot think that Weiss (Meyer, xiv.[5] [1888], p. 15) is justified in saying: "It is certainly a useless quarrel about words to refuse to call such a composition a letter in the sense of the New Testament letter-literature". The question *letter or epistle?* is in effect the necessary pre-condition for the understanding of the historical facts of the case. The '·sense" of the *New Testament letter-literature*, which Weiss seems to assume as something well known, but which forms our *problem*, cannot really be ascertained without first putting that question.—The author does not venture here to give a decision regarding the *Second* and *Third Epistles of John;* the question " *letter or epistle?* " is particularly difficult to answer in these cases.

[1] This idea of a *catholic* writing is implied in the classification of the Aristotelian writings which is given by the philosopher David the Armenian

tions addressed to Christians—one might perhaps say the
Church—in general. The catholicity of the address implies,
of course, a catholicity in the contents. What the Church
calls *catholic*, we require only to call *epistle*, and the unsolved enigma with which, according to Overbeck,[1] they
present us, is brought nearer to a solution. The special
position of these "letters," which is indicated by their
having the attribute *catholic* instinctively applied to them,
is due precisely to their literary character; *catholic* means
in this connection *literary*. The impossibility of recognising
the "letters" of Peter, James and Jude as real letters follows directly from the peculiarity in the form of their
address. Any one who writes *to the elect who are sojourners
of the Diaspora in Pontus, Galatia, Cappadocia, Asia and
Bithynia*, or *to the twelve tribes which are of the Diaspora*, or
even *to them which have obtained a like precious faith with us*,
or *to them that are called, beloved in God the Father and kept
for Jesus Christ*, must surely have reflected on the question
as to what means he must employ in order to convey his
message to those so addressed. Quite similarly does that
other early Christian epistle still bear the address *to the
Hebrews ;* quite similarly does the author of the epistle at
the close of the Apocalypse of Baruch write *to the nine-and-a-
half tribes of the Captivity*, and Pseudo-Diogenes, *ep.* 28,[2] *to
the so-called Hellenes*. The only way by which the letters
could reach such ideal addresses was to have them reproduced
in numbers from the first. But that means that they were
literature. Had the *First Epistle of Peter*,[3] for instance, been
intended as a real letter, then the writer of it, or a substitute,
would have had to spend many a year of his life ere he could
deliver the letter throughout the enormous circuit of the

(end of the fifth cent. A.D.) in his prolegomena to the categories of Aristotle
(*Ed.* Ch. A. Brandis, *Schol. in Arist.*, p. 24*a*, Westermann, iii. [1852], p. 9).
In contrast to μερικός *special*, καθολικός is used as meaning *general;* both
terms refer to the contents of the writings, not to the largeness of the public
for which the author respectively designed them.

[1] P. 431.   [2] Hercher, p. 241 ff.

[3] For the investigation of the *Second Epistle of Peter* see the observations which follow below in the *Spicilegium*.

countries mentioned. The epistle, in fact, could only reach its public as a booklet; at the present day it would not be sent as a circular letter in sealed envelope, but as printed matter by book-post. It is true, indeed, that these Catholic Epistles are *Christian* literature : their authors had no desire to enrich universal literature ; they wrote their books for a definite circle of people with the same views as themselves, that is, for Christians ; but books they wrote. Very few books, indeed, are so arrogant as to aspire to become universal literature ; most address themselves to a section only of the immeasurable public—they are special literature, or party literature, or national literature. It is quite admissible to speak of a literary public, even if the public in question be but a limited one—even if its boundaries be very sharply drawn. Hence the early Christian epistles were, in the first instance, special literature ; to the public at large in the imperial period they were altogether unknown, and, doubtless, many a Christian of the time thought of them as esoteric, and handed them on only to those who were brethren ; but, in spite of all, the epistles were designed for some kind of publicity in a literary sense : they were destined for *the* brethren. The ideal indefiniteness of this destination has the result that the contents have an ecumenical cast. Compare the *Epistle of James*, for instance, with the Letters of Paul, in regard to this point. From the latter we construct the history of the apostolic age ; the former, so long as it is looked upon as a letter, is the enigma of the New Testament. Those to whom the " letter " was addressed have been variously imagined to be Jews, Gentile Christians, Jewish Christians, or Jewish Christians and Gentile Christians together ; the map has been scrutinised in every part without any one having yet ascertained where we are to seek—not to say find—the readers. But if *Diaspora* be not a definite geographical term, no more is the Epistle of "James" a letter. Its pages are inspired by no special motive ; there is nothing whatever to be read between the lines ; its words are of such general interest that they might, for the most part, stand in the *Book of Wisdom*, or the

Imitation of Christ. It is true, indeed, that the epistle reveals that it is of early Christian times, but nothing more. There is nothing uniquely distinctive in its motive, and hence no animating element in its contents. " James " sketches from models, not from nature. Unfortunately there has always been occasion, among Christians, to censure contentions and sins of the tongue, greed and calumny ; indignation at the unmercifulness of the rich and sympathy with the *poor* are common moods of the prophetic or apostolic mind ; the scenes from the synagogue and the harvest-field are familiar types —the epistle, in fact, is pervaded by the expressions and topics of the aphoristic " wisdom " of the Old Testament and of Jesus. Even if it could be demonstrated that the writer was alluding to cases which had actually occurred, yet we cannot perceive how these cases concern him in any special way ; there is no particular personal relation between him and those whom he " addresses ". The picture of the readers and the figure of the writer are equally colourless and indistinct. In the letters of Paul, there speaks to us a commanding personality—though, indeed, he had no wish to speak to us at all ; every sentence is the pulse-throb of a human heart, and, whether charmed or surprised, we feel at least the " touch of nature ". But what meets us in the Epistle of James is a great subject rather than a great man, Christianity itself rather than a Christian personality. It has lately become the custom, in some quarters, to designate the book as a *homily.* We doubt whether much is gained by so doing, for the term *homily,* as applied to any of the writings of early Christianity, is itself ambiguous and in need of elucidation ; it probably needs to be broken up in the same way as " *letter* ". But that designation, at least, gives expression to the conviction that the book in question is wholly different in character from a letter. In the same way, the recognition of the fact that the Catholic Epistles in general are not real letters, is evinced by the instinctive judgment passed on them by the Bible-reading community. The Epistle of James and particularly the First Epistle of Peter, one may say, are examples of those New Testament "letters" which play a most important part in popular religion, while the Second Letter to the Corinthians, for instance, must certainly be counted among the least-known parts of the Bible. And naturally so; the latter, properly speaking, was adapted only to the needs of the Corinthians, while later readers know not what to make of it. They seek out a few detached *sayings*, but the connection is not perceived; in it, truly, they find *some things hard to be understood*. But those epistles were adapted to Christians in general; they are ecumenical, and, as such, have a force the persistence of which is not affected by any vicissitude of time. Moreover, it also follows from their character as epistles that the question of authenticity is not nearly so important for them as for the Pauline letters. It is allowable that in the epistle the personality of the writer should be less prominent; whether it is completely veiled, as, for instance, in the Epistle to the Hebrews, or whether it modestly hides itself behind some great name of the past, as in other cases, does not matter; considered in the light of ancient literary practices, this is not only not strange, but in reality quite natural.—Finally, we may consider the *Pastoral Epistles* and the *Seven Messages in the Apocalypse* in regard to the question whether they are epistles. Though it seems to the author not impossible that the former have had worked into them genuine elements of a letter or letters of Paul, he would answer the question in the affirmative. The Seven Epistles of the Book of Revelation, again, differ from the rest in the fact that they do not form books by themselves, nor constitute one book together, but only a portion of a book. It is still true, however, that they are not letters. All seven are constructed on a single definite plan,—while, taken separately, they are not intelligible, or, at least, not completely so; their chief interest lies in their mutual correspondence, which only becomes clear by a comprehensive comparison of their separate clauses: the censure of one church is only seen in its full severity when contrasted with the praise of another.

16. There is now no need, let us hope, of demon-

strating that the distinction between letters and epistles does
not end in mere judgments as to their respective values.
We would be the last to ignore the great value of, say,
the Epistle of James or the Epistles of Peter; a comparison of these writings with the Epistle of Jeremiah, for
example, and many of the Graeco-Roman epistles, would
be sufficient to guard us against that.   In regard to the
latter, one must frequently marvel at the patience of a public
which could put up with the sorry stuff occasionally given
to it as epistles.   The more definitely we assign to the New
Testament epistles a place in ancient epistolography, the
more clearly will they themselves convince us of their own
special excellence.   But our distinction proves itself, as a
principle of method, to be of some importance in other respects, and we may, in conclusion, gather up our methodological inferences in brief form as follows (some of these
have already been indicated here and there).

(1) The historical criticism of early Christian writings
must guard against conceiving of the New Testament as a
collection of homogeneous compositions, and must give due
weight to the pre-literary character of certain parts of it.
The literary portions must be investigated in regard to their
formal similarity with Graeco-Latin and Jewish literature;
further, this line of connection must be prolonged well into
the Patristic literature.   The much-discussed question,
whether we should view the whole subject as the *History of
Early Christian Literature* or as the *Introduction to the New
Testament*, is a misleading one; the alternatives contain a
similar error, the former implying that some, the latter that
all, of the constituent parts of the New Testament should
be considered from a point of view under which they did not
originally stand: the former, in regarding even the real
letters as literature; the latter, in seeking its facts in a
historical connection in which they did not take their rise.
The history of the collection and publication of the non-
literary writings of primitive Christianity, and the history of
the canonisation of the writings which subsequently became

literature, or were literary from the first, constitute, each of them, a distinct field of study.

(2) The letters of Paul afford a fixed starting-point for the history of the origin of the early Christian "letters". We must ask ourselves whether it is conceivable that the literary temperament and the epistles which were its outcome can be older than the letters of Paul.

(3) The collection and publication[1] of the letters of Paul was indirectly influenced by the analogy of other collections of letters[2] made in ancient times.[3] The only possible motive of such collecting and publishing was reverential love.   Once the letters of Paul had been collected and treated as literature, they in turn, thus misconceived, produced a literary impulse. We must, then, carefully weigh the possibility that their collection and publication may form a *terminus post quem* for the composition of the early Christian epistles.

(4) The sources by means of which we are enabled to judge of the knowledge of the New Testament letters which was possessed by Christians of the post-apostolic period, the so-called *testimonia,* and specially the *testimonia e silentio,* have an altogether different historiacl value according as they relate to letters or epistles.[4] The *silentium* regarding the

---

[1] That is to say, of course, publication within Christianity.

[2] Especially those which were made on behalf of a definite circle of readers.

[3] It is not likely that the collection was made all at one time. It may be assumed that the Letter to Philemon, for instance, was a relatively late addition. The collection was probably begun not very long after the death of Paul.

[4] Upon this point the author would specially desire to recommend a perusal of the sketch of the earliest dissemination of the New Testament letters in B. Weiss's *Lehrbuch der Einleitung in das Neue Testament,* Berlin, 1886, §§ 6, 7, p. 38 ff. Many of the apparently striking facts in the history of the "evidence" which are indicated there might find a simple enough explanation if they were regarded from our point of view.

letters (most striking of all, externally considered, in the Book of Acts), is really explained by the nature of the letter as such, and cannot be employed as an evidence of spuriousness. A *silentium*, on the other hand, regarding epistles is, on account of their public character, to say the least, suspicious. The distinction between letters and epistles has also perhaps a certain importance for the criticism of the traditional texts.

(5) The criticism of the Letters of Paul must always leave room for the probability that their alleged contradictions and impossibilities, from which reasons against their authenticity and integrity have been deduced, are really evidences to the contrary, being but the natural concomitants of letter-writing. The history of the criticism of Cicero's letters,[1] for instance, yields an instructive analogy. The criticism of the early Christian epistles must not leave out of account the considerations which are to be deduced from the history of ancient epistolography.

(6) The exegesis of the letters of Paul must take its special standpoint from the nature of the letter. Its task is to reproduce in detail the Apostle's sayings as they have been investigated in regard to the particular historical occasions of their origin, as phenomena of religious psychology. It must proceed by insight and intuition, and hence it has an unavoidable subjective cast. The exegesis of the early Christian epistles must assume a proper historical attitude with regard to their literary character. Its task is not to penetrate into the knowledge of creative personalities in the religious sphere, but to interpret great texts. As the element of personality is wanting in its object, so must that of subjectivity disappear from its procedure.

(7) The value of the New Testament "letters," as sources for the investigation of the Apostolic age, varies according to their individual character. The classic value of

[1] See p. 31.

the letters of Paul lies in their being actual letters, that is to say, in their being artless and unpremeditated ; in this respect also, they resemble those of Cicero.[1] The value of the epistles as sources is not to be rated so highly, and, in particular, not for the special questions regarding the " constitution " and the external circumstances of Christianity ; many details are only of typical value, while others, again, are but literary exercises, or anticipations of conditions not yet fully realised.

(8) In particular, the New Testament letters and epistles, considered as sources for the history of the Christian religion in its early period, are of different respective values. The letters of Paul are not so much sources for the theology, or even for the religion, of the period, as simply for the personal religion of Paul as an individual; it is only by a literary misconception that they are looked upon as the documents of " Paulinism ". The result of their criticism from the standpoint of the history of religion can be nothing more than a sketch of the character of Paul the letter-writer, and not the system of Paul the epistolographer ; what speaks to us in the letters is his faith, not his dogmatics ; his morality, not his ethics ; his hopes, not his eschatology— here and there, no doubt, in the faltering speech of theology. The early Christian epistles are the monuments of a religion which was gradually accommodating itself to external conditions, which had established itself in the world, which received its stimulus less in the closet than in the church, and which was on the way to express itself in liturgy and as *doctrine*.—

" The Hero who is the centre of all this did not himself . . . become an author; the only recorded occasion of his having written at all was when he wrote upon the ground

[1] *Cf.* p. 29, note 3. One may adduce for comparison other non-literary sources as well, *e.g.*, the " We " source of the Acts. It, too, became literature only subsequently—only after it had been wrought into the work of Luke.

with his finger, and the learning of eighteen centuries has not yet divined what he then wrote." [1] If Jesus is the gospel, then it must hold good that the gospel is non-literary. Jesus had no wish to make a religion ; whoever has such a wish will but make a Koran. It was only lack of understanding on the part of those who came after (*die Epigonen*) which could credit the Son of Man with the writing of epistles—and to a king to boot ! The saints are the epistles of Christ. [2] Nor did the Apostle of Jesus Christ advocate the gospel by literature ; in point of fact, the followers of Christ learned first to pray and then to write—like children. The beginnings of Christian literature are really the beginnings of the secularisation of Christianity : the gospel becomes a book-religion. The church, as a factor in history—which the gospel made no claim to be—required literature, and hence it made literature, and made books out of letters ; hence also at length the New Testament came into existence. The New Testament is an offspring of the Church. The Church is not founded upon the New Testament ; other foundation can no man lay than that is laid, which is Jesus Christ. The gain which accrued to the world by the New Testament carried with it a danger which Christianity—to the detriment of the spirit of it—has not always been able to avoid, *viz.*, the losing of itself as a literary religion in a religion of the letter.

[1] Herder, *Briefe, das Studium der Theologie betreffend*, zweyter Theil, zweyte verbesserte Auflage, Frankfurt and Leipzig, 1790, p. 209.

[2] 2 Cor. 3³.

II.

CONTRIBUTIONS TO THE HISTORY OF THE LANGUAGE OF THE GREEK BIBLE.

ἀνοίγω τὰ μνήματα ὑμῶν καὶ ἀνάξω ὑμᾶς ἐκ τῶν μνημάτων ὑμῶν καὶ
εἰσάξω ὑμᾶς εἰς τὴν γῆν τοῦ Ἰσραήλ.

CONTRIBUTIONS TO THE HISTORY OF THE LANGUAGE OF THE GREEK BIBLE.

Ever since the language of the Greek Bible became a subject of consideration, the most astonishing opinions have been held with regard to the sacred text.

There was a time when the Greek of the New Testament was looked upon as the genuinely classical; it was supposed that the Holy Spirit, using the Apostles merely as a pen, could not but clothe His thoughts in the most worthy garb. That time is past: the doctrine of verbal Inspiration, petrified almost into a dogma, crumbles more and more to pieces from day to day; and among the rubbish of the venerable ruins it is the *human* labours of the more pious past that are waiting, all intact, upon the overjoyed spectator. Whoever surrenders himself frankly to the impression which is made by the language of the early Christians, is fully assured that the historical connecting-points of New Testament Greek are not found in the period of the Epos and the Attic classical literature. Paul did not speak the language of the Homeric poems or of the tragedians and Demosthenes, any more than Luther that of the Nibelungen-Lied.

But much still remains to be done before the influence of the idea of Inspiration upon the investigation of early Christian Greek is got rid of. Though, indeed, the former exaggerated estimate of its value no longer holds good, it yet reveals itself in the unobtrusive though widely-spread opinion that the phrase "the New Testament" represents, in the matter of language, a unity and a distinct entity: it is thought that the canonical writings should form a subject of linguistic investigation by themselves, and that it is possible within such a sphere to trace out the laws of a special "genius of language ". Thus, in theological commentaries, even with regard to expressions which have no special religious significance, we may find the observation that so and so are "New Testament" ἅπαξ λεγόμενα,[1] and in a philological discussion of the linguistic relations of the Atticists we are told, with reference to some peculiar construction, that the like does not occur " in the New Testament "—a remark liable to misconception.[2] Or again the meaning of a word in Acts is to be determined : the word occurs also elsewhere in the New Testament, but with a meaning that does not suit the passage in question nearly so well as one that is vouched for say in Galen. Would not the attempt to enrich the "New Testament" lexicon from Galen stir up the most vigorous opposition in those who hold that the "New Testament" language is materially and formally of a uniform and self-contained character? They would object—with the assertion that in the "New Testament" that word was used in such and such a sense, and, therefore, also in the Acts of the Apostles.

In hundreds of similar short observations found in the literature, the methodological presupposition that "the New

---

[1] The only meaning that can be given to such observations—if they are to have any meaning at all—is when it is presumed that " the genius of the language of the New Testament " is not fond of certain words and constructions. It is of course quite a different matter to speak of the ἅπαξ λεγόμενα of a single definite writer such as Paul.

[2] W. Schmid, Der Atticismus in seinen Hauptvertretern von Dionysius von Halikarnass bis auf den zweiten Philostratus, iii., Stuttgart 1893, p. 338. The καί which is inserted between preposition and substantive is there dealt with. The present writer does not suppose that Schmid, whose book is of the greatest importance for the understanding of the biblical texts, would advocate the perverse notion above referred to, should he be called upon to give judgment upon it on principle : especially as the context of the passage quoted permits one to suppose that he there desires to contrast " the N. T." as a monument of popular literature with the studied elegance [?] of Ælian. But the subsuming of the varied writings of the Canon under the philological concept " New Testament " is a mechanical procedure. Who will tell us that, say, even Paul did not consciously aspire to elegance of expression now and then? Why, the very μετὰ καί which, it is alleged, does not belong to the N. T., seems to the author to occur in Phil. 4[3] (differently Act. Ap. 25[23] σύν τε—καί) : cf. ἅμα σύν 1 Thess. 4[17] and 5[10].

Testament" is a philological department by itself, somewhat like Herodotus or Polybius, reveals itself in the same manner. The notion of the Canon is transferred to the language, and so there is fabricated a "sacred Greek" of Primitive Christianity.[1]

It is only an extension of this presupposition when the "New Testament" Greek is placed in the larger connection of a "Biblical" Greek. "The New Testament" is written in the language of the Septuagint. In this likewise much-favoured dictum lies the double theory that the Seventy used an idiom peculiar to themselves and that the writers of the New Testament appropriated it. Were the theory limited to the vocabulary, it would be to some extent justifiable. But it is extended also to the syntax, and such peculiarities as the prepositional usage of Paul are unhesitatingly explained by what is alleged to be similar usage in the LXX.

The theory indicated is a great power in exegesis, and that it possesses a certain plausibility is not to be denied. It is edifying and, what is more, it is convenient. But it is absurd. It mechanises the marvellous variety of the linguistic elements of the Greek Bible and cannot be established either by the psychology of language or by history. It increases the difficulty of understanding the language of biblical texts in the same degree as the doctrine of verbal Inspiration proved obstructive to the historic and religious estimate of Holy Scripture. It takes the literary products which have been gathered into the Canon, or into the two divisions of the Canon, and which arose in the most various circumstances, times and places, as forming one homogeneous magnitude,

---

[1] It is of course true that the language of the early Christians contained a series of religious terms peculiar to itself, some of which it formed for the first time, while others were raised from among expressions already in use to the status of technical terms. But this phenomenon must not be limited to Christianity : it manifests itself in all new movements of civilization. The representatives of any peculiar opinions are constantly enriching the language with special conceptions. This enrichment, however, does not extend to the "syntax," the laws of which rather originate and are modified on general grounds.

and pays no heed to the footprints which bear their silent testimony to the solemn march of the centuries. The author will illustrate the capabilities of this method by an analogy. If any one were to combine the Canon of Muratori, a fragment or two of the Itala, the chief works of Tertullian, the Confessions of Augustine, the Latin Inscriptions of the Roman Christians in the Catacombs and an old Latin translation of Josephus, into one great volume, and assert that here one had monuments of "the" Latin of the early Church, he would make the same error as the wanderers who follow the phantom of "the" biblical Greek. It cannot be disputed that there would be a certain linguistic unity in such a volume, but this unity would depend, not upon the fact that these writings were, each and all, "ecclesiastical," but upon the valueless truism that they were, each and all, written in late-Latin. Similarly we cannot attribute all the appearances of linguistic unity in the Greek Bible to the accidental circumstance that the texts to which they belong stand side by side between the same two boards of the Canon. The unity rests solely on the historical circumstance that all these texts are late-Greek. The linguistic unity of the Greek Bible appears only against the background of classical, not of contemporary "profane," Greek.

It is important, therefore, in the investigation of the Greek Bible, to free oneself first of all from such a methodological notion as the sacred exclusiveness of its texts. And in breaking through the principle, now become a dogma, of its linguistic seclusion and isolation, we must aspire towards a knowledge of its separate and heterogeneous elements, and investigate these upon their own historical bases.

We have to begin with the *Greek Old Testament*. The Seventy translated a Semitic text into their own language. This language was the Egypto-Alexandrian dialect. Our method of investigation is deduced from these two facts.

If we ignore the fact that the work in question is a translation, we thereby relinquish an important factor for the understanding of its linguistic character. The translation is in method very different from what we nowadays

call such.　We see the difference at once when we compare
the Alexandrian theologians' way of working with, say, the
method which Weizsäcker applied in his translation of the
Epistles of Paul.　Was it mere clumsiness, or was it reverence, which caused them to write as they often did?　Who
shall say?　One thing is certain : in proportion as the idea
of 'making the sacred book accessible in another language
was at that time unheard-of, so helpless must the translators
have felt had they been required to give some account of
the correct method of turning Semitic into Greek.　They
worked in happy and ingenuous ignorance of the laws of
Hermeneutics,[1] and what they accomplished in spite of all
is amazing.　Their chief difficulty lay, not in the lexical,
but in the syntactical, conditions of the subject-matter.　They
frequently stumbled at the syntax of the Hebrew text; over
the Hebrew, with its grave and stately step, they have, so to
speak, thrown their light native garb, without being able to
conceal the alien's peculiar gait beneath its folds.　So arose
a written Semitic-Greek [2] which no one ever spoke, far less
used for literary purposes, either before or after.[3]　The supposition, that they had an easy task because the problem of

---

[1] Some centuries later an important Semitic work was translated into
Greek in a very different manner, *viz.*, the original text of Josephus's *Jewish
War*.　In the preface he states that he had written it first of all in his native
language (*i.e.*, Aramaic).　In the work of translation he had recourse to col-
laborateurs for the sake of the Greek style (*c. Ap.* i. 9), *cf.* Schürer, i. (1890),
p. 60 f. [Eng. Trans., i., i., p. 83].　Here then we have the case of a Semitic text
being translated under Greek superintendence with the conscious intention
of attaining Greek elegance.　Thus the *Jewish War* should not, strictly
speaking, be used as an authority for the style of Josephus the Semite.　The
case is different with the *Antiquities*—unless they likewise have been redacted
in form.　Moreover, it has been shown by Guil. Schmidt, *De Flavii Iosephi
elocutione observationes criticae*, Fleck. *Jahrbb. Suppl.* xx. (1894), p. 514 ff.—
an essay in the highest degree instructive on the question of the " influences "
of the Semitic feeling for language—that at most only one Hebraism is found
in Josephus, and that a lexical one, *viz.*, the use of προστίθεσθαι = יסף.

[2] *Cf.* the remarks of Winer, adopted by Schmiedel, Winer-Schmiedel,
§ 4, 1 *b* (p. 25 f.) [Eng. Trans., p. 28 f.], upon the Greek which was really
spoken by the Jewish common people and was independent of the Greek of
translation.　But see the author's remark on p. 74, note 1.

[3] See below, p. 295 ff.

the syntax was largely solved for them through a "Judæo-
Greek" already long in existence,[1] is hardly tenable. We
have a whole series of other Jewish texts from Alexandria,[2]

[1] In particular, J. Wellhausen formerly advocated this supposition;
cf. his observations in F. Bleek's Einleitung in das A. T.[4], Berlin, 1878, p.
578, and, previously, in Der Text der Bücher Samuelis untersucht, Göttingen,
1871, p. 11. But the very example which he adduces in the latter passage
supports our view. In 1 Sam. 4[2, 3], the verb πταίω is twice found, the first
time intransitively, the second time transitively, corresponding respectively
to the Niphal and Qal of נגף. Wellhausen rightly considers it to be incredible that the Seventy "were unwilling or unable" to express "the distinction
of Qal and Hiphil, etc.," by the use of two different Greek words. When,
however, he traces back the double πταίω, with its distinction of meaning,
to the already existent popular usage of the contemporaries of the LXX (i.e.,
from the context—the Alexandrian Jews), he overlooks the fact that the
transitive sense of πταίω is also Greek. The LXX avoided a change of verb
because they desired to represent the same Hebrew root by the same Greek
word, and in this case a Greek could make no objection.—Regarding another
peculiarity of the LXX, viz., the standing use "of the Greek aorist as an
inchoative answering to the Hebrew perfect," it is admitted by Wellhausen
himself that "for this, connecting links were afforded by classical Greek."
—Wellhausen now no longer advocates the hypothesis of a "Judæo-Greek,"
as he has informed the author by letter.

[2] To the literary sources here indicated there have lately been added
certain fragments of reports which refer to the Jewish War of Trajan, and
which were probably drawn up by an Alexandrian Jew: Pap. Par. 68
(Notices, xviii. 2, p. 383 ff.), and Pap. Lond. 1 (Kenyon, p. 229 f.); cf. Schürer,
i., p. 53; further particulars and a new reading in U. Wilcken, Ein Aktens-
tück zum jüdischen Kriege Trajans, Hermes, xxvii. (1892), p. 464 ff. (see also
Hermes, xxii. [1887], p. 487), and on this GGA. 1894, p. 749. Pap. Berol.
8111 (BU. xi., p. 333, No. 341), is also connected with it. I cannot, however willing, discover the slightest difference in respect of language between the readable part of the fragments, which unfortunately is not very
large, and the non-Jewish Papyri of the same period. Independently of their
historical value, the fragments afford some interesting phenomena, e.g.,
κωστωδία (Matt. 27[65 f.], 28[11] κουστωδία, Matt. 27[66] Cod. A κωστουδία; Cod. D
has κουστουδία), ἀχρεῖοι δοῦλοι (Luke 17[10], cf. Matt. 25[30]). The identification
of the ὅσιοι Ἰουδαῖοι with the successors of the Ἀσιδαῖοι of the Maccabean
period, which Wilcken advances, hardly commends itself; the expression
does not refer to a party within Alexandrian Judaism, but is rather a self-
applied general title of honour.—Wilcken, further, has in view the publication
of another Papyrus fragment (Hermes, xxvii., p. 474), which contains an
account of the reception of a Jewish embassy by the Emperor Claudius at
Rome. (This publication has now seen the light; for all further particulars
see the beginning of the author's sketch, "Neuentdeckte Papyrus-Fragmente
zur Geschichte des griechischen Judenthums," in ThLZ. xxiii. (1898), p. 602 ff.)

but do their idioms bear comparison even in the slightest
with the peculiarities of the LXX, which arose quite incidentally?[1] So long as no one can point to the existence of
actual products of an original Judæo-Greek, we must be permitted to go on advocating the hypothesis, probable enough
in itself, that it was never an actual living language at all.

Thus the fact that the Alexandrian Old Testament is a
translation is of fundamental importance for an all-round
criticism of its syntax.   Its "Hebraisms" permit of no conclusions being drawn from them in respect to the language
actually spoken by the Hellenistic Jews of the period : they
are no more than evidences of the complete disparity between
Semitic and Greek syntax.   It is another question, whether
they may not have exercised an influence upon the speech of
the readers of the next period : it is, of course, possible that
the continually repeated reading of the written Judæo-Greek
may have operated upon and transformed the "feeling for
language" of the later Jews and of the early Christians.   In
respect of certain lexical phenomena, this supposition may of
course be made good without further trouble ; the parts of the
O. T. Apocrypha which were in Greek from the beginning,
Philo, Josephus, Paul, the early Christian Epistle-writers,
move all of them more or less in the range of the ethical and
religious terms furnished by the LXX.   It is also quite conceivable that some of the familiar formulæ and formulaic
turns of expression found in the Psalms or the Law were

---

[1] The relation which the language of the Prologue to Sirach bears to
the translation of the book is of the utmost importance in this question.
(Cf. the similar relation between the Prologue to Luke and the main constituent parts of the Gospel; see below, p. 76, note 2.) The Prologue is
sufficiently long to permit of successful comparison : the impression cannot
be avoided that it is an Alexandrian Greek who speaks here; in the book
itself, a disguised Semite. The translator' himself had a correct apprehension of how such a rendering of a Semitic text into Greek differed from
Greek—the language which he spoke, and used in writing the Prologue.
He begs that allowance should be made for him, if his work in spite of all
his diligence should produce the impression τισὶ τῶν λέξεων ἀδυναμεῖν · οὐ γὰρ
ἰσοδυναμεῖ αὐτὰ ἐν ἑαυτοῖς ἑβραϊστὶ λεγόμενα καὶ ὅταν μεταχθῇ εἰς ἑτέραν γλῶσσαν.
Whoever counts the Greek Sirach among the monuments of a "Judæo-Greek,"
thought of as a living language, must show why the translator uses Alexandrian Greek when he is not writing as a translator.

borrowed from the one or the other, or again, that the occasional literary impressiveness is an intentional imitation of the austere and unfamiliar solemnity of that mode of speech which was deemed to be *biblical*. But any fundamental influence of the LXX upon the syntactic, that is to say, the logical, sense of a native of Asia Minor, or of the West, is improbable, and it is in the highest degree precarious to connect certain grammatical phenomena in, say, Paul's Epistles straightway with casual similarities in the translation of the O. T. A more exact investigation of Alexandrian Greek will, as has been already signified, yield the result that far more of the alleged Hebraisms of the LXX than one usually supposes are really phenomena of Egyptian, or of popular, Greek.[1]

This brings us to the second point: the real language, spoken and written, of the Seventy Interpreters was the Egyptian Greek of the period of the Ptolemies. If, as translators, they had often, in the matter of syntax, to conceal or disguise this fact, the more spontaneously, in regard to their lexical work, could they do justice to the profuse variety of the Bible by drawing from the rich store of terms furnished by their highly-cultured environment. Their work is thus one of the most important documents of Egyptian Greek.[2] Conversely, its specifically Egyptian character can be rendered intelligible only by means of a comparison with all that we possess of the literary memorials of Hellenic Egypt from the time of the Ptolemies till about the time of Origen.[3] Since F. W. Sturz[4] began his studies

[1] References in regard to the truly Greek character of alleged Hebraisms in Josephus are given by U. von Wilamowitz-Moellendorff and Guil. Schmidt in the already-quoted study of the latter, pp. 515 f. and 421.—*See* below, p. 290 f.

[2] *Cf.* the remarks of Buresch, *Rhein. Mus. für Philologie*, N. F., xlvi. (1891), p. 208 ff.

[3] In the rich Patristic literature of Egypt there lies much material for the investigation of Egyptian Greek. One must not overestimate here the "influence" of the LXX, particularly of its vocabulary. The Egyptian Fathers doubtless got much from the colloquial language of their time, and the theory of borrowing from the LXX need not be constantly resorted to. The Papyri of the second and third centuries may be used as a standard of comparison.

[4] *De dialecto Macedonica et Alexandrina liber*, Leipzig, 1808.

in this subject there has passed nearly a century, which has disclosed an infinite number of new sources. Why, if the Inscriptions in Egyptian Greek, when systematically turned to account, could put new life into Septuagint research even then, the Papyrus discoveries have now put us in the position of being able to check the Egyptian dialect by document—so to speak—through hundreds of years. A large part of the Papyri, for us certainly the most valuable, comes from the Ptolemaic period itself; these venerable sheets are in the original of exactly the same age as the work of the Jewish translators[1] which has come down to us in late copies. When we contemplate these sheets, we are seized with a peculiar sense of their most delightful nearness to us—one might almost say, of historical reality raised from the dead. In this very way wrote the Seventy—the renowned, the un-approachable—on the same material, in the same characters, and in the same language! Over their work the history of twenty crowded centuries has passed: originating in the self-consciousness of Judaism at a time of such activity as has never been repeated, it was made to help Christianity to become a universal religion ; it engaged the acuteness and the solicitude of early Christian Theology, and was to be found in libraries in which Homer and Cicero might have been sought for in vain ; then, apparently, it was forgotten, but it continued still to control the many-tongued Christianity by means of its daughter-versions : mutilated, and no longer possessed of its original true form, it has come to us out of the past, and now proffers us so many enigmas and problems as to deter the approach not only of overweening ignorance but often of the diffidence of the ablest as well. Meanwhile the Papyrus documents of the same age remained in their tombs and beneath the rubbish ever being heaped upon them ; but our inquiring age has raised them up, and the information concerning the past which they give in return, is also help-ful towards the understanding of the Greek Old Testament. They preserve for us glimpses into the highly-developed civi-

[1] We have Papyri of the very time of Ptolemy II. Philadelphus, who plays such an important part in the traditions of the LXX.

lization of the Ptolemaic period : we come to know the stilted
speech of the court, the technical terms of its industries, its
agriculture and its jurisprudence; we see into the interior of
the convent of Serapis, and into the family affairs which shrink
from the gaze of history. We hear the talk of the people and
the officials—unaffected because they had no thought of making
literature. Petitions and rescripts, letters, accounts and receipts—of such things do the old documents actually consist;
the historian of national deeds will disappointedly put them
aside; to the investigator of the literature only do they
present some fragments of authors of greater importance.
But in spite of the apparent triviality of their contents at
first sight, the Papyri are of the highest importance for the
understanding of the language of the LXX,[1] simply because
they are direct sources, because they show the same conditions
of life which are recorded in the Bible and which, so to speak,
have been translated into Egyptian Greek. Naturally, the obscure texts of the Papyri will often, in turn, receive illumination from the LXX ; hence editors of intelligence have already
begun to employ the LXX in this way, and the author is of
opinion that good results may yet be obtained thereby. In
some of the following entries he hopes, conversely, to have
demonstrated the value of the Egyptian Papyri and Inscriptions for Septuagint research. It is really the pre-Christian
sources which have been used;[2] but those of the early im-

---

[1] A portion at least of the Papyri might be of importance for the LXX
even with respect to matters of form. The author refers to the official decisions, written by trained public functionaries, and approximately contem-
poraneous with the LXX. While the orthography of the letters and other
private documents is in part, as amongst ourselves, very capricious, there
appears to him to be a certain uniformity in those official papers. One may
assume that the LXX, as "educated" people, took pains to learn the official
orthography of their time. The Papyri have been already referred to in
LXX-investigations by H. W. J. Thiersch, *De Pentateuchi versione Alexandrina
libri tres*, Erlangen, 1841, p. 87 ff.; recently by B. Jacob, *Das Buch Esther
bei den LXX*, *ZAW*. x. (1890), p. 241 ff. The Papyri are likewise of great
value for the criticism of the Epistle of Aristeas; hints of this are given in
the writings of Giac. Lumbroso.

[2] U. Wilcken is preparing a collection of Ptolemaic texts (*DLZ*. xiv.
[1893], p. 265). Until this appears we are limited to texts which are scattered
throughout the various editions, and of which some can hardly be utilised.

perial period also will yet yield rich results. One fact observation appears to put beyond question, *viz.*, the preference of the translators for the technical expressions of their surroundings. They, too, understood how to spoil the Egyptians. They were very ready to represent the technical (frequently also the general) terms of the Hebrew original by the technical terms in use in the Ptolemaic period.[1] In this way they sometimes not only Egyptianised the Bible, but, to speak from their own standpoint, modernised it. Many peculiarities from which it might even be inferred that a text different from our own lay before them, are explained, as the author thinks, by this striving to make themselves intelligible to the Egyptians. Such a striving is not of course justifiable from the modern translator's point of view ; the ancient scholars, who did not know the concept "historic," worked altogether naïvely, and if, on that account, we cannot but pardon their obliteration of many historical and geographical particulars in their Bible, we may, as counterbalancing this, admire the skill which they brought to bear upon their wrongly-conceived task.[2] From such considerations arises the demand that no future lexicon to the LXX[3] shall content itself with the bringing forward of mere equations ; in certain cases the

[1] It is specially instructive to notice that terms belonging to the language of the court were employed to express religious conceptions, just as conversely the word *Grace*, for instance, is prostituted by servility or irony amongst ourselves. Legal phraseology also came to be of great importance in religious usage.

[2] Quite similar modernisings and Germanisings of technical terms are found also in Luther's translation. Luther, too, while translating apparently literally, often gives dogmatic shadings to important terms in theology and ethics ; the author has found it specially instructive to note his translation of Paul's υἱοὶ θεοῦ by *Kinder Gottes* (children of God), of υἱὸς θεοῦ by *Sohn Gottes* (Son of God). Luther's dogmatic sense strove against an identical rendering of υἱός in both cases : he was unwilling to call Christians *sons of God*, or Jesus Christ *the child of God*, and in consequence made a distinction in the word υἱός. We may also remember the translation of νόημα in 2 Cor. 10[5] by *Vernunft* (reason), whereby biblical authority was found for the doctrine *fides praecedit intellectum*.

[3] The clamant need of a Lexicon to the LXX is not to be dismissed by pointing to the miserable condition of the Text. The knowledge of the lexical conditions is itself a preliminary condition of textual criticism.

Greek word chosen does not represent the Hebrew original at all, and it would be a serious mistake to suppose that the LXX everywhere used each particular word in the sense of its corresponding Hebrew. Very frequently the LXX did not translate the original at all, but made a substitution for it, and the actual meaning of the word substituted is, of course, to be ascertained only from Egyptian Greek. A lexicon to the LXX will thus be able to assert a claim to utility only if it informs us of what can be learned, with regard to each word, from Egyptian sources. In some places the original was no longer intelligible to the translators ; we need only remember the instances in which they merely transcribed the Hebrew words—even when these were not proper names. But, in general, they knew Hebrew well, or had been well instructed in it. If then, by comparison of their translation with the original, there should be found a difference in meaning between any Hebrew word and its corresponding Greek, it should not be forthwith concluded that they did not understand it : it is exactly such cases that not seldom reveal to us the thoughtful diligence of these learned men.

What holds good of the investigation of the LXX in the narrower sense must also be taken into consideration *in dealing with the other translations of Semitic originals into Greek.* Peculiarities of syntax and of style should not in the first instance be referred to an alleged Judæo-Greek of the translators, but rather to the character of the original. We must, in our linguistic criticism, apply this principle not only to many of the Old Testament Apocryphal writings, but also to the Synoptic Gospels, in so far, at least, as these contain elements which originally were thought and spoken in Aramaic.[1]

[1] The author cannot assent to the thesis of Winer (see the passage referred to above, p. 67, note 2), *viz.,* that if we are to ascertain what was the "independent" (as distinct, *i.e.,* from the LXX-Greek, which was conditioned by the original) Greek of the Jews, we must rely "upon the narrative style of the Apocryphal books, the Gospels, and the Acts of the Apostles". There are considerable elements in "the" Apocrypha and in "the" Gospels which, as translations, are as little "independent" as the work of the LXX.— With regard also to certain portions of the Apocalypse of John, the question must be raised as to whether they do not in some way go back to a Semitic original.

So far as regards these Apocryphal books, the non-existence
of the original renders the problem more difficult, but the
investigator who approaches it by way of the LXX will be
able to reconstruct the original of many passages with considerable certainty, and to provide himself, at least in some
degree, with the accessories most required.   The case is less
favourable in regard to the Synoptic sayings of Jesus, as also
those of His friends and His opponents, which belong to the
very earliest instalment of the pre-Hellenistic Gospel-tradition.
We know no particulars about the translation into Greek of
those portions which were originally spoken and spread abroad
in the Palestinian vernacular ; we only know, as can be perceived from the threefold text itself, that " they interpreted as
best they could ".[1]   The author is unable' to judge how far
retranslation into Aramaic would enable us to understand
the Semitisms which are more or less clearly perceived in the
three texts, and suspects that the solution of the problem,
precisely in the important small details of it, is rendered
difficult by the present state of the text, in the same way as
the confusion of the traditional text of many portions of the
LXX hinders the knowledge of *its* Greek.   But the work
must be done : the veil, which for the Greek scholar rests
over the Gospel sayings, can be, if not fully drawn aside,
yet at least gently lifted, by the consecrated hand of the
specialist.[2]   Till that is done we must guard against the

---

[1] *Cf.* Jülicher, *Einleitung in das N. T.*, 1st and 2nd ed., Freiburg (Baden)
and Leipzig, 1894, p. 235; important observations by Wellhausen in *GGA*.
1896, p. 266 ff.—We must at all events conceive of this kind of translation as
being quite different from the translation of Josephus's *Jewish War* from
Aramaic, which was undertaken in the same half-century, and which might
be called "scientific" (*cf.* p. 67, note 1 above).   Josephus desired to impress
the literary public : the translators of the Logia desired to delineate Christ
before the eyes of the Greek Christians.   The very qualities which would
have seemed "barbaric" to the taste of the reading and educated classes,
made upon the Greeks who "would see Jesus" the impression of what was
genuine, venerable—in a word, *biblical*.

[2] The author recalls, for instance, what is said in Wellhausen's *Israelitische und Jüdische Geschichte*, Berlin, 1894, p. 312, note 1.—Meanwhile this
important problem has been taken in hand afresh by Arnold Meyer (*Jesu
Muttersprache*, Freiburg (Baden) and Leipzig, 1896) and others; *cf.* especially
G. Dalman, *Die Worte Jesu*, vol. i., Leipzig, 1898.

illusion[1] that an Antiochian or Ephesian Christian (even if,
like Paul, he were a product of Judaism) ever really *spoke* as
he may have translated the Logia-collection, blessed—and
cramped—as he was by the timid consciousness of being
permitted to convey the sacred words of the Son of God to
the Greeks.   Perhaps the same peculiarities which, so far as
the LXX were concerned, arose naturally and unintention-
ally, may, in the translators of the Lord's words, rest upon
a conscious or unconscious liturgical feeling : their reading
of the Bible had made them acquainted with the sound,
solemn as of the days of old, of the language of prophet and
psalmist ; they made the Saviour speak as Jahweh spoke
to the fathers, especially when the original invited to such
a procedure.   Doubtless they themselves spoke differently[2]
and Paul also spoke differently,[3] but then the Saviour also
was different from those that were His.

Among the biblical writings a clear distinction can be
traced between those that are translations, or those portions
that can be referred to a translation, and the other genus,
viz., those in Greek from the first.   The authors of these belonged to Alexandria, to Palestine, or to Asia Minor.   Who
will assert that those of them who were Jews (leaving out
of account those who belonged to Palestine) each and all
spoke Aramaic—to say nothing of Hebrew—as their native

---

[1] Also against the unmethodical way in which peculiarities in the
diction of Paul, for example, are explained by reference to mere external
similarities in the Synoptics.   What a difference there is—to take one instructive example—between the Synoptical ἐν τῷ ἄρχοντι τῶν δαιμονίων (Mark
3 [22, etc.]) and the Pauline ἐν Χριστῷ Ἰησοῦ !   See the author's essay *Die
neutestamentliche Formel " in Christo Jesu " untersucht*, pp. 15 and 60.

[2] Compare the prologue to Luke's Gospel.   The author is unaware
whether the task of a comparative investigation with regard to the languages
of the translated and the independent parts respectively of the Gospels has
as yet been performed.   The task is necessary—and well worth while.

[3] Even in those cases in which Paul introduces his quotations from the
LXX without any special formula of quotation, or without other indication,
the reader may often recognise them by the sound.   They stand out distinctly
from Paul's own writing, very much as quotations from Luther, for example,
stand out from the other parts of a modern controversial pamphlet.

tongue? We may assume that a Semitic dialect was known among the Jews of Alexandria and Asia Minor, but this cannot be exalted into the principle of a full historical criticism of their language. It seems to the writer that their national connection with Judaism is made, too hastily, and with more imagination than judgment, to support the inference of a (so to speak) innate Semitic "feeling for language". But the majority of the Hellenistic Jews of the Dispersion probably spoke Greek as their native tongue: those who spoke the sacred language of the fathers had only learned it later.[1] It is more probable that their Hebrew would be Græcised than that their Greek would be Hebraised. For why was the Greek Old Testament devised at all? Why, after the Alexandrian translation was looked upon as suspicious, were new Greek translations prepared? Why do we find Jewish Inscriptions in the Greek language,[2] even where the Jews lived quite by themselves, viz., in the Roman catacombs? The fact is, the Hellenistic Jews spoke Greek, prayed in Greek, sang psalms in Greek, wrote in Greek, and produced Greek literature; further, their best minds thought in Greek.[3] While we may then continue, in critically examining the Greek of a Palestinian writer, to give due weight to the influence of his Semitic "feeling for language,"—an influence, unfortunately, very difficult to test—the same procedure is not justified with regard to the others. How should the Semitic "spirit of language" have exercised influence

[1] This was probably the case, e.g., with Paul, who according to Acts 21[40] could speak in the "Hebrew language". That means probably the Aramaic.

[2] So far as the author is aware no Jewish Inscription in Hebrew is known outside of Palestine before the sixth century A.D.; cf. Schürer, ii., p. 543 (=[3] iii., p. 93 f.) [Eng. Trans., ii., ii., p. 284], and, generally, the references given there.

[3] Aristotle rejoiced that he had become acquainted with a man, a Jew of Coele-Syria, who Ἑλληνικὸς ἦν, οὐ τῇ διαλέκτῳ μόνον, ἀλλὰ καὶ τῇ ψυχῇ (Josephus, c. Ap. i. 22).—The sentence (De confusione ling. § 26) [M. i., p. 424], ἔστι δὲ ὡς μὲν Ἑβραῖοι λέγουσι " φανουηλ," ὡς δὲ ἡμεῖς " ἀποστροφὴ θεοῦ," is of great interest in regard to Philo's opinion as to his own language: he felt himself to be a Greek. Cf. H. A. A. Kennedy, Sources of New Testament Greek, Edinburgh, 1895, p. 54, and the present writer's critique of this book GGA. 1896, p. 761 ff.

over them? And how, first of all indeed, over those early
Christian authors who may originally have been pagans?

This " spirit " must be kept within its own sphere; the
investigator of the Greek of Paul and of the New Testament
epistle-writers must first of all exorcise it, if he would see
his subject face to face. We must start from the philological
environment in which, as a fact of history, we find these
authors to be, and not from an improbable and, at best, in-
definable, linguistic Traducianism. The materials from which
we can draw the knowledge of that philological environment
have been preserved in sufficient quantity. In regard to the
vocabulary, the Alexandrian Bible stands in the first rank:
it formed part of the environment of the people, irrespective
of whether they wrote in Alexandria, Asia Minor or Europe,
since it was the international book of edification for Hellenistic Judaism and for primitive Christianity. We must, of
course, keep always before us the question whether the terms
of the LXX, in so far as they were employed by those who
came after, had not already undergone some change of meaning in their minds. Little as the lexicon of the LXX can be
built up by merely giving the Greek words with their corresponding Hebrew originals, just as little can Jewish or early
Christian expressions be looked upon as the equivalents of
the same expressions as previously used by the LXX. Even
in express quotations one must constantly reckon with the
possibility that a new content has been poured into the old
forms. The history of religious terms—and not of religious
ones only—shows that they have always the tendency to become richer or poorer; in any case, to be constantly altering.[1]
Take the term *Spirit* (*Geist*). Paul, Augustine, Luther,
Servetus, the modern popular Rationalism: all of these
apprehend it differently, and even the exegete who is well
schooled in history, when he comes to describe the biblical
thoughts about *Spirit*, finds it difficult to free himself from
the philosophical ideas of his century. How differently

---

[1] Acute observations on this point will be found in J. Freudenthal's
Die Flavius Josephus beigelegte Schrift Ueber die Herrschaft der Vernunft,
Breslau, 1869, p. 26 f.

must the Colossians, for example, have conceived of *Angels*,
as compared with the travelling artisan who has grown up
under the powerful influences of ecclesiastical artistic tradition, and who prays to his guardian angel! What changes
has the idea of *God* undergone in the history of Christianity
—from the grossest anthropomorphism to the most refined
spiritualisation! One might write the history of religion
as the history of religious terms, or, more correctly, one
must apprehend the history of religious terms as being a
chapter in the history of religion. In comparison with the
powerful religious development recorded in the Hebrew Old
Testament, the work of the Seventy presents quite a different phase: it does not close the religious history of Israel,
but it stands at the beginning of that of Judaism, and the
saying that the New Testament has its source in the Old
is correct only if by the Old Testament one means the book
as it was read and understood in the time of Jesus. The
Greek Old Testament itself was no longer understood in the
imperial period as it was in the Ptolemaic period, and, again,
a pagan Christian in Rome naturally read it otherwise than
a man like Paul. What the author means may be illustrated
by reference to the Pauline idea of *Faith*. Whether Paul discovered it or not does not in the meantime concern us. At
all events he imagined that it was contained in his Bible,
and, considered outwardly, he was right. In reality, however, his idea of faith is altogether new: no one would think
of identifying the πίστις of the LXX with the πίστις of Paul.
Now the same alteration can be clearly perceived in other
conceptions also; it must be considered as possible in all, at
least in principle; and this possibility demands precise examination. Observe, for example, the terms *Spirit, Flesh,
Life, Death, Law, Works, Angel, Hell, Judgment, Sacrifice,
Righteousness, Love.* The lexicon of the Bible must also
discuss the same problem in respect of expressions which are
more colourless in a religious and ethical sense. The men of
the New Testament resembled the Alexandrian translators in
bringing with them, from their " profane " surroundings, the
most varied extra-biblical elements of thought and speech.

When, then, we undertake to expound the early Christian writings, it is not sufficient to appeal to the LXX, or to the terms which the LXX may use in a sense peculiar to themselves : we must seek to become acquainted with the actual surroundings of the New Testament authors.   In what other way would one undertake an exhaustive examination of these possible peculiar meanings ?   Should we confine ourselves to the LXX, or even to artificially petrified ideas of the LXX,— what were that but a concession to the myth of a " biblical " Greek ?   The early Christian writings, in fact, must be taken out of the narrow and not easily-illuminated cells of the Canon, and placed in the sunshine and under the blue sky of their native land and of their own time.   There they will find companions in speech, perhaps also companions in thought.   There they take their place in the vast phenomenon of the κοινή.   But even this fact, in several aspects of it, must not be conceived of mechanically.   One must neither imagine the κοινή to be a uniform whole, nor look upon the early Christian authors, all and sundry, as co-ordinate with a definite particular phenomenon like Polybius.   In spite of all the consanguinity between those early Christian Greeks and the literary representatives of universal Greek, yet the former are not without their distinguishing characteristics. Certain elements in them of the popular dialect reveal the fact of their derivation from those healthy circles of society to which the Gospel appealed : the victorious future of those obscure brotherhoods impressively announces itself in new technical terms, and the Apostles of the second and third generation employ the turns of expression, understood or not understood, used by Paul, that " great sculptor of language ".[1]

It is thus likewise insufficient to appeal to the vocabulary and the grammar of the contemporary " profane " literature.   This literature will doubtless afford the most instructive discoveries, but, when we compare it with the direct sources which are open to us, it is, so far as regards the language of the early Christian authors, only of secondary importance.

[1] The author adopts this easily enough misunderstood expression from Buresch, *Rh. Mus. f. Phil.*, N. F., xlvi. (1891), p. 207.

These direct sources are the Inscriptions[1] of the imperial period.   Just as we must set our printed Septuagint side by side with the Ptolemaic Papyri, so must we read the New Testament in the light of the opened folios of the Inscriptions.   The classical authors reach us only in the traditional texts of an untrustworthy later period; their late codices cannot give us certain testimony with regard to any so-called matters of form, any more than the most venerable uncials of the New Testament can let us know how, say, the Letter to the Romans may have looked in its original form.   If we are ever in this matter to reach certainty at all, then it is the Inscriptions and the Papyri which will give us the nearest approximation to the truth.   Of course even they do not present us with unity in matters of form; but it would be something gained if the variety which they manifest throughout were at least to overthrow the orthodox confidence in the trustworthiness of the printed text of the New Testament, and place it among the " externals ".   Here, too, must we do battle with a certain ingenuous acceptation of the idea of Inspiration.   Just as formerly there were logically-minded individuals who held that the vowel-points in the Hebrew text were inspired, so even to-day there are those here and there who force the New Testament into the alleged rules of a uniform orthography.   But by what authority—unless by the dictate of the Holy Spirit—will any one support the notion that Paul, for instance, *must* have written the Greek form of the name *David* in exactly the same way as Mark or John the Divine?

But the help which the Inscriptions afford in the correction of our printed texts, is not so important as the service

[1] When the author (in 1894) wrote the above, he was unaware that E. L. Hicks, in *The Classical Review*, 1887, had already begun to apply the Inscriptions to the explanation of the N. T.   W. M. Ramsay called attention to this, and gave new contributions of his own in *The Expository Times*, vol. x., p. 9 ff.   A short while ago I found a very important little work in the University Library at Heidelberg, which shows that the Inscriptions had begun to be drawn from a hundred years ago: the booklet, by Io. E. Imm. Walch, is called *Observationes in Matthaeum ex graecis inscriptionibus*, Jena, 1779, and is not without value even at the present day.

6

they render towards the understanding of the language itself. It may be that their contents are often scanty ; it may be that hundreds of stones, tiresomely repeating the same monotonous formula, have only the value of a single authority, yet, in their totality, these epigraphic remains furnish us with plenty of material—only, one should not expect too much of them, or too little.   The author is not now thinking of the general historical contributions which they afford for the delineation of the period—such as we must make for Egypt, Syria, Asia Minor, Europe, if we would understand the biblical writings (though for that purpose nothing can be substituted for them) ; but rather of their value for the history of the language of the Greek Bible, and particularly of the New Testament.   Those witnesses in stone come before us with exactly the same variety as to time and place as we have to take into account when dealing with these writings : the period of most of them, and the original locality of nearly all, can be determined with certainty.   They afford us wholly trustworthy glimpses into certain sections of the sphere of ideas and of the store of words which belonged to certain definite regions, at a time when Christian churches were taking their rise, and Christian books being written. Further, that the *religious* conceptions of the time may receive similar elucidation is a fact that we owe to the numerous *sacred* Inscriptions.   In these, it may be observed that there existed, here and there, a terminology which was fixed, and which to some extent consisted of liturgical formulæ.   When, then, particular examples of this terminology are found not only in the early Christian authors, but in the LXX as well, the question must be asked : Do the Christian writers employ such and such an expression because they are familiar with the Greek Bible, or because they are unaffectedly speaking the language of their neighbourhood ?   If we are dealing, *e.g.*, with the Inscriptions of Asia Minor and the Christians of Asia Minor, the natural answer will be : Such expressions were known to any such Christian from his environment, before ever he read the LXX, and, when he met them again in that book, he had no feeling of having his store of words

enlarged, but believed himself to be walking, so to speak, on
known ground : since, happily for him, there was no Schleusner at his disposal, when he found those expressions in the
LXX—where, in their connection, they were perhaps more
pregnant in meaning, perhaps less so,—he read them with
the eyes of an inhabitant of Asia Minor, and possibly emasculated them. For him they were moulds into which he
poured, according to his own natural endowment, now good,
now less valuable, metal. The mere use of LXX-words on
the part of an inhabitant of Asia Minor is no guarantee that
he is using the corresponding LXX-conceptions. Take as
examples words like ἁγνός, ἱερός, δίκαιος, γνήσιος, ἀγαθός, εὐσέβεια, θρησκεία, ἀρχιερεύς, προφήτης, κύριος, θεός, ἄγγελος,
κτίστης, σωτηρία, διαθήκη, ἔργον, αἰών. With regard to all
these words, and many others, common to both the LXX
and the Inscriptions of Asia Minor of the imperial period, it
will be necessary to investigate how far the Christians of Asia
Minor introduced definite local shades of meaning into their
reading of the Septuagint, and, further, how far they unconsciously took these shades of meaning into account either
in their own use of them or when they heard them uttered
by the Apostles. The same holds good of such expressions
as embody the specifically favourite conceptions of primitive
Christianity, e.g., the titles of Christ, υἱὸς θεοῦ, ὁ κύριος ἡμῶν
and σωτήρ. The author has, with regard to the first of these,
set forth in the following pages in more detail the reasons
why we should not ignore the extra-biblical technical use
of the expression,—a use which, in particular, is authenticated by the Inscriptions. A similar investigation with
regard to the others could be easily carried out. Even if
it could be established that " the " New Testament always
employs these expressions in their original, pregnant, distinctively Christian sense, yet who will guarantee that hundreds
of those who heard the apostolic preaching, or of the readers
of the Epistles, did not understand the expressions in the
faded formulaic sense, in regard to which they reflected as
little or as much as when they read a votive Inscription
in honour of the υἱὸς θεοῦ Augustus, or of another emperor

who was described as ὁ κύριος ἡμῶν, or of Apollo σωτήρ?
By the time of the New Testament there had set in a
process of mutual assimilation[1] between the religious conceptions already current in Asia Minor on the one hand,
and "biblical" and "Christian" elements on the other.
Biblical expressions became secularised; heathen expressions
gained ecclesiastical colouring, and the Inscriptions, as being
the most impartial witnesses to the linguistic usage previous
to New Testament times, are the sources which most readily
permit us a tentative investigation of the process.

Other elements, too, of the language of certain portions
of the New Testament can not seldom be elucidated by
parallels from the Inscriptions; likewise much of the so-called
syntax. M. Fränkel[2] has indicated what an "extraordinary
agreement in vocabulary and style" obtains between the
Pergamenian Inscriptions of pre-Roman times and Polybius:
it is proved, he thinks, that the latter, "almost entirely
wanting in a distinctive style of his own," has "assumed
the richly but pedantically developed speech of the public
offices of his time". The Inscriptions of Asia Minor have,
as the author thinks, a similar significance for the history
of the language of the New Testament. It may be readily
granted to the outsider that many of the observations which
it is possible to take in this connection have, of course,
"only" a philological value; he who undertakes them knows
that he is obeying not only the voice of science but also the
behests of reverence towards the Book of Humanity.[3]

The author has, here and there throughout the following pages, endeavoured to carry out in practice the ideas of
method thus indicated. He would request that to these

---

[1] So far as the author can judge, this process shows itself more clearly
in the Catholic and the Pastoral Epistles than in Paul.

[2] *Altertümer von Pergamon*, viii. 1, Berlin, 1890, p. xvii.

[3] This matter is further dealt with in the author's little work *Die
sprachliche Erforschung der griechischen Bibel, ihr gegenwärtiger Stand und
ihre Aufgaben*, Giessen, 1898; *cf.* also *GGA.* 1896, pp. 761-769; 1898, pp. 120-
124, and 920-923; *ThLZ.* xxi. (1896), p. 609 ff., and xxiii. (1898), p. 628 ff.;
Theologische Rundschau, i. (1897-98), pp. 463-472.

should be added the observations that lie scattered throughout the other parts of this book. If he makes a further
request for indulgence, he would not omit to emphasise that
he is not thereby accommodating himself to the well-worn
literary habit the real purpose of which is only the *captatio
benevolentiae.* The peculiar nature of the subject-matter,
which first attracted the author, is certainly calculated to
engender the feeling of modesty, unless, indeed, the investigator has been possessed of that quality from the outset.

ἀγγαρεύω.

Herodotus and Xenophon speak of the Persian ἄγγαροι. The word is of Persian origin and denotes the royal *couriers*. From ἄγγαρος is formed the verb ἀγγαρεύω, which is used, Mark 15 [21] = Matt. 27 [32] and Matt. 5 [41] (a saying of the Lord), in the sense of *to compel one to something*. E. Hatch[1] finds the earliest application of the verb in a letter of Demetrius I. Soter to the high-priest Jonathan and the Jewish people: κελεύω δὲ μηδὲ ἀγγαρεύεσθαι τὰ Ἰουδαίων ὑποζύγια, Joseph. *Antt.* xiii. 2 s. The letter was ostensibly written shortly before the death of the king, and, if this were so, we should have to date the passage shortly before the year 150 B.C. But against this assumption is to be placed the consideration that 1 Macc. 10 [25-45], which was the source for the statement of Josephus, and which also quotes the said letter verbally, knows nothing of the passage in question. Indeed it rather appears that Josephus altered the passage, in which the remission of taxes upon the animals is spoken of (ver. [33] καὶ πάντες ἀφιέτωσαν τοὺς φόρους καὶ τῶν κτηνῶν αὐτῶν), so as to make it mean that they should not be forced into public work. Even if, following Grimm,[2] we consider it possible that the passage in Maccabees has the same purport as the paraphrase of Josephus, yet the word—and it is only the word which comes into consideration here—must be assigned to Josephus, and, therefore, can be made to establish nothing in regard to the second century B.C., but only in regard to the first A.D.

[1] *Essays in Biblical Greek*, Oxford, 1889, p. 37.
[2] *HApAT*. iii. (1853), p.155 f.

But we find the verb in use at a time much earlier than
Hatch admitted. The Comedian Menander († 290 B.C.) uses
it in *Sicyon*. iv. (Meineke, p. 952). It is twice employed in
Pap. Flind. Petr. ii. xx.[1] (252 B.C.), both times in reference to
a boat used for postal service: τοῦ ὑπάρχοντος λέμβου ἀγγαρευ-
θέντος ὑπό σου and ἀγγαρεύσας τὸν Ἀντικλέους λέμβον.

This application of the word is established for the
Egyptian dialect[2] of Greek by the Inscription from the
Temple of the Great Oasis (49 A.D.),[3] in which there is other
linguistic material bearing on the Greek Bible, and to which
Hatch has already called attention: μηδὲν λαμβάνειν μηδὲ
ἀγγαρεύειν εἰ μή τινες ἐμὰ διπλώματα ἔχωσι.

In view of these facts the usage of the verb in the
Synoptists[4] and Josephus falls into a more distinct historical
connection: the word, originally applied only to a Persian
institution, had gained a more general sense as early as the
third century B.C.[5] This sense, of course, was itself a technical one at first, as can be seen from the Papyrus and the
Inscription as well as from Josephus, but the word must
have become so familiar that the Evangelists could use it
quite generally for *to compel*.

ἀδελφός.

The employment of the name *brother* to designate the
members of Christian communities is illustrated by the

---

[1] Mahaffy, ii. [64].

[2] The Persian loan-word recalls the Persian dominion over Egypt: *cf.*
παράδεισος below.—It may appear strange that the LXX do not use ἄγγαρος,
etc., though אִגֶּרֶת, perhaps also derived from the Persian, is found in
those portions which belong to the Persian period, and might have prompted
them to use a cognate Greek substantive. But they translate both it and
the Aramaic אִגְּרָא in every passage by ἐπιστολή, just because there was not
any Greek word formed from ἄγγαρος for *letter*.—For the orthography
ἐγγαρεύω *cf.* III. i. 1 below.

[3] *CIG.* iii. No. 4956, A 21.

[4] What is the Aramaic word which is rendered by ἀγγαρεύω in Matt. 5⁴¹?

[5] *Cf.* Buresch, *Rhein. Mus. für Philologie*, N. F., xlvi. (1891), p. 219:
"The Persian loan-word ἀγγαρεύω, which was naturalised at a very early date,
must have come to be much used in the vernacular—it is still found in the
common dialect of Modern Greek".

similar use, made known to us by the Papyri, of ἀδελφός
in the technical language of the Serapeum at Memphis.
See the detailed treatment of it in A. Peyron,[1] Leemans,[2]
Brunet de Presle,[3] and Kenyon.[4]—ἀδελφός also occurs in the
usage of religious associations of the imperial period as
applied to the members, cf. Schürer, in the *Sitzungsberichte
der Berliner Akademie der Wissenschaften*, 1897, p. 207 ff., and
Cumont, *Hypsistos*, Brussels, 1897, p. 13.

ἀναστρέφομαι.

The moral signification *se gerere* in 2 Cor. 1[12], Eph. 2[3],
1 Pet. 1[17], 2 Pet. 2[18], Heb. 10[33], 13[18], 1 Tim. 3[15], is illustrated
by Grimm,[5] needlessly, by the analogy of the Hebrew הָלַךְ.
It is found in the Inscription of Pergamus No. 224 A[6]
(middle of the second century B.C.), where it is said of some
high official of the king ἐν πᾶσιν κα[ιροῖς ἀμέμπτως καὶ ἀδ]εῶς
ἀναστρεφόμενος.—Further examples in III. iii. 1.

ἀναφάλαντος.

LXX Lev. 13[41] = גִּבֵּחַ, *forehead-bald*, frequent in personal
descriptions in the Papyri of 237, 230 and 225 B.C. ;[7] cf. ἀνα-
φαλάντωμα = גַּבַּחַת, LXX Lev. 13[42. 43].

ἀναφέρω.

In 1 Pet. 2[24] it is said of Christ : ὃς τὰς ἁμαρτίας ἡμῶν
αὐτὸς ἀνήνεγκεν ἐν τῷ σώματι αὐτοῦ ἐπὶ τὸ ξύλον, ἵνα ταῖς
ἁμαρτίαις ἀπογενόμενοι τῇ δικαιοσύνῃ ζήσωμεν. Many commentators consider the expression ἀναφέρειν τὰς ἁμαρτίας to

---

[1] *Papyri Graeci regii Taurinensis musei Aegyptii*, i. Turin, 1826, p. 60 ff.

[2] I., pp. 53 and 64.   [3] *Notices*, xviii. 2, p. 308.   [4] P. 31.

[5] *Ch. G. Wilkii Clavis Novi Testamenti philologica*[3], Leipzig, 1888, p. 28.

[6] Fränkel, p. 129. The word occurs also in Polybius in the same sense.
W. Schulze has also called the attention of the author to the Inscription of
Sestos (c. 120 B.C.), line ϖ; on this cf. W. Jerusalem, *Wiener Studien*, i. (1879),
p. 53.

[7] For particular references see Mahaffy, i. (1891), Index [88], cf. Kenyon,
p. 46; *Notices*, xviii. 2, p. 131. For the etymology, W. Schulze, *Quaestiones
epicae*, Gütersloh, 1892, p. 464; the ἀναφαλαντίασις in Aristot. *H. A.* iii. 11
presupposes ἀναφάλαντος.

be a quotation of LXX Is. 53 ^{12} καὶ αὐτὸς ἁμαρτίας πολλῶι
ἀνήνεγκε and demand that it be understood in the same sense
as in Isaiah : [1] *to bear sins*, *i.e.*, *to suffer punishment for sins*.
But even granting that the whole section is pervaded by
reminiscences of Is. 53, yet it is not scientifically justifiable
to assert that the writer *must* have used ἀναφέρειν in the very
sense of the original which he followed.　The cases are not
few in which phrases from the LXX, given word for word,
and introduced by the solemn formulæ of quotation, have
acquired another sense from the particular new context into
which they are brought.　The early Christian authors do not
quote with that precision as to form and substance which
must needs be shown in our own scientific investigations ;
these " practical " exegetes, in their simple devoutness, have
an ethical and religious purpose in their quotations, not a
scientific one.　Thus their references cannot properly be
called *quotations* at all : *sayings*, in our pregnant use of that
term, would be the preferable expression.　The " practical "
exegetes of every age have considered the same absolute
freedom with regard to the letter as their natural privilege.
In regard to our passage, the addition of ἐπὶ τὸ ξύλον makes
it certain that, even if the allusion is to Isaiah, ἀναφέρειν
cannot be explained by its possible [2] meaning in the Greek
translation of the book.　If *to bear* be made to mean *to suffer
punishment*, then the verb would require to be followed [3] by
ἐπὶ τῷ ξύλῳ : ἐπὶ cum acc. at once introduces the meaning *to
carry up to.*

　　What then is meant by Christ *bearing* our sins in His
body *up to* the tree ?　Attention is commonly called to the
frequently occurring collocation ἀναφέρειν τι ἐπὶ τὸ θυσιαστήριον, and from this is deduced the idea that the death of
Christ is an expiatory sacrifice.　But this attempt at explanation breaks down [4] when it is observed that it is certainly
not said that Christ laid *Himself* upon the tree (as the altar) ;

---

[1] So with Heb. 9 ^{28}.

[2] If, that is to say, the LXX treated the *conceptions* ἀναφέρειν and נָשָׂא
as equivalent.

[3] E. Kühl, Meyer, xii. ^{5} (1887), p. 165.　　　[4] *Cf.* Kühl, p. 166 f.

it is rather the ἁμαρτίαι ἡμῶν that form the object of ἀναφέρειν, and it cannot be said of these that they were offered up. That would be at least a strange and unprecedented mode of expression. The simplest explanation will be this : when Christ *bears up to* the cross the sins of men, then men have their sins no more ; the *bearing up to* is a *taking away*. The expression thus signifies quite generally that Christ took away our sins by His death : there is no suggestion whatever of the special ideas of substitution or sacrifice.

This explanation, quite satisfactory in itself, appears to the author to admit of still further confirmation. In the contract *Pap. Flind. Petr.* i. xvi. 2 [1] (230 B.C.), the following passage occurs : περὶ δὲ ὧν ἀντιλέγω ἀναφερομεν [. . . . .] ὀφειλημάτων κριθήσομαι ἐπ' 'Ασκληπιάδου. The editor re- stores the omission by ων εἰς ἐμέ, and so reads ἀναφερομένων εἰς ἐμέ. In this he is, in our opinion, certainly correct as to the main matter. No other completion of the participle is possible, and the connection with the following clauses requires that the ἀναφερόμενα ὀφειλήματα should stand in relation to the "I" of ἀντιλέγω. It can hardly be determined whether precisely the preposition εἰς [2] be the proper restora- tion, but not much depends on that matter. In any case the sense of the passage is this : *as to the ὀφειλήματα ἀναφερόμενα upon* (or *against*) *me, against which I protest, I shall let myself be judged by Asklepiades*.[3] It is *a priori* probable that ἀναφέρειν τὰ ὀφειλήματα is a forensic technical expression : he who imposes[4] the debts of another upon a third desires to free the former

---

[1] Mahaffy, i. [47].

[2] ἐπί were equally possible ; *cf.* p. 91, note 1.

[3] Mahaffy, i. [48], translates : " But concerning the debts charged against me, which I dispute, I shall submit to the decision of Asklepiades ".

[4] It is true that ἀναφέρειν occurs also in the technical sense of *referre* (*cf.*, besides the dictionaries, A. Peyron, i., p. 110), frequently even in the LXX, and one might also translate the clause : *as to the debts alleged* (*before the magistracy*) *against me ;* ἀναφέρειν would then mean something like *sue for*. But the analogies from the Attic Orators support the above explanation. In LXX 1 Sam. 20 [13] ἀνοίσω τὰ κακὰ ἐπὶ σέ, we have ἀναφέρω in a quite similar sense. *Cf.* Wellhausen, *Der Text der Bb. Sam.*, p. 116 f., for the origin of this translation.

from the payment of thé same. The Attic Orators [1] employ
ἀναφέρειν ἐπί in exactly the same way : Æsch. 3, 215, τὰς ἀπὸ
τούτων αἰτίας ἀνοίσειν ἐπ᾽ ἐμέ ; Isocr. 5, 32, ἣν ἀνενέγκῃς αὐτῶν
τὰς πράξεις ἐπὶ τοὺς σοὺς προγόνους.

That the technical expression was known to the writer
of the Epistle cannot of course be proved, but it is not
improbable.[2] In that case his ἀναφέρειν would take on its
local colour. The sins of men are *laid upon* the cross, as, in
a court of law, a debt in money [3] is removed from one and
laid upon another. Of course the expression must not be
pressed : the writer intends merely to establish the fact that
Christ in His death has removed the sins of men. The nerve
of the striking image which he employs lies in the correlative
idea that the sins of men lie no more upon them. The
forensic metaphor in Col. 2 [14] is at least quite as bold, but
is in perfect harmony with the above : Christ has taken the
χειρόγραφον, drawn up against mankind, out of the way,
nailing it to His cross.

ἀντιλήμπτωρ.[4]

Frequent in the LXX, especially in the Psalms ; also in
Sirach 13 [22], Judith 9 [11]; nearly always used of God as the
Helper of the oppressed. Not hitherto authenticated in
extra-biblical literature.[5] The word is found in *Pap. Lond.*
xxiii.[6] (158-157 B.C.), in a petition to the king and queen, in
which the petitioner says that he finds his καταφυγή in them,
and that they are his ἀντιλήμπτορες ; *cf.* the similar conjunction of καταφυγή and ἀντιλήμπτωρ in LXX 2 Sam. 22 [3].

[1] A. Blackert, *De praepositionum apud oratores Atticos usu quaestiones
selectae*, Marp. Catt., 1894, p. 45.

[2] *Cf.* also the other forensic expressions of the section : κρίνειν ver. [23],
and δικαιοσύνη ver. [24].

[3] Sin is often viewed as a debt in the early Christian sphere of thought.
—*Cf.* III. iii. 2 below.

[4] With regard to the orthography, *cf.* the Programme of W. Schulze,
Orthographica, Marburg, 1894, i., p. xiv. ff. ; Winer-Schmiedel, § 5, 30 (p. 64).

[5] "Peculiar to the LXX," Cremer [7], p. 554 (= [8] 587).

[6] Kenyon, p. 38.

ἀντίλημψις.[1]

Frequent, in the LXX and the Apocryphal books, for
Help. This meaning is not[2] peculiar to "biblical" Greek,
but occurs frequently in petitions to the Ptolemies : *Pap. Par.*
26[3] (163-162 B.C.), *Pap. Lond.* xxiii.[4] (158-157 B.C.), *Pap. Par.*
8[5] (131 B.C.), *Pap. Lugd.* A[6] (Ptolemaic period) ; always
synonymous with βοήθεια. The last two passages yield
the combination τυχεῖν ἀντιλήμψεως[7] which also occurs in
2 Macc. 15[7] and 3 Macc. 2[33].—See further III. iii. 3 below.

This meaning of the word (known also to Paul, 1 Cor.
12[28]), like that of ἀντιλήμπτωρ, was found by the LXX,
as it appears, in the obsequious official language of the
Ptolemaic period. One understands how they could, without the slightest difficulty, transfer such terms of the canting
and covetous court speech to religious matters when one reads
of the royal pair being addressed as ὑμᾶς τοὺς θεοὺς μεγίστους
καὶ ἀντιλήμπτορας, *Pap. Lond.* xxiii.[8] (158-157 B.C.) ; the
worship of the monarch had emasculated the conception
θεός, and thus ἀντιλήμπτωρ and ἀντίλημψις had already
acquired a kind of religious nimbus.

ἀξίωμα.

The LXX translate the words בַּקָּשָׁה (Esther 5[3-8], 7[2 f.]),
תְּחִנָּה (Ps. 118 [119][170]) and the Aramaic בָּעוּ (Dan. 6[7]),
which all mean *request, desire*, by ἀξίωμα. The word occurs
in 1 [3] Esd. 8[4] in the same sense. It is " very infrequent
in this signification ; the lexica cite it, in prose, only from
Plutarch, *Conviv. disput.* ii. 1₉ (p. 632 C)"[9]. The Inscriptions
confirm the accuracy of its usage in the LXX : fragment of
a royal decree to the inhabitants of Hierocomé (date ?) from

---

[1] For the orthography *cf.* p. 91, note 4.

[2] Contra Cremer[7], p. 554 (= [8] 587) ; *Clavis*[3], p. 34.

[3] *Notices*, xviii. 2, p. 276.   [4] Kenyon, p. 38.

[5] *Notices*, xviii. 2, p. 175.   [6] Leemans, i., p. 3.

[7] Upon this *cf.* Leemans, i., p. 5.   [8] Kenyon, p. 38.

[9] Fränkel, *Altertümer von Pergamon*, viii. 1, p. 13 f.

Tralles;[1] a decree of the Abderites (before 146 B.C.) from Teos;[2] Inscription of Pergamus No. 13 (soon after 263 B.C.).[2] "In all these examples the word signifies a request preferred before a higher tribunal, thus acquiring the sense of 'petition' or 'memorial'"[4].

ἀπό.

Of the construction 2 Macc. 14 [30] ἀπὸ τοῦ βελτίστου *in the most honourable way*, in which one might suspect an un-Greek turn of expression, many examples can be found in the Inscriptions, as also in Dionysius of Halicarnassus and Plutarch.[5]

ἀρεταλογία.[6]

O. F. Fritzsche[7] still writes Sirach 36 [19] ([14 or 16] in other editions) as follows : πλῆσον Σιὼν ἆραι τὰ λόγιά σου καὶ ἀπὸ τῆς δόξης σου τὸν λαόν σου. M. W. L. de Wette implies the same text by his rendering : *Fill Zion with the praise of Thy promises, and Thy people with Thy glory;* he takes[8] ἆραι in the sense of *laudibus extollere, celebrare*, and thus the verbal translation would run : *Fill Zion, in order to extol Thy declarations, and Thy people with Thy glory.* But against this Fritzsche[9] makes the objection that ἆραι must stand here in the sense of נָשָׂא, and this, again, should be taken as *receive, obtain*, although, indeed, such a meaning cannot be vouched for by any quite analogous example. But leaving aside the fact that it is not good procedure to illustrate an obscure translation by referring

---

[1] Waddington, iii. (Ph. Le Bas *et* W. H. Waddington, *Inscriptions grecques et latines recueillies en Grèce et en Asie Mineure*, vol. iii., part 2, Paris, 1870), No. 1652 (p. 390).

[2] *Bull. de corr. hell.* iv. (1880), p. 50 = Guil. Dittenberger, *Sylloge inscriptionum Graecarum*, Leipzig, 1883, No. 228.

[3] Fränkel, p. 12.   [4] *Ibid.*, p. 14.   [5] References in Fränkel, p. 16.

[6] Upon this *cf.* also the investigations of Meister, *Berichte der [Kgl. Sächsischen Gesellschaft der Wissenschaften*, 1891, p. 13 ff., to which Wendland has called attention (*Deutsche Litteraturzeitung*, 1895, p. 902).

[7] *Libri apocryphi Veteris Testamenti Graece*, Leipzig, 1871, p. 475. Similarly the corrected text of 1887 in the edition of L. van Ess.

[8] *Cf.* on this O. F. Fritzsche, *HApAT.* v. (1859), p. 201.   [9] *Ibid.*

to a meaning of the possible original which cannot be authenticated, the confusion of the *parallelismus membrorum* which,
with their reading, disfigures the verse, must be urged against
de Wette and Fritzsche.[1] What then is the authority for
this reading? The beginning of the verse has been handed
down in the three principal Codices in the following forms :—

       אA   πλησονσιωναρεταλογιασου,

       B   πλησονσιωναρεταλογιασσου,

       B^b   πλησιονσιωναραιταλογιασου.

The last reading, that of the second reviser of B, has
thus become the standard, except that the πλῆσον of the
others has been retained instead of the πλησίον which it
gives. H. B. Swete[2] considers it probable that also the αρε
of אA is to be taken as equivalent to αραι; in such case the
current text would be supported by אA as well. But in
reality the matter stands quite otherwise; it is B which
gives the original text: πλῆσον Σιὼν ἀρεταλογίας σου,[3] אA
is deduced from this by the hemigraphy of the σσ in αρετα-
λογιασσου, and B^b is a correction by the misunderstood אA.
The unwillingness to recognise this true state of the case
(Fritzsche says of B's reading: *sed hoc quidem hic nullo
modo locum habere potest*) and indeed, to go further back, the
alteration[4] which was made by the reviser of B, who misunderstood the text, are due to a misconception of what
ἀρεταλογία meant. If we consult, *e.g.*, Pape,[5] under ἀρετα-

---

[1] De Wette, guided by a true feeling, has obviated this objection by
rendering ἄραι by a substantive.

[2] Textual-critical note to the passage in his edition of the LXX,
Cambridge, 1887 ff.

[3] This is placed in the text by Tischendorf and Swete.

[4] From his standpoint a fairly good conjecture!

[5] Naturally the word is not given in the lexica to the Greek Old Testament or the Apocrypha; nor is it given by Tromm, either in the Concordance
or in the accompanying Lexicon to the Hexapla by B. de Montfaucon and
L. Bos. The Concordance of E. Hatch and H. A. Redpath, Oxford, 1892 ff.,
which takes into account the variants of the most important manuscripts, was
the first to bring the misunderstood word to its rightful position; although
that book seems to err by excess of good when it constructs from the clerical
error of אA a new word ἀρεταλόγιον.

λογία, we find that its meaning is given as *buffoonery* (*Possen-reisserei*).   Now it is clear that God cannot be invited to fill Zion with "aretalogy" in this sense; then comes the too precipitate deduction that the text must read differently, instead of the question whether the lexicon may not perhaps be in need of a correction.   Even Symmachus, Ps. 29 [30]⁶, could have answered the question : in that passage he renders the word רִנָּה (*shouting for joy*) of the original by ἀρεταλογία,¹ while he always translates it elsewhere by εὐφημία.   The equation of Symmachus, ἀρεταλογία = εὐφημία, which can be inferred from this, and the parallelism of the passage in Sirach, ἀρεταλογία ‖ δόξα, mutually explain and support each other, and force us to the assumption that both translators used ἀρεταλογία *sensu bono*, *i.e.*, of the *glorifying of God*.   The assumption is so obvious as to require no further support; for, to argue from the analogies, it is indisputable that the word, the etymology of which is certainly clear enough, at first simply meant, as a matter of course, the *speaking of the* ἀρεταί, and only then received the bad secondary signification. As to the meaning of ἀρετή which is the basis of this usage, *cf.* the next article.

ἀρετή.²

The observations of Hatch³ upon this word have added nothing new to the article ἀρετή in Cremer, and have ignored what is there (as it seems to the author) established beyond doubt, *viz.*, that the LXX, in rendering הוֹד, *magnificence, splendour* (Hab. 3³ and Zech. 6¹³) and תְּהִלָּה, *glory, praise*, by ἀρετή, are availing themselves of an already-existent linguistic usage.⁴   The meaning of ἀρεταλογία is readily deduced from this usage : the word signifies the same as is elsewhere expressed by means of the verbal constructions, LXX Is. 42¹² τὰς ἀρετὰς αὐτοῦ [θεοῦ] ἀναγγέλλειν, LXX

---

¹ Field, ii., p. 130.   The Hexaplar Syriac thereupon in its turn took this word of Symmachus not as = εὐφημία, but as = *acceptio eloquii*, Field, *ibid*.

² *Cf.* p. 93, note 6.   ³ *Essays*, p. 40 f.

⁴ That is, ἀρετή as synonymous with δόξα.   The word may be used in this sense in 4 Macc. 10¹⁰ also (contra Cremer⁷, p. 154 = ⁸, p. 164).

Is. 43 [21] τὰς ἀρετάς μου [θεοῦ] διηγεῖσθαι, 1 Pet. 2 [9] τὰς ἀρετὰς [θεοῦ] ἐξαγγέλλειν.   It seems to the author the most probable interpretation that the ἀρεταί of the last passage stands, as in the LXX, for *laudes*, seeing that the phrase looks like an allusion to LXX Is. 42 [12], more clearly still to Is. 43 [20 f.]. One must nevertheless reckon with the possibility that the word is used here in a different sense, to which reference has recently been made by Sal. Reinach,[1] and which no doubt many a reader of the above-cited passages from the LXX, not knowing the original, found in these phrases.   Reinach, arguing from an Inscription from Asia Minor belonging to the imperial period, advocates the thesis [2] that ἀρετή, even in pre-Christian usage, could mean *miracle, effet surnaturel*.   He thinks that this is confirmed by a hitherto unobserved signi- fication of the word ἀρεταλόγος, which, in several places, should not be interpreted in the usual bad sense of *one who babbles about virtues, buffoon*, etc., but rather as a technical designation of the *interprète de miracles, exégète* who occupied an official position in the personnel of certain sanctuaries.[3] The author is unable to speak more particularly about the latter point, although it does perhaps cast a clearer light upon our ἀρεταλογία.   He believes however that he can point to other passages in which the ἀρετή of God signifies, not the *righteousness*, nor yet the *praise* of God, but the *manifestation of His power*.   Guided by the context, we must translate Joseph. *Antt.* xvii. 5 [6], αὖθις ἐνεπαρῴνει τῇ ἀρετῇ τοῦ θείου: *he sinned, as if intoxicated, against God's manifestation of His power*.[4]   Still clearer is a passage from a hymn to Hermes, *Pap. Lond.* xlvi. 418 ff.[5] :—

ὄφρα τε μαντοσύνας ταῖς σαῖς ἀρεταῖσι λάβοιμι.

---

[1] *Les Arétalogues dans l'antiquité, Bull. de corr. hell.* ix. (1885), p. 257 ff. The present writer is indebted to W. Schulze for the reference to this essay.
[2] P. 264.   [3] P. 264 f.
[4] The correct interpretation in Cremer [7], p. 153 (= [8], p. 163 f.), also points to this.   But in the other passage there discussed after Krebs, Joseph. *Antt.* xvii. 5 [5], ἀρετή most probably denotes *virtue*.
[5] Kenyon, p. 78 f. ; Wessely, i. p. 138; A. Dieterich, *Abraxas*, p. 64. The Papyrus was written in the fourth century A.D. ; the present writer cannot decide as to the date of the composition, particularly of line 400 ff., but considers that it may, without risk, be set still further back.

The original has μαντοσυναις; the emendation μαντοσύνας (better than the alternative μαντοσύνης also given by
Kenyon) seems to be established.[1] It can only mean: *that
I may obtain the art of clairvoyance by the manifestations of Thy
power*, and this meaning allows the text to remain otherwise
unaltered (after A. Dieterich). This sense of ἀρεταί seems
to have been unknown to other two editors; but they, too,
have indicated, by their conjectures, that the word cannot
signify *virtues*. Wessely[2] emends thus:—

$$\text{ὄφρα τε μαντοσύνης τῆς σῆς μέρος ἀντιλάβοιμι,}$$

and Herwerden[3] writes:—

$$\text{ὄφρα τε μαντοσύνην ταῖς σαῖς ἀρεταῖσι (? χαρίτεσσι) λάβοιμι.}$$

We must in any case, in 2 Pet. 1[3], reckon with this
meaning of ἀρετή, still further examples of which could
doubtless be found. A comparison of this passage with the
Inscription which Reinach calls to his aid should exclude
further doubt. This is the Inscription of Stratonicea in
Caria, belonging to the earliest years of the imperial period,[4]
which will subsequently often engage our attention; the
beginning of it is given in full further on, in the remarks
on the Second Epistle of Peter, and the author has there
expressed the supposition that the beginning of the Epistle
is in part marked by the same solemn phrases of sacred emotion as are used in the epigraphic decree. Be it only remarked
here that the θεία δύναμις is spoken of in both passages, and
that ἀρετή, in the context of both, means *marvel*, or, if one
prefers it, *manifestation of power*.[5]

---

[1] A. Dieterich, *Abr.*, p. 65.

[2] In his attempt to restore the hymn, i., p. 29.

[3] *Mnemosyne*, xvi. (1888), p. 11. The present writer quotes from A.
Dieterich, p. 65; *cf.* p. 51.

[4] *CIG.* iii., No. 2715 *a*, *b* = Waddington iii. 2, Nos. 519, 520 (p. 142).

[5] Cremer [7], p. 153 (=[8], p. 163), guided by the context, points to the true
interpretation by giving *self-manifestation;* similarly Kühl, Meyer xii.[5] (1887),
p. 355, *performance, activity* (*Wirksamkeit*); the translation *virtue* (H. von
Soden, *HC.* iii. 2[2] [1892], p. 197) must be rejected altogether. Moreover
Hesychius appears to the present writer to be influenced by 2 Pet. 1[3] when
he, rightly, makes ἀρετή = θεία δύναμις.

7

ἀρχισωματοφύλαξ.

This occurs in the LXX as the translation of *keeper of the threshold* (Esther 2[21]) and *body-guard* (literally, *keeper of the head*, 1 Sam. 28[2]). The translation in the latter passage is correct, although σωματοφύλαξ (Judith 12[7], 1 [3] Esd. 3[4]) would have been sufficient. The title is Egyptianised in the rendering given in Esther :[1] the ἀρχισωματοφύλαξ was originally an officer of high rank in the court of the Ptolemies—the head of the royal body-guard. But the title seems to have lost its primary meaning; it came to be applied to the occupants of various higher offices.[2] Hence even the translation given in Esther is not incorrect. The title is known not only from Egyptian Inscriptions,[3] but also from *Pap. Taur.* i.[4] (third century B.C.), ii.[5] (of the same period), xi.[6] (of the same period), *Pap. Lond.* xvii.[7] (162 B.C.), xxiii.[8] (158-157 B.C.), Ep. Arist. (*ed.* M. Schmidt), *p.* 15[4ι.]; *cf.* Joseph. *Antt.* xii. 2[2].

ἄφεσις.

1. The LXX translate *water-brooks*, Joel 1[20], and *rivers of water*, Lam. 3[47], by ἀφέσεις ὑδάτων, and *channels of the sea*, 2 Sam. 22[16], by ἀφέσεις θαλάσσης. The last rendering is explained by the fact that the original presents the same word as Joel 1[20], אֲפִיקִים, which can mean either *brooks* or *channels*. But how are we to understand the strange[9] rendering of the word by ἀφέσεις?[10] One might be tempted

---

[1] *Cf.* B. Jacob, *ZAW.* x. (1890), p. 283 f.

[2] Giac. Lumbroso, *Recherches sur l'économie politique de l'Égypte sous les Lagides*, Turin, 1870, p. 191.

[3] Jean-Ant. [not M.] Letronne, *Recherches pour servir à l'histoire de l'Égypte pendant la domination des Grecs et des Romains*, Paris, 1823, p. 56; Lumbroso, *Rech.* p. 191. Also in the Inscription of Cyprus, *CIG.* ii., No. 2617 (Ptolemaic period), an Egyptian official, probably the governor, is so named.

[4] A. Peyron, i., p. 24.   [5] *Ibid.*, i., p. 175.   [6] *Ibid.* ii., p. 65.
[7] Kenyon, p. 11.   [8] *Ibid.*, p. 41.

[9] Elsewhere the LXX translate it more naturally by φάραγξ and χείμαρρος.

[10] In Ps. 125 [126][4], the "fifth" translation of the Old Testament also has ἀφέσεις = *streams* (Field, ii., p. 283).

to think that the rendering has been influenced by *aph*,[1] the
initial syllable of the original, but this does not explain
ἀφέσεις = פְּלָגִים Lam. 3 [47], and why is it that such influence
is not perceived in any other passage?

The explanation is given by the Egyptian idiom. We
have in *Pap. Flind. Petr.* ii. xxxvii.[2] official reports from the
Ptolemaic period concerning the irrigation. In these the
technical expression for the *releasing* of the waters by opening
the sluices is ἀφίημι τὸ ὕδωρ; the corresponding substantival
phrase ἄφεσις τοῦ ὕδατος is found in *Pap. Flind. Petr.* ii. xiii. 2 [3]
(258 B.C.), but—and in this the technical meaning reveals

---

[1] Similar cases in Wellhausen, *Der Text der Bb. Sam.*, p. 10 f.—This
supposition must be taken into account in Ezek. 47 [3] διῆλθεν ἐν τῷ ὕδατι ὕδωρ
ἀφέσεως, which, in its connection (it is previously stated that the water
issued from under the αἴθριον = *atrium*), signifies : *he walked in the water, in
the water* (the nominative has been set down mechanically) *of release, i.e., in
the* (previously mentioned) *released water*. So must a reader of the LXX
have understood their words; the remark of Jerome (in Field, ii., p. 895) that
the LXX had rendered it *aqua remissionis*, rests upon a dogmatic misconception; ἄφεσις here can be translated only by *dimissio*. Now the Hebrew text
has *water of the ankles, i.e., water that reaches to the ankles*. This is the only
occurrence of אָפְסַיִם, *ankles*, in the O. T. C. H. Cornill, *Das Buch des
Propheten Ezechiel*, Leipzig, 1886, p. 501, conjectures that what the LXX
translated was אֲפִיקִים. The author thinks it still more probable that
their ἄφεσις represents the dual of אֶפֶס, *cessation*. But the most natural
supposition is that they did not understand the ἅπαξ λεγόμενον, and simply
transcribed *aph'sajim*, the context prompting them not merely to transcribe,
but to make out of their transcription an inflected word. The present
writer will not reject the supposition that this singular passage might also be
explained in the following way: The Greek translator did not understand
the knotty word, and translated—or transcribed—it ὕδωρ ἕως (*cf.* ἕως twice in
ver. [4]) αφες (*cf.* Ezek. 27 [16] LXX, Codd. 23, 62, 147 ἐν αφεκ, Codd. 87, 88, Hexapl.
Syr. ἐν αφεγ; Theodotion ἐν αφεκ, unless ναφεκ [= נָפֶךְ] read by Parsons in a
Cod. Jes. originally stood there; these data are borrowed from Field, ii., p. 842);
Aquila, Symmachus and Theodotion, who understood the strange word, have
a corresponding rendering, ἕως ἀστραγάλων (Field, ii., p. 895). From ὕδωρ
ἕως αφες some inventive brain fabricated ὕδωρ ἀφέσεως, which could then have
the sense explained above. The translator of Ezekiel has, in many other
cases, shown tact in merely transcribing Hebrew words which he did not
understand (Cornill, p. 96).—The reading ὕδωρ ἀφαιρέσεως of the Complutensian seems to be a correction of ὕδωρ ἀφέσεως made purely within the
Greek text itself.

[2] Mahaffy, ii. [119] f.   [3] *Ibid.*, [38].

itself most clearly—the genitive may also be omitted. ἄφεσις standing alone is intelligible to all, and we find it so used in several passages in the first mentioned Papyrus. When one thinks of the great importance to Egypt of the irrigation, it will be found readily conceivable that the particular incidents of it and their technical designations must have been matter of common knowledge. *Canals*[1] were to the Egyptian what *brooks* were to the Palestinian; the bursting forth of the Nile waters from the opened sluices made upon the former the same deep impression as did the roar of the first winter-brook upon the Canaanite peasants and shepherds. Thus the Egyptian translators of Lam. 3 [47] have rendered, by ἀφέσεις ὑδάτων, the *streams of water* breaking forth before the eyes of the people—not indeed verbally, but, on behalf of their own readers, by transferring into the Egyptian dialect, with most effective distinctness, the image that was so expressive for the Palestinians. Similarly the distress of the land in Joel 1 [20] is made more vivid for the Egyptians by the picture of the carefully-collected water of the *canals* becoming dried up shortly after the opening of the sluices (ἐξηράνθησαν ἀφέσεις ὑδάτων), than it would be by speaking of dried-up *brooks*.[2]

2. The LXX translate יוֹבֵל, Lev. 25 [15], used elliptically for *Jobel-year*,[3] by the substantive σημασία sign, signal, a rendering altogether verbal, and one which does not fail to mark the peculiarity of the original. But they translate *Jobel-year* in vv. [10. 11. 12. 13] of the same chapter (apart from the fact that they do not supply the ellipsis that occurs here and there in the Hebrew passages) by ἐνιαυτὸς or ἔτος ἀφέσεως σημασίας, *signal-year of emancipation*.[4] The technical expression *signal-year* was made intelligible to non-Hebrew readers by

[1] ἄφεσις seems to bear the meaning of *sluice* and *canal* exactly.
[2] *Cf.* below, under διῶρυξ.   [3] [English, "Jubilee".]
[4] In this way, and in no other, did the LXX construe the genitives, as we see from ver. [15]; so in ver. [13], where the article belongs to σημασίας. A Greek reader indeed, ignoring the context, might understand the expression thus: *year of the ἄφεσις of the signal*, *i.e.*, in which the signal was given; ἀφίημι does occur in similar combinations.

the addition of ἀφέσεως, which comes from ver. [10] : διαβοησ-
ετε ἄφεσιν ἐπὶ τῆς γῆς, where ἄφεσις = דְּרוֹר. From this,
again, it is explained how *Jobel-year* in the parts of chap. 25
which follow the verse quoted, and in chap. 27, is rendered
by ἔτος or ἐνιαυτὸς τῆς ἀφέσεως, which is not a translation,[1]
but an "explicative paraphrase".[2] Similarly in these passages the elliptical *Jobel* (standing in connection with what
goes before) is imitated in a manner not liable to be mis-
taken by an elliptical ἄφεσις.

Now this usage of the LXX is not to be explained as a
mere mechanical imitation : it found a point of local connection in the legal conditions of the Ptolemaic period.
Pap. Par. 63[3] (165 B.C.) mentions, among various kinds of
landed property, τὰ τῶν ἐν ἀφέσει καὶ τὴν ἱερὰν γῆν.[4]
Lumbroso[5] explains the lands thus said to be ἐν ἀφέσει as
those which were exempted from the payment of taxes, and
points to several passages on the Rosetta Stone[6] (196 B.C.),
in which the king is extolled as having expressly remitted
certain taxes (εἰς τέλος ἀφῆκεν).[7] With this seems to be
connected also *Pap. Flind. Petr.* ii. ii. 1 (260-259 B.C.) :[8] ὅταν
ἡ ἄφεσις δοθῇ ; *cf.* previously τὰ ἐκφόρια.

The LXX might have translated דְּרוֹר Lev. 25[10] (the
rendering of which was determinative for the whole of
their subsequent usage) by a different word, but their imitation of the technical *Jobel* was facilitated just by their
choice of ἄφεσις, a technical word and one which was
current in their locality.

---

[1] The expression Ezek. 46[17] is such.

[2] Cremer[7], p. 439 (= [8], p. 466).

[3] *Notices*, xviii. 2, p. 368.

[4] This ἱερὰ γῆ occurs still in the (Berlin) Egyptian documents of the
second and third centuries A.D. (U. Wilcken, *Observationes ad historiam
Aegypti provinciae Romanae depromptae e papyris Graecis Berolinensibus
ineditis*, Berlin, 1885, p. 29).

[5] *Recherches*, p. 90. Brunet de Presle (*Notices*, xviii. 2, p. 471) gives the
extraordinary explanation—with a mark of interrogation, it is true—*congé
militaire*.

[6] Letronne, *Recueil des inscriptions grecques et latines de l'Égypte*, vol. i.,
Paris, 1842, p. 244 ff. = *CIG.*, iii. No. 4697.

[7] Line 12 and elsewhere.   [8] Mahaffy, ii. [2].

βαστάζω.

In Matt. 8[17] there is quoted, as the word of "the pro
phet Isaiah," αὐτὸς τὰς ἀσθενείας ἡμῶν ἔλαβεν καὶ τὰς νόσους
ἐβάστασεν. "The passage Is. 53[4] is cited according to the
original, but not in the historical sense thereof, ... nor
according to the special typical reference which any one
looking back from the Saviour's healing of diseases to that
prophetic saying, might have perceived to be the intention
of the latter (Meyer) ; but with a free interpretation of the
language. The Evangelist, that is to say, clearly takes λαμβάνειν in the sense of *take away*, as the נָשָׂא of the original
may also signify—though not in this passage. On the other
hand, it is doubtful whether he also understood βαστάζειν
(סָבַל) in the sense of *bear hence* (John 20[15]), an impossible
meaning for the Hebrew . . ., or whether he is not thinking
rather of the trouble and pains which the Saviour's acts of
healing, continued till far on in the evening, cost Him."[1]
H. Holtzmann,[2] like Weiss, similarly identifies λαμβάνειν with
נָשָׂא, and βαστάζειν with סָבַל. But, if the author's judgment is correct, the case is just the opposite : Matthew has
not only discarded the translation given by the LXX, but
has also, in his rendering, transposed the two clauses of the
Hebrew sentence ;[3] he does not translate *He bore our diseases
and took upon Himself our pains*, but *He took upon Hims lf ou
pains, and bore our diseases*. In that case it will not be סָבַל
but נָשָׂא which is represented by βαστάζειν.[5] The LXX
also translate נָשָׂא, in 2 Kings 18[14] and Job 21[3], Cod. A, by
βαστάζειν ; similarly Aquila in the four extant passages
where he uses βαστάζειν : Is. 40[11],[6] 53[11],[7] 66[12],[8] and Jer.

---

[1] B. Weiss, Meyer, i. 1[8] (1890), p. 169.   [2] *HC.* i.[2] (1892), p. 76.

[3] *Cf.* the remark below upon the Gospel quotations, *sub viós.*

[4] *Cf.*, with reference to λαμβάνειν = סָבַל, LXX Is. 46[4], where the same
verb is rendered by ἀναλαμβάνειν.

[5] Thus A. Resch, *Aussercanonische Paralleltexte zu den Evangelien,*
2 Heft (*TU.* x. 2), Leipzig, 1894, p. 115.

[6] Field, ii., p. 510.   [7] *Ibid.*, p. 535.   [8] *Ibid.*, p. 565.

10⁵.¹ Of these last passages, Is. 53 deserves special attention, as it approximates in meaning to the quotation in
Matthew : καὶ τὰς ἁμαρτίας αὐτῶν αὐτὸς βαστάσει. If we
should not assume, with E. Böhl,² that the quotation is taken
from an already-existent version, then it must be said that
Matthew, or his authority, in their independent rendering of
the נָשָׂא of the original by βαστάζειν, were acting in the
same way as do the LXX and the Jewish translator of the
second century A.D. in other passages. It does not of course
necessarily follow from the fact that the LXX, Matthew,
and Aquila all use βαστάζειν as the analogue of נָשָׂא, that
the βαστάζειν of Matt. 8¹⁷ must have the same meaning as
the נָשָׂא of the Hebrew original. One must rather, in regard to this passage, as indeed in regard to all translations
whatever, consider the question whether the translator does
not give a new shade of meaning to his text by the expression he chooses. It will be more correct procedure to ascertain the meaning of βαστάζειν in this verse of Matthew from
the context in which the quotation occurs, than from the original meaning of נָשָׂא—however evident the correspondence
βαστάζειν = נָשָׂא, superficially regarded, may seem. And
all the better, if the meaning bear away, required here by
the context for βαστάζειν,³ is not absolutely foreign to נָשָׂא
—in the sense, at least, which it has in other passages.

The same favourable circumstance does not occur in
connection with ἔλαβεν, for the signification take away, which
the context demands, does not give the sense of סָבַל.

In the religious language of early Christianity the terms
bear and take away, differing from each other more or less
distinctly, and often having sin as their object, play a great

¹ Field, II., Auct., p. 39.

² Die alttestamentlichen Citate im N. T., Vienna, 1878, p. 34. Böhl finds
his Volksbibel (People's Bible) quoted in this passage also. But the Volksbibel,
or, more properly, a version that was different from the LXX, would hardly
have transposed the two clauses of the original.

³ Cf., upon βαστάζειν in Josephus, Guil. Schmidt, De Flav. Ios. elocutione,
Fleck. Jahrbb. Suppl. xx. (1894), p. 521. Upon βαστάζω in Gal. 6¹⁷ see VII.
below, the study on the " Large Letters " and the " Marks of Jesus," Gal. 6.

part; the Synonymic[1] of this usage must raise for itself the problem of investigating words like αἴρω, ἐξαίρω, βαστάζω, λαμβάνω, ἀναλαμβάνω, φέρω, ἀναφέρω, ὑποφέρω in their various shades of meaning.

βεβαίωσις.

"The seller was required, in general, i.e., unless the opposite was stipulated, to deliver to the buyer the thing sold ἀναμφισβήτητον, without dispute, and had to accept of the responsibility if claims should be raised to the thing by others. . . . If he [the buyer], however, had obtained from the seller the promise of guarantee " . . . he could, if claims to the thing were subsequently raised by others, "go back upon the seller (this was called ἀνάγειν εἰς πράτην) and summon him to confirm—as against the person now raising the claim—that he himself had bought from him the thing now claimed, i.e., he could summon him βεβαιῶσαι. If the seller refused to do this, then the buyer could bring against him an action βεβαιώσεως."[2] In the language of the Attic Process, βεβαίωσις confirmation had thus received the technical meaning of a definite obligation of the seller, which among the Romans was termed auctoritas or evictio:[3] the seller did not only make over the thing to the buyer, but assumed the guarantee to defend the validity of the sale against any possible claims of a third party. Among the historians of the ancient Civil Process there exist differences of opinion[4]

---

[1] Had we a discreetly prepared Synonymic of the religious expressions of Early Christianity—of which there is as yet, one may say, a complete want —we should then have a defence against the widely-current mechanical method of the so-called Biblical Theology of the N. T. which looks upon the men whose writings stand in the Canon less as prophets and sons of the prophets than as Talmudists and Tosaphists. This dogmatising method parcels out the inherited territory as if Revelation were a matter of a thousand trifles. Its paragraphs give one the idea that Salvation is an *ordo salutis*. It desecrates the N. T. by making it a mere source for the history of dogma, and does not perceive that it was, in the main, written under the influence of Religion.

[2] M. H. E. Meier and G. F. Schömann, *Der Attische Process*, neu bearbeitet von J. H. Lipsius, Berlin, 1883-1887, ii., pp. 717, 719, 720.

[3] *Ibid.*, p. 717 f.

[4] *Ibid.*, p. 721 f.; K. F. Hermann, *Lehrbuch der Griechischen Rechtsalterthümer*, 3rd edition by Th. Thalheim, Freiburg and Tübingen, 1884, p. 77.

regarding the details of the δίκη βεβαιώσεως that might
possibly be raised by the buyer, but these are immaterial
for the determination of the idea corresponding to the word
βεβαίωσις.

This technical expression found admission into Egypt
in the Ptolemaic period. The Papyrus documents speak not
only of the βεβαιωτής,[1] the *sale-surety*, the *auctor secundus*
of Roman law, but also of the βεβαίωσις itself: *Pap. Taur.*
i.[2] (2nd cent. B.C.), *Pap. Par.* 62[3] (2nd cent. B.C.)—twice
in the latter passage, once in the combination εἰς τὴν
βεβαίωσιν ὑποθῆκαι.[4] How thoroughly the expression had
become naturalised in Egypt is shown by the fact that we
still find the βεβαίωσις in Papyrus documents belonging to
a time which is separated from the Lagides by seven hundred
years. It is, indeed, possible that in these, as well as already
in the Ptolemaic documents, βεβαίωσις has no longer exactly
the same specific meaning as it has in the more accurate
terminology of the highly-polished juristic Greek of Attica:[5]
but the word is certainly used there also in the sense of
guarantee, safe-guarding of a bargain: *Pap. Par.* 21 *bis*[6] (592 A.D.),
Pap. Jomard[7] (592 A.D.), *Pap. Par.* 21[8] (616 A.D.). In these
the formula κατὰ πᾶσαν βεβαίωσιν occurs several times, and
even the formula εἰς βεβαίωσιν comes before us again in
Pap. Par. 20[9] (600 A.D.), having thus[10] maintained itself
through more than seven hundred years.

Reference has already been made by Lumbroso[11] to the

---

[1] Hermann-Thalheim, p. 78.

[2] A. Peyron, i., p. 32, *cf.* p. 120, and E. Revillout, *Études sur divers points
de droit et d'histoire Ptolémaïque*, Paris, 1880, p. xl. f.

[3] *Notices*, xviii. 2, p. 355.

[4] The text is, indeed, mutilated, but is sufficient for our purpose.

[5] According to Hermann-Thalheim, p. 78, note 1, βεβαιωτής, for instance,
has become nothing but an empty form in the Papyri.

[6] *Notices*, xviii. 2, p. 250.

[7] *Ibid.*, pp. 258, 259.   [8] *Ibid.*, p. 244.

[9] *Ibid.*, p. 241.   [10] *Cf.* above, *Pap. Par.* 62 (2nd cent. B.C.).

[11] *Recherches*, p. 78. But the passage belonging to the 2nd cent. B.C.,
indicated above, is more significant than the one of 600 A.D. quoted by him.

striking similarity of a passage in the LXX with this idiom
of Egyptian Civil law. βεβαίωσις is found only once in
the Alexandrian translation, Lev. 25²³, but there in the
characteristic formula εἰς βεβαίωσιν: καὶ ἡ γῆ οὐ πραθή-
σεται εἰς βεβαίωσιν, ἐμὴ γάρ ἐστιν ἡ γῆ. The translation is
not a literal one, but one of great fineness and accuracy.
The Israelites are but strangers and sojourners in the land;
the ground, the soil, belongs to Jahweh—therefore it may
not be sold *absolutely*: such is the bearing of the original
לִצְמִתֻת (properly *unto annihilation, i.e., completely, for ever*).
Looked at superficially, the εἰς βεβαίωσιν of the LXX is the
exact opposite of the *unto annihilation* of the original;[1] considered properly, it testifies to an excellent understanding
of the text.[2] A sale εἰς βεβαίωσιν is a *definitive, legally
guaranteed* sale: mere sojourners could not, of course, sell
the land which they held only in tenure,—least of all εἰς
βεβαίωσιν. The reading εἰς βεβήλωσιν[3] of Codices xi., 19, 29,
and others, also of the Aldine, is a clumsy mistake of later
copyists (occasioned in part by LXX Lev. 21[4]), who only
spoiled the delicately-chosen expression of the LXX by
school-boy literalness; on the other hand, the *in confirma-
tionem* of the *Vetus Latina*[3] is quite correct, while the renderings
of Aquila,[3] εἰς παγκτησίαν, and Symmachus,[3] εἰς ἀλύτρωτον,
though they miss the point proper, yet render the thought
fairly well.

The LXX have shown the same skill in the only other
passage where this Hebrew word occurs, *viz.*, Lev. 25³⁰:
κυρωθήσεται ἡ οἰκία ἡ οὖσα ἐν πόλει τῇ ἐχούσῃ τεῖχος
βεβαίως τῷ κτησαμένῳ αὐτήν. That they did not here
make choice of the formula εἰς βεβαίωσιν, in spite of the
similarity of the original, reveals a true understanding of
the matter, for, as the phrase was primarily used only of the
giving of a guarantee in concluding a bargain, it would not
have answered in this passage.

---

[1] Which fact explains the variants about to be mentioned.

[2] In the same chapter we also found a pertinent application of ἄφεσις
as a legal conception.

[3] Field, i., p. 212.

The Alexandrian Christian to whom we owe the λόγος
τῆς παρακλήσεως in the New Testament, writes, in Heb. 6[16],
ἄνθρωποι γὰρ κατὰ τοῦ μείζονος ὀμνύουσιν καὶ πάσης αὐτοῖς
ἀντιλογίας πέρας εἰς βεβαίωσιν ὁ ὅρκος.   The context of
the passage is permeated by juristic expressions—as is the
Epistle to the Hebrews as a whole.   That this Egyptian
legal formula, persistent through hundreds of years, occurs
here also, deserves our notice.   We do not need to give
it the same sharply-defined sense which it had in Attic
jurisprudence (*guarantee in regard to a sale*):[1] it must be
interpreted more generally ; at all events it is still a technical
expression for a legal *guarantee*.[2]

The use of βεβαίωσις elsewhere in biblical literature likewise appears to the author to be influenced by the technical
meaning of the word.   In Wisd. 6[19], in the magnificent
hymn[3] upon wisdom, occurs the gnomic saying προσοχὴ
δὲ νόμων βεβαίωσις ἀφθαρσίας; here νόμων suggests very
plainly the juristic conception of the word: he who keeps
the *laws* of wisdom has the *legal guarantee* of incorruption ;
he need have no fear that his ἀφθαρσία will be disputed
by another.

βεβαίωσις has been spoken of more definitely still by
the man upon whose juristic terminology the jurist Johannes
Ortwin Westenberg was able to write an important treatise[4]

---

[1] This interpretation is not impossible. For a legitimate sale an oath
was requisite, *e.g.*, according to the " laws of Ainos " (the name is uncertain)
The buyer must sacrifice to the Apollo of the district; should he purchase a
piece of land in the district in which he himself dwells—he must do the same ;
and he must *take an oath*, in presence of the recording authorities and of
three inhabitants of the place, that he buys honourably : similarly the seller
also must swear that he sells without falsity (Theophrastus περὶ συμβολαίων
in Stobaeus, *Flor.* xliv. 22); *cf.* Hermann-Thalheim, p. 130 ff.

[2] *Cf.* the terms βέβαιος, Heb. 2[2], 3[6], 9[17], and βεβαιόω, Heb. 2[3], which
in the light of the above should probably also be considered as technical.

[3] Upon the form of this.(Sorites or Anadiplosis), *cf.* Paul's words in
Rom. 5[3-5], 10[14f.]; also James 1[3f.], and LXX Hos. 2[21f.], Joel 1[3f.]

[4] *Paulus Tarsensis Jurisconsultus, seu dissertatio de jurisprudentia Pauli
Apostoli habita*, Franecker, 1722. The essay has often been reprinted : an
edition Bayreuth, 1738, 36 pp. 4to lies before the present writer. A new treatment of the subject would be no unprofitable task.

a hundred and seventy years ago.   Paul, in Phil. 1 [7], says
καθώς ἐστιν δίκαιον ἐμοὶ τοῦτο φρονεῖν ὑπὲρ πάντων ὑμῶν διὰ
τὸ ἔχειν με ἐν τῇ καρδίᾳ ὑμᾶς ἔν τε τοῖς δεσμοῖς μου καὶ ἐν τῇ
ἀπολογίᾳ καὶ βεβαιώσει τοῦ εὐαγγελίου : he is indeed in
bonds, but he is standing on his defence, and this defence
before the court will be at the same time an *evictio* or *convictio*
of the Gospel.   To the forensic expressions ἐν τοῖς δεσμοῖς
and ἐν τῇ ἀπολογίᾳ, which, of course,[1] are not to be understood as metaphorical, ἐν βεβαιώσει τοῦ εὐαγγελίου corresponds
very well, and forms at the same time the final step of a very
effective climax.

That the Apostle was not ignorant of the older Attic
signification of βεβαίωσις is rendered probable by a striking
correspondence between the mode of expression he uses in
other passages and the terms applied to the legal ideas which
are demonstrably connoted by βεβαίωσις.   Observe how Paul
brackets together the conceptions ἀρραβών and βεβαιοῦν.
Harpocration, the lexicographer of the Attic Orators, who
lived in the Imperial period, writes in his lexicon, *sub*
βεβαίωσις :[2] ἐνίοτε καὶ ἀρραβῶνος μονου δοθέντος εἶτα
ἀμφισβητήσαντος τοῦ πεπρακότος ἐλάγχανε τὴν τῆς βεβαιώσεως δίκην ὁ τὸν ἀρραβῶνα δοὺς τῷ λαβόντι.   Similarly
in the ancient Λέξεις ῥητορικαί, one of the *Lexica Segueriana*,
edited by Imm. Bekker,[3] *sub* βεβαιώσεως : δίκης ὄνομά ἐστιν,
ἣν ἐδικάζοντο οἱ ὠνησάμενοι κατὰ τῶν ἀποδομένων, ὅτε ἔτερος
ἀμφισβητοῖ τοῦ πραθέντος, ἀξιοῦντες βεβαιοῦν αὐτοῖς τε
πραθέν· ἐνίοτε δὲ καὶ ἀρραβῶνος μόνου δοθέντος. ἐπὶ τούτω
οὖν ἐλάγχανον τὴν τῆς βεβαιώσεως δίκην οἱ δόντες τὸν
ἀρραβῶνα τοῖς λαβοῦσιν, ἵνα βεβαιωθῇ ὑπὲρ οὗ ὁ ἀρραβὼν ἐδόθη.   Now, although doubts do exist[4] about the
possibility of basing a δίκη βεβαιώσεως upon the seller's
acceptance of the *earnest-money*, still thus much is clear,
viz., that, in technical usage, ἀρραβών and βεβαιοῦν stand

---

[1] Paul hopes, 2 [23] (as also appears from the tone of the whole letter), for
an early and favourable judgment on his *case*.

[2] In Hermann-Thalheim, p. 77.

[3] *Anecdota Graeca*, i. Berlin, 1814, p. 219 f.

[4] Hermann-Thalheim, p. 77 ; Meier-Schömann-Lipsius, ii., p. 721.

in an essential relation to each other.[1]   It is exactly in this
way that Paul speaks—his indestructible faith representing
the relation of God to believers under the image of a legally
indisputable relation, 2 Cor. 1 [21 f.]: ὁ δὲ βεβαιῶν ἡμᾶς σὺν
ὑμῖν εἰς Χριστὸν καὶ χρίσας ἡμᾶς θεός, ὁ καὶ σφραγισάμενος
ἡμᾶς καὶ δοὺς τὸν ἀρραβῶνα τοῦ πνεύματος ἐν ταῖς καρδίαις
ἡμῶν.   Apt as is the metaphor itself, intelligible as it would
be in this verse and in 5 [5], particularly to the Christians of
that great commercial centre, it is in form equally apt.   The
Apostle, of course, could have chosen another verb [2] equally
well, without rendering the image unintelligible, but the
technical word makes the image still more effective.   A
patristic remark upon the passage in question [3] shows us,
further, how a Greek reader could fully appreciate the specific
nature of the metaphor: ὁ γὰρ ἀρραβὼν εἴωθε βεβαιοῦν
τὸ πᾶν σύνταγμα.

Hence we shall not err in construing βεβαιόω [4] and
βέβαιος,[5] even where they occur elsewhere in the writings of
Paul and his circle, from this standpoint, and especially as
these words sometimes occur among other juristic expressions.
By our taking *confirm* and *sure* in the sense of legally guaranteed security, the statements in which they occur gain in
decisiveness and force.

Symmachus [6] uses βεβαίωσις once: Ps. 88 [89] [25] for
אֱמוּנָה (LXX ἀλήθεια).

γένημα.[7]

Very common in the LXX for the produce of the land;
so also in the Synoptists: its first occurrence not in Polybius; [8]

---

[1] *Cf.* also below, III. iii. 4.

[2] The κυρόω of Gal. 3 [15], for instance, which is likewise forensic, is a
synonym. *Cf.*, besides, *Pap. Par.* 20 (600 A.D., *Notices*, xviii. 2, p. 240):
πράσεως τῆς καὶ κυρίας οὔσης καὶ βεβαίας.

[3] *Catenae Graecorum Patrum in N. T. ed.* J. A. Cramer, v., Oxford, 1844,
p. 357.

[4] 1 Cor. 1 [6, 8] (observe ἀνεγκλήτους and πιστός), Rom. 15 [8]; *cf.* Mark 16 [20].

[5] 2 Cor. 1 [6], Rom. 4 [16]; *cf.* 2 Pet. 1 [10, 19].   [6] Field, ii., p. 243.

[7] In reference to the orthography *cf.* Winer-Schmiedel, § 5, 26 *a* (p. 55 f.)
The Papyri have γένημα; *cf.* below, III. i. 2.

[8] *Clavis* [3], p. 78.

it is already found in connection with Egypt in *Pap. Flind. Petr.* i. xvi. 2¹ (230 B.C.): τὰ γενήματα τῶν ὑπαρχόντων μοι παραδείσων, and in several other passages of the same age.²

γογγύζω.

Very familiar in the LXX, also in Paul,³ Synopt., John; authenticated in the subsequent extra-biblical literature only by Marcus Aurelius and Epictetus;⁴ but already used in the sense of *murmur* in *Pap. Flind. Petr.* ii. ix. 3⁵ (241-239 B.C.): καὶ τὸ πλήρωμα (men) γογγύζει φάμενοι ἀδικεῖσθαι.

γραμματεύς.

In the O. T. the person designated *scribe* (סֹפֵר and שֹׁטֵר) is generally the *official*. The LXX translate verbally—γραμματεύς—even in those passages where *scribe* seems to be used in the military sense, *i.e.*, of *officers*. One might conjecture that in this they were slavishly subjecting themselves to the original, the employment of γραμματεύς in the military sense being foreign to ordinary Greek usage. But their rendering is altogether correct from their own point of view: in Egyptian Greek γραμματεύς is used as the designation of an officer. In *Pap. Par.* 63⁶ (165 B.C.) we find the γραμματεὺς τῶν μαχίμων, and in *Pap. Lond.* xxiii.⁷ (158-157 B.C,) the γραμματεὺς τῶν δυνάμεων. This technical meaning⁸ of the word was familiar to the Alexandrian translators. So, *e.g.*, 2 Chron. 26¹¹, where the γραμματεύς stands with the διάδοχος;⁹ *cf.* also Jer. 44 [37]¹⁵·²⁰—if Jonathan the *scribe*, in this passage, is an officer. Similarly Judg. 5¹⁴·¹⁰ The following passages, again, are of great interest as showing indubitably that the translators employed the technical term as they had learned its use in their locality. The Hebrew of 2 Kings 25¹⁹ is almost verbally repeated in Jer. 52²⁵, as is 2 Kings 24¹⁸⁻

---

¹ Mahaffy, i. [47].   ² *Cf.* Index in Mahaffy, ii. [190].
³ He probably knows the word from his Bible-readings: 1 Cor. 10¹⁰ is an allusion to LXX Num. 14²⁷·
⁴ *Clavis*³, p. 82.   ⁵ Mahaffy, ii. [23].   ⁶ *Notices*, xviii. 2, p. 367.
⁷ Kenyon, p. 41.   ⁸ *Cf.* Lumbroso, *Recherches*, p. 231.
⁹ On the technical meaning of this word see below, *sub* διάδοχος.
¹⁰ Cod. A has quite a different reading.

25 30 as a whole in Jer. 52. The Book of Kings speaks
here of *the scribe, the captain of the host*.[1] But in our text
of Jeremiah we read (the article is wanting before סֹפֵר) *the
scribe of the captain of the host.* The LXX translate the first
passage by τὸν γραμματέα[2] τοῦ ἄρχοντος τῆς δυνάμεως, as if
they had had our text of Jeremiah before them ; Jer. 52 25, on
the other hand, they render by τὸν γραμματέα τῶν δυνάμεων,
which agrees in sense with the traditional text of 2 Kings
25 19. Now, without having the least desire to decide the
question as to the meaning of סֹפֵר in the Hebrew O. T., or
as to the original text of the above two passages, the author
yet thinks it plain that the LXX believed that they had
before them, in Jer. 52 25,[3] the γραμματεὺς τῶν δυνάμεων now
known to us from the London Papyrus, not some sort of
scribe of the commander-in-chief (Generalcommando).[4] The

---

[1] So De Wette renders; similarly E. Reuss: *the scribe, who as captain
. . . .*; A. Kamphausen (in Kautzsch) translates the text as altered in accordance with Jer. 52 25 by *and " the" scribe of the commander-in-chief.* The
present writer cannot perceive why this alteration should be made "as a
matter of course" (W. Nowack, *Lehrbuch der heb. Archäologie*, i., Freiburg
and Leipzig, 1894, p. 360). But it is scarcely possible, with K. H. Graf
(who does not change the text, but explains the article as referring to the
following relative clause, and translates *the scribe of the captain of the host*),
to pronounce categorically that "The captain of the host cannot be called a
סֹפֵר : that title pertains only to the people who use the pen " (*Der Prophet
Jeremia erklärt*, Leipzig, 1862, p. 628).

[2] The γραμματαιαν of Cod. A is the same form (αι = ε) with the affixed *ν*
of the popular dialect (Winer-Schmiedel § 9, 8, p. 89).

[3] If the article was really taken from 2 Kings 25 19 and inserted in the
Hebrew text here, then the translation of the LXX is an altogether pertinent
rendering of the original, and the supposition of Siegfried-Stade, p. 467, viz.,
that the LXX read the passage in Jeremiah without שַׂר, would not be
absolutely necessary. The LXX, in rendering the original by a firmly-fixed
terminus technicus, could leave untranslated the שַׂר, which was irrelevant
for the sense; the taking of it over would have ruptured the established
phrase γραμματεὺς τῶν δυνάμεων.—The author has subsequently noticed that
the most recent editor of Jeremiah actually emends the text here by the Book
of Kings for internal reasons, and explains *the chancellor, under whom the
army was placed*, as a military minister who took his place beside the chancellor mentioned elsewhere (F. Giesebrecht, *Das Buch Jeremia* [*Handkomm.
zum A. T.* iii. 2 1], Göttingen, 1894, p. 263 f.).

[4] Thus O. Thenius, *Die Bücher der Könige* (*Kurzgef. ex. Handb. zum A. T.*
ix.), Leipzig, 1849, p. 463.

choice of the plural δυνάμεων, which was not forced upon
them by the singular of the original, is to be explained only
by the fact that they were adopting a long-established and
fixed connection.

Is. 36 [22] is a most instructive case. Our Hebrew text
has simply a סֹפֵר there, without any addition; the LXX
however, transfer him to the army with the rank of the
γραμματεὺς τῆς δυνάμεως: they understood *scribe* to denote a
military rank.[1]

The military meaning of γραμματεύς has been preserved
in 1 Macc. 5 [42]; [2] probably also in Symmachus Judg. 5 [14],[3]
Jer. 44 [37] [15].[4]

γράφω.

"In the sphere of Divine Revelation the documents
belonging to it assume this [5] regulative position, and the
γέγραπται always implies an appeal to the *incontestable
regulative authority* of the dictum quoted." [6] "The New
Testament usage of ἡ γραφή . . . . . implies the same idea as
is stamped upon the usage of the γέγραπται, viz., a reference
to the regulative character of the particular document as a
whole, which character gives it a unique position, in virtue
of which ἡ γραφή is always spoken of as an authority." [7]
In this explanation of terms Cremer has, without doubt,
accurately defined the bases not only of "New Testament"

---

[1] In this technical γραμματεύς the fundamental meaning of *scribe* seems
to have grown quite indistinct: Is. 22 [15], Cod. A, has preserved the translation
γραμματεύς for *house-steward*, a reading which, as compared with ταμίας (which
is better Greek), *e.g.* of Cod. B, decidedly gives one the impression of its being
the original; with reference to γραμματεύς as a designation of a civil official
in Egypt, *cf.* Lumbroso, *Recherches*, p. 243 ff.   The word is common elsewhere
in the latter sense.   When the LXX speak of the *Egyptian* task-masters, in
Exod. 5 [6. 10. 14. 15. 19], as γραμματεῖς, it is not only a verbal, but, from their standpoint, also an accurate translation.   They subsequently designate Israelitic
officials also in this way.   In LXX Is. 33 [18], γραμματικός is used for γραμματεύς
in this sense.

[2] *Cf.* Grimm, *ad loc.*, and Wellhausen, *Israelitische und Jüdische
Geschichte*, p. 209.

[3] Field, i., p. 413.   [4] *Ibid.*, ii., p. 682.

[5] *Viz.*, the regulative position which falls to the lot of legal documents.
[6] Cremer [7], p. 241 (= [8], p. 255).   [7] *Ibid.*

usage but of the general idea that regulative authority belongs
to *scripture*.   Should the question be asked, whence it comes
that the conception of Holy *Scripture* has been bound up
with the idea of its absolute authority, the answer can only
be a reference to the *juristic* idea of *scripture*, which was
found ready to hand and was applied to the sacred documents.   A religion of documents—considered even historically—is a religion of law.   It is a particularly instructive,
though commonly overlooked, fact in connection with this
juristic conception of the biblical documents that the LXX
translate תּוֹרָה by νόμος in the great majority of passages,
although the two ideas are not by any means identical; and
that they have thus made a *law* out of a *teaching*.[1]   It is
indeed probable that in this they had been already influenced
by the mechanical conception of Scripture of early Rabbinism,
but, in regard to form, they certainly came under the sway
of the Greek juristic language.   Cremer has given a series of
examples from older Greek of this use of γράφειν in legislative
work,[2] and uses these to explain the frequently-occurring
"biblical" γέγραπται.   This formula of quotation is, however,
not "biblical" only, but is found also in juristic Papyrus
documents of the Ptolemaic period and in Inscriptions : *Pap.*
Flind. Petr. ii. xxx. *a* ;[3] further—and this is most instructive
for the frequent καθὼς γέγραπται of the biblical authors[4]—
in the formula καθότι γέγραπται: *Pap. Par.* 13[5] (probably
157 B.C.) ; *Pap. Lugd.* O[6] (89 B.C.) ; Inscription of Mylasa
in Caria, Waddington, iii. 2, No. 416 = *CIG.* ii., No. 2693 *e*
(beginning of the imperial period) ;[7] Inscription from the

---

[1] *Cf.* the similar alteration of the idea of *covenant* into that of *testament*,
and, upon this, Cremer[7], p. 897 (= [8], p. 946).

[2] The ὃ γέγραφα γέγραφα of Pilate, John 19[22], is also to be understood in
this pregnant sense.

[3] Mahaffy, ii. [102].

[4] In the O. T. *cf.*, *e.g.*, LXX Neh. 10[34 ff.] and, in particular, LXX Job
42[18] (in the *Greek* appendix to the Book of Job).

[5] *Notices*, xviii. 2, p. 210.

[6] Leemans, i., p. 77; on this Leemans, i., p. 133, remarks: "γράφειν:
in contractu scribere".

[7] As to the date see below, *sub* ὄνομα.

neighbourhood of Mylasa, Waddington, iii. 2, No. 483
(imperial period ?) : in spite of mutilation the formula is
still legible in four passages here;—and in the formula
καθὰ γέγραπται, *Pap. Par.* 7 [1] (2nd or 1st cent. B.C.), *cf.*
κα(τ)τάπερ . . . γέγραπ[τοι] in line 50 f. of the architectural
Inscription of Tegea (*ca.* 3rd cent. B.C.) [2]—in all of which
reference is made to a definite obligatory clause of the document quoted.[3] Further examples in III. iii. 5 below.

That the juristic conception of sacred writings was
familiar to the Alexandrian translators is directly shown by
Ep. Arist. (*ed.* M. Schmidt), p. 68 1 ff. : when the translation of
the Bible into Greek was finished, then, καθὼς ἔθος αὐτοῖς
ἐστιν, εἴ τις διασκευάσει προστιθεὶς ἢ μεταφέρων τι τὸ σύνολον
τῶν γεγραμμένων ἢ ποιούμενος ἀφαίρεσιν,[4] he was threatened
with a curse. According to this the Greek Bible was placed
under the legal point of view which forbade the altering of a
document; this principle is not universal in Greek law,[5] but
the Apostle Paul gives evidence for it, when, in Gal. 3 [15],
arguing *e concessis*, he says that a διαθήκη κεκυρωμένη can
neither be made void [6] nor have anything added to it.

Speaking from the same point of view, the advocate
Tertullian—to give another very clear example of the further
development of the juristic conception of biblical authority—
describes, *adv. Marc.* 4 2 and elsewhere, the individual portions
of the New *Testament* as *instrumenta, i.e.,* as *legally valid
documents.*[7]

---

[1] *Notices*, xviii. 2, p. 172.

[2] P. Cauer, *Delectus inscriptionum Graecarum propter dialectum memora-
bilium* [2], Leipzig, 1883, No. 457.

[3] It is not in this pregnant sense that Plutarch uses γέγραπται, but simply
as a formula of quotation ; *cf.* J. F. Marcks, *Symbola critica ad epistolographos
Graecos*, Bonn, 1883, p. 27. So also LXX Esth. 10 [2].

[4] *Cf.* Deut. 4 [2], 12 [32], Prov. 30 [6], and later Rev. 22 [18 f.]

[5] It was allowed, *e.g.*, in Attic Law " to add codices to a will, or make
modifications in it " ; *cf.* Meier-Schömann-Lipsius, ii., p. 597.

[6] Upon the revocation of a will *cf.* Meier-Schömann-Lipsius, ii., p. 597 f.

[7] *Cf.* upon this E. Reuss, *Die Geschichte der Heiligen Schriften Neuen
Testaments* [6], Brunswick, 1887, § 303, p. 340, and Jülicher, *Einleitung in das
N. T.*, p. 303.

διάδοχος and διαδεχόμενος.

διάδοχος occurs in the LXX only in 1 Chron. 18[17], as the equivalent of לְיָד, 2 Chron. 26[11] as the translation of מִשְׁנֶה, and 2 Chron. 28[7] as the translation of שַׂר. In none of these three passages is διάδοχος, in its ordinary sense of *successor*, an accurate rendering of the original. It has therefore been asserted by Schleusner[1] that διάδοχος corresponds to the Hebrew words, and thus means something like *proximus a rege;* he refers to Philo, *de Josepho*, M. pp. 58 and 64. Similarly Grimm,[2] in reference to 2 Macc. 4[29], has, on account of the context, rejected the meaning *successor* for that passage and 14[26]; *cf.* also 4[31] διαδεχόμενος. This supposition is confirmed by *Pap. Taur.* i. (1 15 and 6)[3] (2nd cent. B.C.), in which οἱ περὶ αὐλὴν διάδοχοι and οἱ διάδοχοι are higher officials at the court of the Ptolemies;[4] διάδοχος is thus an Egyptian court-title.[5] The Alexandrian translators of the Book of Chronicles and the Alexandrian Philo used the word in this technical sense, and the second Book of Maccabees (compiled from Jason of Cyrene) also manifests a knowledge of the usage.

Allied to the technical meaning of διάδοχος is that of the participle διαδεχόμενος,[6] 2 Chron. 31[12] and Esth. 10[3], as the translation of the מִשְׁנֶה of the original: so 2 Macc. 4[31].

δίκαιος.

The LXX render צַדִּיק or the genitival צֶדֶק by δίκαιος in almost every case, and their translation is accurate even for those passages in which the conception *normal*[7] (which

---

[1] *Novus Thesaurus*, ii. (1820), p. 87.   [2] *HApAT.* iv. (1857), p. 90.

[3] A. Peyron, i., p. 24.

[4] *Ibid.*, p. 56 ff.   On this see Brunet de Presle, *Notices*, xviii. 2, p. 228, and Lumbroso, *Recherches*, p. 195.

[5] As such frequent also in the London Papyri of the 2nd cent. B.C.; *cf.* on these, Kenyon, p. 9.   On the military signification of διάδοχος *cf.* Lumbroso, *Recherches*, p. 224 f.

[6] *Cf.*, in regard to later usage, F. Krebs, *Ägyptische Priester unter römischer Herrschaft*, in *Zeitschr. für ägyptische Sprache und Alterthumskunde*, xxxi. (1893), p. 37.

[7] *Cf.* E. Kautzsch, [*Über*] *die Derivate des Stammes* צדק *im alttestamentlichen Sprachgebrauch*, Tübingen, 1881, p. 59.

lies at the basis of the Hebrew words) has been preserved
most purely, *i.e.*, where *correct* measures are described as
just.[1] That they did not translate mechanically in these
cases appears from Prov. 11[1], where they likewise render
the weight there described as שָׁלֵם, *full*, by σταθμίον δίκαιον.[2]
There can be established also for Greek a usage similar to
the Semitic,[3] but it will be better in this matter to refer to
Egyptian usage than to Xenophon and others,[4] who apply
the attribute δίκαιος to ἵππος, βοῦς, etc., when these animals
correspond to what is expected of them. Thus in the decree
of the inhabitants of Busiris,[5] drawn up in honour of the
emperor Nero, the rise of the Nile is called a δικαία ἀνάβασις;
but more significant—because the reference is to a *measure*
—is the observation of Clemens Alexandrinus, *Strom.* vi. 4
(p. 758, Potter), that, in Egyptian ceremonies, the πῆχυς
τῆς δικαιοσύνης was carried around—*i.e.*, a *correct* cubit.[6]
That is the same idiom as the LXX apply in the ζυγὰ δίκαια
καὶ σταθμία δίκαια καὶ χοῦς δίκαιος, Lev. 19[36], in the μέτρον
ἀληθινὸν καὶ δίκαιον, Deut. 25[15], and in the χοῖνιξ δικαία,
Ezek. 45[10].

διῶρυξ.

The LXX translate *flood* Is. 27[12], *stream* Is. 33[21], and
river Jer. 38 [31][9], by διῶρυξ *canal*. They have thus
Egyptianised the original. Such a course was perhaps quite
natural in the first passage, where the reference is to the
"flood of Egypt": noticing that *stream* and *river* were meta-

---

[1] *Cf.* Kautzsch, p. 56 f., on the inadequacy of the German *gerecht* for
the rendering of the Hebrew word.

[2] Deut. 25[15], ἀληθινόν.

[3] Kautzsch, p. 57 ff. In Arabic the same word is used, according to
Kautzsch, to describe, *e.g.*, a lance or a date [the fruit] as *correct*.

[4] Cremer[7], p. 270 (= [8], p. 284).

[5] Letronne, *Recueil*, ii., p. 467, *cf.* p. 468 f.; also Letronne, *Recherches*,
p. 396 f., Lumbroso, *Recherches*, p. 290. Pliny, *Nat. Hist.* v. 58, speaks in the
same way of the *iustum incrementum*, and Plutarch, *de Isid. et Osirid.*, p. 368,
says: ἡ δὲ μέση ἀνάβασις περὶ Μέμφιν, ὅταν ᾖ δικαία, δεκατεσσάρων πηχῶν.

[6] *Cf.* also the Egyptian measure δικαιότατον μύστρον in F. Hultsch's
Griechische und römische Metrologie[2], Berlin, 1882, p. 636.

phorically used in the other two passages, they made the
metaphors more intelligible to the Alexandrians by giving
them a local colouring—just as was shown above in the case
of ἄφεσις.

εἰς.

"The prepositional construction came easily to the
N. T. writers probably because of the more forcible and
more expressive diction of their native tongue, and we
therefore find εἰς in places where the Dat. commodi or
incommodi would have sufficed for the Greeks, *e.g.*, Acts
24 [17]: ἐλεημοσύνας ποιήσων εἰς τὸ ἔθνος μου . . ." [1]
In answer to this it must, to begin with, be remarked
that "the" New Testament writers were not the first to
find the usage a natural one, for it is already found in the
Greek Old Testament. The author is not now examining
the use of εἰς in that book, but he can point to the following
passages, in which εἰς represents the "dative of advantage " :
LXX Bel [5], ὅσα εἰς αὐτὸν [Bel] δαπανᾶται, ver. [22], τὴν
δαπάνην τὴν εἰς αὐτόν [Bel], with which is to be compared
ver. [2], ἀνηλίσκετο αὐτῷ [2] [Bel]; Ep. Jerem. [9] (ἀργύριον) εἰς
ἑαυτοὺς καταναλοῦσι; Sir. 37 [7], συμβουλεύων εἰς ἑαυτόν (=
ver. [8], ἑαυτῷ βουλεύσεται). In all these passages the original
is wanting, but it seems certain to the author that what we
find here is not one of the LXX's many [3] Hebraisms in the
use of prepositions, but that this employment of εἰς is an
Alexandrian idiom.

In *Pap. Flind. Petr.* ii. xxv. *a–i* [4] (*ca.* 226 B.C.) and elsewhere, we have a number of receipts, from the standing
formulæ of which it appears that εἰς was used to specify the
various purposes of the items of an account. Thus the receipt
a [5] runs : ὁμολογεῖ Κεφάλων ἡνίοχος ἔχειν παρὰ Χάρμου . . . . .

---

[1] Winer-Lünemann, § 31, 5 (p. 200).

[2] Theodotion (ver. [3]) translates the same passage thus : καὶ ἐδαπανῶντε
εἰς αὐτὸν [Bel] σεμιδάλεως ἀρτάβαι δώδεκα (*Libri apocryphi V. T. graece, ed.*
O. F. Fritzsche, p. 87).

[3] *Cf.* the author's work *Die neutest. Formel "in Christo Jesu,"* p. 55 f.

[4] Mahaffy, ii. [72] ff.   [5] *Ibid.*, ii. [72].

εἰς αὐτὸν καὶ ἡνιόχους ζ΄ .'. ἄρτων καθαρῶν β΄ χοίνικας .....
καὶ εἰς ἱπποκόμους ιγ΄ ἄρτων αὐτοπύρων .. κς΄, *i.e.*, *Kephalon
the charioteer certifies that he has received from Charmos for himself
and* 7 *other charioteers,* 2 *chœnices* |*of pure bread, and for* 13
grooms, 26 *measures of bran bread.* Further, εἰς stands before
non-personal words in the same way : καὶ εἰς ἵππον ἐνοχλού-
μενον . εἰς χρῖσιν ἐλαίου κ` γ΄ καὶ .. εἰς λύχνους κίκεως κ` β΄,
i.e., and for a. sick horse 3 *cotylas of oil for rubbing in, and for
the lantern* 2 *cotylas of Kiki-oil.*

Still more clear is the passage from the contract *Pap.
Par.*[5] [1] (114 B.C.) καὶ τὸν εἰς Τάγην οἶκον ᾠκοδομημένον.
Further examples in III. iii. 1, below.

The same usage of εἰς, the examples of which may be
increased from the Papyri, is found specially clearly in Paul :
1 Cor. 16[1] τῆς λογείας τῆς εἰς τοὺς ἁγίους, similarly 2 Cor.
8[4], 9[1. 13], Rom. 15[26]; *cf.* Acts 24[17]; Mark 8[19 f.] should probably be explained in the same way.

ἐκτὸς εἰ μή.

The commonly cited examples, from Lucian, etc., of
this jumbled phrase,[2] long since recognised as late-Greek, in
the Cilician Paul (1 Cor. 14[5], 15[2], *cf.* 1 Tim. 5[19]) are not so
instructive for its use as is the passage of an Inscription of
Mopsuestia in Cilicia, Waddington, iii. 2, No. 1499 (the
author cannot fix the date ; certainly the imperial period) :
ἐκτὸς εἰ μὴ [ἐ]ὰν Μάγνα μόνη θε[λή]σῃ.

ἐν.

The ignoring of the difference between translations of
Semitic originals and works which were in Greek from the
first—a difference of fundamental importance for the grammar
(and the lexicon) of the " biblical " writers—has nowhere
such disastrous consequences as in connection with the pre-

---

[1] *Notices*, xviii. 2, p. 131.—The same words are found in *Pap. Lugd.* M.
(Leemans, i., p. 59) ; Leemans, i., p. 63, explains εἰς as a periphrasis for the
genitive : similarly W. Schmid, *Der Atticismus*, iii. (1893), p. 91. One should
notice in this latter work the other observations upon the prepositions—they
are of importance for biblical philology.

[2] Winer-Lünemann, § 65, 3 (p. 563) ; Schmiedel, *HC.*, ii. 1 (1891), p. 143.

position. The author considers that he has previously shown,
by a not unimportant example, what a difference there is
between a peculiarity of syntax in the originally-Greek
Epistles of Paul and the apparently similar phenomenon in
Greek translations. A similar fact may be observed with
regard to the question of ἐν with the *dativus instrumenti.*
Winer-Lünemann [1] still maintains that ἐν is used " of the
instrument and means (chiefly in the Apocalypse)—not only
(as in the better Greek prose-writers . . . .) where *in* (or
on) would be proper enough . . . . . ., but also, irrespective
of this, where in Greek the dative alone, as *casus instru-
mentalis,* would be used—as an after-effect of the Hebrew בְּ ".
Similarly A. Buttmann.[2] In their enumeration of the examples—in so far as these can come into consideration at all
—both writers, in neglecting this difference, commit the error
of uncritically placing passages from the Gospels and the
Apocalypse, in regard to which one *may* speak of a Semitic
influence, *i.e.,* of a possible Semitic original, alongside of,
say, Pauline passages, without, however, giving any indication of how they imagine the " after-effect " of the בְּ to
have influenced Paul. Thus Winer-Lünemann quotes Rom.
15 [6] ἐν ἑνὶ στόματι δοξάζητε, and Buttmann,[3] 1 Cor. 4 [21] ἐν
ῥάβδῳ ἔλθω πρὸς ὑμᾶς, as Pauline examples of ἐν with the
instrumental dative. The author believes that both passages
are capable of another explanation, and that, as they are
the only ones that can be cited with even an appearance
of reason, this use of ἐν by Paul cannot be made out. For,
to begin with, the passage in Romans is one of those
" where *in* would be proper enough," *i.e.,* where the reference to its primary sense of location is fully adequate to
explain it, and it is thus quite superfluous to make for
such instances a new compartment in the dust-covered re-
pository ; the Romans are to glorify God *in* one mouth—
because, of course, words are formed *in* the mouth, just as,
according to popular psychology, thoughts dwell *in* the

---

[1] § 48, *d* (p. 363).
[2] *Grammatik des neutestamentlichen Sprachgebrauchs,* p. 157.
[3] P. 284.

heart.   In 1 Cor. 4²¹, again, the case seems to be more
favourable for the view of Buttmann, for the LXX frequently
use the very construction ἐν τῇ ῥάβδῳ; what more easy
than to maintain that "the" biblical Greek uses this construction instrumentally throughout?   But here also we
perceive very clearly the difference between the diction of
the translators as cramped by their original, and the unconstrained language of Paul.   In all the passages of the
LXX (Gen. 32¹⁰, Exod. 17⁵, 21²⁰, 1 Sam. 17⁴³, 2 Sam. 7¹⁴,
23²¹, 1 Chron. 11²³, Ps. 2⁹, 88 [89]³³, Is. 10²⁴, Mic. 5¹, 7¹⁴;
cf. Ezek. 39⁹, also Hos. 4¹², where ἐν ῥάβδοις is conformed
to the previous ἐν [= בְּ] συμβόλοις) the ἐν of the phrase ἐν
τῇ ῥάβδῳ is a mechanical imitation of a בְּ in the original: it
cannot therefore be maintained in any way that that construction is peculiar to the indigenous Alexandrian Greek.
With Paul, on the contrary, ἐν ῥάβδῳ is anticipatively
conformed to the following locative ἤ ἐν ἀγάπῃ πνεύματί τε
πραΰτητος; it is but a loose formation of the moment, and
cannot be deduced from any law of syntax.   It is, of course,
not impossible that this anticipative conformation came the
more easily to the Apostle, who knew his Greek Bible, because one or other of those passages of the LXX may have
hovered[1] before his mind, but it is certainly preposterous to
speak of the "after-effect" of a בְּ.   Where in Paul's psychology of language may this powerful particle have had
its dwelling-place?

ἐνταφιαστής.

The LXX correctly translate רֹפֵא physician by ἰατρός;
only in Gen. 50²ᶠ by ἐνταφιαστής.   The original speaks in
that passage of the Egyptian physicians who embalmed the
body of Jacob.   The translation is not affected by the verb
ἐνταφιάζειν simply, but is explained by the endeavour to

---

[1] The ἐν τῇ ῥάβδῳ, which should possibly be restored as the original
reading in line 12 of the leaden tablet of Adrumetum to be discussed in Art.
IV., might be explained as a reminiscence of these LXX passages, in view of
its association with the many other quotations from the LXX found there.—
In the passage in Lucian, *Dial. Mort.* 23₃, καθικόμενον ἐν τῇ ῥάβδῳ the ἐν is
regarded as doubtful (Winer-Lünemann, p. 364).

introduce a term better suited to Egyptian conditions: it was, of course, an embalming in Egypt. But the professional designation of the person [1] entrusted with this work was ἐνταφιαστής, *Pap. Par.* 7 [2] (99 B.C.). Those sections of the Old Testament the scene of which was laid in Egypt, or which had regard to Egyptian conditions, naturally gave the translators most occasion to use Egyptianised expressions.

ἐντυγχάνω, ἔντευξις, ἐντυχία.

In the New Testament writings ἔντευξις is used only in 1 Tim. 2 [1] and 4 [5], having in both passages the sense of *petitionary prayer.* This usage is commonly explained [3] by the employment of the word in the sense of *petition* which is found in extra-biblical literature from the time of Diodorus and Josephus. The Papyri [4] show that in Egypt it had been long familiar in technical language: " ἔντευξις *est ipsa petitio seu voce significata, seu in scripto libello expressa, quam supplex subditus offert; . . . vocem Alexandrini potissimum usurpant ad designandas petitiones vel Regi, vel iis, qui regis nomine rempublicam moderantur, exhibitas* ".[5] This explanation has been fully confirmed by the newly-discovered Papyri of the Ptolemaic period.[6] The technical meaning also occurs in Ep. Arist. (ed. M. Schmidt), p. 58₃; A. Peyron, who has previously drawn attention to this passage, finds it also in 2 Macc. 4 [8]—probably without justification.

ἐντυχία is found in the same sense in *Pap. Lond.* xliv.[3] [7] (161 B.C.) and 3 Macc. 6 [40]—in both passages in the idiomatic phrase ἐντυχίαν ποιεῖσθαι.

The verb ἐντυγχάνω [8] has the corresponding technical

---

[1] *Cf.* on this point Lumbroso, *Recherches*, p. 136 f.

[2] *Notices*, xviii. 2, p. 172.   [3] *Clavis*[3], p. 151.

[4] The word does not occur in the LXX. In 2nd Macc. 4 [8], ἔντευξις signifies *conference.*

[5] A. Peyron, i., p. 101.

[6] *Cf.* the indexes of Leemans, of the *Notices*, xviii. 2, of Mahaffy and Kenyon.

[7] Kenyon, p. 34.

[8] In addition to Wisdom 8 [21], a later testimony, *Pap. Berol.* 7351 (*BU.* viii., p. 244, No. 246₁₃) 2-3 cent. A.D.: εἰδότες ὅτι νυκτὸς καὶ ἡμέρας ἐντυγχάνω τῷ θεῷ ὑπὲρ ὑμῶν, is significant in regard to the use of this word in religious speech. (Rom. 8 [27.34], 11 [2], Heb. 7 [25], Clem. Rom. 1 Cor. 56 [1]).

meaning; the correlative term for the king's *giving an answer* is χρηματίζειν.[1]

Both the verb and the substantive are frequently combined with κατά and ὑπέρ, according to whether the memorial expresses itself *against* or *for* some one; *cf.* the Pauline ὑπερεντυγχάνω, Rom. 8 [26].

ἐργοδιώκτης.

This word, common in the LXX, but hitherto not authenticated elsewhere, is vouched for by *Pap. Flind. Petr.* ii. iv. i.[2] (255-254 B.C.) as a technical term for *overseer of work, foreman*. Philo, who uses it later, *de Vit. Mos.* i. 7 (M., p. 86), can hardly have found it in the LXX first of all, but rather in the current vocabulary of his time. It is in use centuries later in Alexandria: Origen[3] jestingly calls his friend Ambrosius his ἐργοδιώκτης. Even he would not originally get the expression from the LXX.[4]

εὐΐλατος.

Occurring only in LXX Ps. 98 [99][8] (representing נשׂא) and 1 [3] Esd. 8 [53][5] = *very favourable :* already exemplified in *Pap. Flind. Petr.* ii. xiii. 19 [6] (*ca.* 255 B.C.) ; observe that it is the same phrase τυχεῖν τινος εὐϊλάτου which is found here and in the passage in Esd. See a further example, III. iii. 6, *sub* βιάζομαι, below.

εὐχαριστέω.

In regard to the passive,[7] 2 Cor. 1 [11], *Pap. Flind. Petr.* ii. ii. 4 [8] (260-259 B.C.) is instructive ; it is difficult, however, to

[1] A. Peyron, i., p. 102; Lumbroso, *Recherches,* p. 254; Mahaffy, ii., p. 28.

[2] Mahaffy, ii. [6], *cf.* p. 6.

[3] Hieron. *de vir. inl.* 61; *cf.* P. D. Huetii, *Origenianorum,* i. 8 (Lomm. xxii., p. 38 f.).

[4] Upon the usage of the word in ecclesiastical Greek and Latin, *cf.* the Greek and Latin Glossaries of Du Cange. The ἅπαξ λεγόμενον ἐργοπαρέκτης of Clem. Rom. 1 Cor. 34 [1] seems to be allied.

[5] Cod. A reads ἱλάτου (thus the ιλαστου of the second hand should perhaps be restored).

[6] Mahaffy, ii. [45]. The word refers to the king.

[7] *Cf. Clavis*[3], p. 184, in the concluding note, and G. Heinrici, Meyer vi.[i] (1890), p. 25.

[8] Mahaffy, ii. [4].

settle what the εὐχαριστηθείς in this passage refers to, owing
to mutilation of the leaf.

τὸ θεμέλιον.

In deciding the question whether θεμέλιον is to be
construed as masculine or neuter in passages where the
gender of the word is not clearly determined, attention is
usually called to the fact that the neuter form is first found
in Pausanius (2nd cent. A.D.). But it occurs previously in
Pap. Flind. Petr. ii. xiv. 3 [1] (Ptolemaic period). *Cf.* also τὸ
θεμέλιον of an unknown translator of Lev. 4 18. [2]   From this,
the possibility, at least, of taking it as neuter, in the non-
decisive passages [3] Sir. 1 15, Rom. 15 20, Eph. 2 20, Luke 6 48 f.,
14 29, 1 Tim. 6 19, Heb. 6 1, may be inferred.

ἴδιος.

The LXX not seldom (Gen. 47 18, Deut. 15 2, Job 2 11,
7 10. 13, Prov. 6 2, 13 8, 16 23, 27 8, Dan. 1 10) translate the
possessive pronoun (as a suffix) by ἴδιος, though the connection does not require the giving of such an emphasis
to the particular possessive relation.   Such passages as Job
24 12, Prov. 9 12, 22 7, 27 15, might be considered stranger still,
where the translator adds ἴδιος, though the Hebrew text does
not indicate a possessive relation at all, nor the context require the emphasising of any.   This special prominence is,
however, only apparent, and the translation (or addition) is
correct.   We have here probably the earliest examples of the
late-Greek use of ἴδιος for the genitives ἑαυτοῦ and ἑαυτῶν
employed as possessives, a usage which can be pointed to in
Dionysius of Halicarnassus, Philo, Josephus and Plutarch, [4]

---

[1] Mahaffy, ii. [4], p. 30.   [2] Field, i., p. 174.

[3] Winer-Schmiedel notes the " unambiguous " ones, § 8, 13 (p. 85).

[4] References in Guil. Schmidt, *De Flavii Iosephi elocutione,* Fleck. *Jbb.
Suppl.* xx. (1894), p. 369.   Specially important are the many examples given
there from Josephus, in whose writings a similar use of οἰκεῖος is also shown.
—A more out-of-the-way example of this worn-out οἰκεῖος may be mentioned
here.   In the second (spurious) Prologue to Jesus Sirach, near the middle, it
is said : (τὴν βίβλον) Σιρὰχ οὗτος μετ᾽ αὐτὸν πάλιν λαβὼν τῷ οἰκείῳ παιδὶ κατέλιπεν
Ἰησοῦ (*Libri apocr. V. T. ed.* O. F. Fritzsche, p. 388).   O. F. Fritzsche assigns
this Prologue to the 4th-5th cent. A.D., *HApAT.* v. (1859), p. 7 ; in his edition
of 1871, *ad loc.,* he seems to agree with K. A. Credner, who dates it cent. 9-10.

and in the Attic Inscriptions [1] subsequent to 69 B.C. This
usage is also confirmed by the Apocryphal books of the
O. T., specially by those in Greek from the first, and it influences the New Testament writers,[2] and especially Paul,
much more strongly than is implied by Winer-Lünemann.[3]
Exegetes have, in many places, laid a stress upon the ἴδιος
which, in the text, does not belong to it at all. In consideration of the very widely-extended use of the exhausted
ἴδιος in the post-classical age, it will, in point of fact, be the
most proper course in exegesis always to assume it primarily
as most probable, and to take ἴδιος in the old sense only
when the context absolutely requires it. A specially instructive example is 1 Cor. 7[2], διὰ δὲ τὰς πορνείας ἕκαστος τὴν
ἑαυτοῦ γυναῖκα ἐχέτω καὶ ἑκάστη τὸν ἴδιον ἄνδρα ἐχέτω : ἴδιος
is here used only for the sake of variety and is exactly
equivalent to the ἑαυτοῦ.

ἱλαστήριος and ἱλαστήριον.

Of all the errors to be found in exegetical and lexical
literature, that of imagining that ἱλαστήριον in the LXX is
identical in meaning with כַּפֹּרֶת, cover (of the ark of the covenant), and that therefore the word with them means propitiatory cover (Luther: Gnadenstuhl), is one of the most
popular, most pregnant with results, and most baneful. Its
source lies in the fact that the LXX's frequent external
verbal equation, viz., ἱλαστήριον = kappōreth, has been inconsiderately taken as an equation of ideas. But the investigation cannot proceed upon the assumption of this

[1] K. Meisterhans, Grammatik der attischen Inschriften [2], Berlin, 1888,
p. 194.

[2] Genuine examples are readily found in all of these except Revelation,
in which ἴδιος does not occur at all. The reason of this is not, of course, that
they all wrote "New Testament" Greek, but that they wrote at a time
when the force of ἴδιος had been long exhausted. The Latin translations,
in their frequent use of the simple suus (A. Buttmann, p. 102, note), manifest a true understanding of the case.

[3] § 22, 7 (p. 145 f.). Here we read : " no example can be adduced from
the Greeks " ; reference is made only to the Byzantine use of οἰκεῖος and the
late-Latin proprius = suus or ejus. A. Buttmann, p. 102 f., expresses himself
more accurately.

identification of ideas. We must rather, as in all cases where
the Greek expression is not congruent with the Hebrew
original, begin here by establishing the difference, and then
proceed with an attempt to explain it. In the present case
our position is happily such that we can give the explanation
with some certainty, and that the wider philologico-historical
conditions can be ascertained quite as clearly.

To begin with, it is altogether inaccurate to assert that
the LXX *translate kappōreth* by ἱλαστήριον. They first encountered the word in Exod. 25 [16] [17]: *and thou shalt make a
kappōreth of pure gold.* The Greek translator rendered thus :
καὶ ποιήσεις ἱλαστήριον ἐπίθεμα [1] χρυσίου καθαροῦ. His
rendering of *kappōreth* is therefore not ἱλαστήριον, but ἱλαστήριον ἐπίθεμα ; he understood *kappōreth* quite well, and
translates it properly by *cover*,[2] but he has elucidated the
word, used technically in this place, by a theological adjunct
which is not incorrect in substance.[3] ἐπίθεμα is doubtless a
translation of *kappōreth* the *word ;* ἱλαστήριον ἐπίθεμα is a
rendering of *kappōreth* the religious *concept.* How then are
we to understand this theological gloss upon the Hebrew
word? ἱλαστήριον is not a substantive,[4] but, as in 4 Macc.

---

[1] ἐπίθεμα is wanting in Cod. 58 only ; in Codd. 19, 30, etc., it stands
before ἱλαστήριον. A second hand makes a note to ἱλαστήριον in the margin
of Cod. vii. (an Ambrosianus of cent. 5,—Field, i., p. 5), *viz.,* σκέπασμα (*covering*), (Field, i., p. 124). Cremer[7], p. 447 (= [8], p. 475), following Tromm,
quotes also LXX Exod. 37 [6] for *kappōreth* = ἱλαστήριον ἐπίθεμα. But the
Complutensian alone has it there—not the manuscripts.

[2] The Concordance of Hatch and Redpath is therefore inaccurate in
affirming, *sub* ἐπίθεμα, that this word has no corresponding Hebrew in Exod.
25 [16] [17], and also in quoting this passage *sub* ἱλαστήριον instead of *sub*
ἱλαστήριος.

[3] This is also the opinion of Philo, *cf.* p. 128 below.

[4] Against Cremer[7], p. 447 (= [8], p. 475), who has no hesitation in
identifying ἱλαστήριον with *kappōreth.* His taking ἱλαστήριον as a substantive
in this passage would have better support if the word stood after ἐπίθεμα ; it
could then be construed as in apposition to ἐπίθεμα. The passage he quotes,
LXX Exod. 30 [25] [not [35]] is not to the purpose, for, at the end of the verse,
ἔλαιον χρῖσμα ἅγιον ἔσται should be translated *the* (previously mentioned) *oil
shall be a* χρῖσμα ἅγιον, and, at the beginning of the verse, χρῖσμα ἅγιον appears
to be in apposition to ἔλαιον. If Cremer takes ἱλαστήριον as a substantive =
propitiatory cover, then he could only translate LXX Exod. 25 [16] [17] by *and
thou shalt make a propitiatory cover as a cover of pure gold*, which the original
does not say.

17 [22] (if τοῦ ἱλαστηρίου θανάτου is to be read here with the Alexandrinus), an adjective, and signifies *of use for propitiation*.

The same theological gloss upon the ceremonial *kappōreth* is observed when, in the Greek translation of the Pentateuch [1]—first in the passages immediately following upon Exod. 25 [16] [[17]] and also later—it is rendered, breviloquently,[2] by the simple ἱλαστήριον instead of ἱλαστήριον ἐπίθεμα. The word is now a substantive and signifies something like *propitiatory article*. It does not *mean cover*, nor even *propitiatory cover*, but for the concept *cover* it substitutes another, which only expresses the ceremonial purpose of the article. The *kappōreth* was for the translators a σύμβολον τῆς ἵλεω τοῦ θεοῦ δυνάμεως, as Philo, *de vit. Mos.* iii. 8 (M., p. 150), speaking from the same theological standpoint, explains it, and therefore they named this symbol ἱλαστήριον. Any other sacred article having some connection with propitiation might in the very same way be brought under the general conception ἱλαστήριον, and have the latter substituted for it, *i.e.*, if what was required was not a translation but a theological paraphrase. And thus it is of the greatest possible significance that the LXX actually do make a generalising gloss [3] upon another quite different religious conception by ἱλαστήριον, viz., עֲזָרָה, the *ledge* of the altar, Ezek. 43 [14.] [17.] [20]; it also, according to ver. [20], had to be sprinkled with the blood of the sin-offering, and was therefore a kind of *propitiatory article*—hence the theologising rendering of the Greek translators. ἱλαστήριον here also

---

[1] The apparent equation ἱλαστήριον = *kappōreth* is found only in Exod., Lev., Numb.

[2] The present writer cannot understand how Cremer,[7], p. 447 (= [8], p. 475), inverting the facts of the case, can maintain that ἱλαστήριον ἐπίθεμα is an expansion of the simple ἱλαστήριον = *kappōreth*. This is exactly the same as if one should explain the expression *symbolum apostolicum* as an " expansion " of the simple *apostolicum*, which we do in fact use for *Apostolic Symbol*. But, besides, it would be very strange if the LXX had expanded an expression before they had used it at all ! No one can dispute that ἱλαστήριον ἐπίθεμα is their earliest rendering of *kappōreth*. Then it must also be conceded that the simple ἱλαστήριον is an abbreviation. We have in this a case similar to that of the breviloquence *Jobel* and of ἄφεσις (*cf.* p. 100 above.)

[3] This fact is almost always overlooked in the commentaries.

means neither *ledge* nor *ledge of propitiation*, but *propitiatory article.*

The proof of the fact that the LXX did not identify the concept ἱλαστήριον with *kappōreth* and ʿ*azārah* can be supplemented by the following observed facts. The two words paraphrased by ἱλαστήριον have other renderings as well. In Exod. 26 ³⁴ the original runs, *and thou shalt put the kappōreth upon the ark of the testimony in the most holy place;* LXX καὶ κατακαλύψεις τῷ καταπετάσματι τὴν κιβωτὸν τοῦ μαρτυρίου ἐν τῷ ἁγίῳ τῶν ἁγίων. According to Cremer, the LXX have not translated the Hebrew word here at all —let alone by καταπέτασμα. But it is without doubt a more correct conjecture that they read not כַּפֹּרֶת but פָּרֹכֶת, *curtain*, and thus *did* translate the Hebrew word.[1] This conjecture is, however, in no way absolutely necessary; the author thinks it not at all impossible that the LXX read *kappōreth*, and translated it by καταπέτασμα, just as they did, at its first occurrence, by ἐπίθεμα. More significant is 1 Chron. 28 ¹¹, where *house of the kappōreth* is rendered by ὁ οἶκος τοῦ ἐξιλασμοῦ: this also is a theological gloss, not a verbal translation of the original.[2] It may be regarded as specially significant that the ceremonial word should thus be glossed in two different ways. Similarly, ʿ*azārah* in Ezek. 45 ¹⁹ is paraphrased[3] by τὸ ἱερόν, and, in 2 Chron. 4 ⁹ and 6 ¹³, translated by αὐλή.

It thus seems clear to the author that it is not correct to take the LXX's equation of words as being an equation of ideas. ἱλαστήριον, for the translators, signified *propitiatory article*, even where they used it for *kappōreth*. Philo still had a clear conception of the state of the matter. It

---

[1] In the same way they probably read in Amos 9 ¹ כַּפֹּרֶת instead of כַּפְתֹּר, *capital of a column,* and translated ἱλαστήριον, unless the θυσιαστήριον of Cod. A and others (Field, ii., p. 979) should be the original; *cf.* the same variant to ἱλαστήριον in Exod. 38 ⁵ [37 ⁶] (in Field, i., p. 152) and Lev. 16 ¹⁴.

[2] Hardly any one would maintain in regard to this that ἐξιλασμός in the LXX "means" *kappōreth*.

[3] Had the Greek translators understood the construction here, they ought certainly to have written καὶ ἐπὶ τὰς τέσσαρας γωνίας τοῦ ἱεροῦ τοῦ θυσιαστηρίου.

is not correct to assert[1] that, following the example of the LXX, he describes *kappōreth* as ἱλαστήριον : he *describes* it correctly as ἐπίθεμα τῆς κιβωτοῦ, and remarks further that it is called ἱλαστήριον in the Bible: *De Vit. Mos.* iii. 8 (M. p. 150) ἡ δὲ κιβωτὸς . . ., ἧς ἐπίθεμα ὡσανεὶ πῶμα τὸ λεγόμενον ἐν ἱεραῖς βίβλοις ἱλαστήριον, and, further on in the same work, τὸ δὲ ἐπίθεμα τὸ προσαγορευόμενον ἱλαστήριον ; *De Profug.* 19 (M. p. 561) . . . τὸ ἐπίθεμα τῆς κιβωτοῦ, καλεῖ δὲ αὐτὸ ἱλαστήριον. Philo manifestly perceived that the ἱλαστήριον of the Greek Bible was an altogether peculiar designation, and therefore expressly distinguishes it as such : he puts the word, so to speak, in quotation-marks. Thus also, in *De Cherub.* 8 (M. p. 143), καὶ γὰρ ἀντιπρόσωπά φασιν εἶναι νεύοντα πρὸς τὸ ἱλαστήριον ἑτέροις is clearly an allusion to LXX Exod. 25 20 [21], and, instead of saying that Philo here describes the *kappōreth* as ἱλαστήριον,[1] we should rather say that he, following the LXX, asserts that the cherubim over-shadow the ἱλαστήριον.[2] How little one is entitled to speak of a " Sprachgebrauch "[3] (*usage*, or, *habit of speech*), *viz.*, ἱλαστήριον = *kappōreth*, is shown by the fact that Symmachus in Gen. 6 16 [15] twice renders the *Ark* of Noah by ἱλαστήριον,[4] and that Josephus, *Antt.* xvi. 7 1, speaks of a monument of white stone as a ἱλαστήριον : περίφοβος δ' αὐτὸς ἐξῄει καὶ τοῦ

---

[1] Cremer[7], p. 447 (= [8], p. 475).

[2] It is to be doubted whether the Hebrew concept *kappōreth* was present to the mind of the writer at all : in any case it is wrong to assume forthwith that he consciously described *kappōreth* as ἱλαστήριον. It is exactly the same as if one were to assert that wherever the word *Gnadenstuhl* (mercy-seat) occurs in the biblical quotations of German devotional books, the original being *kappōreth*, the writers describe the *kappōreth* as *Gnadenstuhl*. In most cases the writers will be simply dependent upon Luther, and their usage of the word *Gnadenstuhl* furnishes nothing towards deciding the question how they understood *kappōreth*. *Cf.* p. 134 f.—Similarly, Heb. 9[5] is an allusion to LXX Exod. 25 20 [21]; what was said about the passage in Philo holds good here.

[3] Cremer[7], p. 447 (= [8], p. 475).

[4] Field, i., p. 23 f. The present writer agrees with Field in this matter, and believes that Symmachus desired by this rendering to describe the Ark as a *means of propitiation* : God was gracious to such as took refuge in the Ark.

δέους ἱλαστήριον μνῆμα λευκῆς πέτρας ἐπὶ τῷ στομίῳ κατεσ-
κευάσατο, which must certainly be translated : *he set up a
monument of white stone as a ἱλαστήριον.*[1]

What, then, is the meaning of ἱλαστήριον in the important " Christological " statement Rom. 3 [25] ?   Paul says there
of Jesus Christ, ὃν προέθετο ὁ θεὸς ἱλαστήριον διὰ πίστεως ἐν
τῷ αὐτοῦ αἵματι εἰς ἔνδειξιν τῆς δικαιοσύνης αὐτοῦ.   It has
been said that the Roman readers could hardly have known
the expression from any other source than the Greek Bible.[2]
But, even if this assumption were correct, it still requires to
be proved that they could have learned from the Greek Bible
that ἱλαστήριον means the *kapporeth ;* besides, the primary
question must be : what did the term signify to Paul himself ?   The author believes that even the context requires
us to reject the opinion that the Apostle is describing the
crucified Christ as " a " [3] *kapporeth.*   Had the Cross been so
named, then the metaphor might possibly be understood ; as
used of a person, it is infelicitous and unintelligible ; further,
Christ, *the end of the law,* Christ, of whom Paul has just said
that He is the revealer of the δικαιοσύνη θεοῦ χωρὶς νόμου,
would hardly be named by the same Paul, in the same breath,
as the cover of the ark of testimony : the metaphor were as
unlike Paul as possible.   But the whole assumption of the
explanation in question is without support : no " Sprachgebrauch," according to which one *had* to understand ἱλαστήριον as the *kapporeth,* ever existed either in the LXX or
later.   Hence this explanation of the passage in Romans
has long encountered opposition.   Again, it is a popular
interpretation to take ἱλαστήριον as equivalent to *propitiatory*

---

[1] Cremer[8], p. 474, joins ἱλαστήριον with μνῆμα and therefore construes
ἱλαστήριον adjectivally—as did the present writer in the German edition of
this book, pp. 122 and 127—which is not impossible, but improbable. See
note 2 on p. 127 of the German edition.

[2] Cremer[7], p. 448 (= [8], p. 475).

[3] The absence of the article is more important than Cremer supposes ;
if " the " *kapporeth,* " the " ἱλαστήριον, was something so well known to the
readers as Cremer asserts, then it would be exactly a case where the article
could stand with the predicate (*contra* E. Kühl, *Die Heilsbedeutung des
Todes Christi,* Berlin, 1890, p. 25 f.).

sacrifice, after the analogy of σωτήριον, χαριστήριον, καθάρσιον, etc., in connection with which θῦμα is to be supplied. However difficult it would be to find examples of the word being used in this sense,[1] there is no objection to it linguistically. But it is opposed by the context; it can hardly be said of a sacrifice that God προέθετο it. The more general explanation therefore, which of late has been advocated again, specially by B. Weiss,[2] *viz.*, *means of propitiation*, is to be preferred: linguistically it is the most obvious; it is also presupposed in the "usage" of the LXX, and admirably suits the connection—particularly in the more special sense of *propitiatory gift* which is to be referred to just below.

Hitherto the word in this sense had been noted only in Dion Chrysostom (1-2 cent. A.D.), *Or.* xi. p. 355 (Reiske), καταλείψειν γὰρ αὐτοὺς ἀνάθημα κάλλιστον καὶ μέγιστον τῇ Ἀθηνᾷ καὶ ἐπιγράψειν· ἱλαστήριον Ἀχαιοὶ τῇ Ἰλιάδι—and in later authors. The word here means a votive gift, which was brought to the deities in order to induce them to be favourable[3]—a *propitiatory gift*. Even one such example would be sufficient to confirm the view of the passage in Romans advocated above. Its evidential value is not decreased, but rather increased, by the fact that it is taken from a "late" author. It would surely be a mechanical notion of statistical facts to demand that only such concepts in "profane" literature as can be authenticated before, *e.g.*, the time of Paul, should be available for the explanation of the Pauline Epistles. For this would be to uphold the fantastic idea that the first *occurrence* of a word in the slender remains of the ancient literature must be identical with the earliest *use* of it in the history of the Greek language, and to overlook the fact that the annoying caprice of statistics may, in most cases, rather tend to delude the pedants who entertain such an idea.

In the case before us, however, a means has been found

---

[1] Winer-Schmiedel, § 16, 2*b*, note 16 (p. 134) refers only to the Byzantine Theophanes Continuatus.

[2] Meyer, iv.⁸ (1891), p. 164 f. and elsewhere.

[3] This ἱλαστήριον should not be described as a *sacrifice*.

of removing the objection to the " lateness " of the quotation :
ἱλαστήριον in the assigned meaning is found also before the
time of Paul—occurring as it does in a place at which the
Apostle certainly touched in his travels (Acts 21 [1]) : the
Inscription of Cos No. 81 [1] reads thus :—

ὁ δᾶμος ὑπὲρ τᾶς αὐτοκράτορος

Καίσαρος

Θεοῦ υἱοῦ [2] Σεβαστοῦ σωτηρίας

Θεοῖς ἱλαστήριον.

This Inscription is found on a statue or on the base of
a statue,[3]—at all events on a votive-gift which the " people "
of Cos erected to the gods as a ἱλαστήριον for the welfare of
the " son of God," Augustus.   That is exactly the same use
of the word as we find later in Dion Chrysostom, and the
similarity of the respective formulæ is evident.

The word is used in the same way in the Inscription of
Cos No. 347,[4] which the author cannot date exactly, but
which certainly falls within the imperial period : it occurs
upon the fragment of a pillar :—

[ὁ δᾶμος ὁ Ἀλεντίων]

. . . . Σε]βα-

σ[τ]ῷ Διὶ Σ[τ]ρατίῳ ἱλασ-

τήριον δαμαρχεῦν-

τος Γαΐου Νωρ-

βανοῦ Μοσχίω-

νο[ς φι]λοκαίσα-

ρος.

Thus much, then, can be derived from these three passages, as also from Josephus, viz., that, early in the imperial
period, it was a not uncommon custom to dedicate propitiatory gifts to the Gods, which were called ἱλαστήρια.   The

---

[1] W. R. Paton and E. L. Hicks, *The Inscriptions of Cos*, Oxford, 1891,
p. 126.

[2] For this expression see below, *sub* υἱὸς θεοῦ.

[3] The editors, p. 109, number it among the Inscriptions on votive
offerings and statues.

[4] Paton and Hicks, p. 225 f.

author considers it quite impossible that Paul should not have known the word in this sense : if he had not already become familiar with it by living in Cilicia, he had certainly read it here and there in his wanderings through the empire, when he stood before the monuments of paganism and pensively contemplated what the piety of a dying civilisation had to offer to its known or unknown Gods. Similarly, the Christians of the capital, whether one sees in them, as the misleading distinction goes, Jewish Christians or Heathen Christians, would know what a ἱλαστήριον was in their time. To suppose that, in consequence of their "magnificent knowledge of the Old Testament,"[1] they would immediately think of the *kappōreth*, is to overlook two facts. First, that the out-of-the-way[2] passages referring to the ἱλαστήριον may very well have remained unknown even to a Christian who was conversant with the LXX : how many Bible readers of to-day, nay, how many theologians of to-day—who, at least, should be Bible readers,—if their readings have been unforced, and not desecrated by side-glances towards "Ritschlianism" or towards possible examination questions, are acquainted with the *kappōreth* ? The second fact overlooked is, that such Christians of the imperial period as were conversant with those passages, naturally understood the ἱλαστήριον in the sense familiar to them, not in the alleged sense of *propitiatory cover*—just as a Bible reader of to-day, unspoiled by theology, finding the word *Gnadenstuhl* (*mercy-seat*) in Luther, would certainly never think of a *cover*.

That the verb προέθετο admirably suits the ἱλαστήριον taken as *propitiatory gift*, in the sense given to it in the Greek usage of the imperial period, requires no proof. God has *publicly set forth* the crucified Christ in His blood in view of

---

[1] Cremer[7], p. 448 (= [8], p. 476).

[2] By the time of Paul the ceremony in which the *kappōreth* played a part had long disappeared along with the Ark of the Covenant ; we can but conjecture that some mysterious knowledge of it had found a refuge in theological erudition. In practical religion, certainly, the matter had no longer any place at all.

the Cosmos—to the Jews a stumbling block, to the Gentiles
foolishness, to Faith a ἱλαστήριον. The crucified Christ is
the votive-gift of the Divine Love for the salvation of men.
Elsewhere it is human hands which dedicate to the Deity a
dead image of stone in order to gain His favour; here the
God of grace Himself erects the consoling image,—for the
skill and power of men are not sufficient. In the thought
that God Himself has erected the ἱλαστήριον, lies the same
wonderful μωρία of apostolic piety which has so inimitably
diffused the unction of artless genius over other religious
ideas of Paul. God's favour must be obtained—He Himself
fulfils the preliminary conditions; Men can do nothing at
all, they cannot so much as believe—God does all in Christ:
that is the religion of Paul, and our passage in Romans is
but another expression of this same mystery of salvation.

A. Ritschl,[1] one of the most energetic upholders of the
theory that the ἱλαστήριον of the passage in Romans signifies
the kappōreth, has, in his investigation of this question, laid
down the following canon of method: "... for ἱλαστήριον
the meaning *propitiatory sacrifice* is authenticated in heathen
usage, as being a gift by which the anger of the gods is
appeased, and they themselves induced to be gracious. . . .
But . . . the heathen meaning of the disputed word should
be tried as a means of explaining the statement in question
only when the biblical meaning has proved to be wholly
inapplicable to the passage." It would hardly be possible
to find the sacred conception of a "biblical" Greek more
plainly upheld by an opponent of the theory of inspiration
than is the case in these sentences. What has been already
said will show the error, as the author thinks it, of the
actual assertions they contain concerning the meaning of
ἱλαστήριον in "biblical"[2] and in "heathen" usage; his
own reflections about method are contained in the introduction to these investigations. But the case under considera-

---

[1] *Die christliche Lehre von der Rechtfertigung und Versöhnung dargestellt*,
ii.³, Bonn, 1889, p. 171.

[2] *Cf.* A. Ritschl, p. 168; the opinions advanced there have urgent need
of correction.

tion, on account of its importance, may be tested once more by an analogy which has already been indicated above.

In the hymn *O König, dessen Majestät*, by Valentin Ernst Löscher († 1749), there occurs the following couplet[1]:—

> *Mein Abba, schaue Jesum an,*
> *Den Gnadenthron der Sünder.*[2]

Whoever undertakes to explain this couplet has, without doubt, a task similar to that of the exegete of Rom. 3[25]. Just as in the passage from Paul there is applied to Christ a word which occurs in the Bible of Paul, so there is in this hymn a word, similarly used, which stands in the Bible of *its* author. The Apostle calls Christ a ἱλαστήριον; ἱλαστήριον is occasionally found in the Greek Bible, where the Hebrew has *kappōreth: ergo*—Paul describes Christ as the *kappōreth!* The Saxon Poet calls Christ the *Throne of Grace* (*Gnadenthron*); the *Mercy-seat* (*Gnadenstuhl*—not indeed *Throne of Grace*, but an expression equivalent to it) is found in the German Bible, where the Greek has ἱλαστήριον, the Hebrew *kappōreth: ergo*—the poet describes Christ as ἱλαστήριον, as *kappōreth*, i.e., as the *lid of the Ark of the Covenant!* These would be parallel inferences—according to that mechanical method of exegesis. The historical way of looking at the matter, however, gives us the following picture. *Kappōreth* in the Hebrew Bible signifies the *cover* (of the Ark); the Greek translators have given a theological paraphrase of this conception, just as they have occasionally done in other similar cases, in so far as they named the sacred article ἱλαστήριον ἐπίθεμα, *propitiatory cover*, according to the purpose of it, and then, quite generally, ἱλαστήριον, *propitiatory article;* the readers of the Greek Bible understood this ἱλαστήριον in its own proper sense (a sense presupposed also in the LXX) as *propitiatory article*—the more so as it was otherwise known to them in this sense; the German translator, by reason of his knowledge of the Hebrew text,

---

[1] The quotation is from [C. J. Böttcher] *Liederlust für Zionspilger*, 2nd edition, Leipzig, 1869, p. 283.

[2] *I.e.*, literally: My father, look upon Jesus, the sinner's throne of grace! *Tr.*

again specialised the *propitiatory article* into a *vehicle* or *instrument* of propitiation—again imparting to it, however, a theological shading,—in so far as he wrote, not *propitiatory cover* or *cover of mercy*, but *mercy-seat*;[1] the readers of the German Bible, of course, apprehend this word in its own proper sense, and when we read it in Bible or hymn-book, or hear it in preaching, we figure to ourselves some Throne in Heaven, to which we *draw near that we may receive mercy and may find grace to keep us in time of need*, and nobody thinks of anything else.

The LXX and Luther have supplied the place of the original *kappōreth* by words which imply a deflection of the idea. The links—*kappōreth*, ἱλαστήριον, *Gnadenstuhl*—cannot be connected by the sign of equality, not even, indeed, by a straight line, but at best by a curve.

ἱστός.

The Greek usage of this word is also found in the LXX's correct renderings of the corresponding Hebrew words, *viz.*, *mast* (of a ship), Is. 30[17], 33[23], Ezek. 27[5], and *web* (through the connecting-link *weaver's-beam*), Is. 59[5, 6] (likewise Is. 38[12], but without any corresponding word in our text); *cf.* Tobit 2[12] Cod. ℵ. In reference to this, the author would again call attention to a little-known emendation in the text of the Epistle of Aristeas proposed by Lumbroso.[2] M. Schmidt writes, p. 69 16, (ἔπεμψε δὲ καὶ τῷ Ἐλεαζάρῳ . . . .) βυσσίνων ὀθονίων εἰς † τοὺς ἑκατόν, which is altogether meaningless. We must of course read, in accordance with Joseph. *Antt.* xii. 2 14 (βυσσίνης ὀθόνης ἱστοὺς ἑκατόν), βυσσίνων ὀθονίων ἱστοὺς ἑκατόν.

καρπόω, etc.

In Leviticus 2[11] we find the command: *ye shall not burn incense* (תַקְטִירוּ) *of any leaven or honey as an offering made by fire* (אִשֶּׁה) *to Jahweh.* The LXX translate: πᾶσαν

---

[1] Luther undoubtedly took this nuance from Heb. 4[16], where the θρόνος τῆς χάριτος is spoken of: this also he translates by *Gnadenstuhl*.

[2] *Recherches*, p. 109, note 7.

γὰρ ζύμην καὶ πᾶν μέλι οὐ προσοίσετε ἀπ' αὐτοῦ (a mechanical imitation of מִמֶּנּוּ) καρπῶσαι κυρίῳ. This looks like an inadequate rendering of the original: in the equation, προσφέρειν καρπῶσαι = *burn incense as an offering made with fire*, there seems to be retained only the idea of *sacrifice;* the special nuance of the commandment seems to be lost, and to be supplanted by a different one: for καρποῦν of course means "*to make* or *offer as fruit*".[1] The idea of the Seventy, that that which was leavened, or honey, might be named a *fruit-offering,* is certainly more striking than the fact that the offering made by *fire* is here supplanted by the offering of *fruit.* But the vagary cannot have been peculiar to these venerable ancients, for we meet with the same strange notion also in passages which are not reckoned as their work in the narrower sense. According to 1 [3] Esd. 4[52] King Darius permits to the returning Jews, among other things, καὶ ἐπὶ τὸ θυσιαστήριον ὁλοκαυτώματα καρποῦσθαι καθ' ἡμέραν, and, in the Song of the Three Children [14], Azarias laments καὶ οὐκ ἔστιν ἐν τῷ καιρῷ τούτῳ ἄρχων καὶ προφήτης καὶ ἡγούμενος οὐδὲ ὁλοκαύτωσις οὐδὲ θυσία οὐδὲ προσφορὰ οὐδὲ θυμίαμα οὐδὲ τόπος τοῦ καρπῶσαι ἐναντίον σου καὶ εὑρεῖν ἔλεος. If then a *whole burnt-offering* could be spoken of as a *fruit-offering,* wherefore should the same not be done as regards things leavened and honey?

But the LXX can be vindicated in a more honourable way. Even their own usage of καρπόω elsewhere might give the hint: it is elsewhere found[2] only in Deut. 26[14], οὐκ ἐκάρπωσα ἀπ' αὐτῶν εἰς ἀκάθαρτον, which is meant to represent *I have put away nothing thereof* (*i.e.,* of the tithes), *being unclean.* In this the LXX take בְּטָמֵא to mean *for an unclean use,* as did also De Wette, while καρπόω for בִּעַר is apparently intended to signify *put away,* a meaning of the word which is found nowhere else,[3] implying, as it does, almost the

---

[1] O. F. Fritzsche *HApAT.* i. (1851), p. 32, in reference to this passage. Thus also the Greek lexica.

[2] In Josh. 5[12] we should most probably read ἐκαρπίσαντο.

[3] Schleusner explains καρπόω = *aufero* by καρπόω = *decerpo,* but it is only the middle voice which occurs in this sense.

opposite of the primary meaning *to bring forth fruit*. It is
not the LXX, however, who have taken καρπόω and *put
away* as equivalent, but rather the unscientific procedure
which looks upon verbal equations between translation and
original without further ceremony as equations of ideas.
The true intention of the Greek translators is shown by
a comparison of Lev. 2[11] and Deut. 26[14]. In the first
passage, one may doubt as to whether καρπόω is meant to
represent הַקְטִיר or אִשֶּׁה, but whichever of the two be
decided upon does not matter : in either case it represents
some idea like *to offer a sacrifice made with fire*. In the other
passage, καρπόω certainly stands for בִּעֵר, and if, indeed, the
Greek word cannot mean *put away*, yet the Hebrew one can
mean *to burn*. It is quite plain that the LXX thought that
they found this familiar meaning in this passage also : the
two passages, in fact, support one another, and ward off any
suspicion of " the LXX's " having used καρπόω in the sense
of *put away* and *bring forth fruit* at the same time. However
strange the result may appear, the issue of our critical comparison is this : the LXX used καρπόω for *to burn* both in a
ceremonial and in a non-ceremonial sense.

This strange usage, however, has received a brilliant
confirmation. P. Stengel[1] has shown, from four Inscriptions
and from the old lexicographers,[2] that καρπόω must have been
quite commonly used for *to burn* in the ceremonial sense.[3]

Stengel explains as follows how this meaning arose :
καρποῦν properly signifies *to cut into pieces ;* the holocausts
of the Greeks were cut into pieces, and thus, in ceremonial
language, καρπόω must have come to mean *absumere, consu-
mere, ὁλοκαυτεῖν*.

---

[1] *Zu den griechischen Sacralalterthümern, Hermes*, xxvii. (1892), pp.
161 ff.

[2] The passages he brings forward, in which the meaning, at least, of *to
sacrifice* for καρπόω is implied, may be extended by the translation *sacrificium
offero* given by the Itala, as also by the note " καρπῶσαι, θυσιάσαι " in the MS.
glossary (?) cited by Schleusner.   Schleusner also gives references to the
ecclesiastical literature.

[3] He counts also Deut. 26[14] among the LXX passages in this connection, but it is the non-ceremonial sense of *to burn* which καρπόω has there.

The ceremonial sense of καρπόω grows more distinct when we notice the compound form ὁλοκαρπόω,[1] Sir. 45 [14], 4 Macc. 18 [11], Sibyll. Orac. 3 565, as also by the identity in meaning of the substantives ὁλοκάρπωμα = ὁλοκαύτωμα, and ὁλοκάρπωσις = ὁλοκαύτωσις, all of which can be fully established in the LXX and the Apocrypha as meaning, in most cases, *burnt-offering*, just like κάρπωμα = κάρπωσις.

These substantives are all to be derived, not from καρπός *fruit*, but from the ceremonial καρπόω, *to burn*.[2]

κατά.

1. In 3 Macc. 5 [34] and Rom. 12 [5] is found ὁ καθ᾿ εἶς [3] for εἷς ἕκαστος, and in Mark 14 [19] and John 8 [9][4] the formula εἷς καθ᾿ εἷς for *unusquisque*. In these constructions, unknown in classical Greek, we must, it is said, either treat εἷς as an indeclinable numeral, or treat the preposition as an adverb.[5] Only in the Byzantine writers have such constructions been authenticated. But εἷς καθ᾿ ἕκαστος [6] already stands in LXX Lev. 25 [10] (καὶ ἀπελεύσεται εἷς ἕκαστος εἰς τὴν κτῆσιν αὐτοῦ), according to Cod. **A**. This represents אִישׁ, and cannot, therefore, be explained as a mechanical imitation of the original. What we have here (assuming that A has preserved the original reading) will rather be the first example of a special usage of κατά, and thus, since it is ἕκαστος which is now in question, the first, at least, of Buttmann's proposed explanations would fall to the ground.

It is, of course, quite possible that the εἷς καθ᾿ ἕκαστος should be assigned only to the late writer of Cod. A. But

---

[1] This of course does not "properly" signify *to offer a sacrifice which consists wholly of fruits* (Grimm, *HApAT.* iv. [1857], p. 366), but *to burn completely.*

[2] Stengel, p. 161.

[3] For the orthography *cf.* Winer-Schmiedel, § 5, 7 *g* (p. 36).

[4] In the non-Johannine passage about the adulteress.

[5] A. Buttmann, p. 26 *f.*, Winer-Lünemann, § 37, 3 (p. 234).

[6] The Concordance of Hatch and Redpath puts, very strangely, a point of interrogation to καθ᾿. Holmes and Parsons (Oxf. 1798) read "καί *uncis inclus.*" for καθ᾿. But the fac-simile (*ed.* H. H. Baber, London, 1816) shows ΚΑΤ̇ quite distinctly.

the hypothesis of its being the original derives, as the author
thinks, further support from the following facts.   The LXX
translate the absolute אִישׁ by ἕκαστος in innumerable passages.   But in not a single passage except the present (according to the ordinary text), is it rendered by εἶς ἕκαστος.
This combination, already found in Thucydides,[1] frequent
also in the "fourth" Book of Maccabees,[2] in Paul and in
Luke, is used nowhere else in the LXX, a fact which, in
consideration of the great frequency of ἕκαστος = אִישׁ, is certainly worthy of note.   It is in harmony with this that, so
far as the author has seen, no example occurs in the contemporary Papyri.[3]   The phrase seems to be absent from
the Alexandrian dialect in the Ptolemaic period.[4]   Hence it
is *a priori* probable that any other reading which is given by
a trustworthy source should have the preference.   Although
indeed our εἶς καθ᾽ ἕκαστος seems strange and unique, yet
this fact speaks not against, but in favour of, its being the
original.   It can hardly be imagined that the copyist would
have formed the harsh εἶς καθ᾽ ἕκαστος out of the every-day
εἶς ἕκαστος.   But it is quite plain, on the other hand, that
the latter reading could arise from the former—nay, even
had to be made from it by a fairly "educated" copyist.[5]
Our reading is further confirmed not only by the analogies
cited, but also by Rev. 21 [21], ἀνὰ εἶς ἕκαστος τῶν πυλώνων ἦν
ἐξ ἑνὸς μαργαρίτου : here also we have evidently an adverbial
use of a preposition,[6] which should hardly be explained as
one of the Hebraisms of Revelation, since in 4 [8] the distri-

---

[1] A.Buttmann, p. 105.

[2] In O. F. Fritzsche, *Libri apocryphi V. T. graece*, 4 [26], 5 [2], 8 [5. 8], 13 [13] (in
which the connected verb stands in the plural), 13 [17], 14 [12], 15 [5] (καθ᾽ ἕνα ἕκαστον
—according to AB, which codices should not.be confused with the similarly
designated biblical MSS. ; *cf. Praefatio*, p. xxi.), 15 [16], 16 [24].

[3] The author cannot of course assume the responsibility of guarantee-
ing this.

[4] Nor does it occur in the Epistle to the Hebrews.   If we could assign
4 Macc. to an Alexandrian writer, we should have the first example of it in
that book.

[5] Hence also the frequent corrections in Mark 14 [19] and John 8 [9].

[6] *Cf.* also 2 [Hebr.] Ezra 6 [20] ἕως εἶς πάντες, which indeed is perhaps a
Hebraism, and 1 Chron. 5 [10], Cod. A [N.B.] ἕως πάντες (Field, i., p. 708).

butive ἀνά is made, quite correctly, to govern the accusative, and since, further, it would be difficult to say what the original really was which, as it is thought, is thus imitated in Hebraising fashion.

2. "Even more diffuse and more or less *Hebraising* periphrases of simple prepositions are effected by means of the substantives πρόσωπον, χείρ, στόμα, ὀφθαλμός."[1] The author considers that this general assertion fails to stand the test. One of the phrases used by Buttmann as an example, *viz.*, κατὰ πρόσωπόν τινος = κατά, is already found in *Pap. Flind. Petr.* i. xxi.,[2] the will of a Libyan, of the year 237 B.C., in which the text of line 8 can hardly be restored otherwise than τὰ μὲ[ν κα]τὰ πρόσωπον τοῦ ἱεροῦ.

λειτουργέω, λειτουργία, λειτουργικός.

"The LXX took over the word [λειτουργέω] in order to designate the duties of the Priests and Levites in the sanctuary, for which its usage in profane Greek yielded no direct support, as it is only in late and in very isolated cases [according to p. 562, in Dionysius of Halicarnassus and Plutarch] that even one word of this family, λειτουργός, occurs as applied to priests."[3] The Papyri show, however, that λειτουργέω and λειτουργία were commonly used in Egypt in the ceremonial sense. In particular, the services in the Serapeum[4] were so designated. As examples of the verb there should be noted here : *Pap. Par.* 23[5] (165 B.C.), 27[6] (same date), *Pap. Lugd.* B[7] (164 B.C.), E[8] (same date), *Pap. Lond.* xxxiii.[9] (161 B.C.), xli.[10] (161 B.C.), *Pap. Par.* 29[11] (161-160 B.C.) ; of the substantive, *Pap. Lugd.* B[12] (164 B.C.), *Pap.*

---

[1] A. Buttmann, p. 274.   [2] Mahaffy, i. [59].

[3] Cremer[7], p. 560 (= [8], p. 592). But before this there had been noted in the *Thesaurus Graecae Linguae*, Diod. Sic. i. 21, τὸ τρίτον μέρος τῆς χώρας αὐτοῖς δοῦναι πρὸς τὰς τῶν θεῶν θεραπείας τε καὶ λειτουργίας.

[4] *Cf.* upon this H. Weingarten, *Der Ursprung des Mönchtums, ZKG.* i. (1877), p. 30 ff., and *R-E*[2], x. (1882), p. 780 ff.

[5] *Notices*, xviii. 2, p. 268.   [6] *Ibid.*, p. 277.

[7] Leemans, i., p. 9.   [8] *Ibid.*, p. 30.

[9] Kenyon, p. 19.   [10] *Ibid.*, p. 28.

[11] *Notices*, xviii. 2, p. 279.   [12] Leemans, i., p. 11.

Lond. xxii.[1] (164-163 B.C.), xli.[2] (161 B.C.), *Pap. Dresd.* ii.[3] (162 B.C.), *Pap. Par.* 33 [4] (*ca.* 160 B.C.).　But also of other ceremonial services elsewhere there were used λειτουργέω, *Pap. Par.* 5 [5] (113 B.C.) twice ; λειτουργία in the *Papp. Lugd.* G [6], H [7] and J,[8] written 99 B.C.[9]

λειτουργικός is found not "only in biblical and ecclesiastical Greek," [10] but occurs in a non-religious sense six times in a taxation-roll of the Ptolemaic Period, *Pap. Flind. Petr.* ii. xxxix. *e.*[11]　Its use is confined, so far as "biblical" literature is concerned, to the following Alexandrian compositions : LXX Exod. 31 [10], 39 [1],[12] Numb. 4 [12, 26], 7 [5], 2 Chron. 24 [14] ; Heb. 1 [14].

λίψ.

In the three passages, 2 Chron. 32 [30], 33 [14], and Dan. 8 [5], the LXX render the direction *West* by λίψ.　Elsewhere they use λίψ quite accurately for *South*.　But even in the passages cited they have not been guilty of any negligence, but have availed themselves of a special Egyptian usage, which might have been noticed long ago in one of the earliest-known Papyrus documents.　In a Papyrus of date 104 B.C.,

---

[1] Kenyon, p. 7.　　　　　　　　[2] *Ibid.*, p. 28.

[3] Wessely, *Die griechischen Papyri Sachsens, Berichte über die Verhandlungen der Kgl. Sächs. Gesellsch. der Wissenschaften zu Leipzig*, philol.-histor. Classe, xxxvii. (1885), p. 281.

[4] *Notices*, xviii. 2, p. 289.　　　　[5] *Notices*, xviii. 2, pp. 137 and 143.

[6] Leemans, i., p. 43.　　　[7] *Ibid.*, p. 49.　　　[8] *Ibid.*, p. 52.

[9] A Berlin Papyrus of date 134 B.C. (Ph. Buttmann, *AAB.* 1824, hist.-phil. Klasse, p. 92) uses λειτουργία for the duties of the funeral society mentioned below under λογεία.　Similarly in *Pap. Lond.* iii., 146 or 135 B.C. (Kenyon, pp. 46, 47).　But it is doubtful whether such duties were of a ceremonial character.—Further examples of λειτουργεῖν in the religious sense, from the Inscriptions, in H. Anz, *Subsidia ad cognoscendum Graecorum sermonem vulgarem e Pentateuchi versione Alexandrina repetita, Dissertationes Philologicae Halenses*, vol. xii., Halle, 1894, p. 346.

[10] Cremer [7], p. 562 (= [8], p. 595).

[11] Mahaffy, ii. [130].

[12] Tromm and Cremer also give Exod. 39 [43] ; probably they intend 39 [41][19], where the word is found only in Cod. 72 and the Complutensian ; in regard to the confused state of the text, *cf.* Field, i., p. 160.

which was elucidated by Boeckh,[1] there occurs the phrase
λιβὸς οἰκία Τέφιτος. As the South (νότος) has been expressly
mentioned just before, this can mean only *in the West the house
of Tephis*. To this Boeckh [2] observes: "λίψ means *South-
West* in Hellas, *Africus*, because Libya lies South-West from
the Hellenes—whence its name: Libya lies directly West
from the Egyptians; hence λίψ is for them the *West* itself,
as we learn here ". The word had been already used in the
will of a Libyan, *Pap. Flind. Petr.* i. xxi.[3] (237 B.C.), where
similarly the connection yields the meaning *West*.

λογεία.

In 1 Cor. 16 [1] Paul calls the *collection* for " the saints "
(according to the ordinary text) λογία, and in ver. [2] says that
the λογίαι must begin at once. The word is supposed to
occur for the first time here,[4] and to occur elsewhere only in
the Fathers. Grimm [5] derives it from λέγω. Both views
are wrong.

λογεία can be demonstrated to have been used in Egypt
from the 2nd cent. B.C. at the latest: it is found in Papyrus
documents belonging to the Χοαχύται or Χολχύται (the
orthography and etymology of the word are uncertain), a
society which had to perform a part of the ceremonies re
quired in the embalming of bodies: they are named in one
place ἀδελφοὶ οἱ τὰς λειτουργίας ἐν ταῖς νεκρίαις παρεχόμενοι.[6]
They had the right, as members of the guild, to institute
collections, and they could sell this right. Such a *collection*
is čalled λογεία: *Pap. Lond.* iii.[7] (*ca.* 140 B.C.), *Pap. Par.* 5 [8]

---

[1] *Erklärung einer Ägyptischen Urkunde in Griechischer Cursivschrift
vom Jahre 104 vor der Christlichen Zeitrechnung, AAB.* 1820-21 (Berlin, 1822),
hist.-phil. Klasse, p. 4.

[2] P. 30.   [3] Mahaffy, i. [59]; *cf.* [60].

[4] Th. Ch. Edwards, *A Commentary on the First Epistle to the Corinthians,* London, 1885, p. 462, even maintains that Paul coined the word.

[5] *Clavis*[3], p. 263.

[6] *Pap. Taur.* i., 2nd cent. B.C. (A. Peyron, i., p. 24). ʀʼor the name
brother, cf. p. 87 f. above; νεκρία A. Peyron, i., p. 77, takes to be *res mortuaria.*
For these guilds in general, *cf.,* most recently, Kenyon, p. 44 f.

[7] Kenyon, p. 46.   [8] *Notices,* xviii. 2, pp. 143, 147.

(114 B.C.) twice ; *Pap. Lugd.* M ¹ (114 B.C.).   We find the
word, further, in the taxation-roll *Pap. Flind. Petr.* ii. xxxix. *c*,²
of the Ptolemaic period,³ in which it is used six times—probably in the sense of *tax.*

The derivation of the word from λέγω is impossible ;
λογεία belongs to the class ⁴ of substantives in -εία formed
from verbs in -εύω.   Now the verb λογεύω *to collect,* which has
not been noticed in literary compositions, is found in the
following Papyri and Inscriptions : *Pap. Lond.* xxiv.⁵ (163 B.C.),
iii.⁶ (*ca.* 140 B.C.), a Papyrus of date 134 B.C.,⁷ *Pap. Taur.* 8 ⁸
(end of 2nd cent. B.C.), an Egyptian Inscription, *CIG.* iii.,
No. 4956 ₃₇ (49 A.D.) ; *cf.* also the Papyrus-fragment which
proves the presence of Jews in the Fayyûm.⁹

The Papyri yield also the pair παραλογεύω, *Pap. Flind.
Petr.* ii. xxxviii. *b* ¹⁰ (242 B.C.) and παραλογεία, *Pap. Par.* 61 ¹¹
(145 B.C.).

In regard to the orthography of the word, it is to be
observed that the spelling λογεία corresponds to the laws of
word-formation.   Its consistent employment in the relatively
well-written pre-Christian Papyri urges us to assume that
it would also be used by Paul : the Vaticanus still has it, in
1 Cor. 16 ² ¹² at least.

In speaking of the collection for ¹³ the poor in Jerusalem,

---

¹ Leemans, i., p. 60.   ² Mahaffy, ii. [127].

³ This Papyrus, it is true, is not dated, but is " a fine specimen of Ptolemaic writing " (Mahaffy, *ibid.*), and other taxation-rolls which are published
in xxxix. date from the time of Ptolemy II. Philadelphus, *i.e.*, the middle of
the 3rd cent. B.C.   For further particulars see below, III. iii. 2.

⁴ Winer-Schmiedel, § 16, 2*a* (p. 134).

⁵ Kenyon, p. 32.   ⁶ *Ibid.*, p. 47.

⁷ Ph. Buttmann, *AAB.*, 1824, hist.-phil. Kl., p. 92, and, on this, p. 99.

⁸ A. Peyron, ii., p. 45.   ⁹ Issued by Mahaffy, i., p. 43, undated.

¹⁰ Mahaffy, ii. [122].   ¹¹ *Notices,* xviii. 2, p. 351.

¹² The author has subsequently seen that L. Dindorf, in the *Thesaurus
Graecae Linguae,* v. (1842-1846), col. 348, had already noted λογεία in the
London Papyrus (as in the older issue by J. Forshall, 1839).   He certainly
treats λογία and λογεία in separate articles, but identifies the two words and
decides for the form λογεία.

¹³ For the εἰς following λογεία *cf.* p. 117 f. above.

Paul has other synonyms besides λογεία, among them λειτουργία, 2 Cor. 9 [12]. This more general term is similarly
associated with λογεία in *Pap. Lond.* iii. 9.[1]

In 1 Cor. 16 [1] Donnaeus and H. Grotius proposed to
alter "λογία" to εὐλογία,[2] as the collection is named in
2 Cor. 9 [5]. This is of course unnecessary : but it does not
seem to the author to be quite impossible that, conversely,
the first εὐλογίαν in the latter passage should be altered to
λογείαν. If λογείαν were the original, the sentence would
be much more forcible ; the temptation to substitute the
known word for the strange one could come as easily to a
copyist as to the scholars of a later period.

μειζότερος.

With this double comparative in 3 John [4][3] *cf.* the
double superlative μεγιστότατος, *Pap. Lond.* cxxx.[4] (1st or
2nd cent. A.D.).

ὁ μικρός.

In Mark 15 [40] there is mentioned a Ἰάκωβος ὁ μικρός.
It is a question whether the attribute refers to his age or
his stature,[5] and the deciding between these alternatives is
not without importance for the identification of this James
and of Mary his mother. In reference to this the author
would call attention to the following passages. In *Pap. Lugd.*
N [6] (103 B.C.) a Νεχούτης μικρός is named twice. Upon
this Leemans [7] observes : "*quominus vocem μικρός de corporis
altitudine intelligamus prohibent tum ipse verborum ordo quo ante
patris nomen et hic et infra in Trapezitae subscriptione vs. 4 poni-
tur ; tum quae sequitur vox μέσος, qua staturae certe non parvae
fuisse Nechyten docemur. Itaque ad aetatem referendum videtur,
et additum fortasse ut distingueretur ab altero Nechyte, fratre*

---

[1] Kenyon, p. 46.   Also in line 17 of the same Papyrus, λειτουργιων
should doubtless be read instead of λειτουργων.   *Cf.* also line 42 and *Pap. Par.*
5 (*Notices*, xviii. 2, top of p. 143).

[2] Wetstein, *ad loc.*   [3] Winer-Schmiedel, § 11, 4 (p. 97).
[4] Kenyon, p. 134.   [5] B. Weiss, Meyer i. 2 [7] (1885), p. 231,
[6] Leemans, i., p. 69,   [7] *Ibid.*, p. 74.

majore;" it is, in point of fact, shown by *Pap. Taur.* i. that
this Nechytes had a brother of the same name. In a similar manner a Μάνρης μέγας is named in *Pap. Flind. Petr.* ii.
xxv. *i*[1] (Ptolemaic period). Mahaffy,[2] it is true, prefers to
interpret the attribute here as applying to the stature.

The LXX also are acquainted with (not to speak of
the idiom ἀπὸ μικροῦ ἕως μεγάλου) a usage of μικρός to
signify age, *e.g.*, 2 Chron. 22[1].

νομός.

L. van Ess's edition of the LXX (1887)[3] still reads Is.
19[2] thus : καὶ ἐπεγερθήσονται Αἰγύπτιοι ἐπ᾿ Αἰγυπτίους καὶ
πολεμήσει ἄνθρωπος τὸν ἀδελφὸν αὐτοῦ καὶ ἄνθρωπος τὸν
πλησίον αὐτοῦ, πόλις ἐπὶ πόλιν καὶ νόμος ἐπὶ νόμον. In
the original the concluding words of the verse are *kingdom
against kingdom.* The Concordance of Tromm therefore
says νόμος *lex* stands for מַמְלָכָה *regnum*, and the editor
of Van Ess's LXX appears to be of the same opinion. The
correct view has long been known ;[4] the phrase should be
accented thus : νομὸς ἐπὶ νομόν.[5] νομός is a *terminus technicus*
for a political *department* of the country, and was used as
such in Egypt especially, as was already known from Herodotus and Strabo. The Papyri throw fresh light upon this
division into departments, though indeed the great majority
of these Papyri come from the "Archives" of the Nomos of
Arsinoe. This small matter is noted here because the translation of Is. 19, the "ὅρασις Αἰγύπτου," has, as a whole,
been furnished by the LXX, for reasons easily perceived,
with very many instances of specifically Egyptian—in comparison with the original, we might indeed say modern-
Egyptian—local-colouring. This may also be observed in
other passages of the O.T. which refer to Egyptian conditions.

---

[1] Mahaffy, ii. [79].   [2] ii., p. 32.

[3] It is true that the edition is stereotyped, but the plates were corrected
at certain places before each reprint.

[4] *Cf.* Schleusner, *Nov. Thes. s. v.*

[5] Thus also Tischendorf[6] (1880), and Swete (1894).

ὄνομα.

In connection with the characteristic "biblical" construction εἰς τὸ ὄνομά τινος,[1] and, indeed, with the general
usage of ὄνομα in the LXX, etc., the expression ἔντευξις εἰς
τὸ τοῦ βασιλέως ὄνομα, which occurs several times in the
Papyri, deserves very great attention : Pap. Flind. Petr. ii.
ii. 1[2] (260-259 B.C.), Pap. Flind. Petr. ii. xx. ee[3] (241 B.C.) ;
cf., possibly, Pap. Flind. Petr. ii. xlvii.[4] (191 B.C.).

Mahaffy[5] speaks of the phrase as a hitherto unknown
"formula". Its repeated occurrence in indictments certainly suggests the conjecture that it must have had a technical meaning. This is, doubtless, true of ἔντευξις.[6] An
ἔντευξις εἰς τὸ τοῦ βασιλέως ὄνομα would be a direct petition
—a memorial to the King's Majesty ;[7] the name of the King
is the essence of what he is as ruler. We see how nearly
this idea of the ὄνομα approaches to that of the Old Testament שֵׁם, and how convenient it was for the Egyptian translators to be able to render quite literally the expressive word
of the sacred text.

The special colouring which ὄνομα often has in early
Christian writings was doubtless strongly influenced by the
LXX, but the latter did not borrow that colouring first from
the Hebrew ; it was rather a portion of what they took from
the adulatory official vocabulary of their environment. But
current usage in Asia Minor also provided a connecting link
for the solemn formula of the early Christians, viz., εἰς τὸ
ὄνομα with genitive of God, of Christ, etc., after it. In the
Inscription of Mylasa in Caria, Waddington, iii. 2, No. 416
CIG. ii. No. 2693 e, belonging to the beginning of the imperial period,[8] we find γενομένης δὲ τῆς ὠνῆς τῶν προγεγραμ-

---

[1] Passages in Cremer[7], p. 676 f. (= [8], p. 710).　　　[2] Mahaffy, ii. [2].

[3] Ibid. [32].　　　[4] Ibid. [154].　　　[5] Ibid. [32].　　　[6] Cf. above, p. 121 f.

[7] The synonymous phrase ἔντευξιν ἀποδιδόναι (or ἐπιδιδόναι) τῷ βασιλεῖ
occurs frequently in the Papyri of the 2nd cent. B.C. (Kenyon, pp. 9, 41 and
10, 11, 17, 28).

[8] It is undated, but an approximate point is afforded by its affinity with
a long series of similar decrees from Mylasa (Waddington, iii. 2, Nos. 403-
415), of which No. 409 must have been written not long after 76 B.C. The
date given above seems to the author to be too late rather than too early.

μένων τοῖς κτηματώναις εἰς τὸ τοῦ θεοῦ ὄνομα.[1] This means :
"*after the sale of the afore-mentioned objects had been concluded
with the κτηματῶναι εἰς τὸ τοῦ θεοῦ [Zeus] ὄνομα*". In reference to the κτηματώνης, which is to be found in Inscriptions
only, Waddington [2] observes that the word means the *purchaser of an article*, but the person in question, in this connection, is only the nominal purchaser, who represents the
real purchaser, *i.e.*, the Deity ; the κτηματώνης εἰς τὸ τοῦ
θεοῦ ὄνομα is the *fidéicommissaire du domaine sacré*. The passage appears to the author to be the more important in that
it presupposes exactly the same conception of the word
ὄνομα as we find in the solemn forms of expression used in
religion. Just as, in the Inscription, *to buy into the name of
God* means *to buy so that the article bought belongs to God*, so
also the idea underlying, *e.g.*, the expressions *to baptise into
the name of the Lord*, or *to believe into the name of the Son of
God*, is that baptism or faith constitutes the *belonging* to God
or to the Son of God.

The author would therefore take exception to the statement that the non-occurrence of the expression ποιεῖν τι ἐν
ὀνόματί τινος in profane Greek is due to the absence of
this usage of the *Name*.[3] What we have to deal with here
is most likely but a matter of chance ; since the use of ὄνομα
has been established for the impressive language of the court
and of worship, it is quite possible that the phrase ἐν τῷ ὀνόματι
τοῦ βασιλέως or τοῦ θεοῦ may also come to light some day
in Egypt or Asia Minor.

The present example throws much light upon the development of the meaning of the religious terms of primitive
Christianity. It shows us that, when we find, *e.g.*, a
Christian of Asia Minor employing peculiar expressions,
which occur *also* in his Bible, we must be very strictly on

---

[1] The very same formula is found in the Inscription *CIG*. ii. No. 2694 *b*,
which also comes from Mylasa, and in which, as also in *CIG*. ii. No. 2693 *e*,
Boeckh's reading τοῖς κτημάτων δὶς εἰς τὸ τοῦ θεοῦ ὄνομα is to be corrected by
that of Waddington.

[2] In connection with No. 338, p. 104.

[3] Cremer [7], p. 678 (= [8], p. 712).

our guard against summarily asserting a "dependence"
upon the Greek Old Testament, or, in fact, the presence of
any Semitic influence whatever.—Further in III. iii. 1 below,
and *Theol. Literaturzeitung*, xxv. (1900), p. 735.

ὀψώνιον.

The first occurrence of τὰ ὀψώνια is not in Polybius;[1]
it is previously found in *Pap. Flind. Petr.* ii. xiii. 7[2] and
17[3] (258-253 B.C.); τὰ ὀψώνια is found in *Pap. Flind. Petr.*
ii. xxxiii. *a*[4] (Ptolemaic period). In all three places, not
pay of soldiers, but quite generally *wages;* similarly *Pap.
Lond.* xlv.[5] (160-159 B.C.), xv.[6] (131-130 B.C.), *Pap. Par.* 62[7]
(Ptolemaic period). The word is to be found in Inscriptions
onwàrds from 278 B.C.[8] Further remarks below, III. iii. 6.

παράδεισος.

This word resembles ἀγγαρεύω in its having been divested of its original technical meaning, and in its having
become current in a more general sense. It stands for
garden in general already in *Pap. Flind. Petr.* ii. xlvi. *b*[9]
(200 B.C.), *cf.* xxii.,[10] xxx. *c*,[11] xxxix. *i*[12] (all of the Ptolemaic
period);[13] similarly in the Inscription of Pergamus, Waddington, iii. 2, No. 1720 *b* (undated). It is frequent in the
LXX, always for *garden* (in three of the passages, *viz.*, Neh.
2[8], Eccles. 2[5], Cant. 4[13], as representing פַּרְדֵּס[14]); so in Sir.,
Sus., Josephus, etc., frequently. Of course, παράδεισος in
LXX Gen. 2[8 ff.] is also *garden*, not *Paradise*. The first
witness to this new technical meaning[15] is, doubtless, Paul,
2 Cor. 12[4], then Luke 23[43] and Rev. 2[7]; 4 Esd. 7[53], 8[52].

---

[1] *Clavis*[3], p. 328.   [2] Mahaffy, ii. [38].   [3] *Ibid.* [42].   [4] *Ibid.*, [113].
[5] Kenyon, p. 36.   [6] *Ibid.*, pp. 55, 56.   [7] *Notices*, xviii. 2, p. 357.

[8] Examples in Guil. Schmidt, *De Flav. Ios. eloc.* Fleck. *Jbb. Suppl.* xx.
(1894), pp. 511, 531.

[9] Mahaffy, ii. [150].   [10] *Ibid.* [68].   [11] *Ibid.* [104].   [12] *Ibid.* [134].
[13] *Cf.* also *Pap. Lond.* cxxxi., 78-79 A.D. (Kenyon, p. 172).

[14] The Mishna still uses פַּרְדֵּס only for *park* in the natural sense
(Schürer, ii., p. 464, = [3], ii., p. 553) [Eng. Trans., ii., ii., p. 183 f., note 88].

[15] *Cf.* G. Heinrici, *Das zweite Sendschreiben des Apostel Paulus an die
Korinthier erklärt*, Berlin, 1887, p. 494.

παρεπίδημος.

In LXX Gen. 23 [4] and Ps. 38 [39] [13], this is the translation of תּוֹשָׁב ; used, most probably in consequence thereof in 1 Pet. 1 [1], 2 [11], Heb. 11 [13]; authenticated only [1] in Polybius and Athenaeus. But it had been already used in the will of a certain Aphrodisios of Heraklea, *Pap. Flind. Petr.* i. xix. [2] (225 B.C.), who calls himself, with other designations, a παρεπίδημος. Mahaffy [3] remarks upon this : "in the description of the testator we find another new class, παρεπίδημος, a sojourner, so that even such persons had a right to bequeath their property". Of still greater interest is the passage of a will of date 238-237 B.C. [4] which gives the name of a Jewish παρεπίδημος in the Fayyûm : [5] Ἀπολλώνιον παρεπ]ίδημον ὃς καὶ συριστὶ Ἰωνάθας [6] [καλεῖται].

The verb παρεπιδημέω, e.g., *Pap. Flind. Petr.* ii. xiii. 19 [7] (258-253 B.C.).

παστοφόριον.

The LXX use this word in almost all the relatively numerous passages where it occurs, the Apocrypha and Josephus [8] in every case, for the *chambers of the Temple.* Sturz [9] had assigned it to the Egyptian dialect. His conjecture is confirmed by the Papyri. In the numerous documents relating to the Serapeum [10] at Memphis, παστοφόριον is used, in a technical sense, of the Serapeum itself, or of *cells* in the Serapeum : [11] *Pap. Par.* 11 [12] (157 B.C.), 40 [13] (156 B.C.) ; similarly in the contemporary documents *Pap. Par.*

---

[1] *Clavis* [3], p. 339.   [2] Mahaffy, i. [54].

[3] i. [55].   [4] *Ibid.*, ii., p. 23.

[5] Upon Jews in the Fayyûm *cf.* Mahaffy, i., p. 43 f., ii. [14].

[6] Ἀπολλώνιος is a sort of translation of the name Ἰωνάθας.

[7] Mahaffy, ii. [45]. The word is frequently to be found in Inscriptions; references, *e.g.*, in Letronne, *Recueil*, i., p. 340; Dittenberger, *Sylloge* Nos. 246 30 and 267 5.

[8] Particulars in Guil. Schmidt, *De Flav. Ios. eloc.*, Fleck. *Jbb. Suppl.* xx. (1894), p. 511 f. Reference there also to *CIG.* ii., No. 2297.

[9] *De dialecto Macedonica et Alexandrina*, p. 110 f.

[10] *Cf.* p. 140 above.   [11] *Cf.* Lumbroso, *Recherches*, p. 266 t

[12] *Notices*, xviii. 2, p. 207.   [13] *Ibid.*, p. 305.

41 [1] and 37 [2]—in the last passage used of the Ἀσταρτιεῖον
which is described as being contained ἐν τῷ μεγάλῳ Σααρ-
πιείῳ.[3] The LXX have thus very happily rendered the
general term לִשְׁכָּה, wherever it denotes *a chamber of the
Temple*, by a technical name with which they were familiar.
παστοφόριον is also retained by several Codices in 1 Chron.
9 [33], and 2 Esd. [Hebr. Ezra] 8 [29].[4]

περιδέξιον.

In LXX Numb. 31 [50], Exod. 35 [22] and Is. 3 [20] (in the two
latter passages without any corresponding original) for *brace-
let*. To be found in *Pap. Flind. Petr.* i. xii.[5] (238-237 B.C.).
The enumeration given there of articles of finery resembles
Exod. 35 [22], and particularly Is. 3 [20]; in the latter passage
the ἐνώτια [6] (mentioned also in the former) come immediately
after the περιδέξια—so in the Papyrus. As the original has
no corresponding word in either of the LXX passages, we
may perhaps attribute the addition to the fact that the two
ornaments were usually named together.

περίστασις.

In 2 Macc. 4 [16], Symmachus Ps. 33 [34] [57] (here the
LXX has θλῖψις, or παροικία), in the evil sense, for *distress ;*
it is not found first of all in Polybius, but already in *Pap.
Lond.* xlii.[8] (172 B.C.); cf. the Inscription of Pergamus No.
245 A [9] (before 133 B.C.) and the Inscription of Sestos (*ca.*
120 B.C.), line 25.[10]

---

[1] *Notices*, xviii. 2, p. 306.   [2] *Ibid.*, p. 297.

[3] *Cf.* Brunet de Presle, *ibid.*, and Lumbroso, *Recherches*, p. 266.

[4] Field, i., pp. 712, 767. It is these which De Lagarde uses to determine the Lucianus: his accentuation of 1 Chron. 9 [26], παστοφοριῶν, is not
correct.

[5] Better reading than in Mahaffy, i. [37]; see Mahaffy, ii., p. 22.

[6] The Papyrus reads ενωιδια ; that is also the Attic orthography—found
in a large number of Inscriptions from 398 B.C. onwards, Meisterhans [2],
pp. 51, 61.

[7] Field, ii., p. 139.   [8] Kenyon, p. 30.   [9] Fränkel, p. 140.

[10] W. Jerusalem, *Die Inschrift von Sestos und Polybios, Wiener Studien*,
i. (1879), p. 34 ; *cf.* p. 50 f., where the references from Polybius are also given.

περιτέμνω.

The LXX use περιτέμνω always in the technical sense
of the ceremonial act of *circumcision*; this technical meaning
also underlies the passages in which *circumcision* is metaphorically spoken of, *e.g.*, Deut. 10 [16] and Jer. 4 [4]. The word
is never employed by the LXX in any other sense.   The
usual Hebrew word מוּל occurs frequently, it is true, in a
non-technical signification, but in such cases the translators
always choose another word : Ps. 57 [58] [8] ἀσθενέω for *to be
cut off*,[1] Ps. 117 [118] [10, 11, 12], ἀμύνομαι for the *cutting in
pieces* (?) of enemies, Ps. 89 [90],[6] ἀποπίπτω (of grass) for *to
be cut down*.[2]   Even in a passage, Deut. 30 [6], where מוּל, *cir-
cumcise*, is used metaphorically, they reject περιτέμνω and
translate by περικαθαρίζω.[3]   The textual history of Ezek.
16 [4] affords a specially good illustration of their severely
restrained use of language.   To the original (according to
our Hebrew text) *thy navel-string was not cut*, corresponds, in
the LXX (according to the current text), οὐκ ἔδησας τοὺς
μαστούς σου, " quite an absurd translation, which, however,
just because of its absolute meaninglessness, is, without
doubt, ancient tradition ".[4]   But the " translation " is not
so absurd after all, if we read ἔδησαν [5] with the Alexandrinus and the Marchalianus,[6] a reading which is supported
by the remark of Origen : [7] the LXX had translated *non alli-
gaverunt ubera tua*, " *sensum magis eloquii exponentes quam
verbum de verbo exprimentes* ".   That is to say, among the
services mentioned here as requiring to be rendered to the
helpless new-born girl, the Greek translators set down something different from the procedure described by the Hebrew
author ; what they did set down corresponds in some degree

[1] The author does not clearly understand the relation of this translation
to the (corrupt) original.

[2] If the original should not be derived from מלל ; *cf.* Job 14 [2], where
the LXX translate ἐκπίπτω.

[3] *Cf.* Lev. [not *Luc.* as in Cremer [7], p. 886 (= [8], p. 931)] 19 [23].

[4] Cornill, *Das Buch des Propheten Ezechiel*, p. 258.

[5] Which would be translated *they bound*.

[6] For this Codex *cf.* Cornill, p. 15.   [7] Field, ii., p. 803.

with the ἐν σπαργάνοις σπαργανωθῆναι which comes later.[1]
But perhaps they had a different text before them. In any
case the translation given by some Codices,[2] viz., οὐκ ἐτμήθη
ὁ ὀμφαλός σου, is a late correction of the LXX text by our
present Hebrew text ; other Codices read οὐκ ἔδησαν τοὺς
μαστούς σου, and add the emendation οὐκ ἐτμήθη ὁ ὀμφαλός
σου ; others do the same, but substitute περιετμήθη, a form
utterly at variance with LXX usage (and one against which
Jerome's *non ligaverunt mamillas tuas et umbilicus tuus non est
praecisus*[3] still guards), for the ἐτμήθη. It is this late emendation which has occasioned the idea[4] that the LXX in one
case also used τὸν ὀμφαλόν as the object of περιτέμνειν. This
is not correct. One may truly speak here, for once, about
a "usage" of the LXX : περιτέμνω, with them, has always
a ceremonial meaning.[5]

In comparison with the verbs כָּרַת, הֵסִיר and מוּל, which
are rendered by περιτέμνω, the Greek word undoubtedly introduces an additional nuance to the meaning; not one of
the three words contains what the περί implies. The
choice of this particular compound is explained by the fact
that it was familiar to the LXX, being in common use as
a technical term for an Egyptian custom similar to the Old
Testament *circumcision*. "The Egyptians certainly practised
circumcision in the 16th century B.C., probably much earlier."[6]

---

[1] The reading οὐκ ᾔδεισαν, which is given in two late minuscules, and
from which Cornill makes the emendation οὐκ ᾔδεισας (as a 2nd person
singular imperfect founded on a false analogy) as being the original reading
of the LXX, appears to the author to be a correction of the unintelligible
ἔδησαν which was made in the Greek text itself, without reference to the
original at all.

[2] Field, ii., p. 803, where a general discussion is given of the materials
which follow here.

[3] Should have been *circumcisus*, if Jerome was presupposing περιετμήθη.

[4] Cremer[7], p. 886 (= [8], p. 931). The remark is evidently traceable to
the misleading reference of Tromm.

[5] Similarly περιτομή, occurring only in Gen. 17[12] and Ex. 4[26]. In Jer.
11[16] it has crept in through a misunderstanding of the text; *cf.* Cremer[7],
p. 887 (= [8], p. 932).

[6] J. Benzinger, *Hebräische Archäologie*, Freiburg and Leipzig, 1894,
p. 154.

Now even if it cannot be made out with certainty that the Israelites copied the *practice* from the Egyptians, yet it is in the highest degree probable that the Greek Jews are indebted to the Egyptians [1] for the *word*. Herodotus already verifies its use in ii. 36 and 104 : he reports that the Egyptians περιτάμνονται τὰ αἰδοῖα. But the expression is also authenticated by direct Egyptian testimony : *Pap. Lond.* xxiv.[2] (163 B.C.), ὡς ἔθος ἐστὶ τοῖς Αἰγυπτίοις περιτέμνεσθαι, and *Pap. Berol.* 7820 [3] (14th January, 171 A.D., Fayyûm) still speaks several times of the περιτμηθῆναι of a boy κατὰ τὸ ἔθος.

If περιτέμνω is thus one of the words which were taken over by the LXX, yet the supposition [4] that their frequent ἀπερίτμητος *uncircumcised* = עָרֵל was first coined by the Jews of Alexandria may have some degree of probability. In the last-cited Berlin Papyrus, at least, the as yet uncircumcised boy is twice described as ἄσημος.[5] The document appears to be employing fixed expressions. ἄσημος was perhaps the technical term for *uncircumcised* among the Greek Egyptians ; [6] the more definite and, at the same time, harsher ἀπερίτμητος corresponded to the contempt with which the Greek Jews thought of the uncircumcised.

πῆχυς.

We need have no doubt at all about the contracted genitive πηχῶν,[7] LXX 1 Kings 7 [2] (Cod. A), [38] (Cod. A), Esther 5 [14], 7 [9], Ezek. 40 [7], 41 [22] ; John 21 [8], Rev. 21 [17]. It is already found in *Pap. Flind. Petr.* ii. xli.[8] (Ptolemaic

---

[1] The author does not know how the Greek Egyptians came to use the compound with περί. Did the corresponding Egyptian word suggest it to them ? Or did the anatomical process suggest it to them independently ?

[2] Kenyon, p. 32, *cf.* p. 33.   [3] *BU.* xi., p. 337 f., No. 347.

[4] Cremer [7], p. 887 (= [8], p. 932).

[5] And circumcision as σημεῖον : *cf.*, in reference to this, LXX Gen. 17 [11] and Rom. 4 [11].

[6] F. Krebs, *Philologus*, liii. (1894), p. 586, interprets ἄσημος differently, *viz.*, free from bodily marks owing to the presence of which circumcision was forborne.

[7] Winer-Schmiedel, § 9, 6 (p. 88).   [8] Mahaffy, ii. [137].

period) twice; Josephus agrees with the LXX in using
πήχεων and πηχῶν promiscuously.[1]

πcτισμός.

In Aquila Prov. 3[8][2] *watering, irrigation;* to be found in
Pap. Flind. Petr. ii. ix. 4[3] (240 B.C.).

πράκτωρ.

In LXX Is. 3[12] for נֹגֵשׂ *despot.* In the Papyri frequently as the designation of an official; the πράκτωρ[4]
seems to have been *the public accountant*:[5] *Pap. Flind. Petr.*
ii. xiii. 17[6] (258-253 B.C.), and several other undated Papyri
of the Ptolemaic period given in Mahaffy, ii.[7]

In Luke 12[58] also the word has most probably a technical meaning; it does not however denote a finance-official,
but a lower *officer of the court.*

Symmachus Ps. 108 [109][11][8] uses it for נֹשֶׁה *creditor.*

πρεσβύτερος.

The LXX translate זָקֵן *old man* by both πρεσβύτης and
πρεσβύτερος. The most natural rendering was πρεσβύτης,
and the employment of the comparative πρεσβύτερος must
have had some special reason. We usually find πρεσβύτερος
in places where the translators appear to have taken the
זָקֵן of the original as implying an official position. That
they in such cases speak of the *elders* and not of the *old men*
is explained by the fact that they found πρεσβύτερος already
used technically in Egypt for the holder of a communal
office. Thus, in *Pap. Lugd.* A 35 f.[9] (Ptolemaic period), mention

---

[1] Guil. Schmidt, *De Flav. Ios. eloc.*, Fleck. *Jbb. Suppl.* xx. (1894),
p. 498.

[2] Field, ii., p. 315.   [3] Mahaffy, ii. [24].

[4] On the πράκτορες in Athens, *cf.* von Wilamowitz-Moellendorff, *Aristoteles und Athen*, i., Berlin, 1893, p. 196.

[5] Mahaffy, ii. [42].   [6] *Ibid.*

[7] Further details in E. Revillout, *Le Papyrus grec 13 de Turin* in the
Revue égyptologique, ii. (1881-1882), p. 140 f.

[8] Field, ii., p. 265.   [9] Leemans, i., p. 3.

is made of ὁ πρεσβύτερος τῆς κώμης—without doubt an
official designation,—although, indeed, owing to the mutilation of another passage in the same Papyrus (lines 17-23), no
further particulars as to the nature of this office can be
ascertained from it.[1] The author thinks that οἱ πρεσβύτεροι
in *Pap. Flind. Petr.* ii. iv. 6 13 [2] (255-254 B.C.) is also an
official designation ; *cf.* also *Pap. Flind. Petr.* ii. xxxix. *a*,
3 and 14.[3] Similarly, in the decree of the priests at Diospolis
in honour of Callimachus,[4] (*ca.* 40 B.C.), the πρεσβύτεροι are
still mentioned along with the ἱερεῖς τοῦ μεγίστου θεοῦ
᾿Αμονρασωνθήρ. We have a periphrasis of the title πρεσβύτερος in *Pap. Taur.* 8 60 f.[5] (end of the 2nd cent B.C.), in
which the attribute τὸ πρεσβεῖον ἔχων παρὰ τοὺς ἄλλους
τοὺς ἐν τῇ κώμῃ κατοικοῦντας is applied to a certain Erieus.
We still find οἱ πρεσβύτεροι in the 2nd century A.D. as
Egyptian village-magistrates, of whom a certain council of
three men, οἱ τρεῖς, appears to have occupied a special
position.[6]

Here also then the Alexandrian translators have appropriated a technical expression which was current in the
land.

Hence we must not summarily attribute the " New Testament," *i.e.*, the early Christian, passages, in which πρεσβύτεροι occurs as an official designation, to the " Septuagint
idiom," since this is in reality an Alexandrian one.   In
those cases, indeed, where the expression is used to designate Jewish municipal authorities[7] and the Sanhedrin,[8] it
is allowable to suppose that it had been adopted by the
Greek Jews from the Greek Bible,[9] and that the Christians

[1] Leemans, i., foot of p. 3.   [2] Mahaffy, ii. [10].   [3] *Ibid.* [125].

[4] *CIG.* iii., No. 4717 : on this, as on the title πρεσβύτεροι in general, *cf·*
Lumbroso, *Recherches*, p. 259.

[5] A. Peyron, ii., p. 46.

[6] U. Wilcken, *Observationes ad historiam Aegypti provinciae Romanae
depromptae e papyris Graecis Berolinensibus ineditis*, Berlin, 1885, p. 29 f.

[7] Schürer, ii., p. 132 ff. (= [3] ii., p. 176 ff.). [Eng. Trans., ii., i., p. 150 f.]

[8] *Ibid.*, p. 144 ff. (= [3] ii., p. 189 ff.). [Eng. Trans., ii., i., p. 165 ff.]

[9] *Cf.* the use of the word πρεσβύτεροι in the Apocrypha and in Josephus.

who had to translate the term *the old men* found it convenient
to render it by the familiar expression οἱ πρεσβύτεροι. But
that is no reason for deeming this technical term a peculiarity of the Jewish idiom. Just as the Jewish usage is
traceable to Egypt, so is it possible that also the Christian
communities of Asia Minor, which named their superintendents πρεσβύτεροι, may have borrowed the word from their
surroundings, and may not have received it through the
medium of Judaism at all.[1] The Inscriptions of Asia Minor
prove beyond doubt that πρεσβύτεροι was the technical term,
in the most diverse localities, for the members of a corporation :[2] in Chios, *CIG.* ii. Nos. 2220 and 2221 (1st cent. B.C.[3]),
—in both passages the council of the πρεσβύτεροι is also
named τὸ πρεσβυτικόν ; in Cos, *CIG.* ii. No. 2508 = Paton
and Hicks, No. 119 (imperial period[4]) ; in Philadelphia in
Lydia, *CIG.* ii. No. 3417 (imperial period), in which the
συνέδριον τῶν πρεσβυτέρων,[5] mentioned here, is previously
named γερουσία. "It can be demonstrated that in some
islands and in many towns of Asia Minor there was, besides
the Boulē, also a Gerousia, which possessed the privileges of
a corporation, and, as it appears, usually consisted of Bou-
leutes who were delegated to it. Its members were called
γέροντες, γερουσιασταί, πρεσβύτεροι, γεραιοί. They had a

---

[1] In any case it is not correct to contrast, as does Cremer[7], p. 816 (=
[8], p. 858), the word ἐπίσκοπος, as the "Greek-coloured designation," with the
term πρεσβύτεροι (almost certainly of Jewish colouring). The word was a
technical term in Egypt before the Jews began to speak of πρεσβύτεροι, and
it is similarly to be found in the Greek usage of the imperial period in the
most diverse localities of Asia Minor.

[2] This reference to the πρεσβύτεροι of Asia Minor has of course a purely
philological purpose. The author does not wish to touch upon the question
regarding the nature of the presbyterial "Office". It may have been developed quite apart from the name—whatever the origin of that may have
been.

[3] Both Inscriptions are contemporary with No. 2214, which is to be
assigned to the 1st cent. B.C.

[4] Possibly, with Paton and Hicks, p. 148, to be assigned, more exactly,
to the time of Claudius.

[5] *Cf.* the data of Schürer, ii., p. 147 f., note 461. [Eng. Trans. ii., i.,
p. 169, note 461.]

president (ἄρχων, προστάτης, προηγούμενος), a secretary, a special treasury, a special place of assembly (γεροντικὸν, γερουσία), and a palæstra."[1]—See also III. iii. 4. below.

πρόθεσις.

The LXX translate the technical expression *bread of the countenance* (also called *row-bread* [*Schichtbrot*] and *continual bread*), which Luther rendered *Schaubrot* (*show-bread*), in 1 Sam. 21[6] and Neh. 10[33] by οἱ ἄρτοι τοῦ προσώπου, and in Exod. 25[30] by οἱ ἄρτοι οἱ ἐνώπιοι, but their usual rendering is οἱ ἄρτοι τῆς προθέσεως. The usual explanation of this πρόθεσις is *setting forth*, *i.e.*, of the bread before God. The author leaves it undecided whether this explanation is correct; but, in any case, it is to be asked how the LXX came to use this free translation, while they rendered the original verbally in the other three passages. The author thinks it not unlikely that they were influenced by the reminiscence of a ceremonial custom of their time : "*Au culte se rattachaient des institutions philantropiques telle que la suivante : Le médecin Dioclès cité par Athénée (3, 110), nous apprend qu'il y avait une* πρόθησις[sic] *de pains périodique à Alexandrie, dans le temple de Saturne* ('Αλεξανδρεῖς τῷ Κρόνῳ ἀφιεροῦντες προτιθέασιν ἐσθίειν τῷ βουλομένῳ ἐν τῷ τοῦ Κρόνου ἱερῷ). *Cette* πρόθεσις τῶν ἄρτων *se retrouve dans un papyrus du Louvre* (60bis)." [2] The expression πρόθεσις ἄρτων is also found in LXX 2 Chron. 13[11]; *cf.* 2 Macc. 10[3].

πυρράκης.

Hitherto known only from LXX Gen. 25[25], 1 Sam. 16[12], 17[42], for *ruddy*. To be found in *Pap. Flind. Petr.* i. xvi. 1[3] (237 B.C.), xxi.[4] (237 B.C.), possibly also in xiv.[5] (237 B.C.).

---

[1] O. Benndorf and G. Niemann, *Reisen in Lykien und Karien*, Vienna, 1884, p. 72.

[2] Lumbroso, *Recherches*, p. 280; the Papyrus passage—certainly not fully legible—in *Notices*, xviii. 2, p. 347. Lumbroso defends his reading in *Recherches*, p. 23, note 1.

[3] Mahaffy, i. [47].   [4] *Ibid.* [59].

[5] *Ibid.* [43]. The passage is mutilated.

σιτομέτριον.

In Luke 12 [42] for *portio frumenti;* referred to in this
passage only : to be verified by *Pap. Flind. Petr.* ii. xxxiii. *a* [1]
(Ptolemaic period).   *Cf.* σιτομετρέω in Gen. 47 [12] (said of
Joseph in *Egypt*).

σκευοφύλαξ.

Earliest occurrence in the Recension of Lucianus,[2] 1
Sam. 17 [22], as the literal translation of שׁוֹמֵר הַכֵּלִים *keeper of
the baggage.*[3] The supposition that the word was not first
applied as a mere momentary creation of the recensionist,
but came to him on good authority, is supported by its
occurrence in *Pap. Flind. Petr.* ii. xiii. 10 [4] (258-253 B.C.) :
σκεοφυλακα there is to be read σκευοφύλακα, in accordance
with σκευοφυλάκιον in *Pap. Flind. Petr.* ii. v. *a* [5] (before 250
B.C.).

σπυρίς, σφυρίς.

With the σφυρίς (vernacular aspiration [6]) handed down
on good authority in Mark 8 [8. 20], Matt. 15 [37], 16 [10], Acts 9 [25],
cf. σφυρίδα in *Pap. Flind. Petr.* ii. xviii. 2 *a* [7] (246 B.C.), though
we should observe the reading σπυριδίου in *Pap. Flind. Petr.*
Z *d* [8] (Ptolemaic period). Further remarks in III. i. 2, below.

στάσις.

Among other words, the translation of which by στάσις
is more or less intelligible, מָעוֹז *stronghold* Nah. 3 [11], and
הֲדֹם *footstool* 1 Chron. 28 [2], are rendered in the same way

---

[1] Mahaffy, ii. [113]. In this an οἰκονόμος submits an account of his house-
keeping. The present writer thinks that the σιτομετρια which occurs in this
account should be taken as the plural of σιτομέτριον, and not as a singular,
σιτομετρία. The passage is mutilated.

[2] Edited by De Lagarde, *Librorum V. T. canonicorum pars prior graece,*
Göttingen, 1883.

[3] The simple φύλακος of our LXX text is marked with an *asteriscus* by
Origen, Field, i., p. 516.

[4] Mahaffy, ii. [39].   [5] *Ibid.* [16].   On σκευοφυλάκιον *cf.* Suidas.

[6] Winer-Schmiedel, § 5, 27 *e* (p. 60).

[7] Mahaffy, ii. [59].   [8] *Ibid.*, p. 33.

by the LXX, and Symmachus [1] uses στάσις in Is. 6 [13] for
מַצֶּבֶת root-stock (truncus) or young tree, cutting ; [2] certainly
a very remarkable use of the word, and one hardly explained
by the extraordinary note which Schleusner [3] makes to the
passage in Nahum: " στάσις est firmitas, consistentia, modus
et via subsistendi ac resistendi ". What is common to the
above three words translated by στάσις is the idea of secure
elevation above the ground, of upright position, and this fact
seems to warrant the conjecture that the translators were
acquainted with a quite general usage of στάσις for any
upright object. [4]

This conjecture is confirmed by Pap. Flind. Petr. ii. xiv.
3 [5] (Ptolemaic period ?), i.e., if the στάσεις which is found
in this certainly very difficult passage be rightly interpreted
as erections, buildings. [6] This use of the word seems to the
author to be more certain in an Inscription from Mylasa in
Caria, CIG. ii. Nó. 2694 a (imperial period), in which Boeckh
interprets the word στάσεις (so restored by him) as stabula.

συγγενής.

In the Old Testament Apocryphal books there is found
not infrequently the expression kinsman of a king. Like
riend, [7] etc., it is a court-title, which was transferred from
the Persian usage to the language of Alexander the Great's
court, and thence became very common among the Diadochi.
Compare, in regard to Egypt, the exhaustive references in
Lumbroso ; [8] in regard to Pergamus, the Inscription No.
248, line 28f. (135-134 B.C.). [9]

---

[1] Field, ii., p. 442.

[2] In the LXX this passage is wanting; Aquila translates στήλωσις;
Theodotion, στήλωμα (Field, ibid.).

[3] Novus Thesaurus, v. (1821), p. 91.

[4] Cf. the German Stand for market-stall. [Also the English stand =
support, grand-stand, etc.—Tr.]

[5] Mahaffy, ii. [51].   [6] Ibid., p. 30.   [7] Cf. sub φίλος below.

[8] Recherches, p. 189 f. Also the Inscription of Delos (3rd cent. B.C.),
Bull. de corr. hell. iii. (1879), p. 470, comes into consideration for Egypt : the
Χρύσερμος there named is συγγενὴς βασιλέως Πτολεμαίου.

[9] Fränkel, pp. 166 and 505.

συνέχω.

Used in Luke 22 [63] of the officers who held Jesus *in charge;* in the same sense *Pap. Flind. Petr.* ii. xx.[1] (252 B.C.).

σῶμα.

In Rev. 18 [13] σώματα stands for *slaves.* σῶμα was used for *person* in very early times, and already in classical Greek the slaves were called σώματα οἰκετικά or δοῦλα.[2] σῶμα alone—without any such addition—is not found used for *slave* earlier than in LXX Gen. 34 [29] (36 [6]),[3] Tob. 10 [10], Bel and the Dragon [32], 2 Macc. 8 [11], Ep. Arist. (*ed.* M. Schmidt), p. 16 [29], in Polybius and later writers. The Greek translators of the O. T. found the usage in Egypt: the Papyri of the Ptolemaic period yield a large number of examples, *cf.* especially *Pap. Flind. Petr.* ii. xxxix.[4]

ὑποζύγιον.

The LXX translate חֲמוֹר *ass* in very many places by ὑποζύγιον (*cf.* also Theodotion Judg. 5 [10],[5] 19 [10] [6] [also the Alexandrinus and the recension of Lucianus read ὑποζυγίων in both passages], Symmachus Gen. 36 [24] [7]). Similarly, ὑποζύγιον stands for *ass* in Matt. 21 [5] (*cf.* Zech. 9 [9]) and 2 Pet. 2 [16].[8] This specialising of the original general term *draught animal, beast of burden,* is described by Grimm [9] as a usage peculiar to Holy Scripture, which is explained by the importance of the ass as the beast of burden κατ᾽ ἐξοχήν in the East. A statistical examination of the word, however, might teach us that what we have to deal with here is no " biblical "

---

[1] Mahaffy, ii. [61].

[2] Ch. A. Lobeck *ad Phryn.* (Leipzig, 1820), p. 378.

[3] *Cf.* the old scholium to the passage, σώματα τοὺς δούλους ἴσως λέγει (Field, i., p. 52).

[4] Mahaffy, ii. [125] ff.   [5] Field, i., p. 412.

[6] *Ibid.*, p. 464.   [7] *Ibid.*, p. 52 f.

[8] In this passage the interpretation *ass* is not in any way necessary; the she-ass of Balaam, which is called ἡ ὄνος in the LXX, might quite well be designated there by the general term *beast of burden.*

[9] *Clavis* [3], p. 447.

peculiarity, but, at most, a special usage of the LXX which
may possibly have influenced other writings.   But even the
LXX do not occupy an isolated position in regard to it ;
the truth is rather that they avail themselves of an already-
current Egyptian idiom.   It seems to the author, at least,
that the "biblical" usage of ὑποζύγιον is already shown in
the following passages : *Pap. Flind. Petr.* ii. xxii.[1] (Ptolemaic
period), where βοῦς [2] ἢ ὑποζύγιον ἢ πρόβατον are mentioned
after one another ; *Pap. Flind. Petr.* ii. xxv. *d* [3] (2nd half of
3rd cent. B.C.), where the *donkey*-driver Horos gives a receipt
for money due to him by a certain Charmos in respect of
ὑποζύγια : ὁμολογεῖ ῏Ωρος ὀνηλάτης ἔχειν παρὰ Χάρμου δέοντα
ὑποζυγίων κατὰ σύμβολον ; similarly in the same Papyrus *i*.[4]

Grimm's remark may, of course, be turned to account
in the explanation of *this* idiom.

υἱός (τέκνον).

Those circumlocutions by which certain adjectival conceptions are represented by υἱός or τέκνον followed by a
genitive, and which are very frequent in the early Christian
writings, are traced back by A. Buttmann [5] to an "influence
of the oriental spirit of language" ; they are explained
by Winer-Lünemann [6] as "Hebrew-like circumlocution,"
which however is no mere idle circumlocution, but is due
to the more vivid imagination of the oriental, who looked
upon any very intimate relationship—whether of connection,
origin or dependence—as a relation of sonship, even in the
spiritual sphere.   According to Grimm,[7] these periphrases
spring "*ex ingenio linguae hebraeae*," and Cremer [8] describes
them as "Hebrew-like turns of expression in which υἱός . . .
is used analogously to the Hebr. בֵּן ".

In order to understand this "New Testament" idiom,
it is also necessary to distinguish here between the cases in

---

[1] Mahaffy, ii. [68].   [2] It should be stated that Mahaffy sets a ? to βους.
[3] Mahaffy, ii. [75].   [4] *Ibid.* [79].
[5] *Gramm. des neutest. Sprachgebrauchs*, p. 141.
[6] § 34, 3b, note 2 (p. 223 f.).   [7] *Clavis*[3], p. 441.
[8] 7th edition, p. 907 = [8], p. 956.

which this "periphrastic" υἱός or τέκνον[1] occurs in translations of Semitic originals, and the instances found in texts
which were in Greek from the first. This distinction gives
us at once the statistical result that the circumlocution is
more frequent in the former class than in the latter. One
should not, therefore, uniformly trace the "New Testament"
passages back to the influence of an un-Greek "spirit of
language," but, in the majority of cases, should rather speak
merely of a *translation* from the Semitic. What occasioned
the frequent υἱός or τέκνον was no "spirit of language"
which the translators may have brought to their task, but
rather the hermeneutic method into which they were unconsciously drawn by the original.

First as regards υἱός: such *translations* occur in the following passages,—Mark 2[19] = Matt. 9[15] = Luke 5[34], οἱ υἱοὶ
τοῦ νυμφῶνος, a saying of Jesus.—Mark 3[17], υἱοὶ βροντῆς,
where the original, Βοανεργες or Βοανηργες, is also given,
and the equation βοανε or βοανη = בְּנֵי is certainly evident.
—Matt. 8[12] = 13[38], οἱ υἱοὶ τῆς βασιλείας, sayings of Jesus.
—Matt. 13[38], οἱ υἱοὶ τοῦ πονηροῦ, a saying of Jesus.—Matt.
23[15], υἱὸν γεέννης, a saying of Jesus.—Matt. 21[5], υἱὸν
ὑποζυγίου, translation[2] of the Hebrew בֶּן־אֲתֹנוֹת, Zech. 9[9].

---

[1] The solemn expression υἱοὶ or τέκνα θεοῦ has, of course, no connection
with this, as it forms the correlative to θεὸς πατήρ.

[2] One dare hardly say, with respect to this passage, that "Matthew"
"quotes" from the original Hebrew text; the present writer conjectures that
"Matthew," or whoever wrote this Greek verse, translated its Hebrew
original, which, already a quotation, had come to him from Semitic tradition.
The Old Testament quotations of "Matthew" agree, in most passages, with
the LXX: wherever the Semitic tradition contained words from the Hebrew
Bible, the Greek translator just used the Greek Bible in his work, *i.e.*, of
course, only when he succeeded in finding the passages there. The tradition
gave him, in Matt. 21[5], a free combination of Zech. 9[9] and Is. 62[11] as a word
of "the Prophet": he could not identify it and so translated it for himself.
A similar case is Matt. 13[35]; here the tradition gave him, as a word of "the
Prophet Isaiah," a saying which occurs in Ps. 78[2], not in Isaiah at all; but
as he could not find the passage, ἡρμήνευσε δ' αὐτὰ ὡς ἦν δυνατός. Similarly,
in Mark 1[2 f.], a combination of Mal. 3[1] and Is. 40[3] is handed down as a
word of "the Prophet Isaiah": only the second half was found in Isaiah
and therefore it is quoted from the LXX; the first half, however, which the
Greek Christian translator could not find, was translated independently, and,

—Luke 10⁶, υἱὸς εἰρήνης, a saying of Jesus.—Luke 16⁸ and
20³⁴, οἱ υἱοὶ τοῦ αἰῶνος τούτου, sayings of Jesus.—Luke 16⁸,
τοὺς υἱοὺς τοῦ φωτός, a saying of Jesus.—Luke 20³⁶, τῆς
ἀναστάσεως υἱοί, a saying of Jesus.—Acts 4³⁶, υἱὸς παρακλήσεως, where the ostensible original, Βαρναβᾶς,¹ is also
given.—The υἱὲ διαβόλου, Acts 13¹⁰, should also be mentioned here, as the expression clearly forms a sarcastic
antithesis to Βαριησοῦ, son of Jesus (verse 6).

As regards τέκνον, we have the same phenomenon in
(Matt. 11¹⁹ =) Luke 7³⁵, τῶν τέκνων αὐτῆς [σοφίας], a saying
of Jesus.

Similarly *quotations* and manifest *analogical formations*
should not be taken into consideration in a critical examination of the original idiom; e.g., υἱοὶ φωτός in 1 Thess. 5⁵
(here also the analogical formation υἱοὶ ἡμέρας) and John
12³⁶ (cf. τέκνα φωτός, Ephes. 5⁸) should probably be taken
as a quotation from Luke 16⁸, or of the saying of Jesus preserved there, but in any case as an already familiar phrase;
οἱ υἱοὶ τῶν προφητῶν, Acts 3²⁵, is a quotation of a combination which had become familiar from LXX 1 Kings 20³⁵, 2
Kings 2³· ⁵· ⁷—the following καὶ [υἱοὶ] τῆς διαθήκης is an
analogical formation; ὁ υἱὸς τῆς ἀπωλείας, 2 Thess. 2³ and
John 17¹² is an echo of LXX Is. 57⁴ τέκνα ἀπωλειας; τὰ
τέκνα τοῦ διαβόλου 1 John 3¹⁰ is perhaps an analogical formation from οἱ υἱοὶ τοῦ πονηροῦ, Matt. 13³⁸.

There remain, then, the combination υἱοὶ τῆς ἀπειθείας
(Col. 3⁶), Eph. 2², 5⁶, and its antithesis τέκνα ὑπακοῆς, 1 Pet.
1¹⁴; τὰ τέκνα τῆς ἐπαγγελίας, Gal. 4²⁸, Rom. 9⁸, and its

---

in the form in which it occurs in Matt. 11¹⁰ and Luke 7²⁷, it is taken over
as an anonymous biblical saying.—In all these passages we have to do with
biblical sayings which do not form part of the discourses of Jesus or of His
friends or opponents, and which therefore do not belong to the earliest
material of the pre-Synoptic Gospel tradition.   But the peculiar character
of the quotations just discussed, which the author cannot interpret in any
other way, requires us to postulate that a sort of "synthetic text" (*verbin-
dender Text*), and, in particular, the application of certain definite O. T.
words to Christ, had been added, at a very early period, to this primitive
Semitic tradition; here and there in the Gospels we can still see, as above,
the method by which they were rendered into Greek.

¹ See further p. 307 f. below.

antitheses κατάρας τέκνα, 2 Pet. 2 [14], τέκνα ὀργῆς, Eph. 2 [3]
But it is not at all necessary, even for the explanation of
these expressions, to go back to the Hebrew spirit or to the
oriental genius of language. The system followed by the
Alexandrian translators of the Old Testament may furnish
us here with an instructive hint. In innumerable cases
their task was to render into Greek an exceedingly large
number of those characteristic Semitic turns of expression
formed with בֵּן. True, they rendered not a few of those
cases by the corresponding constructions with υἱός; but
very frequently, too, translating freely (as we might say),
they found substitutes for them in Greek expressions of a
different character. But such a procedure, in view of the
comparative scrupulosity with which in general they follow
the original, must surely surprise us, if we are to pre-suppose
in them, as in the early Christian writers, a certain Semitic
"genius of language" lying in reserve, as it were, and
behind their "feeling" for the Greek tongue. Had they
always imitated that characteristic בֵּן by using υἱός, then it
might have been maintained with some plausibility that
they had seized the welcome opportunity of translating
literally and, at the same time, of giving scope to the non-
Hellenic tendencies of their nature in the matter of language;
as they, however, did not do this, we may be permitted
to say that they had no such tendency at all. We give
the following cases,[1] from which this fact may be deduced
with certainty : "*Son*" *of Man*, Is. 56 [2], Prov. 15 [11] = ἄνθρωπος; *son of the uncle*, Numb. 36 [11] = ἀνεψιός ; *son of the she-
asses*, Zech. 9 [9] = πῶλος νέος ; [2] "*son*" *of the month*, often, =
μηνιαῖος ; "*son*" *of the dawn*, Is. 14 [12] = πρωΐ ἀνατέλλων ;
"*son*" *of strangers*, often, = ἀλλογενής or ἀλλόφυλος ; "*son*"
of the people, Gen. 23 [11] = πολίτης ; "*son*" *of the quiver*, Lam.
3 [13] = ἰοὶ [3] φαρέτρας ; "*son*" *of strength*, 2 Chron. 28 [6] = δυνα-

---

[1] These might be added to.

[2] The translator of the same combination in Matt. 21 [5] has scrupulously
imitated the original by his υἱὸς ὑποζυγίου.

[3] Thus the unanimous tradition of all the Codices except 239 and the
Syro-Hexaplar (Field, ii., p. 754) which read υἱοὶ φαρέτρας, an emendation
prompted by the Hebrew text.

τὸς ἰσχύϊ; "*son*" *of misery*, Prov. 31[5] = ἀσθενής; "*son*" *of strokes*, Deut. 25[2] = ἄξιος πληγῶν. And if, on the other hand, cases can be pointed out in which the LXX imitate[1] the characteristic בֶּן, then the υἱός of the Greek text is not to be forthwith explained as caused by the translators' oriental way of thinking, but rather as due to the original. At the very most we might speak of a "Hebraism of translation," but not of a Hebraism simply.[2] But we are of opinion that it is not at all necessary, in this matter, to have recourse to a Hebraism in every case; we cannot, at least, perceive why such constructions[3] as LXX Judg. 19[22] υἱοὶ παρανόμων, 1 Sam. 20[31] υἱὸς θανάτου,[4] 2 Sam. 13[28] υἱοὶ δυνάμεως, 2 Esd. [Hebr. Ezra] 4[1], 10[7, 16] [not 6[19]] υἱοὶ ἀποικίας, Hos. [not Ezek.] 2[4] τέκνα πορνείας, Is. 57[4] τέκνα ἀπωλείας, should be looked upon as un-Greek.[5] It is true, of course, that a Corinthian baggage-carrier or an Alexandrian donkey-driver would not so speak—the expressions are meant to be in elevated style and to have an impressive sound; but for that very reason they might have been used by a Greek poet. Plato uses the word ἔκγονος[6] in exactly the same way: *Phaedr.*, p. 275 D, ἔκγονα τῆς ζωγραφίας and *Rep.*, pp. 506 E and 507 A, ἔκγονος τοῦ ἀγαθοῦ (genitive of τὸ ἀγαθόν). In the impressive style of speech on inscriptions and coins we find υἱός in a number of formal titles of honour[7] such as υἱὸς τῆς γερουσίας, υἱὸς τῆς πόλεως, υἱὸς τοῦ δήμου,[8]

---

[1] The author does not know in what proportion these cases are distributed among the several books of the LXX, or to what degree the special method of the particular translator influenced the matter.

[2] The genus "Hebraisms" must be divided into two species, thus: "Hebraisms of translation," and "ordinary Hebraisms".

[3] These are the passages given by Cremer[7], pp. 907 and 901 (= [8], pp. 956 and 950) with the references corrected.

[4] In the passage 2 Sam. 2[7], cited by Cremer for υἱὸς θανάτου, stands υἱοὺς δυνατούς. Probably 2 Sam. 12[5] is meant.

[5] LXX Ps. 88 [89][23] υἱὸς ἀνομίας, and 1 Macc. 2[47] υἱὸς τῆς ὑπερηφανίας may be added to these.

[6] The references to this in the *Clavis*[3], p. 429, at the end of the article τέκνον, are not accurate.

[7] Particulars in Waddington, iii. 2, p. 26.

[8] On this *cf.* also Paton and Hicks, *The Inscriptions of Cos*, p. 125 f. υἱὸς γερουσίας is also found in these, Nos. 95–97.

υἱὸς 'Αφροδισιέων, etc. And thus, though the υἱός of the biblical passages above may have been occasioned, in the first instance, by the original, yet no one can call it un-Greek.—W. Schulze has also directed the author's attention to the υἱὸς τύχης in the Tragedians, and *filius fortunae* in Horace.

Our judgment, then, in regard to the philological history of the above-cited expressions (Greek from the first) in Paul and the Epistles of Peter, may be formulated somewhat in this way. In no case whatever are they un-Greek; they might quite well have been coined by a Greek who wished to use impressive language. Since, however, similar turns of expression are found in the Greek Bible, and are in part cited by Paul and others, the theory of analogical formations will be found a sufficient explanation.

ὁ υἱὸς τοῦ θεοῦ.

It is very highly probable that the " New Testament " designation of Christ as the *Son of God* goes back to an " Old Testament " form of expression. But when the question is raised as to the manner in which the " Heathen-Christians " of Asia Minor, of Rome, or of Alexandria, understood this designation, it seems equally probable that such " Old Testament presuppositions " were not extant among them. We are therefore brought face to face with the problem whether they could in any way understand the Saviour's title of dignity in the light of the ideas of their locality. If this solemn form of expression was already current among them in any sense whatever, that would be the very sense in which they understood it when they heard it in the discourses of the missionary strangers : how much more so, then, seeing that among the " heathen " the expression *Son of God* was a technical term, and one which therefore stamped itself all the more firmly upon the mind. When the author came upon the expression for the first time in a non-Christian document (*Pap. Berol.* 7006 [1] (Fayyûm, 22nd August, 7 A.D.): ἔτους ἕ[κ]του καὶ τριακοστοῦ [τῆς] Καίσαρος κρατήσεως θεοῦ

---

[1] *BU.* vi., p. 180, No. 174.

υἱοῦ, where without doubt the Emperor Augustus is described as θεοῦ υἱός), he had no idea how very frequently
the title is used for Augustus in the Inscriptions. Since
that time he has become convinced that the matter stands
thus : υἱὸς θεοῦ is a translation of the *divi filius* which is
equally frequent in Latin Inscriptions.

Since, then, it is established that the expression υἱὸς
θεοῦ was a familiar one in the Graeco-Roman world from
the beginning of the first century,[1] we can no longer ignore
the fact; it is indirectly of great importance for the history
of the early-Christian title of Christ. The fact does not of
course explain its origin or its primary signification, but it
yields a contribution to the question as to how it might be
understood in the empire.[2] It must be placed in due connection with what is said by Harnack[3] about the term θεός
as used in the imperial period.

φίλος.

Friend was the title of honour given at the court of the
Ptolemies to the highest royal officials. " Greek writers, it
is true, already used this name for the officials of the Persian
king ; from the Persian kings the practice was adopted by
Alexander, and from him again by all the Diadochi ; but we
meet it particularly often as an Egyptian title." [4] The LXX

---

[1] Particular references are unnecessary. The author would name only
the Inscription of Tarsus, interesting to us by reason of its place of origin,
Waddington, iii. 2, No. 1476 (p. 348), also in honour of Augustus :—

Αὐτοκράτορα Καί]σαρα θεοῦ υἱὸν Σεβαστὸν

ὁ δῆμ]ος ὁ Ταρσέων.

Perhaps the young Paul may have seen here the expression *Son of God* for
the first time—long before it came to him with another meaning.

[2] It may be just indicated here that the history of the terms used by
Christians of the earlier time teaches us that other solemn expressions of
the language of the imperial period were transferred to Christ.

[3] *Lehrbuch der Dogmengeschichte*, i.[2], Freiburg, 1888, pp. 103, 159. [Eng.
Trans., i., pp. 116 f., 179 f.]

[4] Jacob, *ZAW.* x., p. 283. The examples in the Papyri and the Inscriptions are exceedingly numerous. *Cf.*, in addition to the literature instanced
by Jacob, Letronne, *Rech.*, p. 58, A. Peyron, i., p. 56, Grimm, *HApAT.* iii.
(1853), p. 38, Letronne, *Notices*, xviii. 2, p. 165, Bernays, *Die heraklitischen
Briefe*, p. 20, Lumbroso, *Rech.*, pp. 191 ff., 228.

were, therefore, quite correct (from their standpoint) in translating שַׂר *prince* by φίλος, Esth. 1³, 2¹⁸, 6⁹,—a fact not
taken into consideration in the Concordance of Hatch and
Redpath—and the same usage is exceedingly frequent in
the Books of Maccabees.[1] We think it probable that the
Alexandrian writer of the Book of Wisdom was following
this idiom when he spoke of the pious as φίλους θεοῦ (Wisd.
7²⁷, *cf.* v.¹⁴) ; similarly the Alexandrian Philo, *Fragm.* (M.)
ii., p. 652, πᾶς σοφὸς θεοῦ φίλος, and *De Sobr.* (M.) i., p. 401,
where he quotes the saying in LXX Gen. 18¹⁷ (in our text
οὐ μὴ κρύψω ἐγὼ ἀπὸ Ἀβραὰμ τοῦ παιδός μου) thus : μὴ
ἐπικαλύψω ἐγὼ ἀπὸ Ἀβραὰμ τοῦ φίλου[2] μου. In explaining
this, reference is usually made to Plato *Legg.* iv., p. 716, ὁ
μὲν σώφρων θεῷ φίλος, ὅμοιος γάρ ; but, although it is not to
be denied that this passage may perhaps have exercised an
influence in regard to the choice of the expression, yet the
Alexandrians would, in the first instance, understand it[3] in
the sense to which they had been pre-disposed by the above-
mentioned familiar technical usage of φίλος : φίλος θεοῦ
denotes high honour in the sight of God[4]—nothing more
nor less. The question whether *friend of God* is to be interpreted as *one who loved God* or as *one whom God loved*, is not
only insoluble[5] but superfluous. Philo and the others would
hardly be thinking of a " relation of the will . . . . , such, however, that the benevolence and love of God towards men are
to be emphasised as its main element ".[6]

In John 15¹⁵ οὐκέτι λέγω ὑμᾶς δούλους . . . ὑμᾶς δὲ

[1] The expression φίλος τοῦ Καίσαρος, John 19¹², is doubtless to be understood in the light of Roman usage ; but, again, *amicus Caesaris* is most likely
dependent upon the court speech of the Diadochi.

[2] *Cf.* James 2²³, Clem. Rom. 1 Cor. 10¹, 17².

[3] The expression *Gottesfreund* (friend of God), again, used by the German mystics, is certainly dependent on the biblical passages, but they use
it in a sense different from that mentioned in the text.

[4] The designation of Abraham in particular (the standard personality
of Judaism and of earlier Christianity) as the φίλος θεοῦ accords with the
position of honour which he had in Heaven.

[5] W. Beyschlag, Meyer, xv.⁵ (1888), p. 144.

[6] Grimm, *HApAT.* vi. (1860), p. 145.

εἴρηκα φίλους, as can be seen by the contrast, φίλος has, of course, its simple sense of *friend*.

———

In Corinth the Gospel was understood otherwise than in Jerusalem, in Egypt otherwise than in Ephesus. The history of our Religion, in its further course, manifestly shows distinct phases of Christianity : we see, in succession or side by side, a Jewish Christianity and an International— a Roman, a Greek, a German and a Modern. The historical conditions of this vigorous development are to be found to a large extent in the profusion of the individual forms which were available for the ideas of the Evangelists and the Apostles. The variation in the meaning of religious terms has not always been to the disadvantage of religion itself : the Kingdom of God is not in *words*.

III.

FURTHER CONTRIBUTIONS TO THE HISTORY OF THE LANGUAGE OF THE GREEK BIBLE,

BEING *NEUE BIBELSTUDIEN*, MARBURG, 1897.

ὁ δὲ ἀγρός ἐστιν ὁ κόσμος.

FURTHER CONTRIBUTIONS TO THE HISTORY OF THE LANGUAGE OF THE GREEK BIBLE.

In the third article[1] of *Bibelstudien* we endeavoured to correct the widespread notion that the New Testament presents us with a uniform and isolated linguistic phenomenon. Most of the lexical articles in that section were intended to make good the thesis that a philological understanding of the history of New Testament (and also of Septuagint) texts could be attained to only when these were set in their proper historical connection, that is to say, when they were considered as products of later Greek.

Friedrich Blass in his critique[2] of *Bibelstudien* has expressed himself with regard to this inquiry in the following manner :—

The third treatise again[3] begins with general reflections, the purport of which is that it is erroneous to regard New Testament, or even biblical, Greek as something distinct and isolated, seeing that the Papyrus documents and the Inscriptions are essentially of the same character, and belong similarly to that "Book of Humanity" to which "reverence" (*Pietät*) is due.[4]

[1] *I.e.* the foregoing article. The present article was published later by itself.

[2] *ThLZ.* **xx.** (1895), p. 487.

[3] This *again* refers to a previous remark in which Blass had "willingly conceded" to the author his "general, and not always short, reflections".

[4] Blass has here fallen into a misunderstanding. The present writer remarked (above, p. 84) that he who undertakes to glean materials from the Inscriptions for the history of the New Testament language, is not merely obeying the voice of science, "but also the behests of reverence towards the Book of Humanity". The "Book of Humanity" is the New Testament. We are of opinion that every real contribution, even the slightest, to the historical understanding of the N. T. has not only scientific value, but should also be made welcome out of reverence for the sacred Book. We cannot honour the Bible more highly than by an endeavour to attain to the truest possible apprehension of its literal sense.

This appears to us to be the language of naturalism rather than of theology ; but, this apart, it remains an incontestable fact that, in the sphere of Greek literature, the New Testament books form a special group—one to be primarily explained by itself; first, because they manifest a peculiar genius, and, secondly, because they alone, or almost alone, represent the popular— in contrast to the literary—speech of their time in a form not indeed wholly, but yet comparatively, unadulterated, and in fragments of large extent. All the Papyri in the world cannot alter this—even were there never so many more of them : they lack the peculiar genius, and with it the intrinsic value ; further, they are to a considerable extent composed in the language of the office or in that of books. True, no one would maintain that the N. T. occupies an absolutely isolated position, or would be other than grateful[1] if some peculiar expression therein were to derive illumination and clearness from cognate instances in a Papyrus. But it would be well not to expect too much.

The author must confess that he did not expect this opposition from the philological side.[2] The objections of such a renowned Graecist—renowned also in theological circles—certainly did not fail to make an impression upon him. They prompted him to investigate his thesis again, and more thoroughly, and to test its soundness by minute and detailed research. But the more opportunity he had of examining non-literary Greek texts of the imperial Roman period, the more clearly did he see himself compelled to stand out against the objections of the Halle Scholar.

Blass has meanwhile published his Grammar of New Testament Greek.[3] In the Introduction, as was to be expected, he expresses his view of the whole question. The astonishment with which the present writer read the following, p. 2, may be conceived :—

. . . The spoken tongue in its various gradations (which, according to the rank and education of those who spoke it, were, of course, not absent from it) comes to us quite pure—in fact even purer than in the New Testament itself—in the private records, the number and importance of which are

---

[1] Blass writes *denkbar, conceivable*, but the sentence in that case seems to defy analysis. After consultation with the author, the translator has substituted *dankbar*, and rendered as above.—*Tr.*

[2] He noticed only later that Blass had previously, *ThLZ.* xix. (1894), p. 338, incidentally made the statement that the New Testament Greek should " be recognised as something distinct and subject to its own laws ".

[3] Göttingen, 1896. [Eng. Trans., London, 1898.]

constantly being increased by the ever-growing discoveries in Egypt. Thus the New Testament language may be quite justly placed in this connection, and whoever would write a grammar of the popular language of that period on the basis of all these various witnesses and remains, would be, from the grammarian's point of view, taking perhaps a more correct course than one who should limit himself to the language of the N. T.[1]

If the present writer judges rightly, Blass has, in these sentences, abandoned his opposition to the thesis above mentioned. For his own part, at least, he does not perceive what objection he could take to these words, or in what respect they differ from the statements the accuracy of which had previously been impugned by Blass. When in the Grammar we read further :—

Nevertheless those practical considerations from which we started will more and more impose such a limitation, for that which some Egyptian or other may write in a letter or in a deed of sale is not of equal value with that which the New Testament authors have written—

it can hardly need any asseveration on the author's part that with such words in themselves he again finds no fault. For practical reasons, on account of the necessities of biblical study, the linguistic relations of the New Testament, and of the Greek Bible as a whole, may continue to be treated by themselves, but certainly not as the phenomena of a special idiom requiring to be judged according to its own laws.

Moreover, that view of the inherent value of the ideas of the New Testament which Blass again emphasises in the words quoted from his Grammar, does not enter into the present connection. It must remain a matter of indifference to the grammarian whether he finds ἐάν used for ἄν in the New Testament or in a bill of sale from the Fayyûm, and the lexicographer must register the κυριακός found in the pagan Papyri and Inscriptions with the same care as when it occurs in the writings of the Apostle Paul.

The following investigations have been, in part, arranged on a plan which is polemical. For although the author is now exempted, on account of Blass's present attitude, from any need of controversy with him as regards principles, still

---

[1] In the note to this Blass refers to the author's *Bibelstudien*, p. 57 f. (above, p. 63 f.).

the historical method of biblical philology has very many opponents even yet.

In this matter, one thinks first of all of the unconscious opponents, *viz.*, those who in the particular questions of exegesis and also of textual criticism stand under the charm of the " New Testament " Greek without ever feeling any necessity to probe the whole matter to the bottom. Among these the author reckons Willibald Grimm (not without the highest esteem for his lasting services towards the reinvigoration of exegetical studies), the late reviser of Wilke's *Clavis Novi Testamenti Philologica.* A comparison of the second,[1] and the little-changed third,[2] edition of his work with the English revision of Joseph Henry Thayer [3]—the best, because the most reliable of all dictionaries to the N. T. known to us—reveals many errors, not only in its materials, but also in its method. His book reflects the condition of philological research in, say, the fifties and sixties. At least, the notion of the specifically peculiar character of New Testament Greek could be upheld with more plausibility then than now ; the New Testament texts were decidedly the most characteristic of all the products of non-literary and of later Greek which were then known. But materials have now been discovered in face of which the linguistic isolation of the New Testament—even that more modest variety of it which diffuses an atmosphere of venerable romanticism around so many of our commentaries— must lose its last shadow of justification.

Among the conscious opponents, *i.e.*, those who oppose in matters of principle, we reckon Hermann Cremer. His *Biblisch-theologisches Wörterbuch der neutestamentlichen Gräcität* [4] has for its fundamental principle the idea of the formative power of Christianity in the sphere of language. This idea, as a canon of historical philology, becomes a fetter upon investigation. Further, it breaks down at once in the department of morphology. But the most conspicu-

---

[1] Leipzig, 1879.   [2] *Ibid.*, 1888 [quoted in this article as *Clavis* [3]].
[3] The author quotes the *Corrected Edition*, New York, 1896.
[4] 8th Edition, Gotha, 1895.

ous peculiarity of " New Testament " Greek—let us allow
the phrase for once—is just the morphology. The canon
breaks down very often in the syntax also. There are
many very striking phenomena in this department which
we cannot isolate, however much we may wish. The few
Hebraising expressions in those parts of the New Testament
which were in Greek from the first[1] are but an *accidens*
which does not essentially alter the fundamental character
of its language. The case in regard to these is similar to
that of the Hebraisms in the German Bible, which, in spite
of the many Semitic constructions underlying it, is yet a
German book. There remains, then, only the lexical element in the narrower sense, with which Cremer's book is,
indeed, almost exclusively occupied. In many (not in all,
nor in all the more important) of its articles, there appears,
more or less clearly, the tendency to establish new " biblical "
or " New Testament " words, or new " biblical " or " New
Testament " meanings of old Greek words. That there are
" biblical " and " New Testament " words—or, more correctly, words formed for the first time by Greek Jews and
Christians—and alterations of meaning, cannot be denied.
Every movement of civilisation which makes its mark in
history enriches language with new terms and fills the old
speech with new meanings. Cremer's fundamental idea
is, therefore, quite admissible if it be intended as nothing
more than a means for investigating the history of religion.
But it not infrequently becomes a philologico-historical
principle : it is not the ideas of the early Christians
which are presented to us, but their " Greek ". The correct
attitude of a lexicon, so far as concerns the history of
language, is only attained when its primary and persistent
endeavour is to answer the question : To what extent do the
single words and conceptions have links of connection with
contemporary usage ? Cremer, on the other hand, prefers
to ask : To what extent does Christian usage differ from
heathen ? In cases of doubt, as we think, the natural course

---

[1] Those parts of the N. T. which go back to translations must be considered by themselves.

is to betake oneself placidly to the hypothesis of ordinary usage ; Cremer prefers in such cases to demonstrate something which is distinctively Christian or, at least, distinctively biblical.

In spite of the partially polemical plan of the following investigations, polemics are not their chief aim. Their purpose is to offer,[1] towards the understanding of the New Testament, positive materials [2] from the approximately contemporary products of later Greek, and to assist, in what degree they can, in the liberation of biblical study from the bonds of tradition, in the secularising of it—in the good sense of that term. They take up again, one might say, the work of the industrious collectors of " observations " in last century. The reasons why the new spheres of observation disclosed since that time are of special importance for the linguistic investigation of the Greek Bible in particular, have been already set forth and corroborated by examples.[3] In these pages the following works have been laid under contribution :—

1. Collections of Inscriptions : the Inscriptions of Pergamus [4] and those of the Islands of the Ægean Sea, fasc. 1.[5]

---

[1] On the other hand, the Greek Bible contains much, of course, which may promote the understanding of the Inscriptions and Papyri.

[2] No intelligent reader will blame the author for having, in his investigations regarding the orthography and morphology, confined himself simply to the giving of materials without adding any judgment. Nothing is more dangerous, in Textual Criticism as elsewhere, than making general judgments on the basis of isolated phenomena. But such details may occasionally be of service to the investigator who is at home in the problems and has a general view of their connections.

[3] Above, pp. 61-169 ; cf. also GGA. 1896, pp. 761-769 : and ThLZ. xxi. (1896), pp. 609-615, and the other papers cited above, p. 84.

[4] Altertümer von Pergamon herausgegeben im Auftrage des Königlich Preussischen Ministers der geistlichen, Unterrichts- und Medicinal-Angelegenheiten, Band viii. : Die Inschriften von Pergamon unter Mitwirkung von Ernst Fabricius und Carl Schuchhardt herausgegeben von Max Fränkel, (1) Bis zum Ende der Königszeit, Berlin, 1890, (2) Römische Zeit.—Inschriften auf Thon, Berlin, 1895 [subsequently cited as Perg. or Fränkel].

[5] Inscriptiones Graecae insularum Maris Aegaei consilio et auctoritate Academiae Litterarum Regiae Borussicae editae. Fasciculus primus : Inscriptiones Graecae insularum Rhodi Chalces Carpathi cum Saro Casi . . . edidit Fridericus Hiller de Gaertringen, Berolini, 1895 [subsequently cited as IMAe.].

2. Issues of Papyri : the Berlin Egyptian Documents, vol. i. and vol. ii., parts 1-9 ;[1] also the Papyri of the Archduke Rainer, vol. i.[2]

In reading these the author had in view chiefly the lexical element, but he would expressly state that a reperusal having regard to the orthographical and morphological features would assuredly repay itself. He desiderates, in general, a very strict scrutiny of his own selections. It is only the most important lexical features that are given here. The author, not having in Herborn the necessary materials for the investigation of the LXX at his disposal, had, very reluctantly, to leave it almost entirely out of consideration. But he has reason for believing that the Berlin and Vienna Papyri in particular, in spite of their comparative lateness, will yet yield considerable contributions towards the lexicon of the LXX, and that the same holds good especially of the Inscriptions of Pergamus in connection with the Books of Maccabees.

It may be said that the two groups of authorities have been arbitrarily associated together here. But that is not altogether the case. They represent linguistic remains from Asia Minor [3] and Egypt, that is to say, from the regions which, above all others, come into consideration in connection with Greek Christianity. And, doubtless, the greater part of the materials they yield will not be merely local, or confined only to the districts in question.

The gains from the Papyri are of much wider extent than those from the Inscriptions. The reason is obvious. We might almost say that this difference is determined by the disparity of the respective materials on which the writing

---

[1] *Aegyptische Urkunden aus den Königlichen Museen zu Berlin herausgegeben von der Generalverwaltung: Griechische Urkunden.* *Erster Band,* Berlin, [completed] 1895 ; *Zweiter Band, Heft* 1-9, Berlin, 1894 ff. [subsequently cited as *BU.*].

[2] *Corpus Papyrorum Raineri Archiducis Austriae, vol. i.* *Griechische Texte herausgegeben von* Carl Wessely, *i. Band : Rechtsurkunden unter Mitwirkung von* Ludwig Mitteis, Vienna, 1895 [subsequently cited as *PER.*].

[3] We need only think of the importance of Pergamus for the earlier period of Christianity.

was made. Papyrus is accommodating and is available for
private purposes ; stone is unyielding, and stands open to
every eye in the market-place, in the temple, or beside the
tomb. The Inscriptions, particularly the more lengthy and
the official ones, often approximate in style to the literary
language, and are thus readily liable to affectation and
mannerism ; what the papyrus leaves contain is much less
affected, proceeding, as it does, from the thousand requirements and circumstances of the daily life of unimportant
people. If the legal documents among the Papyri show
a certain fixed mode of speech, marked by the formal-
ism of the office, yet the many letter-writers, male and
female, express themselves all the more unconstrainedly.
This holds good, in particular, in regard to all that is, relatively speaking, matter of form. But also in regard to the
vocabulary, the Inscriptions afford materials which well repay
the labour spent on them. What will yet be yielded by the
comprehensive collections of Inscriptions, which have not
yet been read by the author in their continuity, may be
surmised from the incidental discoveries to which he has
been guided by the citations given by Fränkel. What
might we not learn, *e.g.*, from the one inscription of
Xanthus the Lycian ! [1]

Would that the numerous memorials of antiquity which
our age has restored to us, and which have been already
so successfully turned to account in other branches of
science, were also explored, in ever-increasing degree, in
the interest of the philologico-historical investigation of the
Greek Bible ! Here is a great opportunity for the ascertain-
ment of *facts !*

---

[1] See below, *sub* καθαρίζω, βιάζομαι, ἱλάσκομαι.

I.

NOTES ON THE ORTHOGRAPHY.

The orthographical problems of the New Testament writings are complicated in the extreme. But, at all events, one thing is certain, *viz.*, that it is a delusion to search for a "New Testament" orthography—if that is understood to signify the spelling originally employed by the writers. In that respect one can, at most, attain to conjectures regarding some particular author: "the" New Testament cannot really be a subject of investigation.[1] The present writer would here emphasise the fact that — notwithstanding all other differences—he finds himself, in this matter, in happy agreement with Cremer, who has overtly opposed the notion that an identical orthography may, without further consideration, be forced upon, *e.g.*, Luke, Paul and the author of the Epistle to the Hebrews.[2] The first aim of the investigation should perhaps be this :—to establish what forms of spelling were possible in the imperial period in Asia Minor, Egypt, etc. We need not, of course, pay any attention to manifest errors in writing. The following observed facts are intended to yield materials for this purpose.

1. VARIATION OF VOWELS.

(a) *The feminine termination* -ιa *for* -$\epsilon \iota a$.[3] That in 2 Cor. 10[4] $\sigma \tau \rho a \tau \iota a \varsigma$ (= $\sigma \tau \rho a \tau \epsilon \iota a \varsigma$), and not $\sigma \tau \rho a \tau \iota \hat{a} \varsigma$, is

---

[1] See above, p. 81. W. Schmid makes some pertinent remarks in *GGA*. 1895, p. 36 f.

[2] Cremer[8], p. xiii. (Preface to the 4th edition).

[3] Winer-Schmiedel, § 5, 13 c (p. 44) ; Blass, *Grammatik*, p. 9 [Eng. Trans., p. 8].

intended, should no longer be contested. It is really superfluous to collect proofs of the fact that στρατεία could also
be written στρατία. Nevertheless, the mode of spelling the
word in the Fayyûm Papyri should be noted. In these
there is frequent mention of campaigns, the documents
having not seldom to do with the concerns of soldiers either
in service or retired. στρατεία is given by *PER.* i.3 (83-84
A.D.), *BU.* 140 11. 23 (*ca.* 100 A.D.) 581 4. 15 (133 A.D.), 256 15
(reign of Antoninus Pius), 180 15 (172 A.D.), 592, i.6 (2nd
cent. A.D.), 625 14 (2nd-3rd cent. A.D.); στρατία by 195 39
(161 A.D.), 448 [= 161] 14 (2nd half of 2nd cent. A.D.), 614 20
(217 A.D.). Also in 613 23 (reign of Antoninus Pius), where
Viereck has στρατιαῖς, the author would prefer the accentuation στρατίαις.

(b) *Interchange of a and ε.* Of ἐγγαρεύω (Matt. 5 41
ℵ, Mark 15 21 ℵ*B*) for ἀγγαρεύω,[1] Tischendorf says in connection with the latter passage, " *quam formam in usu fuisse
haud incredibile est, hinc nec aliena a textu* ". A papyrus of
cent. 4 shows also the spelling with ε, in the substantive :
BU. 21, iii. 16 (locality uncertain, 340 A.D.) ἐνγαρίας.

Δελματία, 2 Tim. 4 10 C and others (A., Δερματία) for
Δαλματία,[2] according to Winer-Schmiedel, § 5, 20 c (p. 50),
is "probably Alexandrian, but perhaps also the original
form ". *BU.* 93 7 (Fayyûm, 2-3 cent. A.D.) gives ε in
δελματική ; on the other hand, *PER.* xxi. 16 (Fayyûm,
230 A.D.) has δαλματική. We should hardly postulate an
" Alexandrian " spelling.

(c) *The contraction of ιει = ii to ι long*[3] in the (New
Testament) cases ταμεῖον and πεῖν, occurs also in the

---

[1] Winer-Schmiedel, § 5, 20 c (p. 50); Blass, *Grammatik*, p. 21 [Eng.
Trans., p. 20 f.].

[2] " *Delm.* as well as *Dalm.* occurs also in Latin " (Blass, *Gramm.*,
p. 21. [Eng. Trans., p. 21.] P. Jürges has called the author's attention
also to the excursus *CIL.* iii. 1, p. 280.

[3] Winer-Schmiedel, § 5, 23 *b* (p. 53 f.); Blass, *Gramm.*, p. 23 [Eng.
Trans., p. 23].

Papyri. The author met with ταμιεῖον only once, *BU*. 106 5 (Fayyûm, 199 A.D.) ; everywhere else [1] ταμεῖον : *PER*. 1 13. 30 (83-84 A.D.), *BU*. 75 ii. 12 (2nd cent. A.D.), 15 ii. 16 (197 A.D. ?), 156 6 (201 A.D.) 7 i. 8 (247 A.D.), 8 ii. 30 (248 A.D.), 96 8 (2nd half of 3rd cent. A.D.). Πεῖν occurs in *BU*. 34 ii. 7. 17. 22. 23, iii. 2, iv. 3. 10 (place and date ?), πῖν *ibid*. iv. 25 [2] and once more *BU*. 551 6 (Fayyûm, Arabian period).

2. VARIATION OF CONSONANTS.

(*a*) *Duplication*. The materials with regard to ἀρραβών given in Winer-Schmiedel, § 5, 26 *c* (p. 56 f.) may be supplemented : the author found ἀρραβών only in *BU*. 240 6 (Fayyûm, 167-168 A.D.) ; [3] ἀραβών, on the other hand, in *BU*. 446 [= 80] 5. 17. 18 (reign of Marcus Aurelius, a fairly well written contract), (in line 26 of the same document, in the imperfect signature of one of the contracting parties, we find ἀλαβών), 601 11 (Fayyûm, 2nd cent. A.D., a badly written private letter), *PER*. xix. 9. 16. 21. 24 (Fayyûm, 330 A.D. a well written record of a legal action). The assertion of Westcott and Hort (in view of their usual precision a suspicious one), that ἀραβών is a purely " Western " reading, is hardly tenable. The author, moreover, would question the scientific procedure of Winer-Schmiedel's assertion that the spelling ἀρραβών is " established " by the Hebrew origin of the word. [4] It would be established only if we were forced to presuppose a correct etymological judgment in all who used the word. [5] But we cannot say by what considerations they

---

[1] All the Papyri cited here are from the Fayyûm.

[2] F. Krebs, the editor of this document, erroneously remarks on p. 46 : " πεῖν = πίνειν ". In connection with this and with other details W. Schmid, *GGA*. 1895, pp. 26-47, has already called attention to the Papyri.

[3] This passage is also referred to by Blass, *Gramm*., p. 11. [Eng. Trans., p. 10, note 4.]

[4] Blass similarly asserts, *Gramm*., p. 11 [Eng. Trans., p. 10], that the duplication is " established " in the Semitic form.

[5] The matter is still more evident in proper names. For example, Ἀρέθας, as the name of Nabatæan kings, is undoubtedly " established " by etymological considerations; on the other hand, the Inscriptions and other ancient evidence, so far as the author knows, all give Ἀρέτας, and thus Ἀρέτα in 2 Cor. 11 [32] may be considered " established " without the slightest

were influenced in orthographical matters. It can no longer be questioned that the spelling ἀραβών was very common. Who knows whether some one or other did not associate the non-Greek word with the *Arabs* ?[1] A popular tradition of this kind might, in the particular case, invalidate the etymological considerations advanced by us from the standpoint of our present knowledge, and so induce us to uphold an etymologically *false* spelling as " established ".

γέννημα and γένημα. The spelling with a single ν and, consequently, the derivation from γίνεσθαι have been already established by the Ptolemaic Papyri.[2] It is confirmed by the following passages from Fayyûm Papyri of the first four Christian centuries, all of which have to do with *fruits of the field :* [3] *BU.* 197₁₃ (17 A.D.), 171₃ (156 A.D.), 49₅ ⟨179 A.D.), 188₉ (186 A.D.), 81₇ (189 A.D.), 67₈ (199 A.D.), 61 *i.* ₈ (200 A.D.), 529₆ and 336₇ (216 A.D.), 64₅ (217 A.D.), 8 i.₂₈ (middle of 3rd cent. A.D.), 411₆ (314 A.D.) ; *cf.* also γενηματο-γραφεῖν in *BU.* 282₁₉ (after 175 A.D.).

A fluctuation in the orthography of those forms of γεννάω and γίνομαι which are identical except for the ν (νν) has often been remarked ;[4] thus, γενηθέντα, undoubtedly from γεννάω, occurs also in the Papyri : *BU.* 110₁₄ (Fayyûm, 138-139 A.D.) and 28₁₆ (Fayyûm, 183 A.D.). Both documents are official birth-notices. On the other hand, the " correct " γεννηθείς is thrice found in vol. i. of the Berlin Papyri. The uncertainty of the orthography[5] is well indicated in

misgiving. It is exceedingly probable (according to the excellent conjecture of Schürer, *Gesch. d. jüd. Volkes im Zeitalter Jesu Christi,* i., Leipzig, 1890, p. 619 [Eng. Trans., i., ii., p. 359]) that this spelling was influenced by the desire to Hellenise the barbaric name by assimilation to ἀρετή.—Moreover, also Blass, *Gramm.,* p. 11 [Eng. Trans., p. 11], takes this view in regard to Ἰωάνης.

[1] *Cf.* the case of ἀλαβών for ἀραβών, as above, with the well-known ἀλαβάρχης for ἀραβάρχης.

[2] Above, p. 109 f. ; *cf.* Blass, *Gramm.,* p. 11 [Eng. Trans., p. 11].

[3] The author has not found the spelling with νν anywhere in the Papyri.

[4] Winer-Schmiedel, § 5, 26 *a* (p. 56).

[5] The problem of orthography became later a point of controversy in the History of Dogma ; *cf.* A. Harnack, *Lehrbuch der Dogmengeschichte,* ii.³, Freiburg and Leipzig, 1894, p. 191 f. [Eng. Trans., iv., p. 12 ff.]

BU. 111 (Fayyûm, 138-139 A.D.), where line 21 has ἐπι-γεννήσεως ; line 24, ἐπιγενήσεως.

(b) *Interchange of consonants.* Σμύρνα, Ζμύρνα.[1] *Perg.* 203 8. 11. 17 (pre-Christian) Σμύρνα, *IMAe.* 148 1 (Rhodes, date ?) Σμυρναῖος, 468 (Rhodes, date ?) Σμυρναῖος. On the other hand, *Perg.* 1274 (2nd cent. B.C., *cf.* Fränkel, p. 432) Ζμυρ-ναῖος, *BU.* 1 11 (Fayyûm, 3rd cent. A.D.) μύρου καὶ ζμύρνης.[2]

σπυρίς, σφυρίς. The Ptolemaic Papyri have both spellings ;[3] the author found the diminutive twice in the later Papyri from the Fayyûm, and, indeed, with the vulgar aspiration : σφυρίδιον *PER.* xlvii. 5 (2nd-3rd cent. A.D.) and (a vulgar abbreviation)[4] σφυρίτιν *sic*, *BU.* 247 3. 4. 6. (2nd-3rd cent. A.D.).

---

[1] *Cf.* Winer-Schmiedel, § 5, 27 *d* (p. 59) ; Blass, *Gramm.*, p. 10. [Eng. Trans., p. 10.]

[2] *Cf.* also *BU.* 69 6 (Fayyûm, 120 A.D.) νομίζματος.   [3] Above, p. 158.

[4] Examples of this abbreviation from the Inscriptions are given by Fränkel, p. 341.

II.

NOTES ON THE MORPHOLOGY.

The New Testament references are again very seldom given in the following; they can easily be found in the cited passages of the Grammars.

1. DECLENSION.

(*a*) $\sigma\pi\epsilon\acute{\iota}\rho\alpha\varsigma$ was not found by the author in the Papyri: they seem always to have $\sigma\pi\epsilon\acute{\iota}\rho\eta\varsigma$:[1] *BU.* 73 2 (Fayyûm, 135 A.D.), 136 22 (Fayyûm, 135 A.D.), 142 10 (159 A.D.), 447 [= 26] 12 (Fayyûm, 175 A.D.), 241 3 (Fayyûm, 177 A.D.). The materials from the Inscriptions of Italy and Asia Minor which Fränkel adduces in connection with $\sigma\pi\epsilon\acute{\iota}\rho\alpha = Thiasos$, also exhibit η in the genitive and dative.

(*b*) The Genitive $\dot{\eta}\mu\acute{\iota}\sigma o\nu\varsigma$[2] is found in *PER.* xii. 6 (93 A.D.), *BU.* 328 ii. 22 (138-139 A.D.), *PER.* cxcviii. 17 etc. (139 A.D.), *BU.* 78 11 (148-149 A.D.), 223 6 f. (210-211 A.D.), *PER.* clxxvi. 13 (225 A.D.); all these Papyri are from the Fayyûm. A form noteworthy on account of the genitive $\tau o\hat{\nu}\ \dot{\eta}\mu\acute{\iota}\sigma o\nu$ in the LXX,[3] occurs in *BU.* 183 41 (Fayyûm, 85 A.D.), *viz.*, $\H{\eta}\mu\iota\sigma o\nu\ \mu\acute{\epsilon}\rho o\varsigma$. This may be a clerical error (line 21 has the correct $\H{\eta}\mu\iota\sigma o\iota\ [o\iota = \nu]\ \mu\acute{\epsilon}\rho o\varsigma$), but it is more probable that here also we have a vulgar form $\H{\eta}\mu\iota\sigma o\varsigma$ which was common in Egypt.

---

[1] Winer-Schmiedel, § 8, 1 (p. 80 f.); Blass, *Gramm.*, p. 25 [Eng. Trans., p. 25], gives other examples from the Papyri.

[2] Winer-Schmiedel, § 9, 6 (p. 87); Blass, *Gramm.*, p. 27 [Eng. Trans., p. 27].

[3] Winer-Schmiedel, § 9, 6 (p. 87), note 4; here we already find the Papyrus, *Notices*, xviii. 2, 230 (154 A.D.), cited in reference to the form.

(c) δύο.[1] The following forms in the Fayyûm Papyri
are worthy of notice:[2] δύω *BU.* 208₄ (158-159 A.D.), δυῶν
BU. 282₂₅ (after 175 A.D.), δυεῖν *BU.* 256₅ (reign of Antoninus Pius), δυσί *BU.* 197₈ (17 A.D.) *PER.* ccxlii. ₁₀ (40 A.D.),
i.₇ (83-84 A.D.), *BU.* 538₆ (100 A.D.), 86₆ (155 A.D.), 166₇
(157 A.D.), 282₁₀ (after 175 A.D.), 326 ii.₇ (189 A.D.), 303₁₉
(586 A.D.).

2. PROPER NAMES.

Abraham is Graecised Ἄβραμος (as in Josephus) in *BU.*
585 ii.₃ (Fayyûm, after 212 A.D.) Πααβῶς Ἀβράμου; on the
other hand, in Fayyûm documents of the Christian period,
Ἀβραάμιος 395₇ (599-600 A.D.), 401₁₃ (618 A.D.), 367₅ etc.
(Arabian period); not Graecised, Ἀβραάμ 103, verso ₁
(6th-7th cent. A.D.).

Ἀκύλας. *Clavis*[3], p. 16, simply gives Ἀκύλου as the
genitive for the N. T., although a genitive does not occur
in it. The Fayyûm Papyri yield both Ἀκύλου *BU.* 484₆
(201-202 A.D.) and Ἀκύλα 71₂₁ (189 A.D.).—The name of
the veteran C. Longinus Aquila, which occurs in the last-
mentioned document, is written Ἀκύλας in 326 ii.₁₉ (end
of the 2nd cent. A.D.) and Ἀκύλλας in the fragment of a
duplicate of the same document which is there cited; this
doubling of the λ is not unknown also in New Testament
manuscripts.[3]

Ἀντίπα[τρο]ς. It is not wholly without interest
that the name of an inhabitant of Pergamus, which occurs
in Rev. 2¹³, is still found in Pergamus in the beginning of
the 3rd cent. A.D.: *Perg.* 524₂ (not older than the time of
Caracalla?) [Ἀ]ντιπάτρου.

Βαρναβᾶς. On p. 310 below the author expresses
the conjecture that the name *Barnabas*[4] arose from the

---

[1] Winer-Schmiedel, § 9, 11 (p. 90).

[2] Exhaustiveness is not guaranteed: it was only lately that the author
directed his attention to the point. In particular, he has no general idea as
to the usage of the common forms in the Papyri.

[3] *Cf.* Tischendorf on Rom. 16³ and Acts 18².

[4] *Cf.* A. Meyer, *Jesu Muttersprache*, Freiburg and Leipzig, 1896, p. 47 f.,
and E. Nestle, *Philologica sacra*, Berlin, 1896, p. 19 f.

Graecising of the Semitic $Βαρνεβοῦς$ [1] or $Βαρναβοῦς$, which could readily happen by the alteration of the Semitic termination -$οῦς$ into -$ᾶς$.[2] The termination -$ᾶς$ was in general a very popular one in the Graecising of Semitic proper names: of this there occur numerous biblical examples. An example somewhat out of the way, but in itself worthy of notice, may be noted here. Probably the oldest of the Inscriptions found at Pergamus is the dedicatory Inscription *Perg.* 1, $Παρταρας \ Ἀθηναίηι$, which, from the character of the writing, is to be assigned to the 4th cent. A.D. "The Greek dedicatory Inscription is preceded by two lines, the script of which I am unable to determine; but there is no doubt that they contain the dedication in the language of the dedicator, whose name marks him as a foreigner. The foreign script runs from right to left, since, assuming this direction, we can recognise without difficulty the name of the dedicator with its initial B, as the beginning of the second line" (Fränkel, p. 1, *ad loc.*). There is no mention here of a fact which could certainly not remain unnoticed, *viz.*, that the "foreign" script, at least at the beginning (*i.e.*, at the right) of the second line, is plainly Greek with the letters reversed: Greek letters undoubtedly occur also in other parts of the mutilated text. One may assume that the Semitic (?) text is given in Greek "reverse-

---

[1] The reference from the Inscriptions for this name which is given below belongs to the 3rd or 4th century A.D. P. Jensen has called the author's attention to a much older passage. In the Aramaic Inscription of Palmyra No. 73, of the year 114 B.C. (in M. de Vogüé's *Syrie Centrale, Inscriptions Sémitiques . . .*, Paris, 1868, p. 53) mention is made of a *Barnebo* (ברנבו).

[2] Blass, *ThLZ.* xx. (1895), p. 488, holds this supposition to be absolutely impossible. According to A. Hilgenfeld, *Berl. Philol. Wochenschr.*, 1896, p. 650, it deserves consideration, but also requires to be tested. The author stands by his hypothesis quite confidently—the more so as Blass has not mentioned his counter-reasons. He has been informed by several well-known Semitists that they accept it; *cf.* most recently, G. Dalman, *Die Worte Jesu*, vol. i., Leipzig, 1898, p. 32.—From the genitive $Βαρνα$, *CIG.* 4477 (Larissa in Syria, *ca.* 200 A.D.) we may most likely infer a nominative $Βαρνᾶς$. The author does not venture to decide whether this might be a pet form of $Βαρναβᾶς$ (*cf.* Heinrici, Meyer, v[8]. [1896], p. 525).

script" (Spiegelschrift) in the first two lines. The stone-cutter who, as Fränkel also thinks, was perhaps the dedi-cator himself, had, on this view, the Semitic (?) text before him, transcribed it letter by letter into Greek, and, more-over, lighted upon the original idea of one by one revers-ing the Greek letters (now standing in Semitic order). It is, of course, possible that this hypothesis is fundamentally wrong. It is certain, however, that the Greek name Παρταρας occurs in the "foreign" text in the doubly-divergent form Βαρταρα. The letter which follows Βαρταρα cannot be a sigma; the non-Greek form is Βαρταρα,—by all analogies a personal name formed with בַּר son. The author does not venture to make any assertion with regard to the second constituent -ταρα;[1] he has not met with the name elsewhere. By the addition of a ς the name has been Graecised, Βαρταρᾶς or according to the carver, Παρταρᾶς.[2]

Δορκάς. The examples[3] in connection with Acts 9 36. 39, may be supplemented by IMAe. 569 (Rhodes, date?).

'Ισακ. The spelling 'Ισακ (for 'Ισαακ), in Cod. א, in both of D, often implied in the old Latin versions, and probably also underlying the Graecised "Ισακος of Josephus, is found in PER. xliv. 9 (Fayyûm, 3rd-4th cent., A.D.), in which an Αὐρήλιος 'Ισακ is mentioned; often also in the Fayyûm documents of the Christian period: BU. 305 5 (556 A.D.), 303 7 (586 A.D.), 47 6 and 173 5 (6th-7th cent. A.D.).

3. VERB.

(a) Augment. ἠνοίγην[4] (Mark 7 35, Acts 12 10, Rev. 11 19, 15 5): BU. 326 ii. 10 (Fayyûm, 194 A.D.) ἠνύγη [υ = οι], said of a will.[5]

---

[1] Aram. תֶּרָע ? i.e., son of the palace? Or son of Therach, Terah (LXX Θαρρα and Θαρα, but, as a place-name, with τ for ח, Numb. 33 27 1. Ταραθ) ? ?

[2] The author does not know of any other examples of π for ב. The accentuation -âς should probably be preferred to the Παρτάρας given by Fränkel.

[3] Cf. Wendt, Meyer, iii. 6/7 (1888), p. 235.

[4] Winer-Schmiedel, § 12, 7 (p. 103).

[5] For the reading see ibid., Supplement, p. 359.

(b) *Conjugation.* τέτευχα[1] is fairly well authenticated in Heb. 8⁶; *cf. BU.* 332₆ (Fayyûm, 2nd-3rd cent. A.D.) ἐπι- τετευχότας, unnecessarily altered by the editor to ἐπιτετυ- χότας.

ἦξα[2] (Luke 13³⁴, 2 Pet. 2⁵, Acts 14²⁷ D): *BU.* 607₁₅ (Fayyûm, 163 A.D.) κατῆξαν.

ἔλειψα[3] (Acts 6², Luke 5¹¹ D, Mark 12¹⁹ א, always in the compound κατέλειψα) also occurs in the following Fayyûm Papyri: *BU.* 183₁₉ (85 A.D.) καταλείψῃ, 176₁₀ (reign of Hadrian) καταλεῖψαι, 86₇.₁₃ (155 A.D.) καταλείψῃ,[4] 467₆ (no note of place, *ca.* 177 A.D.) καταλείψας, 164₁₃ (2nd-3rd cent. A.D.) καταλεῖψαι. The same compound is found also in the passages Clem. 2 Cor. 5¹, 10¹, and Herm. Similit. 8, 3⁵ cited by Blass, also in LXX 1 Chron. 28⁹, and *CIG.* 4137₃ₜ. (Montalub in Galatia, date?); 4063₆ₜ. (Ancyra, date?) has ἐνκατάλιψε. It is possible that the use of the form is confined to this compound.

ἡρπάγην[5] (2 Cor. 12², ⁴) occurs also in the fragment of a document[6] which relates to the Jewish war of Trajan, *BU.* 341₁₂ (Fayyûm, 2nd cent. A.D.). On p. 359 of vol. i. of that collection, ἡρπάγησαν is given as the corrected reading of this.

The attaching of 1st *aorist terminations to the* 2nd *aorist*[7] is of course very frequent in the Papyri. The author has noted the following:—

---

[1] Winer-Schmiedel, § 13, 2, Note 2 (p. 104); Blass, *Gramm.*, p. 57. [Eng. Trans., p. 57.]

[2] Winer-Schmiedel, § 13, 10 (p. 109); Blass, *Gramm.*, p. 42. [Eng. Trans., p. 43.]

[3] Winer-Schmiedel, § 13, 10 (p. 109); Blass, *Gramm.*, p. 43. [Eng. Trans., p. 43.]

[4] The Editor, P. Viereck, makes the unnecessary observation, " *l.* [read] καταλίπῃ ".

[5] Winer-Schmiedel, § 13, 10 (p. 110); Blass, *Gramm.*, p. 43. [Eng. Trans., p. 43.]

[6] *Cf.* above, p. 68.

[7] Winer-Schmiedel, § 13, 13 (p. 111 f.); Blass, *Gramm.*, p. 44 f. [Eng. Trans., p. 45 f.]

ἐγενάμην: *PER.* i. 26 (Fayyûm, 83-84 A.D.) γενάμενος along with the frequent γενόμενος, *BU.* 464 7 (132-133 A.D.) γενάμενα together with γενομένη[ν] in line 10, 300 11 (Fayyûm, 148 A.D.) παραγενάμενος, 301 4 (Fayyûm, 157 A.D.) γεναμένου, 115 ii. 25 (Fayyûm, 189 A.D.) γεναμένοις, 490 5 (Fayyûm, 2nd cent. A.D.) γεναμένη, 531 ii. 17 (Fayyûm, 2nd cent. A.D.) πα[ρ]αγενάμενος, 21 ii. 2 (340 A.D.) γεναμένου, 3 24 (Fayyûm. 605 A.D.) γεναμένων.

ἦλθα: *BU.* 530 11 (1st cent. A.D.) ἦλθας, 72 6 (191 A.D.) ἐπῆλθαν, 515 13 (193 A.D.) ἐπε[ι]σῆλθαν, 146 5 (2nd-3rd cent. A.D.) ἐπῆλθαν, 103 1 (6th-7th cent. A.D.) ἦλθαν; all these Papyri come from the Fayyûm.

ἔσχα (Acts 7 57 D, συνέσχαν): *BU.* 451 8 (1st-2nd cent. A.D.) ἔσχαμεν.

ἔλαβα: *BU.* 562 21 (Fayyûm, beginning of 2nd cent. A.D.) ἐξέλαβα, 423 9 (2nd cent. A.D.) ἔλαβα, 261 13 and 449 8 (both from the Fayyûm, 2nd-3rd cent. A.D.) ἔλαβα.

The use of the terminations -a, -aς *in the imperfect*[1] is shown in *BU.* 595 9 (Fayyûm, 70-80 A.D.) ἔλεγας, 515 5 (Fayyûm, 193 A.D.) ὠφείλαμεν, 157 8 (Fayyûm, 2nd-3rd cent. A.D.) ἐβάσταζαν. We might add 44 8 (Fayyûm, 102 A.D.) ὀφίλατε: the augment is wanting, as in *BU.* 281 12 (Fayyûm, reign of Trajan) ὄφ[ι]λεν, and 340 11 (Fayyûm, 148-149 A.D.) ὄφιλεν.

The termination -σαν *for* -ν *in the 3rd plural*[3] is attested by *BU.* 36 9 (Fayyûm, 2nd-3rd cent. A.D.) ἐπήλθοσαν, and (in a contracted verb) 251 4 (Fayyûm, 81 A.D.) προεγ[αμ]οῦσαν; also in the document by the same hand 183 6 (Fayyûm, 85 A.D.) προεγαμοῦσαν;[4] the last two examples occur in the phrase καθὼς καὶ προεγαμοῦσαν, most likely a formula in marriage-contracts.

[1] Winer-Schmiedel, § 13, 13 (p. 112); Blass, *Gramm.*, p. 45. [Eng. Trans., p. 46.]

[2] Most likely an assimilation to ὄφελον.

[3] Winer-Schmiedel, § 13, 14 (p. 112 f.); Biass, *Gramm.*, p. 45 f. [Eng. Trans., p. 46.]

[4] The editors accentuate προεγάμουσαν.

The termination -αν for -ασι in the 3rd plural perfect[1] occurs in BU. 597₁₉ (Fayyûm, 75 A.D.) γέγοναν (Rom. 16[7] א AB, Rev. 21[6] א[c] A) and 328 i.₆ (Fayyûm, 138-139 A.D.) μετεπιγέγραφαν.[2]

The termination -ες for -ας in the 2nd singular perfect and aorist[3] is found with remarkable frequency in the badly-written private letter BU. 261 (Fayyûm, 2nd-3rd cent. A.D.?): line 14 δέδωκες, 17 ἤρηχες (= εἴρηκες), 23 σὺ οἶδες, 24 f. ἔγραψες: the last form occurs also in the private letter 38₁₄ (Fayyûm 1st cent. A.D.).

δίδωμι:[4] The Papyri yield a number of examples of δίδω (διδῶ?) for δίδωμι—all from the Fayyûm. In BU. 261₂₁ (2nd-3rd cent. A.D.?, badly written) is found οὐδὲν ἐγὼ δίδω (διδῶ?),[5] 97₂₁ (201-202 A.D.) ἐπιδίδω,[6] 38₁₉ (1st cent. A.D.) δίδι as 3rd sing. pres. (= δίδει).—δ ι δ ῶ (= διδόω) is indicated by 86₂₂ (155 A.D.) διδοῦντος, and already by 44₁₅ (102 A.D.) ἀνδιδοῦντα[7] (but in line 14 διδόντα).

τίθημι. According to Winer-Schmiedel, § 14, note 11 (p. 121) there appear to be no indubitable derivations from a verb τίθω. But the well-written Papyrus BU. 326 i.₁₆

---

[1] Winer-Schmiedel, § 13, 15 (p. 113); Blass, Gramm., p. 45. [Eng. Trans., p. 46.]

[2] Conversely, -ασι for -αν in BU. 275₅ (Fayyûm, 215 A.D.) ἐπῆλθασι.

[3] Winer-Schmiedel, § 13, 16 (p. 113 f.); Blass, Gramm., p. 46. [Eng. Trans., p. 46.]

[4] Winer-Schmiedel, § 14, 11 ff. (p. 121 f.); Blass, Gramm., p. 48 f. [Eng Trans., p. 49 f.] Neither writer takes notice of 1 Cor. 7[3] A ἀποδιδέτω.

[5] It is true that line 23 has μὴ διδι αὐτῇ (cf. Supplement, p. 358). The editor, F. Krebs, accentuates δίδι, and explains thus: "l. [read] δίδει = δίδωσι". The present writer considers this impossible: δίδι (= δίδει) is rather an imperative of δίδωμι, formed in accordance with τίθει. Similarly BU. 602₆ Fayyûm, 2nd cent. A.D.) ἐδείδι (= ἐδίδει) on the analogy of ἐτίθει. Other assimilations to the formation of τίθημι in the Fayyûm Papyri are: 360₈ (108-109 A.D.) the imperative παράδετε, and 159₃ (216 A.D.) ἐξέδετο; the latter form already in PER. ccxxii. ₁₈ (2nd cent. A.D.).

[6] ἐπιδίδω could also be an abbreviation of ἐπιδίδωμι, specially as it occurs in a common formula. Hence the editor, U. Wilcken, writes ἐπιδίδω(μι).

[7] Apocope of the preposition, like BU. 86₇ (Fayyûm, 155 A.D.) καλείψῃ; in contrast with line 12 of the same Papyrus καταλείψῃ (not, however, παδώσω BU. 39₂₀ which has been corrected, in accordance with a more exact reading p. 354, to ἀποδώσω). Cf. Winer-Schmiedel, § 5, 22 c, note 47 (p. 53).

(Fayyûm, 189 A.D.) yields παρακατατίθομαι.—τ ι θ ῶ (= τιθέω) is indicated by *BU.* 350 13 (Fayyûm, reign of Trajan) ὑπο-τιθοῦσα, which, however, perhaps depends in this place merely on euphony; it stands in the following connection: ἐνοικοδομοῦσα καὶ ἐπισκευάζουσα καὶ πολοῦσα *sic* καὶ ὑποτι-θοῦσα καὶ ἑτέροις μεταδιδοῦσα.

δύνομαι [1] is often attested in the Fayyûm Papyri: *BU.* 246 10 (2nd-3rd cent. A.D.), 388 ii. 8 (2nd-3rd cent. A.D.), 159 5 (216 A.D.) δυνόμενος,—also 614 20 (217 A.D.).   In 348 8 (156 A.D.) there occurs ὡς ἂν δύνοι, which must certainly be 3rd singular; this would involve a δύνω. [2]

---

[1] Winer-Schmiedel, § 14, 17 (p. 123); Blass, *Gramm.*, p. 48. [Eng. Trans., p. 49.]

[2] The particular sentence (from a private letter) is not quite clear to the author, but he considers it impossible that the form could be derived from the well-known δύνω.   F. Krebs also places δύνοι in connection with δύναμαι in his index.

III.

NOTES ON THE VOCABULARY AND THE SYNTAX.

1. So-called Hebraisms.

ἀναστρέφομαι and ἀναστροφή.

Quite a multitude of examples, all of the Roman period (after 133 B.C.), of the moral signification of the verb,[1] which is not to be explained as a Hebraism, and to which attention was called above, p. 88, are yielded by the since-published second volume of the Inscriptions of Pergamus. Putting aside *Perg.* 252 39, where the word is got only by a violent restoration, the author would refer to 459 5 καλῶς καὶ ἐνδόξως ἀναστραφῆναι (*cf.* Heb. 13 18 καλῶς ἀναστρέφεσθαι, James 3 13, 1 Pet. 2 12 καλὴ ἀναστροφή), 470 4 [ἐν πᾶσ]ιν ἀνεσ[τραμ]μένον ἀξίως [τῆς πόλεως] and 496 5 ff. [ἀ]ναστρεφομένην καλῶς καὶ εὐσεβῶς καὶ ἀξίως τῆς πόλεως (*cf.* the Pauline περιπατεῖν ἀξίως c. gen.); also 545 ἀναστραφέν[τα]. *IMAe.* 1033 7 f. (Carpathus, 2nd cent. B.C. ?) φιλοδόξως ἀνέ[σ]τραπ[ται] may be still older than any of these. Fränkel, p. 16, cites further *CIG.* 1770 (letter of Flaminin) οἱ οὐκ ἀπὸ τοῦ βελτίστου εἰωθότες ἀναστρέφεσθαι.[2]

For ἀναστροφή, in the ethical sense, *IMAe.* 1032 6 (Carpathos, 2nd cent. B.C.) should be noted.

εἰς.

The use of εἰς for expressing the purpose of donations, collections or other expenditure (discussed above, p. 117 f.),

---

[1] It is significant that Thayer should note this usage in Xenophon (*An.* 2, 5, 14) and Polybius (1, 9, 7 ; 74, 13 ; 86, 5, etc.), while *Clavis* 3 does not.

[2] P. Wendland, *Deutsche Litteraturzeitung*, 1895, col. 902, refers further to Schenkl's Index to Epictetus, and to Viereck, *Sermo graecus*, p. 75.

which is not to be interpreted as a Hebraism, is confirmed
also by the later Papyri. For example, in the very comprehensive account *BU.* 34 (date and place uncertain), the
separate items of expenditure are very often introduced by
εἰς. τὰς εἰς τὸν Μάρωνα . . . . οἰκονομίας, *PER.* i. 11 (Fayyûm,
83-84 A.D.) is correctly translated by the editor as *the endorsement of Maron's account;* cf. *PER.* xviii. 12 f. (Fayyûm,
124 A.D.) εἰς ἄλλον τινὰ γράφειν διαθήκην, *to draw up a will in
favour of any other person.* Leaving aside the New Testament passages, we find this εἰς elsewhere as well; the usage is
therefore no mere Egyptian idiom. Thus, in a list of donors
to a religious collection, *Perg.* 554 (after 105 A.D.), the purpose
of the various items of expenditure is expressed by εἰς,[1] *e.g.*,
line 10, εἰς ταυροβόλιον. The abrupt εἰς in the expenses-list
Perg. 553 K (reign of Trajan) may also be mentioned as an
example. The author has found this εἰς in other Inscriptions
as well.

ἐρωτάω.

Cremer[8], p 415, says: "in New Testament Greek also
request . . . . . . — an application of the word which
manifestly arose through the influence of the Hebr. שָׁאַל ".
But, as against this, Winer-Lünemann, p. 30, had already made
reference to some profane passages,[2] which *Clavis*,[3] p. 175,
appropriates and extends—though with the accompanying
remark, " *ex imitatione hebr.* שָׁאַל, *significatu ap. profanos
rarissimo* ". The author has already expressed his disagree-
ment with the limitation of this really vulgar-Greek usage
to the Bible.[3] The Fayyûm Papyri yield new material:
ἐρωτᾶν *request* occurs in *BU.* 50 9 (115 A.D.), 423 11 (2nd cent.
A.D.), 417 2 f. (2nd-3rd cent. A.D.), 624 15 (reign of Diocletian).

---

[1] Fränkel, p. 353.

[2] Winer-Schmiedel, § 4, 2 *a* (p. 27), counts this usage among the "imperfect" Hebraisms. It would be better to abolish this term from Winer's
Grammar.

[3] Below, p. 290 f., with a reference to the examples of Wilamowitz-Moellendorff in Guil. Schmidt, *De Flavii Iosephi elocutione observationes criticae*,
Fleck. *Jbb. Suppl.* xx. (1894), p. 516.

To these should be added the adjuration-tablet of Adrumetum (probably belonging to the 2nd cent. A.D.), line 31.
(See p. 276.)

καθαρὸς ἀπό τινος.

The erroneous idea that this construction (Acts 20 [26] and
in Old Testament passages) is a Hebraism, has been long
refuted not only by passages from late-Greek writers, but
even by Demosthenes, 59 73.[1]   That the error, in spite of all,
is still prevalent is shown by *Clavis* [3], p. 217, "*ex hebr. add. ἀπό
τινος, ... ap. nativos Graecos c. nudo gen.*".   It will therefore do no harm to supplement the extra-biblical examples
by the following passages from the Fayyûm Papyri: *BU.*
197 14 (17 A.D.), 177 12 (46-47 A.D.), 112 11 (*ca.* 60 A.D.), 184 25
(72 A.D.), *PER.* i. 16 (83-84 A.D.), *BU.* 536 6 (reign of Domitian),
193 19 (136 A.D.), 240 24 (167-168 A.D.), *PER.* ccxx. 10 (1st or
2nd cent. A.D.), *BU.* 94 13 (289 A.D.).   In all these passages,
which are distributed over a period of nearly three hundred
years, we find the formula *free of a money-debt*.   To these
there may be added a still older example in the Inscription
of Pergamus 255 7 ff. (early Roman period), ἀπὸ δὲ τάφου καὶ
ἐκφορ[ᾶς] . . . καθαροὶ ἔστωσαν.

ὄνομα.

1. This word occurs in Acts 1 [15], Rev. 3 [4], 11 [13], with
the meaning of *person*.   *Clavis* [3], p. 312, explains this usage
ex imitatione hebr. שֵׁמוֹת.   But the hypothesis of a Hebraism
is unnecessary; the Papyri demonstrate the same usage,
which, of course, sufficiently explains itself: *BU.* 113 11 (143
A.D.) ἑκάστῳ ὀνόματι παρα(γενομένῳ), 265 18 (Fayyûm, 148
A.D.) [ἑκάστῳ ὀνόμ]ατι παράκ[ει]ται,[2] 531 ii. 9 t. (Fayyûm, 2nd

---

[1] The passage in Demosthenes had been cited by G. D. Kypke, *Observationes sacrae*, Wratisl. 1755, ii., p. 109; after him by Winer for example (*e.g.*,
4[1836], p. 183, 7[1867], p. 185, and Blass, *Gramm.*, p. 104 [Eng. Trans., p.
106].   The author's attention was called to Kypke by Wendt on Acts 20 [26]
(Meyer, iii. 6/7 [1888], p. 444.   The right view is advocated also by Cremer [8],
p. 489.

[2] In regard to both of these passages, Professor Wilcken of Breslau
observes, in a letter to the author, that ὄνομα is there used "for the possessor

cent. A.D.) τὰ περιγεινόμενα^{sic} ἐνοίκια πρὸς ἕκαστον ὄνομα
τῶν τρυγώντων γραφήτωι ^{sic}, 388 i. 16 (Fayyûm, 2nd-3rd cent.
A.D.) ταβέλλαι δύ[ο] ἐλευθερώσεων τοῦ αὐτοῦ ὀνόματος δια-
φόροις χρόνοις (cf. ii. 35 πῶς [ο]ῦν τοῦ Εὐκαίρου δύ[ο] ταβέλλαι
ἐλευθερίας εὐ[ρί]σ[κον]ται ;).

2. To the authorities for the formula εἰς τὸ ὄνομά
τινος, given on p. 146 ff. above, may be added BU. 256 5
(Fayyûm, reign of Antoninus Pius) τὰ ὑπάρχοντ[α] εἰς ὄνομα
δυεῖν ^{sic}, that which belongs to the name (i.e., property or means)
of the two; here the form is used in the same way as in the
expression (belonging to Asia Minor) κτηματώνης εἰς τὸ τοῦ
θεοῦ ὄνομα, p. 147 above. For other examples see ThLZ.
xxv. (1900), p. 73 f. The formula ἐπ᾽ ὀνόματος is similarly
used in the Papyri—BU. 226 15 f. (Fayyûm, 99 A.D.) πάντων
τῶν ἐπ᾽ ὀνόματος τῆς μητρός μου . . . εἰς αὐτοὺς ὑπαρχόντων ; [1]
further, BU. 231 9 (Fayyûm, reign of Hadrian) should possibly be restored thus : [ἐπ᾽ ὀνό]ματος τῆς θυγατρός σου.[2]

3. On p. 147 above, the conjecture was made that the non-
discovery hitherto of the phrase ποιεῖν τι ἐν τῷ ὀνόματί τινος in
any extra-biblical source is to be attributed solely to chance.
But the author has meanwhile met with it—not, indeed, in
the construction with ἐν, but in the very similar one with
the dative alone. The oath of fealty to the Emperor Cali-
gula taken by the inhabitants of Assos in Troas (Ephemeris
epigraphica, v. [1884], p. 156, 37 A.D.) is signed by 5 πρεσ-
βευταί, after which group of names occur the concluding

of the name, the *person*," but that the translation *name* answers quite well.
—The present writer would, with Luther, render the word by *name* in the
New Testament passages also, so that the special character of the usage
might not be obliterated.

[1] In *Corpus Papyrorum Raineri*, i. 1, 270, note, L. Mitteis translates
this passage : alles Vermögen meiner Mutter ist in seinem Besitz [all the property of my mother is in his possession].

[2] A different case is 153 27 (Fayyûm, 152 A.D.) ἀπογράψασθαι ἐν τῇ τῶν
καμήλων ἀπογραφῇ . . . ἐπ᾽ ὀνόματος αὐτῶν. What we have here is the entering
on the list of a camel *under the name* of its new owner. Still, that which is
specified as ἐπ᾽ ὀνόματος of any one is, in point of fact, his property. One
sees that here, as also in the above formulæ, there can be no thought of a
new *meaning* of the word, but only of a realising of its pregnant fundamental
meaning.

words : οἵτινες καὶ ὑπὲρ τῆς Γαίου Καίσαρος Σεβαστοῦ Γερμανικοῦ σωτηρίας εὐξάμενοι Διὶ Καπιτωλίῳ ^{sic} ἔθυσαν τῷ τῆς
πόλεως ὀνόματι. Here we have most likely the same usage
as in James 5¹⁰ A ἐλάλησαν τῷ ὀνόματι κυρίου ;¹ and the
hypothesis of Cremer ³, p. 712, viz., that " it was Christianity
which first introduced the use of the phrase ' in the name of,
etc.,' into occidental languages " should thus be rejected.

2. SO-CALLED " JEWISH-GREEK " " BIBLICAL " OR " NEW TESTAMENT " WORDS AND CONSTRUCTIONS.

The articles which follow should make it clear that the
non-occurrence in extra-biblical literature of many biblical
words is a matter solely of statistical contingency. (In some
cases the question, moreover, is not one of non-occurrence at
all, but merely of non-notification.) Many of this particular
class of words have been already noticed in the second treatise
of this work. The author observes, further, that reference
is made by Blass, *Grammatik des Neutest. Griechisch*, p. xii.
[see Eng. Trans., p. 127, note], to ἔναντι in Inscriptions ; p.
69 [Eng. Trans., p. 68], to φιλοπρωτεύω in an Inscription,
and p. 68 [Eng. Trans., p. 68] to φρεναπάτης in a Papyrus.
The number of " biblical " or " New Testament " words
will certainly still further melt away—and without prejudice
to the distinctive inner character of biblical ideas.

ἀγάπη.

In the German edition of *Bibelstudien* (Marburg, 1895),
p. 80, there was cited, in reference to ἀγάπη, the Paris
Papyrus 49 (between 164 and 158 B.C.), in which citation
the author adopted the reading of the French editor (1865).
Subsequently, Blass, in his critique,² questioned the accuracy
of this reading, and, in virtue of the facsimile, proposed
ταραχήν instead of ἀγάπην. The facsimile is not a photo-
graphic one ; the author considered that ἀγάπην was, at
least, not impossible. Blass, however, is most probably
right. A re-examination of the passage in the original, as

---

¹ But not in Mark 9³⁸ A and Matt. 7²², where the dative is instrumental.
² *ThLZ.* xx. (1895), p. 488.

has been kindly communicated to us by M. Pierret, the
Conservator of Egyptian Antiquities in the Louvre, has had
the result "*qu'on ne trouve, dans le papyrus N⁰ 49, aucune
trace du mot ἀγάπην, mais seulement à la ligne 6 la vraisemblance
d'une lecture ταραχήν*". The author, therefore, has no hesitation in here withdrawing his reference to this Papyrus.[1]
[The note in question has, of course, been omitted in this
translation.]

Nevertheless, this does not imply the removal of the
doubt as to whether the word is a specifically " biblical "
one, and the conjecture that it was used in Egypt can now
be confirmed. Only, one does not need to go to Paris in
order to find the word. The statements of v. Zezschwitz,[2]
Clavis[3] and Cremer[4] notwithstanding, it is found in Philo, to
which fact, so far as the present writer is aware, Thayer
alone has called attention in his lexicon.[5] In *Quod Deus
immut.* § 14 (M., p. 283), it is said : παρ' ὅ μοι δοκεῖ τοῖς
προειρημένοις δυσὶ κεφαλαίοις, τῷ τε "ὡς ἄνθρωπος" καὶ τῷ
"οὐχ ὡς ἄνθρωπος ὁ θεός,"[6] ἕτερα δύο συνυφῆναι ἀκόλουθα καὶ
συγγενῆ, φόβον τε καὶ ἀγάπην. Here then we have ἀγάπη,
and in such manner as to repel the supposition that Philo
adopted the word from the LXX. Further, ἀγάπη is here
used already in its religious-ethical sense, for the connection
shows that the reference is to *love to God*, the antithesis of
which is *fear of God* (cf., in the next sentence, ἢ πρὸς τὸ
ἀγαπᾶν ἢ πρὸς τὸ φοβεῖσθαι τὸν ὄντα. The analogy to 1 John
4 18 is quite apparent.

---

[1] *Cf.* W. M. Ramsay, *The Expository Times*, vol. ix., p. 567 f.

[2] *Profangraecitaet und biblischer Sprachgeist*, Leipzig, 1859, p. 62:
"'Αγάπη does not occur as a genuine term, so far as the references in the Lexica
avail, in the κοινή either ".

[3] *Clavis*[3], p. 3 : " *In Philone et Josepho legi non memini* " (after Bret-
schneider).

[4] Cremer[8], p. 14, " this word, apparently formed by the LXX, or, at any
rate, in their circle (Philo and Josephus do not have it) . . . . .".

[5] The present writer had not the book by him when he wrote the article
ἀγάπη in the German *Bibelstudien*.

[6] The passage relates to the apparent contradiction between LXX Deut.
1 31 and Numb. 23 19.

For the sake of completeness it may be permitted to notify still another passage, which, however, does not afford an altogether certain contribution to the answering of our question either way. In a scholion to Thuc. ii. 51, 5, we find φιλανθρωπίας καὶ ἀγάπης as a gloss to ἀρετῆς (ed. Poppo, ii. 2, p. 92, or A. Schoene [1874], p. 209 25). Our opinion of the gloss will depend upon our answer to the question whether the glossator was a Christian or not. But no certain answer to this question can be given. In the present state of scholiastic research it is impossible to speak definitely about the age of any particular scholium or of any philological term in the scholia. Still, the sort of gloss which savours of interlinear explanation, and which explains only by remodelling the expression, has always against it (in the opinion of Professor G. Wissowa of Halle, who has most willingly furnished us with this information) the disadvantage of late age.

ἀκατάγνωστος.

Hitherto authenticated only in 2 Macc. 4 [47], Tit. 2 [8] and in ecclesiastical writers. *Clavis* [3], p. 14, is content to confirm this state of the matter; Cremer [8], p. 245, isolates the word thus: "only in biblical and ecclesiastical Greek". The formation and meaning of the word, however, support the hypothesis that we have to reckon here with a matter of statistical chance. In point of fact, the word occurs in the epitaph *CIG.* 1971 *b* 5 (Thessalonica, 165 A.D.), applied to the deceased; also in the poetical epitaph in the Capitoline Museum at Rome *IGrSI.* [1] 2139 3 (date ?), applied to the deceased (ἄμεμπτος, ἀκατάγνωστος) [2]; finally, also in a deed of tenure, which certainly belongs to the Christian period, but which can hardly be deemed a memorial of "ecclesi-

[1] *Inscriptiones Graecae Siciliae et Italiae additis Graecis Galliae Hispaniae Britanniae Germaniae inscriptionibus consilio et auctoritate Academiae Litterarum Regiae Borussicae edidit* Georgivs Kaibel, . . . *Berolini* 1890.

[2] Kaibel, *Epigrammata Graeca ex lapidibus conlecta*, Berlin, 1878, p. 295 f., treats the Inscription under No. 728 as a Christian one, but without giving his reasons.

astical" Greek in Cremer's sense: *BU.* 308 8 (Fayyûm, Byzant. period) ἐπάναγκες ἐπιτελέσωμεν τὰ πρὸς τὴν καλλιερ-γίαν τῶν ἀρουρῶν ἔργα πάντα ἀκαταγνώστ[ως].[1]

ἐάν.

1. A. Buttmann [2] observes in reference to *ἐάν* with the indicative [3]: "It cannot be denied, indeed, that the examples of this construction are almost as nothing compared with the mass of those which are grammatically regular, whatever doubts may be raised by the fact that hardly a single quite trustworthy passage with the indicative has come down to us". But he is right, with regard to those passages in which both the indicative and the subjunctive appear in the text, in attributing the latter to the copyists. Only a very few absolutely certain examples, belonging to a relatively early period, can be pointed out. The following have been noticed by the author in Papyri: *BU.* 300 5 (Fayyûm, 148 A.D.) κἂν δέον ἦν,[4] 48 13 (Fayyûm, 2nd-3rd cent. A.D.) ἐὰν δὲ μὴ ἐνῆν [5]; in each case the form is properly a perfect.[6] Further, with the present or future indicative following, we have the Paris Papyrus 18 (imperial period?),[7] in the middle, ἐὰν μαχουσιν μετ᾽ ἐσοῦ οἱ ἀδελφοί σου, according as we accentuate μάχουσιν or μαχοῦσιν [8]; *BU.* 597 6 (Fayyûm, 75 A.D.) καὶ ἐὰν εἰπόσει,[9]

---

[1] So the editor, Wilcken, restores; the author considers that ἀκατά-γνωστ[οι] is also possible.

[2] *Grammatik des neutestamentlichen Sprachgebrauchs*, Berlin, 1859, p. 192.

[3] Strictly speaking, this point is out of place in the above paragraph, but it is discussed here in order to avoid breaking up the article ἐάν.

[4] The editor's proposal to change ἦν into ᾖ seems to the present writer wrong. *Cf.* also the passage *B U.* 543 5 quoted below.

[5] ἐάν with the subjunctive is found three times (lines 4. 12. 17) in the same Papyrus.

[6] Winer-Lünemann, p. 277, β at the foot.

[7] *Notices et extraits des manuscrits de la bibliothèque impériale*, vol. xviii., part 2, Paris, 1865, p. 232 f.

[8] For μάχω cf. the analogous cases in Winer-Lünemann, top of p. 244.

[9] This peculiar form (developed from εἶπον?) must in any case be inter-preted as indicative.

cf. 607 23 (Fayyûm, 163 A.D.) ὁπόταν ¹ ἀναιρ[ο]ῦνται and the passages cited below, 86 19, 22.

2. Winer-Lünemann, p. 291, writes as follows, in reference to the frequent ἐάν instead of ἄν in relative clauses: "In the text of the N. T. (as in the LXX and the Apocrypha . . ., now and then in the Byzantine writers, . . .), ἄν after relatives is frequently displaced, according to most authorities and the best, by ἐάν [here the passages are given], as not seldom in the Codices of Greek, even of Attic, writers. Modern philologists . . . substitute ἄν throughout. . . . The editors of the N. T. have not as yet ventured to do this, and in point of fact ἐάν for ἄν may well have been a peculiarity of the popular language in later (if not, indeed, in earlier) times." A. Buttmann, p. 63 f., is of a like opinion: "We may at least infer with certainty, from the frequent occurrence of this substitution, that this form, certainly incorrect (but still not quite groundless), was extant among later writers". Schmiedel ² also recognises this ἐάν as late-Greek. But even in 1888 Grimm, *Clavis*,³ p. 112, had explained it "*ex usu ap. profanos maxime dubio*". The case is extremely instructive in regard to the fundamental question as to the character of the language of the Greek Bible. That this small formal peculiarity, occurring abundantly ³ in the Greek Bible, should be, as is said, very doubtful among "profane" writers, is conceivable only on the view that "biblical Greek" constitutes a philological-historical magnitude by itself. If, however, we take the philological phenomena of the Bible out of the charmed circle of the

---

¹ ὁπόταν and ὅταν with the future indicative in the Sibyllists are treated of by A. Rzach, *Zur Kritik der Sibyllinischen Orakel, Philologus*, liii. (1894), p. 283.

² *HC.* ii. 1 (1891), p. 98, *ad loc.* 1 Cor. 6¹⁸.

³ In the LXX in innumerable passages (H. W. J. Thiersch, *De Pentateuchi versione Alexandrina libri tres*, Erlangen, 1841, p. 108) ; in the Apocrypha, Ch. A. Wahl, *Clavis librorum V. T. Apocryphorum philologica*, Leipzig, 1853, p. 137 f., enumerates 28 cases ; in the N.T. Clavis ³ gives 17. Many other cases, without doubt, have been suppressed by copyists or editors.— U. von Wilamowitz-Moellendorff considers ὃ ἐάν, 3 John⁵, to be an "orthographic blunder" (*Hermes*, xxxiii. [1898], p. 531), but this is a mistake.

dogma of "biblical Greek," we may then characterise the
possible non-occurrence of "profane" examples of the present
phenomenon as, at most, a matter of accident. But the
Papyri prove that the biblical ἐάν—so far at least as regards
New Testament times [1]—was in very frequent use in Egypt;
they confirm in the most marvellous way the conjecture of
Winer and A. Buttmann. The New Testament is, in this
matter, virtually surrounded by a cloud of witnesses: the
author has no doubt that the Ptolemaic Papyri [2] and the
Inscriptions yield further material, which would similarly
substantiate the ἐάν of the LXX and the Apocrypha. On
account of the representative importance of the matter, a
number of passages from the Papyri [3] may be noted here,
which furnish, so to speak, the linguistic-historical framework for the New Testament passages: BU. 543 5 (Hawarah,
27 B.C.) ἢ ὅσων ἐὰν ἦν, PER. ccxxiv. 10 (Fayyûm, 5th-6th
cent. A.D.) ἢ ὅσων ἐνὰν �sⁱᶜ ᾖ,[4] BU. 197 10 (F., 17 A.D.) ἢ ὅσων
ἐὰν αἱρ[ῆται], ibid. 19 οἷς ἐὰν αἱρῆται, 177 7 (F., 46-47 A.D.) ἢ
ὅσων ἐὰν ὦσιν, PER. iv. 11 (F., 52-53 A.D.) ἢ ὅσων ἐὰν ὦσι,
ibid. 23 ὡς ἐὰν βούληται, BU. 251 6 (F., 81 A.D.) [ἀ]φ' ἧ[ς ἐ]ὰν
[ἀπ]αιτήσει �sⁱᶜ, PER. i. 19 (F., 83-84 A.D.) ὡς ἐὰν [βούλω]νται,
ibid. 26 ἢ ὅσαι ἐὰν ὦσι, BU. 183 8 (F., 85 A.D.) ἀφ' ἧς ἐὰν
ἀπαιτηθῇ, ibid. 19 ὅσα ποτὲ ἐὰν καταλείψῃ �sⁱᶜ, ibid. 25 οἷς ἐὰν
βούληται, 260 6 (F., 90 A.D.) ὁπόδε �sⁱᶜ ἐὰν αἱρῇ, 252 9 (F., 98
A.D.) ἀφ' ἧς [ἐὰ]ν ἀπα[ι]τ[η]θῇ, 538 8 (F., 100 A.D.) ἢ ὅσων ἐὰν
ὦσι, PER. clxxxviii. 20 (F., 105-106 A.D.) ὡς ἐὰν αἱρῶνται,
ibid. 31 ἢ [ὅσα]ι ἐὰν ὦσι, xi. 26 (F., 108 A.D.) ἃ[ς] ἐὰν αἱρῆται,

---

[1] It is only the Papyri of the (early and late) imperial period which
have been collated by the author in regard to this question.

[2] This conjecture is confirmed by a Papyrus in the British Museum,
from the Thebaid, belonging to the year 132 A.D.; given in Grenfell's *An
Alexandrian Erotic Fragment and other Greek Papyri chiefly Ptolemaic*, Oxford, 1896, No. xviii. 27, p. 40: καὶ ἐξ οὗ ἐὰν αἱρῆται.

[3] In almost every case the editors of the Berlin and the Vienna Papyri
prefer to read ἄν instead of ἐάν, but what we have to do with here is not really
a clerical error. ἐάν should be read in every case, just as it is written. In
Vol. II. of the Berlin documents, ἐάν has for the most part been allowed to
remain, and rightly so.

[4] Pap.: η. Wessely, p. 255, accentuates ᾖ ᵃⁱᶜ.

xxviii.7 (F., 110 A.D.) οἷα ἐὰν ἐγβῇ*sic*, *ibid.* 14 ἢ ὅσων ἐὰν ὦσι, BU. 101 9 (F., 114 A.D.) ἐξ οὗ ἐὰν αἱρῇ μέρους, *ibid.* 18 ἐφ᾽ ὃν ἐὰν . . . χρόνον, 444 7 (reign of Trajan) ἢ ὅσηι *sic* ἐὰν ᾖ, 113 4 (143 A.D.) πρὸς ἃς ἐὰν μεταξὺ ἀγάγωσι, 300 11 (F., 148 A.D.) οἷς ἐὰν πρὸς ταῦτα ἐπιτελέσῃ, 86 7. 13 (F., 155 A.D.) ὧν ἐὰν καταλείψῃ *sic*, *ibid.* 19 μέχρι ἐὰν . . . γένο[νται] *sic*, *ibid.* 22 ὀπ[ό]τε ἐὰν . . . γένονται *sic*, 80 [= 446] 14 (F., 158-159 A.D.) ὁπότε ἐὰ[ν αἱρῆται], *ibid.* 24 ὁπότε αἰὰν *sic* αἱρ[ῇ], 542 13 (F., 165 A.D.) ὃ ἐὰν αἱρῆται, 282 28 (F., after 175 A.D.) ἢ ὅσοι ἐὰν ὦσι, *ibid.* 36 ὡς ἐὰν αἱρῆται, 241 25 (F., 177 A.D.) [ἢ ὅσαι] ἐὰν ὦσι, *ibid.* 28 ἢ ὅσαι [ἐὰ]ν ὦσι, *ibid.* 38 ὡ[ς ἐ]ὰν αἱρῆται, 326 i. 10 (F., 189 A.D.) εἴ τι ἐὰν ἀν[θ]ρώπιν[ον] πά[θῃ], *ibid.* ii. 2 εἴ τι ἐὰν ἐγὼ . . . καταλίπω,[1] 432 ii. 2 9 (190 A.D.) ὅ,τι ἐὰν πράξῃς, 46 17 (F., 193 A.D.) ἐν οἷς ἐὰν βούλωμαι τόποις, 233 15 (F., 2nd cent. A.D.) ὅ,τι ἐὰν αἱρ[ῶνται], 236 4 (F., 2nd cent. A.D.) ἢ ὅσων ἐὰν ὦσι, 248 19 (F., 2nd cent. A.D.) ὡς ἐὰν δοκιμάζῃς, 33 16 (F., 2nd-3rd cent. A.D.) ὅπου ἐὰν θέλῃς, *ibid.* 21 ἢ διὰ οἵου ἐὰν εὕρῃς, 13 10 (F., 289 A.D.) ὡς ἐὰν αἱρῇ, 380 18 (F., 3rd cent. A.D.) μετὰ οὗ ἐὰν εὕρω, PER. xix. 23 (F., 330 A.D.) ὧν ἐὰν . . προσφωνήσῃ, BU. 364 10 (F., 553 A.D.) ὅσων ἐὰν ὦσιν, 303 12 (F., 586 A.D.) ὅσας ἐὰν ὦσιν, *ibid.* verso 1 ὅσων [ἐ]ὰν ὦσι.

Surveying this long list, one is struck by the fact that ἐάν is used in many constantly recurring formulæ, but, nevertheless, in spontaneously-formed clauses as well. We should also notice that the documents in which it occurs

---

[1] Proceeding from this twice-occurring εἰ with (ἐάν =) ἄν following, we can understand the peculiar negative εἰ μή τι ἄν in 1 Cor. 7 5. Schmiedel, HC. ii. 1 (1891), p. 100, explains thus: "εἰ μή τι ἄν = ἐὰν μή τι, as Origen reads". This equation ought not to be made; it only explains the meaning of the combination, but not its special syntactic character. εἰ μή τι ἄν has philologically nothing to do with the ἐάν in ἐὰν μή τι; ἄν, occurring here after εἰ, is rather exactly the same as if it occurred after a hypothetical relative, thus: *unless in a given case, unless perhaps.* The fact that the verb (say, ἀποστερῆτε or γένηται) has to be supplied is absolutely without importance for the grammatical determination of the case. —Blass, *Gramm.*, p. 211 [Eng. Trans., p. 216], counts εἰ μή τι ἄν among the combinations in which εἰ and ἐάν are blended together. We consider this hypothesis untenable, on account of the ἄν. A. Buttmann, p. 190, note, agrees with it, though indeed he also refers to the explanation which we consider to be the correct one, pp. 189, bottom line, and 190, first two lines. It is confirmed by the εἰ ἄν of the Papyrus.

are of very various kinds, and are not merely official papers, with regard to which we might always be justified in supposing that what we had there was only a peculiarity of the official language. The first and second centuries A.D. constitute its definite classical period ; it seems to become less frequent later. The author has met with the "correct" ἄν only in the following passages : *BU.* 372, ii. 17 (Fayyûm, 154 A.D.) ἐξ οὗ ἄν . . . προτεθῇ, 619 7 (F., 155 A.D.) ἄχρι ἂν ἐξετασθῇ, 348 5 (F., 156 A.D.) ὡς ἂν δοκειμάσῃς *sic*, *ibid.* 7, ὡς ἂν δύνοι *sic*, 419 11 (F., 276-277 A.D.) ἄχρις ἂν παραγένωμαι, 316 21 (Askalon in Phœnicia, 359 A.D.) ὃν ἂν αἱρῆτε *sic* τρόπον, *ibid.* 26. 32 καὶ ὅσον ἂν . . . . διαφέρῃ, 36 ὧν ἂν . . ἐπικτή-ση[τ]ε *sic* ; he does not of course guarantee that this is an exhaustive list. The hypothesis that ἐάν for ἄν is an Alexandrianism, in support of which the repeated ἄν of the last-mentioned document from Askalon might be put forward, seems to the present writer to be groundless. We must deal very circumspectly with all such tendencies to isolate We actually find ὅσοι ἐὰν συνζευχθῶσιν twice on a leaden tablet from Carthage (imperial period), *CIL.* viii. suppl. 12511.

Blass also refers to the use of ἐάν for ἄν in the Papyri, *Gramm.*, p. 61 [Eng. Trans., p. 61], where he cites *BU.* 12, 13, 33, 46, "etc." ; and also p. 212 [Eng. Trans., p. 217], where he cites the London Aristotelian Papyrus (end of 1st cent. A.D.).

εἰ (εἶ ?) μήν.

εἰ μήν occurs on good authority in Heb. 6 [14] (as already in LXX, *e.g.*, Ezek. 33 [27], 34 [8], 35 [6], 36 [5], 38 [19], Numb. 14 [28], Job. 27 [3], Judith 1 [12], Baruch 2 [29]) as used to express an oath. F. Bleek, *ad loc.*,[1] has gone into the matter most thoroughly ; he concludes his investigation as follows : "These examples [*i.e.*, from the LXX] prove that εἰ μήν in the present passage also was, for the Alexandrian Jews, no meaningless form, as Tholuck describes it ; and this case may serve to convince us how much we must be on our guard

---

[1] *Der Brief an die Hebräer erläutert*, part 2, Berlin, 1840, pp. 248-250.

against the temptation to reject forthwith a reading which
is vouched for by the agreement of the oldest authorities of
various classes and from various localities, on the alleged
ground of its meaninglessness, and without more strict inquiry as to whether it may not be established or defended
by biblical usage ". This "biblical" usage, according to
him, arises from " a blending together of the Greek form of
oath ἦ μήν with the wholly un-Greek εἰ μὴ, which originates
in a literal imitation of the Hebrew form " (top of p. 250).
Clavis[3], p. 118, and Winer-Schmiedel, § 5, 15 (p. 46), still
consider this blending as possible, unless, perhaps, it be
a case of itacistic confusion of η with ει, and ἦ μήν be
intended. But O. F. Fritzsche,[1] again, asserts this latter
supposition to be the only admissible one, and finds in the
opinion of Bleek an example of "how easily the obstinate
adherence to the letter of the traditional text leads to confusion and phantasy".

The whole matter is exceedingly instructive. How
plausible does an assertion like Bleek's, accepted from him
by so many others, seem to an adherent of the notion of
"biblical" Greek! On the one hand the Greek ἦ μήν, on
the other the Hebrew אִם לֹא = εἰ μή—by blending the two
the genius of the biblical diction constructs an εἰ μήν! True,
it might have made an ἦ μή from them, but it did not—it
preferred εἰ μήν. Pity, that this fine idea should be put out
of existence by the Papyri.[2] *BU*. 543 2 ff. (Hawarah, 28-27
B.C.) runs: ὄμνυμι Καίσαρα Αὐτοκράτορα θεοῦ υἱὸν εἰ μὴν
παραχωρήσειν . . . τὸν . . κλῆρο[ν], and we read, in *PER*.
ccxxiv. 1 ff. (Soknopaiu Nesos in the Fayyûm, 5-6 A.D.):
ὀμνύω sic [. . Καίσαρα] Αὐτοκράτορα θεοῦ υ[ἱὸν] . . . .
εἰ μὴν ἐνμένειν ἐν πᾶσι τοῖς γεγε[νημένοις κατὰ τὴ]ν γραφὴν
. . . . Here, in two mutually independent cases, we have εἰ

---

[1] *HApAT*. ii. (1853), p. 138; *cf.* i. (1851), p. 186.

[2] Further, the hypothesis of blending, considered purely by itself,
is inconceivable. If εἰ μήν is a Hebraising form, as regards one half of
it, then εἰ must have the sense of אִם. But then also the formula takes on
a negative sense, so that, *e.g.*, Hebr. 6 [14] would read: *Truly if I bless thee and
multiply thee*—[*scil.*: *then will I not be God*, or something similar].

(εἰ?) μήν as a form of oath—on Papyrus leaves which are some hundred years older than the original text of Hebrews, and which come from the same country in which the LXX and, most probably, the Epistle to the Hebrews, were written. Whatever, then, may be its relation to this εἰ (εἰ?) μήν, thus much, at all events, is clear : it is no specific phenomenon of biblical or of Jewish[1] Greek. It is either a case of mere itacistic confusion of η with ει,[2] as Fritzsche assumes in regard to the biblical, Krebs[3] and Wessely[4] in regard to the Papyrus passages; or else the expression is a peculiar form of oath, only authenticated as regards Egypt, about the origin of which the author does not venture to express an opinion. The abundant and excellent evidence in biblical MSS. for the ει in this particular combination,[5] and its occurrence, in the same combination, in two mutually independent Papyrus passages, deserve in any case our fullest consideration.

Blass, too, has not failed to notice the εἰ μήν, at least of the first passage, BU. 543 : he writes thus, Gramm., p. 9 [Eng. Trans., p. 9] : "Εἰ μήν for ἦ μήν, Heb. 6[14] (ℵABD[1]), is also attested by the LXX and Papyri [Note 4, to this word, is a reference to BU. 543, and to Blass, Ausspr. d. Gr.[3], pp. 33, 77] ; all this, moreover, properly belongs to orthoepy, and not to orthography ". Then on p. 60 [Eng. Trans., p. 60] : "ἦ, more correctly εἰ, in εἰ μήν," and p. 254 [Eng. Trans., p. 260] : "Asseverative sentences, direct and indirect (the latter infinitive sentences) are, in Classical Greek, intro-

---

[1] That the author of either Papyrus was a Jew is impossible.

[2] Thus, e.g., in the Berlin MS., immediately before, we have, conversely, χρηων for χρειων. (The document is otherwise well-written, like that of Vienna). Cf. also BU. 316 12 (Askalon, 359 A.D.) εἰ [= ἦ] καὶ εἴ τινι ἑτέρῳ ὀνόματι καλῖτε, and, conversely, 261 13 (Fayyûm, 2nd-3rd cent. A.D.) ἢ μή, without doubt for εἰ μή.

[3] Krebs writes εἰ in the Berlin MS., and adds the note : " l. [i.e., read] ἦ ".

[4] Wessely writes ει sic μην, and adds " l. [= read] ἦ μήν ".

[5] The note on p. 416 of the Etymologicum magnum, viz., ἦ · ἐπίρρημα ὀρκικόν · ὅπερ καὶ διὰ διφθόγγου γράφεται, has in itself no weight ; it but repeats the documentary information found in the passage quoted in connection with it, Hebr. 6[14] = Gen. 22[17].

duced by ἦ μήν, for which, in Hellenistic-Roman times, we find εἶ (accent?) μήν written; so LXX and consequently Heb. 6 [14]". The author cannot rightly judge from this as to the opinion of Blass concerning the spelling and the origin of the formula : in any case it is evident from the last-quoted observation that he does not consider the accentuation εἶ, which he seems to uphold, to be wholly free from doubt.

The above-quoted work of Blass, *Über die Aussprache des Griechischen* [3], Berlin, 1888, p. 33, shows that this formula of swearing is used also in the Doric Mystery-Inscription of Andania in the Peloponnesus (93 or 91 B.C.); the ὅρκος γυναικονόμου begins, in line 27, εἶ μὰν ἕξειν ἐπιμέλειαν περί τε τοῦ εἱματισμοῦ (Dittenberger, *Sylloge*, No. 388, p. 570). Blass observes regarding this : "*Εἶ μάν* seems, nevertheless, rather to be a *jussum speciale* of the language than to rest upon general rules".

ἐλαιών.

This word is undoubtedly found in Acts 1 [12], ἀπὸ ὄρους τοῦ καλουμένου ἐλαιῶνος; according to *Clavis* [3], elsewhere only in the LXX and Josephus : "*apud Graecos non exstat*". A matter of statistical chance: in the Berlin Papyri, vol. i., alone, ἐλαιών, olive-grove or olive-garden, occurs in nine different documents, of which *BU.* 37 5 (51 A.D.), 50 6 (115 A.D.) are of "New Testament" times; there may be added from vol. ii., *BU.* 379 12. 14 (67 A.D.), 595 10 (perhaps 70-80 A.D.). The Papyri named are all from the Fayyûm. The formation of the word is correctly given in *Clavis*, [3] [1] but it is a misleading half-truth to say: *terminatio ών est nominum derivatorum indicantium locum iis arboribus consitum, quae nomine primitivo designantur.* The termination -ών is used, quite generally, and not only in regard to the names of trees, to form words which designate the place where the particular objects are found. Equally strange is the identification with which Grimm supplements the above : *olivetum, locus oleis consitus, i.e.* [!] *mons olearum.* As if an ἐλαιών could not

---

[1] A. Buttmann, p. 20, refers to the similarly-formed Greek names of mountains (Κιθαιρών, Ἑλικών, etc.).

just as well be in a valley or anywhere else. ἐλαιών does
not, of course, *mean* " Olive-*Mount* " in Acts 1¹² either, but
" place of olives " or, if one prefers, " olive-wood ".¹ The
word is, doubtless, used here as a place-name ; but when a
particular mountain has the name ἐλαιών, it cannot be inferred therefrom that the lexicographer has a right to render
ἐλαιών by "*mons*" *olearum.* To do so would be quite as preposterous as to translate λεγιών, in Mark 5⁹, etc., by *legion
of demons.*

The circumstance that the word has been but scantily
authenticated hitherto must have had a share in sometimes
keeping it from its rights in another respect. Luke 19²⁹
reads, according to universal testimony, πρὸς τὸ ὄρος τὸ
καλούμενον ἐλαιων ; similarly 21³⁷, εἰς τὸ ὄρος τὸ καλούμενον
ἐλαιων, and,² in Mark 11¹, the Vaticanus reads πρὸς τὸ
ὄρος τὸ ἐλαιων, the Bobbiensis, *ad montem eleon ;* in Luke
22³⁹, Δ Sangallensis has εἰς τὸ ὄρος ἐλαιων. In the two
first-named passages, ἐλαιων was formerly taken as the
genitive plural of ἐλαία—probably universally, and accentu-
ated ἐλαιῶν. Schmiedel³ still considers this view possible,
and, in point of fact, the abbreviated form of speech which
we must in such case admit would not be without analogy :
in *BU.* 227₁₀ (Fayyûm, 151 A.D.) the author finds ἐν τόπ(ῳ)
Καινῆς Διώρυγος λεγο[μένῳ] ; similarly in 282₂₁ (Fayyûm,
after 175 A.D.), ἐν τόπῳ Οἰκίας Κανν[. λ]εγομένου *sic*, and in

---

¹ The author is not quite able to determine whether the mistake in procedure which underlies the above-named identification should be attributed
to W. Grimm, or whether it is a result of the erroneous view of Chr. G.
Wilke. In any case we may characterise the mistake in the pertinent words
of the latter (*Die Hermeneutik des Neuen Testaments systematisch dargestellt,*
zweiter Theil : *die hermeneutische Methodenlehre,* Leipzig, 1844, p. 181) :
" Exegetes are frequently in the habit of giving to this or the other word a
meaning which belongs only to some word which is *combined with it,* and
which does not apply to the word in question, either in this combination or
elsewhere ".

² The passages which follow, so far as the author knows, have in no case
been previously noticed.

³ Winer-Schmiedel, § 10, 4 (p. 93) ; the author perceives here that also
Niese and Bekker always write ἐλαιῶν in Josephus. The relevant passages
are cited in *Clavis*³, p. 140.

line 24 *l.*, ἐν τόπῳ Οἰκίας [1] Σα[. . . . .]λοχ [λεγο]μένου *sic* ;
PER. xxxviii. 9 (F., 263 A.D.) ἐν τόπῳ Ψιβιστάνεως λεγομ(ένῳ).
Nevertheless the case is a somewhat different one in the
Papyrus passages ; the author would only bring the above
forward in case of extreme necessity. But such a case would
only exist if ἐλαιων were necessarily a genitive. Now, since
we may without misgiving accentuate ἐλαιών [2], the question
alone remains whether this form, which is urged upon us
by Acts 1 [12], and which is *à priori* more probable than ἐλαιῶν
without the article (which never occurs in Luke), is grammatically tenable. And the answer must unquestionably
be in the affirmative. Not, indeed, as A. Buttmann, p. 20,
thinks, because the word is to be "treated altogether as
an *indeclinabile*, and therefore as a neuter," [3] but by reference
to the more lax usage of later Greek, [4] our knowledge of
which is enlarged by the Papyri. In these the formulæ, ὁ
καλούμενος, ἐπικαλούμενος, ἐπικεκλημένος, λεγόμενος, for introducing the names of persons and places, are extremely
frequent. As a rule these words are construed with the
proper case ; thus, in Vol. I. alone of the Berlin Documents,
we find some thirty examples of the years 121-586 A.D. But
in several passages from the Fayyûm Papyri, we may note
the more lax usage as well : in *BU.* 526 15 *l.* (86 A.D.) ἐν τῇ
Τεσσβῶβις λε[γομ]ένης *sic*, and 235 6 (137 A.D.) Π[α]σ[ί]ων[ος]
Ἀφροδισίου ἐπικ(αλουμένου) Κέννις, Τεσσβῶβις and Κέννις will
be nominatives ; in 277 i. 27 (2nd. cent. A.D.) we find ἐν
ἐποικίῳ Ἀμύντας, even without a participle, and in 349 7*l.*
(313 A.D.) there occurs ἐν κλήρῳ καλουμένου *sic* Ἀφρικιανός.

Thus hardly any further objections can be made to the
accentuation ἐλαιών in Luke 19 [29] and 21 [37] ; it should also be
applied in Mark 11 [1] B and Luke 22 [39] Δ. Another question

---

[1] The editor, Krebs, writes οἰκίας, but the word most likely belongs to the
name of the field, and should thus, according to our custom, be written with
a capital. The two names, in the author's opinion, should be set in the
Index *sub* Οἰκίας Κανν[.] and Οἰκίας Σα[. . . . .]λοχ.

[2] The later editors accentuate thus.

[3] This could be asserted only of the reading in Mark 11 [1] according to B

[4] Winer-Schmiedel, § 10, 4 (p. 93), and Winer [7], § 29, 1 (p. 171).

which appears to the author to deserve a more exact investigation, can only be slightly touched upon here, *viz.*, Which Greek reading for the name of the Mount of Olives is implied by the Vulgate? In Matthew, according to our texts, the Mount of Olives is always (21¹, 24³, 26³⁰) called τὸ ὄρος τῶν ἐλαιῶν, in the corresponding passages in the Vulgate *mons oliveti;* similarly (except in Luke 19²⁹, 21³⁷ and Acts 1¹², passages which on account of ἐλαιών require no explanation) in Luke 19³⁷ and John 8¹, where also *mons oliveti* corresponds to the ὄρος τῶν ἐλαιῶν. The matter would have no further importance if the Mount of Olives were always designated thus in the Vulgate. But in Mark always (11¹, 13³, 14²⁶) and Luke 22³⁹, as in Zech. 14⁴, τὸ ὄρος τῶν ἐλαιῶν is rendered by *mons olivarum.*[1] Does this state of the case not prompt the conjecture that the Vulgate somehow implies ἐλαιών in the first-mentioned passages? How is the Mount of Olives named in the other ancient versions?[2]

Blass, in his Grammar of New Testament Greek, several times expresses himself with regard to the question in a manner that evokes the present writer's strongest opposition. On p. 32 [Eng. Trans., p. 32] he says : " Ἐλαιών, *olive-mountain*, as a Greek translation, cannot be indeclinable; hence, like the τὸ ὄρος τ ῶ ν ἐλαιῶν elsewhere, so ὄρος (acc.) τὸ καλούμενον ἐλαιῶν (not Ἐλαιών) in Luke 19²⁹, 21³⁷; in Acts 1¹² all MSS., ὄρους τοῦ καλουμένου Ἐλαιῶνος, it is wrongly inflected for ἐλαιῶν; *cf.* § 33, 1 ". In § 33, 1 (p. 84) [Eng. Trans., p. 84 f.], again, we read: "When names are introduced without regard to the construction they seem sometimes to be put in the *nominative* case, instead of the case which the construction would require. . . . . . But otherwise they are always made to agree in case. . . . . Accordingly, it is incredible that the Mt. of Olives should be translated ὁ Ἐλαιών and that this word should be used as an indeclinable in Luke 19²⁹, 21³⁷ ὄρος (acc.) τὸ καλούμενον ἐλαιών, but we

---

[1] Tischendorf's Apparatus ignores the whole matter.

[2] Specially the Peschito must be taken into consideration ; *cf.* Winer, p. 171. So far as the author can decide, it implies ἐλαιών in all the passages in Luke. But he cannot guarantee this.

must read ἐλαιῶν (τὸ ὄρος τ ῶ ν ἐλ. in Luke 19 [37] and elsewhere), and, in the single passage Acts 1 [12] (ὄρους τοῦ καλουμένου) ἐλαιῶνος, we must correct to ἐλαιῶν (as also in
Josephus, *A.* 7, 9 ₂)." But, in the first place, the nominative
does not merely "seem" to be used sometimes in a more lax
way : it actually *is* sometimes so used : to the already well-
known biblical and extra-biblical passages there are to be
added the above-quoted examples from the Papyri. "But
otherwise they are always made to agree in case,"—without
doubt! For that more lax usage of the nominative is of
course an exception. But it cannot be doubted that the
exception is possible. Hence it does not seem particularly
convincing that Blass should base upon his "otherwise
always " the opinion : "Accordingly it is incredible that the
Mt. of Olives should be translated ὁ Ἐλαιών, and that this
word should be used as an indeclinable". This sentence,
moreover, contains at the same time a slight but important
displacement of the problem. We have no concern whatever with the question whether ἐλαιών is used, in the passages
quoted, as an indeclinable word (*cf.* Blass, p. 32 "indecl."),
but only with the question whether, according to more lax
usage, the nominative is used there instead of the proper
case.[1] Why should the more lax usage not be possible here ?
Had it been, indeed, the acceptance of the more lax usage of
the nominative in Luke 19 [29] and 21 [37] *only*, which compelled
us to admit ἐλαιών into the New Testament lexicon, then
we might have had our doubts. But the word comes to us
in Acts 1 [12] on the unanimous testimony of all authorities,
and, moreover, in a form which is not liable to doubt, *viz.*,
the genitive. We may well admire the boldness with which
Blass here corrects ἐλαιῶνος into ἐλαιῶν, but we are unable
to follow his example.

[1] To mention a similar case : When we read the title of a book, *e.g.*,
" Jesu Predigt in ihrem Gegensatz zum Judenthum. Ein religionsgeschicht-
licher Vergleich von Lic. W. Bousset, Privatdocent in Göttingen," we would
not say that Privatdocent is used as an indeclinable, but would decide that it
is one of the many cases of a more lax usage of the nominative in titles of
books. [In German we ought, properly speaking, to write "Privatdocent*en*,"
i.e., the dative.—TR.]

ἐνώπιον.

H. A. A. Kennedy[1] assigns the "adverb" ἐνώπιον, which is used in the Bible as a preposition, to the class of "biblical" words, *i.e.*, those belonging to the LXX and the N. T. only. According to A. Buttmann, p. 273, the "preposition" is "probably of Eastern" origin, and according to Winer-Lünemann, p. 201, "the preposition ἐνώπιον (לִפְנֵי) itself," may be said to belong almost entirely to "the Hebrew colouring of the language." These statements are not particularly informative; but, at all events, their purport is easily gathered, *viz.*, ἐνώπιον is a new formation of "biblical" Greek.[2] But *BU.* 578 (Fayyûm, 189 A.D.) attests the adverbial use of the word as regards Egypt. That the Papyrus is comparatively late does not signify. Line 1 runs: μετάδ(ος) ἐνώπι(ον) ὡς καθήκ(ει) τοῖς προστεταγμ(ένοις) ἀκολού[θως];[3] similarly line 7 t. might be restored thus: τοῦ δεδομένου ὑπομνήματος ἀντίγρ(αφον) μεταδοθήτω ὡς ὑπόκ[ειται ἐνώπιον]. It is evident that μεταδιδόναι ἐνώπιον is an official formula. Professor Wilcken of Breslau was good enough to give the author the following information on this point. He thinks that the formula, which is otherwise unknown to him, signifies *to deliver personally*: "the demand for payment shall be made to the debtor, face to face, for the greater security of the creditor".

It is not an impossible, but an improbable, supposition that this adverbial ἐνώπιον was used first of all with the genitive in the LXX: ἐ[ν]ώπιό[ν] τινων is already found in a Papyrus of the British Museum—from the Thebaid, and of the 2nd or 1st cent. B.C.—in Grenfell,[4] No. xxxviii. 11, p. 70.

---

[1] *Sources of New Testament Greek*, Edinburgh, 1895, p. 90.

[2] *Cf.* also Blass, *Gramm.*, p. 125 [Eng. Trans., p. 127 f.] " ἐνώπιον . . . . , κατενώπιον . . . . , ἔναντι . . , κατέναντι . . are derived from the LXX, and are unknown in profane authors even of later times ".—Yet on p. xii. Blass refers to ἔναντι as being profane Greek !!

[3] Also in line 6 the editor, Krebs, restores ἐν[ώπι]ον; in that case the combination μεταδιδόναι ἐνώπιον would be repeated here also. Wilcken, however, questions the correctness of this restoration, and proposes ἔν[τειλ]ον, as he has informed the author by letter.

[4] See above, p. 203, note 2.

ἐπιούσιος.[1]

In the discussion of this word, so far as we have
seen, no attention has been paid to an interesting observation of Grimm—not even by himself in the *Clavis*. He
makes a note to 2 Macc. 1[8] (προσηνέγκαμεν θυσίαν καὶ σεμί-
δαλιν καὶ ἐξήψαμεν τοὺς λύχνους καὶ προεθήκαμεν τοὺς ἄρτους)
as follows : "An arbitrary but, on account of Matt. 6[11] and
Luke 11[3], a remarkable amplification in three Codd.
Sergii, *viz.*, τοὺς ἐπιουσίους".[2] This signifies the *show-bread*
offerings. What connection has it with this reading ? What
can be learned of these MSS. (unknown to the author) ?

We are now (1900) in a position to answer these
questions through a friendly communication of Professor
Nestle of Maulbronn (*cf.* also B[lass], *Lit. Centralblatt*, 1898,
p. 1810).

The "Codices Sergii" are not, as one might expect,
Greek MSS., but are probably identical with the Armenian
codices mentioned in the *Praefatio ad Genesin* of Holmes [and
Parsons'] edition of the LXX, i., Oxford, 1798, p. v., which
were collated in 1773, in the Library of St. James at
Jerusalem, by the Armenian priest Sergius Malea (Novum
Testamentum Graece, *ed.* Tischendorf, 8th edition, vol. iii.,
by Gregory, p. 914). So far as we are aware, it has not
been shown that Malea collated Greek MSS. also. In 2
Macc. 1[8], Malea has probably re-translated an amplification
found in his Armenian MSS. into Greek. Thus there still
remain the following questions to be answered :—

1. How does this addition run in these Armenian MSS.?

2. Is this Armenian word identical with the Armenian
word for ἐπιούσιος in the Lord's Prayer ?

εὐάρεστος (and εὐαρέστως).

Cremer[8], p. 160 f. says of εὐάρεστος : "except in Xen.
Mem. 3, 5, 5 : δοκεῖ μοι ἄρχοντι εὐαρεστέρως *sic* [read εὐαρεστο-
τέρως] διακεῖσθαι ἡ πόλις—unless (contra Lobeck, *Phryn.*, p.

---

[1] The testimony of Origen renders it probable that this word is actually
a "biblical" one ; thus, strictly speaking, it should not be treated here.

[2] *HApAT.* iv. (1857), p. 35.

621) εὐαρεσκοτέρως should be read here as better suiting the meaning—only in bibl. and eccles. Greek. In any case, like its derivatives, belonging otherwise only to later Greek." As this passage from Xenophon possibly authenticates the adverb, it should not be mentioned in connection with the adjective; the adverb is specially discussed by Cremer, and, indeed, with the correct piece of information, p. 161 : "now and then in Epictetus ". The adverbial cases being put aside, Cremer's statement that εὐάρεστος is " only " biblical and ecclesiastical, seems to become more probable : though, indeed, the " otherwise " in the next sentence leaves open the possibility that the word also occurs elsewhere. All doubt as to the point, however, must disappear in the light of the passage from an Inscription of Nisyros (undated, pre-Christian? *Mittheilungen des athen. Instituts* 15, p. 134) line 11 f.: γενόμενον εὐάρεστον πᾶσι.[1] Moreover, the occurrence of the adverb in [Xenophon (?) and] Epictetus ought to have warned against the isolating of the adjective. εὐαρέστως is also found in *CIG.* 2885 = Lebas, *Asie*, 33 (Branchidae, B.C.): τελέσασα τὴν ὑδροφορίαν εὐαρέστως τοῖς πολείταις.

ἱερατεύω.

Cremer,[8] p. 462 : " not used in profane Greek; only occasionally in later writers, *e.g.*, Herodian, Heliodorus, Pausanias". Now, first of all, Josephus, the earliest of the " later writers," is omitted here. Next, it is a contradiction to say, first, that the word is not used, and then to bring forward a number of authors who *do* use it. It would have been more accurate to say : "used in later Greek". This would imply of course that it is no longer justifiable to isolate the word as a biblical one. Kennedy[2] draws the conclusions of the theory of Cremer by making the conjecture that since ἱερατεύω does not occur before the LXX, it was possibly formed by them and was transmitted from " Jewish-Greek " into the common

---

[1] The author is indebted for this and the following passage to a reference of Fränkel, p. 315, relating to *Perg. 461.*

[2] *Sources of N. T. Greek*, p. 119.

tongue.[1] In these circumstances it is very fortunate that the
Inscriptions yield quite a multitude of examples of this very
word, which go back to the age of the LXX, and infallibly
prove that one may safely say: "very common in later
Greek". Of the examples which occur in the two collections
of Inscriptions investigated by the author, *viz.*, those of the
Ægean Sea (fasc. i.) and of Pergamos, let it suffice here to
mention only the pre-Christian ones: IMAe. 808 2 (Rhodes,
3rd cent. B.C.), 811 (Rhodes, 3rd cent. B.C.), 63 1. 2 (Rhodes,
2nd cent. B.C.), 3 5 (Rhodes, 1st cent. B.C.); *Perg.* 167 3. 5. 15
(*ca.* 166 B.C.), 129 and 130 (before 133 B.C.).

καθαρίζω.

Cremer,[3] p. 490, asserts it to be a fact "that καθαρίζω
is found only in Biblical[2] and (seldom indeed) in ecclesiastical
Greek". But already *Clavis* 2. 3 quotes Joseph. *Antt.* 11, 5, 4,
ἐκαθάριζε τὴν περὶ ταῦτα συνήθειαν. More important still is
the occurrence of the word in the Inscriptions in a ceremonial
sense. The Mystery-Inscription of Andania in the Peloponnesus (93 or 91 B.C.) prescribes, in line 37 : ἀναγραψάντω
δὲ καὶ ἀφ' ὧν δεῖ καθαρίζειν καὶ ἃ μὴ δεῖ ἔχοντας εἰσπορεύεσθαι
(Dittenberger, *Sylloge* No. 388, p. 571). Further, there come
into consideration the directions (preserved in a double form[3]
in the Inscriptions) of Xanthos the Lycian for the sanctuary
of Men Tyrannos, a deity of Asia Minor, which he had founded:
CIA. iii. 74,[4] *cf.* 73 (found near Sunium, not older than the
imperial period). No unclean person shall enter the temple:
καθαριζέστω *sic* δὲ ἀπὸ σ[κ]όρδων κα[ὶ χοιρέων] κα[ὶ γυναικός],
λουσαμένους δὲ κατακέφαλα αὐθημερὸν εἰ[σπορεύ]εσθαι. In the
rough draught *CIA.* iii. 73 we find, further, καὶ ἀπὸ νεκροῦ
καθαρίσζεται *sic* δεκα[ταί]αν. The construction with ἀπό in
these instances is the same as in, *e.g.*, 2 Cor. 7 1, Hebr. 9 14,

[1] He certainly discusses the other possibility, *viz.*, that the word was
used previously to the LXX.

[2] Italics from Cremer.

[3] The one copy *CIA.* iii. 73 is the rough draught, so to speak: the
other has had the language corrected, and gives a longer text.

[4] = Dittenberger, *Sylloge* No. 379.

which latter passage is to be interpreted in the light of
the well-known idea, exemplified in the above-mentioned
Inscription and frequently elsewhere, *viz.*, that the touching
of a corpse renders one ceremonially unclean.[1]

κυριακός.

1. *Clavis*[3], p. 254, still describes the word as *vox solum
biblica et eccles.*, and A. Jülicher[2] maintains, indeed, that the
Apostle Paul invented this "new" word. On the other hand,
Cremer,[8] p. 583, notes the extra-biblical usage : "belonging to
the lord, the ruler, *e.g.*, τὸ κυριακόν, public or fiscal property;
synon. τὸ βασιλικὸν (rare)". This statement is probably to
be traced back to Stephanus, who cites "*Inscript. Richteri,
p. 416*". But since the publication of the Richter Inscriptions by Johann Valentin Francke (Berlin, 1830), κυριακός
has been comparatively frequently noticed in Inscriptions
and Papyri. We note the following cases. In the decree of
Ti. Julius Alexander, Prefect of Egypt, *CIG.* 4957 18 (El-
Khargeh or Ghirgé in the Great Oasis, 68 A.D), to which
Professor Wilcken of Breslau has called the author's attention, there occurs τῶν ὀφειλόντων εἰς κυριακὸν λόγον. The
κυριακὸς λόγος is the *Imperial Treasury* : the κύριος to which
the word relates is the Emperor[3] himself. Similarly, in *BU.*
1 15 f. (Fayyûm, 3rd cent. A.D.) we read : a[ἱ] καὶ δ[ια]γραφό-
μεναι εἰς τὸν κυριακὸν λόγον ὑπὲρ ἐπικεφαλίο[υ] τῶν ὑπεραι-
ρόντων ἱερέων, *and these* [the afore-mentioned sums] *have also
been paid into the imperial treasury for the poll-tax of the super-
numerary priests*[4] ; and, in *BU.* 266 17 f. (Fayyûm, 216-217
A.D.), we find the *imperial service* : εἰς τὰς ἐν Συρίᾳ κυρι[α]κὰς
ὑπηρεσίας τῶν γενναιοτάτω[ν] στρατευμάτων τοῦ κυρίου ἡμῶν
Αὐτοκράτορος Σε[ου]ήρου Ἀντωνίνου. But there are also

---

[1] Examples from classical antiquity in Fränkel, p. 188 f.

[2] *Einleitung in das Neue Testament*, 1st and 2nd edn. Freiburg and
Leipzig, 1894, p. 31.

[3] *Cf.*, in line 13 of the same edict, ταῖς κυριακαῖς ψήφοις.

[4] This [*i.e.*, the German] translation is from a letter of Wilcken. The
author has since found in *BU.* 620 15 (Fayyûm, 3rd cent. A.D.) προσετέθη ἐν
τοῖς κυριακοῖς λόγο[ις].

examples from Asia Minor—all of the imperial period. The
κυριακὸς φίσκος is mentioned in *CIG*. 3919 (Hierapolis in
Phrygia),[1] and is to be obtained by restoration in the Inscriptions *CIG*. 3953 *h* and *i*, also from Phrygia; it occurs also in
CIG. 2842 (Aphrodisias in Caria), *cf.* 2827. Finally, the
κυριακαὶ ὑπηρεσίαι are again found in *CIG*. 3490 (Thyatira
in Lydia).[2]

2. With reference to the early Christian designation of
Sunday as ἡ κυριακὴ ἡμέρα or, shortly, ἡ κυριακή,[3] Cremer,[8]
p. 583, observes that it appears to be analogous to the expression κυριακὸν δεῖπνον; H. Holtzmann[4] says still more
definitely: "The expression, moreover, is formed after the
analogy of δεῖπνον κυριακόν". If we are to seek for an
analogy at all, there is another, found in the idiom of the
imperial period, which seems to the author to be much more
obvious. He gives it here—though, of course, he would not
maintain that the Christians consciously took it as the pattern
for the formation of their own technical expression. In the
Inscription of Pergamus 374 B 4. 8 and D 10 (consecration of
the Pergamenian association of the ὑμνῳδοὶ θεοῦ Σεβαστοῦ
καὶ θεᾶς Ῥώμης, reign of Hadrian), the abbreviation "Σεβ."
occurs three times. Mommsen (in Fränkel, p. 265) gives the
following explanation of this: "Σεβ. in B 4. 8 and D 10 is
Σεβαστῇ, and affords a brilliant confirmation of the conjecture of Usener, *viz.*, that the first of every month was called
Σεβαστή in Asia Minor, just as the same is now established
in regard to Egypt; *cf. e.g.*, Lightfoot, *The Apostolic Fathers*,
part ii., vol. i., p. 695";[5] and Fränkel, p. 512, cites a new

---

[1] This is the Richter Inscription named above.

[2] θεῖος is also used in a corresponding manner: the θεῖαι διατάξεις, in
Pap. Par. 69 iii. 20 (Elephantiné, 232 A.D.), edited by Wilcken, *Philologus*,
liii. (1894), p. 83, *cf.* p. 95, are *imperial* arrangements.

[3] The earliest passages are given in A. Harnack's *Bruchstücke des
Evangeliums und der Apokalypse des Petrus*[2] (*TU.* ix. 2), Leipzig, 1893, p. 67.

[4] *HC.* iv[2] (1893), p. 318.

[5] The author is indebted to a communication of his friend B. Bess of
Göttingen for the information that Lightfoot, p. 694 f., gives the following
references for Σεβαστή: *CIG*. 4715 and *Add*. 5866 *c* (both of the time of Augus-

authority for Σεβαστή as *first day of the month* in the Inscription of Iasos,—given by Th. Reinach in the *Revue des Études Grecques*, vi. (1893), p. 159,—line 25, καὶ τὸν κατ᾽ ἐνιαυτὸν γενόμενον τόκον δώσει αἰεὶ τοῦ παρελθόντος ἐνιαυτοῦ μηνὶ πρώτῳ Σεβαστῇ. Just as the first day of the month was thus called *Emperor's day*, so the first day of the week—with all its significant connection with the Gospel history—would be named, by the Christians, the *Lord's day*. The analogy obtains its full importance when considered in relation to the entire usage of κύριος.[1]

λογεία.

We have succeeded in tracing this word in other quarters;[2] first, in *Pap.* Grenfell and Hunt (Oxford, 1897), No. xxxviii. 15 (81 B.C.) and *BU.* 515 7 f. (Fayyûm, 193 A.D.)—adopting the corrected reading of Wilcken given in vol. ii. of the Berlin MSS., p. 357; also in a compound: *BU.* 538 16 f. (Fayyûm, 100 A.D.) βοτανισμοὺς καὶ σιφονολογείας[3] καὶ τὴν ἄλλην γεωργικὴν [ὑπη]ρ[εσί]αν. We would next call attention to 2 Macc. 12 43. O. F. Fritzsche there reads: ποιησάμενός τε κατ᾽ ἀνδρολογίαν κατασκευάσματα εἰς ἀργυρίου δραχμὰς δισχιλίας ἀπέστειλεν εἰς Ἱεροσόλυμα προσαγαγεῖν περὶ ἁμαρτίας θυσίαν. Grimm[4] translates the first words *when by means of a collection he had provided himself with money-supplies*, and explains thus: "ἀνδρολογία, on the analogy of ξενολογία, *levying, collecting of soldiers for military service*, can here mean nothing else than *collectio viritim facta*: cf. λογία, which similarly does not occur in profane Greek, for συλλογή.

---

tus), 4957 (Galba) from Egypt; from Ephesus, an Inscription of the year 104 A.D.; from Traianopolis, Lebas and Waddington, 1676 (130 A.D.). The investigations of Usener are given in the *Bullettino dell' Instit. di Corr. Archeol.*, 1874, p. 73 ff.

[1] The author hopes at some future time to be able to make an investigation of the use of ὁ κύριος and ὁ κύριος ἡμῶν to designate deities and emperors in the imperial period.

[2] *Cf.* p. 142 ff. above.

[3] So reads the Papyrus: which σίφωνες are meant the author does not clearly understand.

[4] *HApAT.* iv. (1857), p. 183 f.

Since Codd. 44 and 71 give κατ᾽ ἄνδρα λογίαν (74 : κατ᾽ ἀνδρα-
λογίαν), and again Codd. 52, 55, 74, 106, and 243 omit
κατασκευάσματα, one might feel tempted to regard the former
as the original reading and the latter as a gloss to λογίαν
—unless perhaps κατασκευάσμ. was too uncommon a word,
and the more familiar συλλογή was a more obvious gloss ".
We cannot comprehend how Grimm can thus speak of
ἀνδρολογία [1] as analogous to ξενολογία : for this analogy
would precisely imply that ἀνδρολογία means *a levying of men.*
Quite as certainly must it be questioned that the word can
signify *a collection from each single man.* But since this signification is required by the connection, the reading κατ᾽ ἄνδρα
λογίαν (read λογείαν [2]) certainly deserves serious consideration ; on this view, κατασκευάσματα may quite well be
retained : *after he had taken a collection from each individual he
sent money to the amount of about 2000 drachmas of silver* [3] *to
Jerusalem.* [4]

νεόφυτος.

Used in LXX Ps. 127 [Hebr. 128] [3], 143 [144] [12], Is. 5 [7],
Job 14 [9], in its proper sense ; in 1 Tim. 3 [6], *novice.* Cremer [8],
p. 987, says : " a new growth ; elsewhere only in bibl. and
eccles. Greek (according to Poll. also used by Aristoph.) " ;
Clavis [3], p. 295, quotes the Biblical passages, adding only
"*script. eccles.*". But the reference of Pollux to Aristophanes
ought to have warned against isolating the word in this way,
a procedure not supported in the slightest by its form or meaning. νεόφυτος is found in *BU.* 563 i. 9. 14. 16, ii. 6. 12 (Fayyûm,
2nd cent. A.D.), [5] applied to newly-planted palm-trees (*cf.* LXX

---

[1] The edition of Van Ess, like Wahl in the *Clavis librorum V.T. Apocryphorum,* p. 44, reads ἀνδραλογία. This is a printer's error in Wahl, as is
ἀνδραφονέω a little farther on (*cf.* the alphabetical order). The author cannot
say whether ἀνδραλογία is a possible form.

[2] Above, p. 143.

[3] A construction like *e.g.,* εἰς ἑξήκοντα ταλάντων λόγος, *a sum of about
sixty talents.*

[4] Swete writes ποιησάμενός τε κατ᾽ ἀνδρολογεῖον εἰς ἀργυρίου δραχμὰς
δισχιλίας. . . . What κατ᾽ ἀνδρολογεῖον is meant to signify we do not understand.

[5] " Of the time of Hadrian at the earliest " (Wilcken *re* this Papyrus).

Ps. 127 [128]³, νεόφυτα ἐλαιῶν; similarly in *BU.* 565 ₁₁ and
566 ₃ (fragments of the same document as 563).

ὀφειλή.

*Clavis*³, p. 326, "*Neque in graeco V. Ti. cod., neque ap.
profanos offenditur*". This negative statement is at all events
more cautious than the positive one of Cremer⁸, p. 737:
"only in New Testament Greek". But both are invalidated
by the Papyri.¹ The word, meaning *debt* (in the literal sense,
as in Matt. 18 ³²), is found in formulae in *BU.* 112 ₁₁ (*ca.* 60
A.D.) καθαρὰ ἀπό τε ὀφιλῆς *sic* καὶ ὑ[π]οθήκης καὶ παντὸς διεγγυήματος, 184 ₂₅ (72 A.D.) [καθ]αρὸν ἀπὸ [ὀ]φειλ(ῆς) [καὶ] ὑποθήκ[ης
καὶ παντὸς] δ[ι]ενγυ[ήμ(ατος)] *sic*, 536 ₆ ₜ. (reign of Domitian)
καθ[αρ]ὰ ἀπό τε ὀφειλ(ῆς) [καὶ ὑπο]θήκης καὶ παντὸς διεγ-
γ(υήματος), *PER.* ccxx. ₁₀ (1st cent. A.D.²) καθαρὸν ἀπ' ὀφειλῆς
[πά]ση(ς) καὶ παντὸς διεγγυήματος *sic*, further in *BU.* 624 ₁₉
(time of Diocletian) ἱερᾶς μὴ ἀμέλει ὀφιλῆ[ς] *sic*.³ All these
Papyri are from the Fayyûm.

ἀπὸ πέρυσι.

"Many of these compounds [*i.e.* combinations of prepositions with adverbs of place and time] are found only
in writers later than Alexander, some only in the Scholiasts
. . . . .; others, such as ἀπὸ πέρυσι (for which προπέρυσι
or ἐκπέρυσι was used) are not to be met with even there."⁴
But we find ἀπὸ πέρυσι (2 Cor. 8 ¹⁰, 9 ²) in the Papyrus letter
BU. 531 ii. ₁ (Fayyûm, 2nd cent. A.D.), also in the Oxyrhyn-
chos Papyrus (ed. by Grenfell and Hunt, London, 1898), No.
cxiv. ₁₂ (2nd-3rd cent. A.D.): ἀπὸ Τῦβι πέρυσι.

¹ The author has subsequently noticed in Pape that even the *Etymologicum Magnum* quotes the word from Xenophon ! ! The New Testament
lexicographers really ought to have noted this. The note of the *Et. M.* in
regard to ὀφειλή is as follows: . . . σπανίως δὲ εὕρηται ἐν χρήσει· εὑρίσκεται δὲ
παρὰ Ξενοφῶντι ἐν τοῖς Περὶ Πόρων.

² But on p. 296 this Papyrus is assigned to the 2nd cent.

³ We do not quite understand this; the *sacred debt* is perhaps a debt
owing to the temple treasury.

⁴ Winer-Lünemann, p. 394.

$$\pi\rho o\sigma\epsilon\upsilon\chi\acute{\eta}.$$

1. According to Cremer[8], p. 420, the word appears "not to occur at all in profane Greek . . . and therefore to be a word of Hellenistic formation, which follows the change which had taken place in the use of προσεύχεσθαι, and which is at the same time a characteristic mark of the difference between Israel and the Gentile world ". But the fact that προσευχή, *place of prayer*,[1] is found also in connection with pagan worship[2] tells against this isolating of the word.

2. The authorities for προσευχή in the sense of a Jewish place of prayer[3] which up till now have been known and applied are most likely all surpassed in age by an Inscription from Lower Egypt, which probably belongs to the 3rd cent. B.C., *viz.*, *CIL.* iii. *Suppl.* 6583 (original in the Berlin Egyptian Museum): "*Βασιλίσσης καὶ βασιλέως προσταξάντων ἀντὶ τῆς προανακειμένης περὶ τῆς ἀναθέσεως τῆς προσευχῆς πλακὸς ἡ ὑπογεγραμμένη ἐπιγραφήτω. Βασιλεὺς Πτολεμαῖος Εὐεργέτης τὴν προσευχὴν ἄσυλον. Regina et rex iusserunt.*" "As Mommsen has recognised, the queen and the king who caused the synagogue Inscription to be renewed are Zenobia and Vaballath [*ca.* 270 A.D.]. Whether the founder is Euergetes I. or II. he leaves an open question."[4] Wilcken decides for Euergetes I. († 222 B.C.) in opposition to Willrich, who contends for Euergetes II. († 117 B.C.). The reasons given by the former have satisfied the present writer: to go into the matter more particularly would meanwhile carry us too far from the point. But it may be permitted to reproduce Wilcken's interesting con-

---

[1] The author has not as yet met with the word, in the sense of *prayer*, in heathen usage. But the question as to its "formation" is sufficiently answered by showing that it occurs outside of the Bible. It is improbable that the heathen usage is in any way to be traced back to Jewish influence.

[2] References in Schürer, *Geschichte des jüdischen Volkes im Zeitalter Jesu Christi*, ii. (1886), p. 370 = [3] ii., p. 444 (Eng. Trans. ii., ii., p. 69).

[3] References *ibid.*, and in Thayer *s. v.* The latter cites also Cleomedes 71, 16.

[4] Wilcken, *Berl. Philol. Wochenschr.*, xvi. (1896), col. 1493 (Review of Willrich, *Juden und Griechen vor der makkab. Erhebung*, Göttingen, 1895.

cluding remark about the Inscription (col. 1419): "Most probably it has hitherto remained unnoticed that the omission of θεός before Ευεργέτης is a unique phenomenon, as the ascription of Divinity ought, according to rule, to stand in official papers. We gather, then, that the king has here renounced the use of θεός in consideration of the sensitiveness of the Jews."

σουδάριον.

Neither *Clavis*[3] nor Thayer gives any example of this[1] outside of the N.T. But in the marriage-contracts, *PER.* xxvii. 7f. (190 A.D.) and xxi. 19 (230 A.D.), the σουδάριον is mentioned among the toilet articles of the dowry.

ὑποπόδιον.

Winer-Schmiedel, § 3, 2 e (p. 23), continues to count ὑποπόδιον (found first in the LXX) among the words which the Jews themselves may possibly have formed by analogy, but which may have been already current in the popular tongue, though not as yet so found by us. *Clavis*[3] gives extra-biblical examples from Lucian and Athenaeus. These would, in the author's opinion, be sufficient to do away with the idea of the Jewish origin of the word. But still more decisive is its occurrence in the Papyri. In the two marriage-contracts from the Fayyûm, *PER.* xxii. 8 (reign of Antoninus Pius) and xxvii. 11 (190 A.D.), among the articles of furniture belonging to the bride there is mentioned a settle, with its accompanying footstool, καθέδρα σὺν ὑποποδίῳ.

3. Supposed Special "Biblical" or "New Testament" Meanings and Constructions.

ἀντίλημψις.

To the older passages from the Ptolemaic Papyri, in which the word is secularised (meaning *help*[2]), there is to be

---

[1] In the case of a Graecism like σουδάριον (authenticated hitherto only for the N.T.), if anywhere at all, we have to deal with a simple case of chance.

[2] Above, p. 92.

added *BU.* 613 13 (Fayyûm, probably of the reign of Antoninus
Pius).

ἀρεσκεία.

"Even those terms which, among the Greeks, are debased
to common uses on account of their exclusive human application, such as ἀρέσκεια [sic], the obsequiousness which suits
itself to everybody, obtain in the scriptures a higher con-
notation by reason of the predominance of their relation to
the Divine standard. The word occurs in Col. 1 [10] in an
undoubtedly good sense, and this transformation is to be
attributed chiefly to the prevailing usage of ἀρεστός and
εὐάρεστος in the LXX and the New Testament." This assertion of G. von Zezschwitz [1] ought not to have been made,
since Lösner had long before pointed out quite a number
of passages in Philo in which the word has unquestionably
a good sense—indeed, that of a relation towards God.[2]
ἀρεσκεία is also used in a good sense in the Inscription in
Latyschev's *Inscriptiones regni Bosporani,* ii. 5 (date?): χάριν
τῆς εἰς τὴν πόλιν ἀρεσκείας.[3]

ἐπιθυμητής.

Used by the Greeks, according to Cremer [8], p. 456, in a
good sense ; "on the other hand" in 1 Cor. 10 [6], ἐπιθυμητὴς
κακῶν, "corresponding to the development of the idea which
has been noted under ἐπιθυμία". But it is found in a bad
sense also in *BU.* 531 ii. 22 (Fayyûm, 2nd cent. A.D.): οὔτε
εἰμὶ ἄδικος οὔτε ἀ[λ]λοτρίων ἐπιθυμητής.[4]

ἱλάσκομαι.

According to Cremer [8], p. 471, the construction of this
word in "biblical" Greek deviates from the usage of profane
authors "in a striking manner". In proof of this, the com-

---

[1] *Profangraecitaet und biblischer Sprachgeist,* Leipzig, 1859, p. 61.

[2] These references have rightly been adopted by Cremer [8], p. 159.

[3] This quotation is from Fränkel, p. 315.

[4] We have in this combination a synonym for ἀλλοτριοεπίσκοπος, hitherto
authenticated only for Christian usage; this compound becomes intelligible
by comparison with ἄδικος.

pound ἐξιλάσκομαι is specially adduced, the usage of which
in "biblical" Greek, as contrasted with the constructions
of profane Greek, is said to be "all the more noteworthy
and all the more deserving of serious consideration". Cremer
deems the biblical phrase ἐξιλάσκεσθαι τὰς ἁμαρτίας to be
one of the "most striking in comparison with profane Greek".[1]
It is, however, to be met with outside the Bible. In
the directions (preserved in a duplicated Inscription) of the
Lycian Xanthus for the sanctuary, founded by him, of Men
Tyrannos, a deity of Asia Minor, CIA. iii. 74,[2] cf. 73 (found
near Sunium, not older than the imperial period), there
occurs the peculiar passage : ὃς ἂν δὲ πολυπραγμονήσῃ τὰ τοῦ
θεοῦ ἢ περιεργάσηται,[3] ἁμαρτίαν ὀφ(ε)ιλέτω Μηνὶ Τυράννῳ, ἣν
οὐ μὴ δύνηται ἐξειλάσασθαι sic.

Further, the ἁμαρτίαν ὀφείλω in this passage is also very
interesting; it is manifestly used like χρέος ὀφείλω, ἁμαρτία
being thought of as *debt*.

λικμάω.

In Luke 20[18] (cf. possibly Matt. 21[44]) πᾶς ὁ πεσὼν ἐπ᾽
ἐκεῖνον τὸν λίθον συνθλασθήσεται · ἐφ᾽ ὃν δ᾽ ἂν πέσῃ, λικμήσει
αὐτόν, B. Weiss[4] and H. Holtzmann[5] take λικμᾶν as *winnow*,
the only meaning hitherto authenticated. But, for one
thing, this does away altogether with the parallelism of the
two clauses, and, for another, gives us a figure which is
hardly conceivable, viz., *every one upon whom the stone falls, it
will winnow.* Should we decide, then, on internal grounds, we
arrive at a meaning for λικμᾶν which is synonymous with
συνθλᾶν. In point of fact, the Vulgate understood the word
in this sense : Matt. 21[44] *conteret*, Luke 20[18] *comminuet;* so
also Luther and most others : *it will grind to powder* (zer-

[1] Cf. also Blass, *Gramm.*, p. 88, note 1 [Eng. Trans., p. 88, note 3]:
"Ἰλάσκεσθαι ἁμαρτίας, Heb. 2[17], strikes as being strange by reason of the
object: the classical (ἐξ)ιλάσκ. θεόν means 'to dispose Him in mercy towards
one'. Similarly, however (= *expiare*), also LXX and Philo."

[2] Dittenberger, *Sylloge*, No. 379. Cf. p. 216 above in reference to
καθαρίζω.

[3] Cf. 2 Thess. 3[11].   [4] Meyer, i. 1[8] (1890), p. 363.
[5] HC. i.[2] (1892), p. 239 f.

malmen). *Clavis*[3], p. 263, adopts this view, with the note
"*usu a profanis alieno*". This is most probably one of the
cases where no reason whatever can be given for the particular alteration of meaning having taken place in "biblical"
Greek. If λικμάω = *grind to powder* be possible at all, then
it is only a matter of contingency that the word has not yet
been found with that meaning outside the Bible. There
is, however, a Papyrus which appears to the author to supply
the want. In the fragment of a speech for the prosecution,
BU. 146 5 ff. (Fayyûm, 2nd-3rd cent. A.D.), the prosecutor
reports : ἐπῆλθαν Ἀγαθοκλῆς καὶ δοῦλος Σαραπίωνος Ὀννώ-
φρεως κ[αὶ ἄ]λλος ξένο[ς] ἐργά[της αὐ]τοῦ τῇ ἁλωνίᾳ μου καὶ
ἐλίκμησάν μου τὸ λάχανον [1] καὶ οὐχ [ὁ]λ[ί]γην ζη[μ]είαν *sic*
μοι ἐζημιωσάμην. What the crime of the three rogues
was is not altogether evident, but it is clear, nevertheless, that they had not *winnowed* the λάχανον : they had
trodden upon it, *stamped* upon it, or *ruined* [2] it in some way.
We might, perhaps, have recourse to the more general
meaning of *destroy*, which, moreover, will be found to
suit the New Testament passages exceedingly well. It is
conceivable that *winnow* might come to have this meaning : the connecting link would be something like *scatter*,
which *Clavis*[3] has established for LXX Jer. 38 [31][10] and
other passages : the heap of corn mingled with chaff is,
by winnowing, separated into its constituent substances, is
scattered. This conjecture has at all events better support
than that made by Carr,[3] viz., that the meanings *winnow* and
crush were associated together in Egypt because in that
country there was drawn over the corn, before winnowing,
a threshing-board which crushed the straw (!).

λούω.

Cremer [8], p. 623 : "While νίζειν or νίπτειν was the usual
word for ceremonial washing in profane Greek—. . . . . .,
the LXX use λούειν as the rendering of the Heb. רחץ, for

---

[1] There is a second *a* placed above the first *a* in the original.
[2] *Cf.* Judith 2 [27] τὰ πεδία ἐξελίκμησε.
[3] Quoted in Kennedy, *Sources of N.T. Greek*, p. 126 f.

the washings required under the theocracy for purposes of
purification". The sets up an unjustifiable antithesis between "profane" Greek and biblical, which Cremer himself
is unable to maintain, for immediately afterwards he finds it
necessary to grant that the word "does not, indeed, seem to
have been altogether unused in profane Greek for ceremonial
washing; Plut. *Probl. Rom.* 264, D : λούσασθαι πρὸ τῆς
θυσίας; Soph. *Ant.* 1186 : τὸν μὲν λούσαντες ἁγνὸν λουτρόν".
Instead, then, of "not altogether unused" one may, since
the above antithesis does not need to be defended, quite well
say "used". Up to the present other three "profane"
passages have become known to the author; the first two
are interesting also from a grammatical point of view on
account of the construction with ἀπό (Acts 16 [33]). *Perg.* 255,
an Inscription of the early Roman period relating to the
regulations of the temple of Athena at Pergamus, ordains in
line 4 ff. that only οἱ . . ἀπὸ μὲν τῆς ἰδίας γ[υναι]κὸς καὶ τοῦ
ἰδίου ἀνδρὸς αὐθημερόν, ἀπὸ δὲ ἀλλοτρίας κ[αὶ] ἀλλοτρίου
δευτεραῖοι λουσάμενοι, ὡσαύτως δὲ καὶ ἀπὸ κήδους κ[α]ὶ τεκούσης
γυναικὸς δευτεραῖο(ι) shall enter the sanctuary. Fränkel, p.
188, makes the following remark upon this : "It is well-
known that sexual intercourse, the touching of the dead or
of women with child, rendered necessary a religious purification previous to communion with the gods". The other
two passages are adopted from the references of Fränkel, p.
189. In the regulations of the Lycian Xanthus for the
sanctuary of Men Tyrannos which he founded in Athens,
CIA. iii. 73 (found near Sunium, not older than the imperial
period), occurs quite similarly ἀπὸ δὲ γυναικὸς λουσάμενο[ν ?].
Finally, the stone from Julis, given in Röhl, *Inscr. antiqu.*, p.
395 (= Dittenberger, *Sylloge*, p. 468), contains the regulation
that those who have become unclean by touching a corpse
are purified if λουσαμένους περὶ πάντα τὸν χρῶτα ὕδατος χύσι.

πάροικος.

According to Cremer [8], p. 695, it appears as if "profane"
and "biblical" Greek diverged from each other in the use of
this word, and, in particular, as if πάροικος in the sense of

alien were unknown in the former, which is said to use
μέτοικος instead. But even in *Clavis*[3], p. 341, we find a
reference to Philo, *De Cherub.* § 34 (p. 160 f. M.), where
πάροικος is used several times in contradistinction to πολίτης.
And if Philo is not to be counted a profane author in the
strict sense of the term, we have the Inscriptions to fall
back upon. In *IMAe.* 1033 9 (Carpathos, 2nd cent. B.C. ?) the
population is divided into πολῖται and πάροικοι; still clearer
is *Perg.* 249 12. 20. 34 (133 B.C.), in regard to which Fränkel, p.
173, remarks: "We are informed of the following classes of
the population: 1. Citizens (πολῖται), 2. Aliens (πάροικοι),
3. Various classes of soldiers (στρατιῶται . .), 4. Emancipated
persons (ἐξελεύθεροι), 5. Slaves, ... Since the offspring
of manumitted slaves come to be counted as aliens in terms
of line 20 *t.* of the edict under notice, it is evident that the
ἐξελεύθεροι were not, as such, transferred to the rank of the
paroikoi, but in the first instance formed an intermediate
class. It was the same in Ceos, according to the Inscription
in Dittenberger's *Sylloge*, 348 10, and in Ephesus at the time
of the Mithridatic war—according to Lebas, *Asie*, 136 *a*
(Dittenberger, *Sylloge*, 253), line 43 ff., where also, as in our
document, the δημόσιοι [= the public slaves] are immediately
raised to the class of πάροικοι, not having first to pass
through that of the ἐξελεύθεροι."[1]

4. TECHNICAL TERMS.

ἀθέτησις (and εἰς ἀθέτησιν).

Clavis[3], p. 9, "*raro apud profanos inferioris aetatis, ut Cic.
ad Att.* 6, 9. *Diog. Laert.* 3. 39, 66, *ap. grammat. improbatio;
saepius ap. ecclesiasticos scriptores*". The usage of the word
in Papyri from the Fayyûm is particularly instructive in
regard to its employment in the Epistle to the Hebrews (7 18,
9 26): *BU.* 44 16 (102 A.D.), conjoined with ἀκύρωσις in reference

---

[1] The author gives this quotation because it yields further epigraphic
materials. Kennedy, *Sources of N. T. Greek*, p. 102, also refers to the
Inscriptions (*CIG.* 3595, " etc.").—*Cf.* now also A. Schulten, *Mittheilungen
des Kaiserlich-Deutschen Archäol. Instituts*, Römische Abtheilung, xiii. (1898).
p. 237

to a document; quite similarly in 196 21 t. (109 A.D.), 281 18 t. (reign of Trajan), and 394 14 t. (137 A.D.). In all these passages ἀθέτησις is used in a technical juristic sense, being found in the formula εἰς ἀθέτησιν καὶ ἀκύρωσιν. Compare these with εἰς ἀθέτησιν in Heb. 9 26, and with the usage of the contrary formula εἰς βεβαίωσιν in LXX Lev. 25 23, Heb. 6 16 and the Papyri.[1] The formula was maintained for long afterwards: we still find εἰς ἀθέτησιν καὶ ἀκύρωσιν in PER. xiv. 17 t. (Fayyûm, 166 A.D.) and ix. 10 (Hermopolis, 271 A.D.).

ἀναπέμπω.

The references given by Clavis[3], p. 27, and Thayer, p. 41, for the meaning ad personam dignitate, auctoritate, potestate superiorem sursum mitto (Luke 23 7, Acts 25 21) from Philo, Josephus and Plutarch can be largely increased from the Fayyûm Papyri: BU. 19 i. 20 (135 A.D.), 5 ii. 19 t. (138 A.D.), 613 4 (reign of Antoninus Pius?), 15 i. 17 (194 A.D.), 168 25 (2nd-3rd cent. A.D.).

ἀπέχω.

In regard to the use of this word in Matt. 6 2. 5. 16, Luke 6 24, Phil. 4 18, as meaning I have received, its constant occurrence in receipts in the Papyri is worthy of consideration. Two cases may be given which are significant on account of their contiguity in time to the above passages, viz., BU. 584 5 t. (Fayyûm, 29th December, 44 A.D.) καὶ ἀπέχω τὴν συνκεχωρημένην τιμὴν πᾶσαν ἐκ πλήρους, and 612 21. (Fayyûm, 6th September, 57 A.D.) ἀπέχω παρ᾽ ὑμῶν τὸν φόρον τοῦ ἐλα[ι]ουργίου, ὧν ἔχετέ [μο]υ ἐν μισθώσει. The words they have their reward in the Sermon on the Mount, when considered in the light of the above, acquire the more pungent ironical meaning they can sign the receipt of their reward : their right to receive their reward is realised, precisely as if they had already given a receipt for it. ἀποχή means receipt exactly, and in Byzantine times we also find μισθαποχή.[2]

---

[1] See p. 105 ff. above.

[2] Wessely, Corpus Papyrorum Raineri, i. 1, 151 ; but no example is given there. The word might signify receipt for rent or hire, not deed of conveyance as Wessely supposes.

βεβαίωσις.

The conjunction of the terms βεβαιοῦν or βεβαίωσις and ἀρραβών [1] is also found in *BU.* 446 [= 80] [18] (reign of Marcus Aurelius) ; the sentence is unfortunately mutilated.

διακούω.

In the technical sense of *to try, to hear judicially* (Acts 23 [35] ; *cf.* LXX Deut. 1 [16], Dion Cass. 36, 53 [36]), also *BU.* 168 [28] (Fayyûm, 2nd-3rd cent. A.D.).

τὸ ἐπιβάλλον μέρος.

Frequent references given in connection with Luke 15 [12] ; a technical formula, also used in the Papyri : *BU.* 234 13. 8 (Fayyûm, 121 A.D.) τὸ καὶ αὐτῷ ἐπιβάλλον μέρος, 419 5 f. (276-277 A.D.) τὸ ἐπιβάλλον μοι μέρος of the paternal inheritance ; similarly 614 17 f. (Fayyûm, 216 A.D.) τὴν ἐπι-βάλλουσαν αὐτῇ τῶν πατρῴω[ν] μερίδα.

ἐπίσκοπος.

Of this word as an official title Cremer [8], p. 889, follow-ing Pape, gives only one example outside the N. T. : "In Athens the name was applied in particular to the able men in the subject states who conducted the affairs of the same ". But we find ἐπίσκοποι as communal officials in Rhodes ; thus in *IMAe.* 49 43 ff. (2nd-1st cent. B.C.) there is named a council of five ἐπίσκοποι ; in 50 34 ff. (1st cent. B.C.) three ἐπίσκοποι are enumerated. Neither Inscription gives any information as to their functions ; in the first, the ἐπίσκοποι are found among the following officials : [πρυτανεῖς (?)], γραμματεὺς βουλᾶς, ὑπογραμματεὺς [β]ου[λᾶ]ι καὶ π[ρ]υτανεῦσ[ι], στρα-ταγοί, [ἐπὶ] τὰν χώραν, [ἐπὶ] τὸ πέραν, γραμματεύς, [ταμίαι], γραμματεύς, ἐ π ί σ κ ο π ο ι, γραμματεύς, ἐπιμεληταὶ τῶν ξέ[νων], γραμματεύς, ἀγεμὼν ἐπὶ Καύνο[υ], ἀγεμὼν ἐπὶ Καρίας, ἀγεμὼν ἐπὶ Λυκίας. In the second the order is as follows : [πρυτανεῖς (?)], [στρα]ταγοί, ταμίαι, ἐ π ί σ κ ο π ο ι, ὑπογραμ-ματεὺς βουλᾶι καὶ [πρυτανεῦσι (?)]. But it is perhaps a still more important fact that likewise in Rhodes ἐπίσκοπος was

[1] Above, p. 108 f.

a technical term for the holder of a *religious* office.   The
pre-Christian Inscription *IMAe.* 731 enumerates the following
officials of the temple of Apollo : three ἐπιστάται, one
γραμματεὺς ἱεροφυλάκων, one ἐ π ί σ κ ο π ο ς [1] in line 8,   six
ἱερο[π]οιοί, one [ταμί]ας, one ὑπο[γραμματε]ὺς ἱερ[οφ]υλάκων.
We must abstain from theorising as to the duties of this
ἐπίσκοπος.   The fact that the word had already been admitted
into the technical religious diction of pre-Christian times is
sufficiently important in itself.

θεολόγος.

This word has been admitted into the *Clavis* on account
of its occurrence in several MSS.[2] as the designation of John
the writer of the Apocalypse.   Fränkel, p. 264 f., in connection with *Perg.* 374 A 30 (dedication of the Pergamenian
Association of the ὑμνῳδοὶ θεοῦ Σεβαστοῦ καὶ θεᾶς 'Ρώμης,
reign of Hadrian) has collected valuable materials for the
usage of Asia Minor: his notes are given as follows—the
author was unable to test the quotations : " The office of a
θεολόγος (line 30) is elsewhere shown to have existed in
Pergamus, and, in fact, seems to have been conferred as a
permanent one, since one and the same person, Ti. Claudius
Alexandros, held it under Caracalla and under Elagabalus
(see below, in reference to No. 525, line 8).   Another theologian, Glykon, as an eponymous magistrate, is met with, in
Pergamon, upon a coin bearing the image of Herennius
Etruscus (Mionnet, *Suppl.* v., p. 472, No. 1160).   It is strange
that P. Aelius Pompeianus, μελοποιὸς καὶ ῥαψῳδὸς θεοῦ
'Αδριανοῦ, who, according to an Inscription of Nysa (*Bullet.
de corr. hellén.* 9, 125 f., lines 4 and 63) was a θεολόγος ναῶν τῶν
ἐν Περγάμῳ, is described as a citizen of Sidë, Tarsus and
Rhodes, but not of Pergamus.   It can be no matter of chance

---

[1] ἐπισκοπο can be read quite plainly, thereafter either an ι or the fragment of another letter.   The editor writes ἐπίσκοποι in his transcription.   But
as only one name follows it would be more correct to read ἐπίσκοπο[ς].   It
appears thus in the index, p. 235, which contains many a tacit correction.

[2] Wessely reads PER. xxx. 3 f. (Fayyûm, 6th cent. A.D.) του αγιου ιωαννου
του ευλογου και ευαγγελιστου, and translates *of Saint John, the apostle and
evangelist.*   Should not θεολόγου be read ?

that we find the title θεολόγος in the two cities of Asia
Minor (invested like Pergamus with the Neokoria) in connection with which we were able to demonstrate the existence of the imperial Hymnodia as well: for Smyrna the
existence of theologians is attested by the passage from *CIG.*
3148, copied out above (p. 205, end) in connection with No.
269 [lines 34 ff.: ὅσα ἐνετύχομεν παρὰ τοῦ κυρίου Καίσαρος
᾿Αδριανοῦ διὰ ᾿Αντωνίου Πολέμωνος · δεύτερον δόγμα συγκλήτου,
καθ᾽ ὃ δὶς νεωκόροι γεγόναμεν, ἀγῶνα ἱερόν, ἀτέλειαν, θεολόγους,
ὑμνῳδούς], and by *CIG.* 3348, where, as in our Inscription,
the same individual is ὑμνῳδὸς καὶ θεολόγος; for Ephesus by
the *Greek Inscr. in the Brit. Mus.* iii. 2, No. 481, line 191 f.: ὁμοίως
καὶ τοῖς θεολόγοις καὶ ὑμνῳδοῖς, in which one must, in consequence of the article being used but once, likewise interpret
as 'theologians who were also hymnodists'. In Heraklea
in the Pontus there is a theologian for the mysteries: *CIG.*
3803, ὑπατικὸν καὶ θεολόγον τῶν τῇδε μυστηρίων,—and also
in Smyrna the female theologians, αἱ θεολόγοι, whom we
find there along with the male, are engaged in the mysteries
of Demeter Thesmophoros: *CIG.* 3199, 3200."

πλῆθος.

This word, followed by a national name in the genitive,
often signifies not *multitude* simply, but *people* in the official
political sense. Thus we have τὸ πλῆθος τῶν ᾿Ιουδαίων
in 1 Macc. 8²⁰, 2 Macc. 11¹⁶ (like ὁ δῆμος τῶν ᾿Ιουδαίων, ver.
³⁴), Ep. Arist., p. 67 18 (Schm.), and most likely also in Acts
25²⁴. The Inscriptions yield further material in regard to
this usage: *IMAe.* 85 4 (Rhodes, 3rd cent. B.C.) τὸ πλῆθος τὸ
῾Ροδίων, similarly 90 7 (Rhodes, 1st cent. B.C.) ; further, 846 10
τὸ πλῆθος τὸ Λινδίων (Rhodes, date ?), similarly 847 14 (Rhodes,
1st cent. A.D.) and many other Inscriptions from Rhodes.

The word has a technical sense also in the usage of the
religious associations: it designates the associates in their
totality, the *community* or *congregation*, *IMAe.* 155 6 (Rhodes,
2nd cent. B.C.) τ[ὸ] πλῆθος τὸ ῾Αλιαδᾶν καὶ [῾Αλια]στᾶν ;
similarly 156 5.[1] Compare with these Luke 1¹⁰, 19³⁷, Acts

---

[1] The editor, in the index, p. 238, remarks upon this " πλῆθος, *i.q.*, κοινόν ".

2⁶, but especially 15³⁰, where the Christian Church at Antioch is called τὸ πλῆθος. Thus also τὸ πλῆθος in 4³² should hardly be interpreted as *multitude, mass,* but as *community;* similarly in 6²·⁵, 15¹², 19⁹, 21²².

πρᾶγμα ἔχω πρός τινα.

πρᾶγμα is very frequently used in the Papyri in the forensic sense of *law-suit;* we cite only *BU.* 22 st. (Fayyûm, 114 A.D.) ἁπλῶς μηδὲν ἔχουσα πρᾶγμα πρὸς ἐμέ, in connection with 1 Cor. 6¹ τὶς ὑμῶν πρᾶγμα ἔχων πρὸς τὸν ἕτερον.

πρεσβύτερος.

At p. 154 f. the attempt was made to demonstrate, first, that πρεσβύτερος was, till late ·in the imperial period, the technical term in Egypt for the occupant of an office in civil communities,—a usage by which the LXX did not fail to be influenced ; secondly, that a similar usage could be established for Asia Minor. The application of the word in its *religious* sense among Catholic Christians, which can be made clear by the series π ρ ε σ β ύ τ ε ρ ο ς—*presbyter—priest,* is illustrated by the fact that πρεσβύτεροι can also be shown to have been an official title of pagan *priests* in Egypt. In confirmation of this, a few sentences from F. Krebs ¹ may be given here. " The organisation of the priesthood in the different temples in the Roman period was still the same as it had been, according to the testimony of the decree of Kanopus, in the Ptolemaic period. To begin with, the priesthood is divided according to descent into 5 φυλαί as at that time " (p. 34). . . . " In Ptolemaic times the affairs of the whole Egyptian priesthood were conducted by an annually changing council of 25 members (πρεσβύτεροι ²

---

¹ *Ägyptische Priester unter römischer Herrschaft* in the *Zeitschrift für ägypt. Sprache und Alterthumskunde,* xxxi. (1893), p. 31 ff.—Reference is made on p. 34 to Wilcken, *Kaiserl. Tempelverwaltung in Ägypten, Hermes,* xxiii., p. 592, and *Arsinoitische Tempelrechnungen, Hermes,* xx., p. 430.

² There is one passage belonging to the Ptolemaic period attesting πρεσβύτεροι in this sense which is not cited here by Krebs. In *CIG.* 4717 2 f. (Thebes in Lower Egypt, between 45 and 37 B.C.) it is said: [ἔδο]ξε τοῖς ἀπὸ Διοσπόλεως τῆ[s μεγάλης ἱ]ερεῦσι το[ῦ μεγίστου θεοῦ Ἀμο]νρασωνθὴρ καὶ τοῖς πρεσβυτέροις καὶ τοῖς ἄλλοις πᾶσι. Here the πρεσβύτεροι plainly belong to the priesthood.

or βουλευταί). In our little provincial temple [1] we find
.. corresponding to it, a council—also changed yearly—
of 'five of the oldest of the five phylæ of the god Sokno-
paios for the present 23rd year' (*i.e.*, of Antoninus Pius =
159-160 A.D.). This council gives in a report which the
Roman authorities had demanded from it concerning disci-
plinary proceedings against a priest of the temple" (p. 35).
The author has met with these Egyptian πρεσβύτεροι in the
following Papyri from the Fayyûm : *BU.* 16 5 ff. (159-160 A.D.
—the passage quoted by Krebs), τῶν ε΄ πρεσβυτέρων ἱερέων
πενταφυλίας θεοῦ Σοκνο[π]αίου ; 347 i. 5 f. (171 A.D.), Σατα-
βοῦτος π[ρεσ]βυτέρο[υ ἱερέω]ς [2] ; in 387 i. 7 f. (between 177 and
181 A.D., much mutilated) the 5 πρεσβύτεροι ἱερεῖς of Sokno-
paios are undoubtedly again spoken of ; 433 5 f. (*ca.* 190 A.D.)
τῶν γ΄ [πρεσβ]υτέρων ἱε[ρ]έων [π]ρώτης φυλῆς ; *ibid.*, line 9 f.,
τῶν ε΄ πρεσβυτέρω[ν ἱερέων πενταφυλ]ίας Σοκνοπ[αίου θε]οῦ ;
392 6 f. (207-208 A.D.), καὶ διὰ τῶν ἱερέων πρεσβυτέρων (here
follow the names, partly mutilated) τῶν δ΄. What the col-
legiate [3] relations of these πρεσβύτεροι ἱερεῖς actually were
we do not definitely understand ; but thus much is certain,
viz., that πρεσβύτεροι occurs here in the technical religious
sense of pagan usage in imperial times, which, according to
Krebs, goes back to the Ptolemaic period. [4]

The Papyrus passages are the more important, as no
other examples of this usage, so far as we know, have
been found in pagan writers. That is to say, indubitable
examples. It is true that the πρεσβύτεροι of towns and
islands in Asia Minor, mentioned on p. 156, are considered
by many investigators, as we have meanwhile learned, to
have been a corporation which exercised authority in sacred
matters, but this hypothesis is opposed by others [5] ; were it

---

[1] The Soknopaios-temple in the Fayyûm, belonging to imperial times,
is meant.

[2] See the corrected reading in the Supplement, p. 397.

[3] They seem always to have formed a college (of 3, 4 or 5 persons).

[4] According to Krebs, p. 35, πρεσβύτεροι was thus used—without the
addition of ἱερεῖς—even in the Ptolemaic period [as above, *CIG.* 4717 2 f.].

[5] Fränkel, p. 321, in ref. to *Perg.* 477 (time of Claudius or Nero): "This
and the following Inscription (478, imperial period) prove the existence in

proved, we should thus have two valuable analogies of the early Christian πρεσβύτεροι. But, nevertheless, the word in the passages from Asia Minor would be used rather in its original signification, and not in the more special sense which finally developed into the idea of *priest*. In the Papyri it has this sense—or rather shows a tendency towards this sense. We do not assert that it *means* "priest": that is impossible in view of the following ἱερεύς. What is of importance for the history of the word is the circumstance that it was used as a distinctive appellation of priests in particular. The transformation of the early Christian *elders* into the Catholic *priests*, so extremely important in its consequences,[1] was of course facilitated by the fact that there already existed *elder priests* or *priestly elders*, of whom both the designation and the institution were but waiting for admission into a church which was gradually becoming secularised.[2]

προφήτης.

"The higher classes of the priesthood [in Egypt], according to the decree of Kanopus (l. 3 f.) and Rosetta (l. 6 f.), were, in ascending scale, the ἱερογραμματεῖς, the πτεροφόροι, the ἱεροστολισταί (πρὸς τὸν στολισμὸν τῶν θεῶν), the προφῆται, and the ἀρχιερεῖς."[3] In Roman times we meet with a προφήτης Σούχου θ[εοῦ μεγάλ]ου μεγάλου, *BU.* 149 3 f. (Fayyûm, 2nd-3rd cent. A.D.). "This 'prophet' receives for his work 344 drachmas and half an obol annually—a salary from

Pergamus of a Gerousia, for which institution, particularly frequent in Roman Asia Minor, reference may be made to the careful discussion of Menadier (*Ephesii*, p. 48 ff.) and its continuation by Hicks (*Greek Inscriptions in the Brit. Mus.*, iii. 2, p. 74 ff.). According to these, the Gerousia is to be thought of as an official body whose authority lay in sacred affairs. Otherwise Mommsen, *Röm. Gesch.* 5, 326."

[1] A. Harnack, *Lehrbuch der Dogmengeschichte*, i.[2] (Freiburg, 1888), p. 385 [Eng. Trans., ii., p. 131]: "One might perhaps say that the internal form of the churches was altered by no other development so thoroughly as by that which made priests of the bishops and elders".

[2] *Cf.* the similar circumstances in regard to προφήτης, p. 236.

[3] F. Krebs, *Ägyptische Priester unter römischer Herrschaft* in the *Zeitschrift für ägypt. Sprache und Alterthumskunde*, xxxi. (1893), p. 36.

the smallness of which we may perhaps infer that the duties
of this office were not his chief occupation."[1] In *BU.* 488 3 f.
(Fayyûm, 2nd cent. A.D.), if the restoration be correct, we
find a προφήτης of a god Συκατοῖμις. The author knows
nothing as to the duties of these Egyptian προφῆται. But
the fact that in Egypt[2] the *prophets* were priests is sufficiently
important for us. It helps us to understand the view held
by the Christians in the second century, *viz.*, that "the
prophets and teachers, as the commissioned preachers of the
word, are the priests";[3] we can better understand such a
strange saying as Didache 13 3, δώσεις τὴν ἀπαρχὴν τοῖς προφή-
ταις· αὐτοὶ γάρ εἰσιν οἱ ἀρχιερεῖς ὑμῶν—particularly as it was
written in the country in which the προφῆται were priests.

Supplementary : An interesting piece of epigraphic
evidence for the priestly προφῆται is found on a statue in the
collection of Consul-General Loytved at Beirut, which has
been published by A. Erman.[4] The statue comes from
Tyre, and represents a worshipper of Osiris, who holds before
him the image of his god. The workmanship is altogether
Egyptian ; the pillar at the back bears an Inscription in
small hieroglyphics, which the editor cannot fully make out,
but from which he translates *inter alia*, "*the Prophet* . . .
of Osiris," which is meant to signify the person represented.
Then, on the right side of the pillar at the back, the following
Inscription is roughly scratched :—

SACERDOS · OSIRIM

FERENS · ΠΡΟΦΗ//////

ΟΣΕΙΡΙΝΚΩΜ///////

ΖΣ/////

---

[1] F. Krebs, *Agyptische Priester unter römischer Herrschaft* in the *Zeit-schrift für ägypt. Sprache und Alterthumskunde*, xxxi. (1893), p. 36.

[2] There were priestly *prophets* in other places. We doubt indeed,
whether, in *IMAe.* 833 6 ff. (Rhodes, 1st cent. B.C.) προφατεύσας ἐν τῷ ἄστει καὶ
ἐπιλαχὼν ἱερεὺς 'Αλίου, the προφατεύσας actually refers to priestly duties. Compare, however, the passages in Kaibel, *IGrSI.* Index, p. 740 *sub* προφήτης.

[3] A. Harnack, *Lehrbuch der Dogmengeschichte*, i 2, p. 183 [Eng. Trans.,
i., p. 214].

[4] *Eine ägyptische Statue aus Tyrus* in the *Zeitschr. für ägypt. Sprache
und Alterthumskunde*, xxxi. (1893), p. 102.

This is to be read: *Sacerdos Osirim ferens.* Προφή[της]
Ὄσειριν κωμ[ά]ζω[ν].[1]

On this Erman remarks as follows: "That the superscription, 'Priest who carries Osiris,' did not come from the
dedicator himself is evident, and is also confirmed by the
way in which it is applied. It is more likely that, in Roman
times, the votive gifts of the Tyrian temple were furnished
with altogether fresh inscriptions, and that, further, for purposes of classification, the category under which they were
catalogued was marked upon them. In this way the statue,
the strange inscription on which was undecipherable, has been
made, not quite accurately, to represent a 'priest' in general,
taking care of the image of his god." The present writer
does not quite see wherein the want of accuracy lies, since
the Greek part of the Inscription speaks of a προφήτης.
But be that as it may, it is of interest to us that in this
Inscription of Roman times *sacerdos* is translated by προφήτης, and is itself most probably a translation of the Egyptian
word for *prophet.* We cannot permit ourselves an opinion
on the latter point, but it appears to us perfectly possible
that the writer of the bilingual Inscription understood
the hieroglyphic text: how otherwise should he have
rendered *sacerdos* by προφήτης? The reason, then, for his
not translating the Egyptian word for *prophet* by *propheta* is
either that this word had not yet become naturalised in
Latin, or that it did not seem capable of expressing the
specific sense of the Egyptian word. The case was very
different with προφήτης, the use of which, for a definite
class of priests, can be demonstrated in Egypt from Ptolemaic times. If this hypothesis be correct, then our Inscription, in spite of its Phœnician origin, would have to
be added to the Egyptian proofs for the existence of the
priest-prophets; if not, it would be evidence for the fact that
προφήτης as the designation of a priest is also found in use
outside Egypt—or, at least, outside the Egyptian range of
ideas.

---

[1] κωμάζων, *carrying in the procession.* This Inscription is a little remini
scent of the passage from the Leiden Papyri on p. 354.

συμβούλιον.

This (as it appears) rare word is mentioned by New Testament lexica as occurring outside the N. T. in Plutarch only. In reference to the unfortunately mutilated passage, *Perg.* 254₃ (Roman period), in which it occurs, Fränkel quotes the following note from Mommsen,[1] which gives what is most likely the oldest example of the word :—

"It appears that the word συμβούλιον is, properly speaking, not Greek, but is formed in the Graeco-Latin official style, in order to represent the untranslateable *consilium*. It is so found in a document of the year 610 A.U.C. [*CIG.* 1543 = Dittenberger, *Sylloge*, 242]. *Cf.* Plutarch, *Rom.* 14 : ὠνόμαζον δὲ τὸν θεὸν Κῶνσον, εἴτε βουλαῖον ὄντα· κωνσίλιον γὰρ ἔτι νῦν τὸ συμβούλιον καλοῦσι."

The author found the word also in *BU.* 288₁₄ (reign of Antoninus Pius) κ[α]θημένων ἐν συμβουλίῳ ἐν τῷ πραι[τωρίῳ], and 511₁₅ (*ca.* 200 A.D.[2]) [ἐ]ν συμβουλείῳ . . . . . . ἐκάθισεν.

σφραγίζω.

In Rom. 15²⁸ Paul describes the collection on behalf of Jerusalem which he had gathered among the Gentile Christians as καρπός : *when I have sealed to them this fruit I shall travel to Spain.* καρπὸν σφραγίζεσθαι is certainly a very remarkable expression. B. Weiss[3] sees in it an indication "that Paul is assuring them by personal testimony how love for the mother-church had brought this gift of love to it ". Others, again, follow Theodore of Mopsuestia in thinking that the apostle merely alludes to the regular method of delivering the money to the church at Jerusalem ; so most recently Lipsius : *deliver properly into their possession.*[4] We are of opinion that the latter view is confirmed by the Papyri. In *BU.* 249₂₁ (Fayyûm, 2nd cent. A.D.) Chairemon writes to Apollonios, σφράγεισον ᶳⁱᶜ τὸ σειτάριον ᶳⁱᶜ καὶ τὴν κρειθήν ᶳⁱᶜ, *seal the wheat and the barley.* Here we have quite

---

[1] *Hermes*, xx., p. 287, note 7.

[2] The Papyrus was written about this time ; the text itself may be older.

[3] Meyer, iv.⁸ (1891), p. 595.   [4] *HC.* ii. 2 (1891), p. 184.

an analogous expression,[1] which Professor Wilcken, in a
letter to the author, explains as follows : *seal (the sacks con-
taining) the wheat and the barley*. The same thing is meant
in 15 ii. 21 [Fayyûm, 197 (?) A.D., ὑμᾶς δὲ σφραγῖδαν *sic* ἐπι-
βά[λ]λιν *sic* ἑκάστῳ ὄνῳ]: *Ye shall set your seal upon every
ass, i.e.,* upon the sacks of every ass ". Our conjecture is
that the sealing of the sacks of fruit was to guarantee the
correctness of the contents. If the *fruit* is *sealed*, then
everything is in order : the sealing is the last thing that
must be done prior to delivery. In the light of this the
metaphorical expression used by the Apostle assumes a more
definite shape. He will act like a conscientious merchant.
We know well that in his labour of love he did not escape
base calumnies ; a sufficient reason for him that he should
perform everything with the greater precision.

υἱοθεσια.

This word is one of the few in regard to which the
"profane" usage of the Inscriptions is taken into consideration in the New Testament lexica.   Cremer[8], p. 972,
observes : "rare in the literature, but more frequent in the
Inscriptions ". His examples may be supplemented by innumerable passages from the pre-Christian Inscriptions of
the Islands of the Ægean Sea. Particular references are
superfluous.[2] The word is always found in the formula καθ'
υἱοθεσίαν δέ: *A., son of B., καθ' υἱοθεσίαν δέ son of C.*
The corresponding formula for the adoption of females is
κατὰ θυγατροποίαν[3] δέ, which occurs seven times. The
frequency with which these formulae occur permits of an
inference as to the frequency of adoptions, and lets us
understand that Paul was availing himself of a generally
intelligible figure when he utilised the term υἱοθέσια in the
language of religion.

---

[1] *BU.* 248 40 (letter from the same person and to the same as in 249)
τὰ ἀμύγδαλα σφραγ(ιζόμενα) might also be added.

[2] *Cf.* the Index of personal names in the *IMAe.* These Inscriptions
have ὑοθεσίαν. The formula κατὰ γένεσιν, 19 10, 884 14 (?) 964 *add.,* expresses
the antithesis to it.

[3] The *IMAe.* mostly read so ; also θυγατροποιΐαν in 646 2.

χάραγμα

The *other beast* of Revelation 13 [11 ff.], causes [16] *all, the small and the great, and the rich and the poor, and the free and the bond,* ἵνα δῶσιν αὐτοῖς χάραγμα ἐπὶ τῆς χειρὸς αὐτῶν τῆς δεξιᾶς ἢ ἐπὶ τὸ μέτωπον αὐτῶν, [17] ἵνα μή τις δύνηται ἀγοράσαι ἢ πωλῆσαι εἰ μὴ ὁ ἔχων τὸ χάραγμα τὸ ὄνομα τοῦ θηρίου ἢ τὸν ἀριθμὸν τοῦ ὀνόματος αὐτοῦ. A recent commentator, W. Bousset,[1] thinks that the fruitless guessing of exegetes about the χάραγμα proves " that here again there has been adopted from some lost older tradition a feature which no longer accords with the figure before us or its application ". But one is not entitled to speak of a *proof* in this connection, even if it were an established fact that the exegetes had sought "fruitlessly ". One might with equal justification suppose that we have here an allusion to some familiar detail, not as yet known to us, of the circumstances of the imperial period, and the only question is, Which interpretation is the more plausible : the reference to an ancient apocalyptic tradition, or the hypothesis of an allusion to a definite fact in the history of the times ? " A cautious mode of investigation will accept the results obtained by reference to contemporary history wherever such reference is unforced— . . . . . it will recognise genuine proofs and results arrived at by the traditional-historical method ; but, where neither is sufficient, it will be content to leave matters undecided—as also the possibility of allusions to contemporary events which we do not know. Finally, it will in many cases apply both methods at once." The following attempt to explain the matter is to be understood in the light of these statements of Bousset,[2] with which the present writer is in absolute agreement.

In his commentary, Bousset rightly repudiates the reference to the stigmatising of slaves and soldiers. One might preferably, he thinks, take the χάραγμα as being a religious protective-mark (*Schutzzeichen*). Other expositors have thought of the Roman coinage with image and superscription of the Emperor. But these explanations also, he thinks, must be

[1] Meyer, xvi. [5] (1896), p. 427.   [2] *Der Antichrist*, Göttingen, 1895, p. 7.

rejected.   The enigma can be solved only by the traditional-historical method which sets the passage in the light of the time-hallowed apocalyptic ideas.   "It is, in fact, the ancient figure of Antichrist that . . . . . has been turned to account in the second half of chap. 13." [1]   The legend of Antichrist, however, has it "that the Antichrist compels the inhabitants of the earth to assume his mark, and that only those who have the mark on forehead and hand may buy bread in times of want.   Here we have the explanation of the enigmatic verses 16 and 17." [2]

Bousset is certainly well aware that to trace backwards is not to *explain*.[3]   And yet, should it be successfully demonstrated that the χάραγμα belonged in some way to the substance of the apocalyptic tradition of ancestral times, our investigation would be substantially furthered thereby.   With no little suspense, therefore, the author examined the references which Bousset adduces elsewhere.[4]   But the citations there are relatively very late passages at best, in regard to which it seems quite possible, and to the author also probable, that Rev. 13 has rather influenced *them*.   And even if the *mark* had been borrowed by John, the special characteristics of the passage would still remain unexplained, *viz.*, the fact that the mark embodies the *name* or the *number* of the beast,[5] that it has some general connection with *buying and selling*,[6] and, most important of all, that it has some special reference to the Roman *emperor* who is signified by the *beast*.   The traditional-historical method is hardly adequate to the elucidation of these three points, and, this being so, the possibility of an

[1] Meyer, xvi.[5], p. 431.   [2] *Ibid.*, p. 432.

[3] *Cf. Der Antichrist*, p. 8: "At the same time I am quite conscious that in the last resort I do not attain to an understanding of the eschatological-mythological ideas".

[4] *Der Antichrist*, p. 132 ff.

[5] According to Bousset, the mark seems to have been originally a serpent-mark: the reference to the name of the beast was added by the writer of the Apocalypse (*Der Antichrist*, p. 133).   But nothing is added: and therefore in Meyer, xvi.[5], p. 432, it is more accurately put that the mark is "changed in meaning".

[6] In the passages cited by Bousset the *buying* (and *selling*) is intimately connected with the famine.

allusion to something in the history of the time, hitherto unknown, presses for consideration.

Now the Papyri put us in a position where we can do justice to this possibility. They inform us of a *mark* which was commonly used in imperial times,[1] which

(1) Is connected with the Roman Emperor,

(2) Contains his name (possibly also his effigy) and the year of his reign,

(3) Was necessary upon documents relating to buying, selling, etc., and

(4) Was technically known as χάραγμα.

1. On Papyri of the 1st and 2nd centuries A.D. are often found " traces, now more distinct, now very faint, of a red seal, which, at first sight, resembles a red maculation ; but the regular, for the most part concentric, arrangement of the spots shows that they are really traces of written charac- ters ".[2] But in addition to those seal-*impressions* on papyrus, which will be discussed presently in greater detail, there has also been preserved a circular stamp-plate of soft lime- stone having a diameter of 5·5 centimetres and a thick- ness of 2·8 centimetres. On the face of the stamp are vestiges of the red pigment. The plate is now in the Museum at Berlin, and a fac-simile was issued by F. Krebs in con- nection with *BU.* 183. We are enabled, by the kind permission of the authorities of the Imperial Museum, to give here a reproduction of the fac-simile.

The legend, in uncial characters, reversed of course, is arranged in a circle, and runs as follows :—

$$\text{L } λε' \text{ } Καίσαρος,$$

i.e., in the 35th year[3] of Caesar (= 5-6 A.D.).

---

[1] Whether the use of this imperial χάραγμα is found elsewhere is unknown to the author. But he is of opinion that it is not; otherwise it would be inconceivable that Mommsen, who finds in John 13[16 f.] an allusion to the imperial *money* (Römische Geschichte, v.[4], Berlin, 1894, p. 522), should not have lighted upon the author's conjecture. Wessely also, in his issue of *PER.*, treats the matter as something new.

[2] Wessely in ref. to *PER.* xi., p. 11.

[3] L is the common abbreviation for ἔτους.

In the middle, surrounded by the circle of these letters, there are also the letters γρ, which we do not understand. Krebs resolves them thus: γρ(αφεῖον); in that case the seal must also have contained the names of the authorities.

IMPERIAL SEAL OF AUGUSTUS.   BERLIN MUSEUM.

It was with such plates that the imperial seals[1] which have been more or less distinctly preserved on some Papyrus documents, were impressed. The following instances have become known to us:—

(a) *PER.* i. (Fayyûm, 83-84 A.D.), a bill of sale, has endorsed on it the remains of two red seals of which the words [Αὐτ]οκρ[άτορος] and Δομ[ιτιανοῦ], besides other traces of writing, can still be recognised.

(b) *BU.* 183 (Fayyûm, 26th April, 85 A.D.), a document about the arrangement of the property and inheritance of a married couple, has an endorsement of three almost wholly obliterated lines by the same hand that wrote the text of the document, and two impressions of a seal in red ink; diameter 7·8 centimetres, length of the letters 0·7 centimetre. The characters (uncial) in a circular line, are as follows:—

Ⳑ δʹ Αὐτοκράτορος Καίσαρος Δομιτιανοῦ Σεβαστοῦ Γερμανικοῦ.

[1] We have found only imperial seals in the Papyri.

(c) *PER.* xi. (Fayyûm, 108 A.D.), an agreement regarding the sharing of two parts of a house, is a specially finely preserved copy which Wessely has issued in fac-simile.[1] " On the back is the red stamp, circular, and having a diameter of 9·7 centimetres; close to the outer edge there is a circular line, then, inside this, a circle formed by the letters (each 1 centimetre in length) :—

L *ιβ′ Αὐτοκράτορος Καισαρος Νέρουα Τραιανοῦ.*

" Within this, again, is a smaller circle, which consists of the letters (beginning under the **L**) :—

Σεβαστοῦ Γερμανικοῦ Δακικοῦ,

and, lastly, in the middle, the bust of the emperor, looking to the right.

" Under the seal there is written in black ink :—

μαρ^ω σεσ^η (Μάρων σεσημείωμαι)."

(d) *PER.* clxx. (Fayyûm, reign of Trajan), a bill of sale, bears on the back the red seal, of which about a third is preserved, and of which there can still be read, in the outer circle :—

[Αὐτ]οκράτορος Καισαρος Ν[έρουα Τραιανοῦ],

in the inner :—

[Σεβασ]τοῦ Γερμανικοῦ.

2. All these imperial seals, including that of Augustus, have this in common, *viz.*, that they contain the name of the emperor; one may assume with certainty, from the analogy of those that are preserved in their completeness, that those which are mutilated also originally contained the year of his reign. One seal has also the effigy of the emperor: how far this may be the case, or may be conjectured, in regard to the others cannot be made out from the reproductions which

---

[1] The author applied, March 15, 1897, to the directors of the Imperial and Royal Printing Establishment at Vienna with the request to lend him the cast of this fac-simile for his book. The directors, to their great regret, could not grant this request, "as the editors of the work *Corpus Papyrorum Raineri* are unable, on principle, to give their consent to it". [Reply of 22nd March.]

have been issued.   At all events, the seal of Augustus bears no effigy.

3. As to the purpose of the seal there can hardly be any doubt.   Wessely[1] thinks indeed that one might "take it to be a credential that the material written upon was produced in the imperial manufactory; or to be the credential of an autograph document ".   But, in our opinion, the former alternative cannot be entertained.   The seal in *PER.* xi., for instance, is much too large for the factory-mark of the Papyrus; so considerable a space of the valuable material would surely not have been from the first rendered unfit for use by stamping.   And there is yet another reason. So far as the date of the preserved seals can still be made out, it corresponds to the year of the particular document. Now, if the seal be a factory-mark, this would be a remarkable coincidence.   It is rather intended to be the guarantee of an autograph document.   It is affixed to a contract by the competent authorities, making the document legally valid. This hypothesis is confirmed by the under-mentioned copy of a similar document: on it there is no seal, but the legend is faithfully copied on the margin.   The seal, then, belongs to the document as such, not to the papyrus.

Looking now at the stamped documents with respect to their contents, we find that in five instances (including the under-mentioned copy) there are three bills of sale or purchase.   The other two documents are in contents closely allied to these.   Wessely[2] has already called special attention to this in regard to the deed of partition; but *BU.* 183 also relates to a similar matter.[3]

4. We are indebted to a fortunate coincidence for the knowledge of the official name of this imperial seal.   *PER.*

---

[1] In connection with *PER.* xi., p. 37.

[2] In connection with *PER.* xi., p. 34.

[3] We are of opinion that, by a more exact examination of the fragments of bills of sale and similar documents of the 1st and 2nd centuries, so far as their originals are extant, we might discover traces of a seal in other instances.

iv. is the copy of a bill of sale from the Fayyûm, belonging
to the 12th year of the Emperor Claudius (52-53 A.D.). It
consists of three parts, *viz.*, the actual substance of the agreement, the procuratorial signature, and the attestation by the
γραφεῖον, an authority whom Wessely describes as the
"graphische Registeramt". Each of these three parts is
prefaced by a note stating it to be a copy, thus: ἀντίγραφον
οἰκονομίας[1] line 1, ἀντίγραφον ὑπογραφῆς line 30; finally, on
the left margin, running vertically, ἀντίγραφον χαράγματος.
Wessely translates "copy of the signature," but the "signature," or rather the necessary stamping, of the original has
been effected precisely by means of the imperial seal. This
is supported by the wording as copied:—

L [ι]β′ Τιβερίου Κλαυδίου Καίσαρος Σεβαστοῦ Γερμανικοῦ
                    Αὐτοκράτορος.

This is exactly the legend whose form is made known to
us by such of the original seals as have been preserved. The
term χάραγμα suits it excellently. In the lines which follow
we must needs recognise the manuscript note of the γραφεῖον,
placed below the seal, such as we find in *PER.* xi., and most
likely in *BU.* 183 also. He adds the day of the month,[2]
μηνὸς Καισαρεί(ου) ιδ′, and the designation of the attesting
authority, ἀναγ(έγραπται) διὰ τοῦ ἐν Ἡρακλείᾳ γραφείου.

To sum up: χάραγμα is the name of the imperial seal,
giving the year and the name of the reigning emperor
(possibly also his effigy), and found on bills of sale and
similar documents of the 1st and 2nd centuries.

It is not asserting too much to say that in this ascertained fact we have something to proceed upon. If the *beast*
be correctly interpreted as referring to a Roman emperor,
which the author does not doubt in the least, then, from

---

[1] οἰκονομία = *document* is often found in the Papyri.

[2] The supposition that the day of the month also belonged to the
seal is in itself improbable, as, in that case, the plate must have been altered
daily; it is further opposed by the fact that the preserved seals only give the
year.

what we now know of the emperor's χάραγμα, we can very
well understand the χάραγμα of the beast.   The χάραγμα of
the Apocalypse is not, of course, wholly identical with its
contemporary prototype.   The seer acted with a free hand ;
he has it that the mark is impressed on forehead or hand,[1]
and he gives the *number* a new meaning.   It is in this point
that ancient (apocalyptic ?) tradition may possibly have
made its influence felt.   But it has only modified ; the
characteristic, not to say charagmatic, features of the prototype can be recognised without difficulty.

χειρόγραφον.

The technical signification *bond, certificate of debt*, authen-
ticated in reference to Col. 2 [14] by *Clavis* [3] and Thayer in
Plutarch and Artemidorus only, is very common in the
Papyri.   Many of the original χειρόγραφα, indeed, have been
preserved ; some of these are scored through and thus
cancelled (*e.g.* *BU.* 179, 272, *PER.* ccxxix).   The following
passages from Fayyûm Papyri may be cited for the word :
PER. i. 29 (83-84 A.D.), xiii. 3 (110-111 A.D.), *BU.* 50 5. 16. 18 (115
A.D.), 69 12 (120 A.D.), 272 4. 16 (138-139 A.D.), 300 3. 12 (148
A.D.), 301 17 (157 A.D.), 179 (reign of Antoninus Pius), *PER.*
ix. 6. 9 (Hermopolis, 271 A.D.).

χωρίζομαι.

As in 1 Cor. 7 [10. 11. 15], a technical expression for divorce
also in the Fayyûm Papyri.[2]   In the marriage-contracts there
are usually stated conditions for the possibility of separation ;
these are introduced by the formula ἐὰν δὲ [οἱ γαμοῦντες]
χωρίζωνται ἀπ᾽ ἀλλήλων ; thus *BU.* 251 6 (81 A.D., restoration
certain), 252 7 (98 A.D.), *PER.* xxiv. 27 (136 A.D.), xxvii. 16 (190
A.D.).

---

[1] Even if all the imperial seals were as large as that of Trajan in *PER.*
xi., which, with its diameter of 9·7 centimetres, could find sufficient room
only on the brows of thinkers and the hands of the proletariat, yet our hypothesis would lose nothing in probability ; surely we do not wish to control
the seer with the centimetre rod.   But there was manifestly no prescribed
standard diameter for the seal ; *cf.* that on *BU.* 183, or even the original
stamp of Augustus ; a seal of its size could quite well have found room on
forehead or hand.

[2] Examples are also to be found in other places.

5. PHRASES AND FORMULAE.

ἐκ τῶν τεσσάρων ἀνέμων.

One might imagine the formula (LXX Zech. 11 [6], Mark 13 [27], Matt. 24 [31]) to be a mere imitation of the corresponding Hebrew one. But it occurs also in *PER.* cxv. [6] (Fayyûm, 2nd cent. A.D.) [γείτο]νες ἐκ τεσσάρων ἀνέμων; notwithstanding the mutilation of the document, there can be no doubt that *the four cardinal points* are meant.

ἀξίως τοῦ θεοῦ.

In 1 Thess. 2 [12] we have περιπατεῖν ἀξίως τοῦ θεοῦ, in Col. 1 [10] περιπατῆσαι ἀξίως τοῦ κυρίου εἰς πᾶσαν ἀρεσκείαν, in 3 John [6] προπέμψας ἀξίως τοῦ θεοῦ (*cf.* possibly Wisdom 3 [5] καὶ εὗρεν αὐτοὺς ἀξίους ἑαυτοῦ [= θεοῦ] and Matt. 10 [37 f.]). The formula was a very popular one in Pergamus (and doubtless also in other localities). In *Perg.* 248 [7 ff.] (142-141 B.C.), Athenaios, a priest of Dionysus and Sabazius, is extolled as συ[ν]τετελεκότος τὰ ἱερὰ . . . . εὐσεβῶς [μ]ὲγ καὶ ἀξίως τοῦ θεοῦ; [1] in *Perg.* 521 (after 136 A.D.), ἱερασαμένην ἀξίως τῆς θεοῦ καὶ τῆς πατρίδος, of a priestess of Athena, and in *Perg.* 485 [3 ff.] (beginning of 1st cent. A.D.), an ἀρχιβούκολος is honoured διὰ τὸ εὐσεβῶς καὶ ἀξίως τοῦ Καθηγεμόνος Διονύσου προΐστασθαι τῶν θείων μυστηρίων. In *Perg.* 522 [7 ff.] (3rd cent. A.D.) two priestesses of Athena are similarly commemorated as ἱερασαμένων . . . . . . ἐνδόξως καὶ ἐπιφανῶς κατὰ τὸ ἀξίωμα καὶ τὸ μέγεθος τῆς θεοῦ. The Inscription of Sestos (*Wiener Studien*, i., p. 33 ff., *ca.* 120 B.C.) has, in line 87, λαμπρὰν ποιησάμενος τὴν ὑποδοχὴν καὶ ἀξίαν τῶν θεῶν καὶ τοῦ δήμου.

ἐμμένω (ἐν) πᾶσι τοῖς γεγραμμένοις.

LXX Deut. 27 [26] ἐπικατάρατος πᾶς ἄνθρωπος ὃς οὐκ ἐμμένει ἐν πᾶσι τοῖς λόγοις τοῦ νόμου τούτου is quoted "freely" by Paul in Gal. 3 [10] thus: ἐπικατάρατος πᾶς ὃς οὐκ ἐμμένει ἐν πᾶσιν τοῖς γεγραμμένοις ἐν τῷ βιβλίῳ τοῦ νόμου. Certainly an immaterial alteration, such as any one may unconsciously make in a quotation from memory. We should not need to

---

[1] *Cf.*, if the restoration be correct, *Perg.* 223 (*ca.* 156 B.C.) ἀναστ[ρεφο. μένη]ν καλ[ῶς] καὶ εὐσεβῶς καὶ ἀ[ξίως τῆς θεᾶς], said of Bito, a priestess of Athena.

trouble any further about it, were it not that the Papyri indicate how Paul may have come to make this particular insignificant change. In the deed of partition *PER.* xi. 23 f. (Fayyûm, 108 A.D.) we read ἐνμενέτωσαν [οἱ] ὁμολο-γοῦντες . . . . ἐν τοῖς ἑκουσίως ὡμολογη[μένοις] καὶ διειρη-μένοις. Here we have a legal formula familiar in the official style of such documents, which occurs earlier in a similar form in the Turin Papyrus 8 (2nd cent. A.D.): ἐμμένειν δὲ ἀμφοτέρους ἐν τοῖς πρὸς ἑαυτοὺς διωμολογημένοις.[1] The formula varies as to its verb, but preserves the constancy of its form—intelligible in the case of a legal expression—by the fact that ἐμμένειν, with or without ἐν, is followed by the dative of a participle, mostly in the plural. It so runs in *PER.* ccxxiv. 5 f. (Fayyûm, 5-6 A.D.) ἐνμένειν ἐν πᾶσι τοῖς γεγε[νημένοις κατὰ τὴ]ν γραφὴν τῆς ὁμολ(ογίας[2]) ἣν συνγέ-γραμμαί σοι. Note here the addition of a new word, πᾶσι. And, finally, let us read *BU.* 600 6 (Fayyûm, 2nd-3rd cent. A.D.) ἐνμένω πᾶσι ταῖς προγεγραμμέν[α]ις sic [ἐν]τολαῖς, a form of which the biblical quotation of Paul, with its distinctive variation, is undoubtedly reminiscent. In these circumstances, the Apostle may be supposed to have continued the biblical ἐμμένει ἐν πᾶσι τοῖς . . . by a participle, unconsciously adopting the cadence of the legal formula. We are unaware whether this form of expression is to be found elsewhere, or outside Egypt; its unquestionably formulaic character speaks for its having belonged—albeit in manifold variation—to the more widely known material of the language. Moreover, the use of a legal form of expression is particularly easy to understand in the case of Paul.[3]

καθὼς γέγραπται, etc.

The authorities given on p. 113 f. for the legal character of the formula of quotation καθὼς (καθάπερ) γέγραπται can still be largely added to.[4] In *IMAe.* 761 41 (Rhodes, 3rd cent.

---

[1] As the author has not the Turin Papyri by him, he quotes according to *Corp. Papp. Raineri,* i. 1, p. 12.

[2] ὁμολογία = *contract.*   [3] See p. 107 f.

[4] It was remarked on p. 114, note 3, that the formula is also found without this technical meaning. As examples of this we have the ἀναγέγραπται

B.C.) we have καθὰ καὶ ἐν τοῖς νόμοις γέγραπται. In the decree *Perg.* 251 ₃₅ (2nd cent. B.C.), with reference to a passage immediately preceding, there occur the words καθάπερ γέγραπται ; similarly, in the documents *BU.* 252 ₉ (Fayyûm 98 A.D.) καθὰ γέγραπται, and *PER.* cliv. ₁₁ (Fayyûm, 180 A.D.) καθὼς γ[έγρ]απται. There may also be added καθότι προγέγραπται *BU.* 189 (Fayyûm, 7 A.D.), and *PER.* iv. ₁₇ ₜ. (Fayyûm, 52-53 A.D.) ; καθώς ὑπογέγραπται, relating to an oracle quoted later, in the Inscription of Sidyma No. 53 Db ₁₁ ₜ.[1] (post-Hadrianic) ; καθὰ διαγέγραπται in an Inscription from Cos [2] (date ?)

Other formulae of quotation used by the New Testament writers are vouched for by the legal language : κατὰ τὰ προγεγραμμένα *PER.* iv. ₂₄ (Fayyûm, 52-53 A.D.) *cf.* κατὰ τὸ γεγραμμένον 2 Cor. 4 ₁₃ ; [κατὰ τὴ]ν γραφήν, with reference to a contract, *PER.* ccxxiv. ₆ (Fayyûm, 5-6 A.D.), and κατὰ γραφάς, with reference to the laws, *BU.* 136 ₁₀ (135 A.D.), *cf.* κατὰ τὰς γραφάς 1 Cor. 15 ³ ᶠ·, and κατὰ τὴν γραφήν James 2 ⁸.

τὸ γνήσιον.

2 Cor. 8 ⁸ τὸ τῆς ὑμετέρας ἀγάπης γνήσιον : *cf.* Inscription of Sestos (*Wiener Studien*, i., p. 33 ff., *ca.* 120 B.C.), line ₇, πρὸ πλείστου θέμενος τὸ πρὸς τὴν πατρίδα γνήσιον καὶ ἐκτενές.

δέησιν, δεήσεις ποιοῦμαι.

δέησιν ποιοῦμαι (Phil. 1 ⁴ of *supplication*) is used quite generally for *request* in *BU.* 180 ₁₇ (Fayyûm, 172 A.D.) δικαίαν δέ[ησ]ιν ποιούμενος ; on the other hand, δεήσεις ποιοῦμαι, as in Luke 5 ³³, 1 Tim. 2 ¹, of *supplication*, also in *Pap. Par.* 69

of Josephus (references in Hans Drüner, *Untersuchungen über Josephus*, Thesis, Marburg, 1896, pp. 54 note 1, and 85), Arrian (*cf.* Wilcken, *Philologus*, liii. [1894], p. 117 f.), and most likely of other authors as well. I am indebted to a kind communication of Dr. Hans Drüner for the information that Josephus frequently employs ἀναγέγραπται for O.T. references also, while he certainly uses γέγραπται very seldom for these ; γέγραπται in *c. Ap.* ii. 18 refers to a non-biblical quotation.

[1] Benndorf and Niemann, *Reisen in Lykien und Karien*, i., Vienna, 1894, p. 77 ; for the date see p. 75.

[2] *Hermes* xvi. (1881), p. 172, note ; cited by Fränkel, p. 16.

ii. 11 (Elephantiné, 232 A.D.) ἔνθα σπονδά[ς τε καὶ δε]ήσεις ποιησάμενος.¹

δεξιὰν δίδωμι.

In *Perg.* 268 C (98 B.C.) the Pergamenians offer themselves as peace-makers in the quarrel between the cities of
Sardis and Ephesus: they send a mediator (line 10 *t.*): [τὸν
παρακα]λέσοντα δοῦναι τ[ὰ]ς χεῖρας ἡμῖν εἰ[ς σύλλυσιν].² On
this Fränkel observes, p. 201: "'to give the hands towards
an agreement (to be brought about by us)'. I have not
found any other example of this use (corresponding to the
German) of the phrase δοῦναι τὰς χεῖρας." We have here a
case where the elucidation of the Inscriptions can be to some
extent assisted by the sacred text; the expression *give the
hand* or *hands*³ is very common in the Greek Bible—though
in the form δεξιὰν (or δεξιὰς) διδόναι: 1 Macc. 6⁵⁸, 11⁵⁰·⁶²,
13⁵⁰, 2 Macc. 11²⁶, 12¹¹, 13²², Gal. 2⁹ (δεξιὰς ἔδωκαν . . .
κοινωνίας; *cf.* δεξιὰν (or δεξιὰς) λαμβάνειν 1 Macc. 11⁶⁶, 13⁵⁰,
2 Macc. 12¹², 14¹⁹.⁴ Then exegetes have also adduced classical analogies; most exhaustively Joannes Dougtæus,
Analecta sacra, 2nd ed., Amsterdam, 1694, Part ii., p. 123.
*Clavis*³, p. 88, cites only Xen. *Anab.* 1, 6, 6; 2, 5, 3; Joseph.
Antt. 18, 19 [should be 9], 3.

εἰς τὸ διηνεκές.

Apart from the Epistle to the Hebrews, authenticated in
Appian, *B. civ.* 1, 4; found in *IMAe.* 786 16 (Rhodes, imperial
period): τετειμημένος *sic* ἐς τὸ διενεκές *sic*, also in Apollodorus
of Damascus, 42.

ἔθος, κατὰ τὸ ἔθος.

The word is used in the Fayyûm Papyri almost entirely
for *law, ritus*, in the narrower sense, as often in Luke and

¹ The citation is made from the issue of this Papyrus (from *Notices et
extraits*, xviii. 2, pp. 390-399) by Wilcken in *Philologus*, liii. (1894), p. 82.

² The restorations are certain.

³ With this we must not confound ἐκδιδόναι τὴν χεῖρα, *BU.* 405.
(Fayyûm, 348 A.D.) where χείρ means *manuscript, document.*

⁴ See also Grimm on 2 Macc. 4³⁴, *HApAT.* iv. (1857), p. 93.

Acts.   Note especially the formula κατὰ τὸ ἔθος (Luke 1⁹,
2⁴²): *BU.* 250₁₇ (reign of Hadrian) καθαρὸς κατὰ τὸ ἔθος,
131₅ (2nd-3rd cent. A.D.) and 96₁₅ (2nd half of 3rd cent. A.D.)
κατὰ τὰ ʿΡωμαίων ἔθη,¹ 347 i. ₁₇, ii. ₁₅ (171 A.D.) and 82₁₂ (185
A.D.) περιτμηθῆναι κατὰ τὸ ἔθος (*cf.* Acts 15¹ περιτμηθῆτε τῷ
ἔθει Μωϋσέως).

ἑτοίμως ἔχω.

Manifold authorities for the phrase in connection with
2 Cor. 12¹⁴, 1 Pet. 4⁵, Acts 21¹³; it is found also in the Fayyûm
documents of the reign of Marcus Aurelius, *BU.* 240₂₇ and
80[= 446]₁₇.   The construction can be made out in the
latter passage only; as in all the New Testament passages it
is followed by the infinitive.

τοῦ θεοῦ θέλοντος, etc.

Similar pagan formulae have long since been referred
to in connection with the New Testament passages.   The
Fayyûm Papyri reveal how widespread its use must have
been, even in the lower strata of society.   With τοῦ θεοῦ
θέλοντος in Acts 18²¹ is connected τῶν θε[ῶ]ν θελόντων *BU.*
423₁₈ (2nd cent. A.D., a soldier's letter to his father);
615₄ᵣ. (2nd cent. A.D., private letter) ἐπιγνοῦσα ὅτι θεῶν
θελόντων διεσώθης, used in reference to the past; similarly in
line₂₁ᵣ.; further, θεῶν δὲ βουλομένων 248₁₁ᵣ. (2nd cent. A.D.,
private letter), 249₁₃ (2nd cent. A.D., private letter).   With
ἐὰν ὁ κύριος ἐπιτρέψῃ 1 Cor. 16⁷, ἐάνπερ ἐπιτρέπῃ ὁ θεός
Heb. 6³, compare θεῶν ἐπιτρεπόν[τ]ων 451₁₀ᵣ. (1st-2nd cent.
A.D., private letter), also τῆς τύχης ἐπιτρεπούσης 248₁₅ᵣ. (2nd
cent. A.D., private letter).   Allied to καθὼς [ὁ θεὸς] ἠθέλησεν
1 Cor. 12¹⁸, 15³⁸ is ὡς ὁ θεὸς ἤθελεν in *BU.* 27₁₁ (2nd-3rd
cent. A.D., private letter).   It is a specially significant fact
that it is precisely in private letters that we find the
specified examples of the use of these formulae.

ἐκ τοῦ μέσου αἴρω.

Thayer, p. 402, cites Plut. *De Curios.* 9, *Is.* 57, 2 in connection with Col. 2¹⁴.   The phrase is used in *BU.* 388 ii. ₂₃

---

¹ This formula often occurs in the *PER.* also.

(Fayyûm, 2nd-3rd cent. A.D.) like *e medio tollo* in the proper sense.

ἀπὸ τοῦ νῦν.

This formula, employed in 2 Cor. 5[16], as also often by Luke (Gospel, and Acts 18[6]), is very common in the Fayyûm legal documents. We find it in the following combinations: ἀπὸ τοῦ νῦν ἐπὶ τὸν ἅπαντα χρόνον *PER.* iv. 9. 17 (52-53 A.D.), xi. 6 (108 A.D.), *BU.* 350 19 (reign of Trajan), 193 ii. 11 (136 A.D.); ἀπὸ τοῦ νῦν εἰς τὸν ἀεὶ χρόνον 282 5 (after 175 A.D.); [ἀπ]ὸ τοῦ νῦν ἐπὶ τὸν ἀεὶ καὶ ἅπαντα [χρόνον] 456 9 (348 A.D.); also standing by itself, ἀπὸ τοῦ νῦν 153 14 (152 A.D.) and 13 9 (289 A.D.).

A corresponding form, μέχρ[ι] τ[οῦ] νῦν (cf. ἄχρι τοῦ νῦν Rom. 8[22], Phil. 1[5]), is found in *BU.* 256 9 (Fayyûm, reign of Antoninus Pius).

κατ' ὄναρ.

The references for this phrase, as found in Matt. 1[20], 2[12 f. 19. 22], 27[19], cannot be supplemented by *Perg.* 357[8] (Roman times) [κ]ατ' ὄναρ or *IMAe.* 979 4 f. (Carpathus, 3rd cent. A.D.) κατὰ ὄναρ; in these cases the phrase does not mean *in a dream*, but *in consequence of a dream*, like κατ' ὄνειρον in *Perg.* 327 (late Roman[1]).

παραίτιος ἀγαθῶν.

In the letter of Lysias to the Jews, 2 Macc. 11[19], it is said καὶ εἰς τὸ λοιπὸν πειράσομαι παραίτιος ὑμῖν ἀγαθῶν γενέσθαι. Similarly in Ep. Arist. p. 67 21 (Schm.) we have ὡς ἂν μεγάλων ἀγαθῶν παραίτιοι γεγονότες. The formula is often found in the Inscriptions. In reference to *Perg.* 246 54 f. (decree of the city of Elaia in honour of Attalus iii., *ca.* 150 B.C.) [ἀ]εί τινος [ἀ]γα[θ]οῦ παραίτ[ι]ον γίνεσθαι αὐτόν, Fränkel, p. 159, observes: "The phrase was received as a formula into the official Greek of the Romans: so a quaestor's letter to the Letaeans, 118 B.C., in Dittenberger, *Sylloge* 247, 44 f.; two letters, from Caesar and Octavian,

---

[1] *Cf.* Fränkel, p. 55.

to the Mitylenians, *Sitzungsber. d. Berl. Akad.* 1889, pp. 960,
965. Elsewhere also, *e.g.* in Dittenberger, 252, 2; 280,
23 ". *IMAe.* 1032 11 (Carpathus, 2nd cent. B.C.) παραίτιος
γεγόνει τᾶς σωτηρ[ί]ας should also be compared.

παρέχομαι ἐμαυτόν.

Clavis[3], p. 340, finds examples of this reflexive phrase
(Tit. 2[7]) only in Xen. *Cyr.* 8, 1, 39; Thayer, p. 488, adds
Joseph. c. *Ap.* 2, 15, 4. It occurs also in *IMAe.* 1032 6 (Car-
pathus, 2nd cent. B.C.) ἀνέγκλητον αὐτὸν παρέσχηται, and
Lebas, *Asie* 409 6 (Mylasa, 1st cent. B.C.), χρήσιμον ἑαυτὸν
παρεσχηται.[1]

παρίστημι θυσίαν.

In reference to Rom. 12[1] B. Weiss[2] rejects the sacri-
ficial meaning of *to present, lay down* (*the sacrifice upon the
altar*), for παριστάναι, as the word "most probably occurs in
Greek in this sense"—here follow the references—"but it is
certainly not . . . in any way a standing technical term in
the O. T. "; it is to be taken as *to place at one's disposal.*
The present writer has two objections to this view. For one
thing he cannot see wherein the two interpretations differ;
even if the latter be preferred, it yet embraces, in this very
combination παριστάναι θυσίαν, the meaning of the former.
And, again, he cannot understand how a form of expression
used by the Apostle Paul can be set up as something to be
contrasted with Greek.

The references given by Weiss for the usage of the word
in Greek can be supplemented by *Perg.* 246 17. 43 (decree of the
city of Elaia in honour of Attalus III., *ca.* 150 B.C.) παραστα-
θείσης θυσίας, 256 14. 21 (imperial period) παρασταθῆναι [θ]υσίαν
αὐτῷ, or [ἀφ' ο]ῦ [ἂ]ν . . παριστῇ τὴν θυσί[α]ν.

μετὰ πάσης προθυμίας.

With Acts 17[11] οἵτινες ἐδέξαντο τὸν λόγον μετὰ πάσης
προθυμίας cf. *Perg.* 13 30 f. (oath of allegiance of the mercen-

[1] This passage is quoted from Fränkel, p. 186, who also refers to the
active παρασχόντα χρήσιμον ἑαυτὸν τῇ πατρίδι, *CIG.* 2771 i. 10 (Aphrodisias), and
would restore *Perg.* 253 15 in a similar way.

[2] Meyer, iv.[8] (1891), p. 512.

aries of King Eumenes I., soon after 263 A.D.) [παρ]έξομαι δὲ
καὶ τὴν [ἄ]λλην χρείαν εὐνόως καὶ ἀπροφα[σ]ί[σ]τως [με]τὰ
πάσης προθυμ[ί]ας εἰς δύναμιν εἶναι τὴν ἐμήν.   The idiom will,
without doubt, be found elsewhere.

ἐκ συμφώνου.

As in 1 Cor. 7 [5], the formula occurs in the following
Fayyûm documents: *BU.* 446 [= 80] 13 (reign of Marcus
Aurelius) κ[α]θὼς ἐκ συνφώνου ὑπηγόρευσαν, *PER.* cxci. 9 (2nd
cent. A.D.) [κ]αθὼς ἐξυμφώνου *sic* ὑπηγόρευσαν, and cxcvii. 8
(2nd cent. A.D.) καδὼς *sic* ἐξυμφώνου *sic* π[. . . . .] ὑπηγ[ό-
ρευσαν].

οὐχ ὁ τυχών.

For *extraordinary*, as in 3 Macc. 3 [7], Acts 19 [11], 28 [2], the
phrase occurs also in *BU.* 36 [*cf.* 436] 9 (Fayyûm, 2nd-3rd
cent. A.D.) ὕβριν οὐ τὴν τυχοῦσαν συνετελέσαντο and in an
earlier Inscription from Ptolemais in Egypt, of the time of
Euergetes, *Bulletin de correspondance hellénique*, xxi. (1897), p.
190.

οἱ ἐν ὑπεροχῇ ὄντες.

Hitherto noted in 1 Tim. 2 [2] only ; *cf.* 2 Macc. 3 [11] ἀνδρὸς
ἐν ὑπεροχῇ κειμένου. Already in *Perg.* 252 [20] (early Roman
period, after 133 B.C.), we find τῶν ἐν ὑπεροχῇ ὄντων, probably used generally of *persons of consequence.*

φίλανδρος καὶ φιλότεκνος.

In regard to Tit. 2 [4] τὰς νέας φιλάνδρους εἶναι, φιλοτέκνους,
v. Soden [1] observes, "both expressions here only," and also
in the last edition of Meyer (xi. [6] [1894], p. 382) they are
described as " ἅπ. λεγ.," although both are already given in
the *Clavis* as occurring elsewhere. More important than the
correction of this error, however, is the ascertained fact that
the two words must have been current in this very combination. Already in *Clavis* [3] we find cited for it Plut. *Mor.*, p.
769 C. To this may be added an epitaph from Pergamus,
Perg. 604 (about the time of Hadrian), which, on account
of its simple beauty, is given here in full :—

[1] *HC.* iii. 1 (1891), p. 209.

'Ιούλιος Βάσσος
'Οτακιλία Πώλλη
τῇ γλυκυτάτῃ
[γ]υναικί, φιλάνδρ[ῳ]
καὶ φιλοτέκνῳ,
συνβιωσάσῃ
ἀμέμπτως
ἔτη λ'.

An Inscription of the imperial period, from Paros, *CIG.* 2384 [1], similarly extols a wife as φίλανδρον καὶ φιλόπαιδα. We need no evidence to prove that precisely a combination of this kind could readily become popular.

τὸ αὐτὸ φρονεῖν.

This formula and others of similar formation which are current in the writings of the Apostle Paul have been found in Herodotus and other writers.[2] The epitaph *IMAe.* 149 (Rhodes, 2nd cent. B.C.), in which it is said of a married couple, ταὐτὰ λέγοντες ταὐτὰ φρονοῦντες ἤλθομεν τὰν ἀμέτρη-τον ὁδὸν εἰς 'Αΐδαν, permits of the supposition that it was familiarly used in popular speech.

6. RARER WORDS, MEANINGS AND CONSTRUCTIONS.

ἄδολος.

In reference to 1 Pet. 2 [2] ὡς ἀρτιγέννητα βρέφη τὸ λογικὸν ἄδολον γάλα ἐπιποθήσατε, E. Kühl [3] observes that the second attribute ἄδολος is not meant to apply to the meta-phorical γάλα, but only to the word of God as symbolised by it. But *BU.* 290₁₃ (Fayyûm, 150 A.D.) makes it probable that this adjective ·could quite well be applied to milk ; the word is there used, alongside of καθαρός, of *unadulterated* wheat. Thus the word need not have been chosen as merely relating to the meaning of the metaphor, nor, again, as merely referring to πάντα δόλον in verse [1].

---

[1] Citation from Fränkel, p. 134.
[2] *Cf.* A. H. Franke on Phil. 2 [2] (Meyer, ix.[5] [1886], p. 84).
[3] Meyer, xii. [6] (1897), p. 136.

ἀμετανόητος.

According to *Clavis* [3], p. 21, found only in Lucian, *Abdic.* 11; Thayer, p. 32, adds Philo, *De Praem. et Poen.* § 3 (M. p. 410). In *PER.* ccxvi. 5 (Fayyûm, 1st-2nd cent. A.D.), the word is used, passively, of a sale (κυρίαν καὶ βεβαίαν καὶ ἀμετανόητον).

ἀπόκριμα.

For this manifestly very rare word in 2 Cor. 1 [9], *Clavis* [3], p. 43, gives only the reference Joseph. *Antt.* 14, 10, 6; Thayer, p. 63, supplements this by Polyb. *Excpt. Vat.* 12, 26 [b], 1; in both passages an official *decision* is meant. The word occurs in the same sense in the Inscription (particularly worthy of consideration by reason of its proximity in time to the Pauline passage) *IMAe.* 2 4 (Rhodes, 51 A.D.), in which τὰ εὐκταιότατα ἀποκρίματα certainly relates to favourable *decisions* of the Emperor Claudius.

ἀρκετός.

Outside the N. T. only authenticated hitherto in Chrysippus (in Athen. 3, 79, p. 113 *b*); is also found in the Fayyûm Papyri *BU.* 531 ii. 24 (2nd cent. A.D.) and 33 5 (2nd-3rd cent. A.D.).

ἀσπάζομαι.

With the meaning *pay one's respects* (Acts 25 [13], Joseph. *Antt.* 1, 19, 5; 6, 11, 1), also in the Fayyûm Papyri *BU.* 347 i. 3, ii. 2 (171 A.D.) and 248 12 (2nd cent. A.D.).

βαστάζω.

Of the special meaning [1] *furtim sepono* in John 12 [6] the Fayyûm Papyri yield a number of fresh examples: *BU.* 361 iii. 10 (end of 2nd cent. A.D.), 46 10 (193 A.D.), 157 8 (2nd-3rd cent. A.D.). The last two documents contain speeches of the public prosecutor in regard to cases of theft.

---

[1] The more general meaning also is found in *BU.* 388 ii. 24 (Fayyûm, 2nd-3rd cent. A.D.).

βιάζομαι.

Without entering into the controversy over Matt. 11[12] and Luke 16[16], the author wishes only to establish the following facts. Cremer[8], p. 215, thinks that it may be considered as "demonstrable" that the word in Matthew *must* be taken as a passive : "As a deponent it would give no sense whatever, since *βιάζεσθαι cannot stand without an object or a substitute therefor, like* πρόσω, εἴσω, *and does not so stand* [1] . . . ; it represents no independent idea such as *do violence, come forward violently.* At least this passage would afford, so far as can be seen, the sole example of such a meaning." But in opposition to this we may refer to the epigraphic regulations of Xanthus the Lycian for the sanctuary of Men Tyrannos founded by him, *CIA.* iii. 74,[2] *cf.* 73 (found near Sunium, not earlier than the imperial period), where *βιάζομαι* is without doubt reflexive and absolute. After the ceremonial purifications are stated, the performance of which is the condition of entrance into the temple, it is further said that no one may sacrifice in the temple ἄνε[υ] τοῦ καθειδρυσαμένου [sic] τὸ ἱερόν (meaning most likely, *without permission from the founder of the temple*) ; ἐὰν δέ τις βιάσηται, the regulation continues, ἀπρόσδεκτος[3] ἡ θυσία παρὰ τοῦ θεοῦ, *but if any one comes forward violently,* or *enters by force, his offering is not pleasing to the god.* But for such as, on the contrary, have rightly performed all that is prescribed, the founder wishes, further on, καὶ εὐείλατος [sic][4] γένοι[τ]ο ὁ θεὸς τοῖς θεραπεύουσιν ἀπλῇ τῇ ψυχῇ. This antithesis is decisive for the sense of *βιάσηται.*

διετία.

Authenticated only in Philo ; Thayer (p. 148) adds to this the *Graecus Venetus* of Gen. 41[1], 45[5]. The word (Acts 24[27], 28[30]) occurs also in *BU.* 180[7] (Fayyûm, 172 A.D.) and *Perg.* 525[13] (after 217 A.D.).

---

[1] Italics from Cremer.

[2] = Dittenberger, *Sylloge,* No. 379. See, in reference to καθαρίζω, p. 216.

[3] *Cf.* its antithesis, εὐπρόσδεκτος, also said of a sacrifice, Rom. 15[16] and 1 Pet. 2[5], like θυσία δεκτή Phil. 4[18] and LXX.

[4] An additional reference for this word ; *cf.* p. 122.

δοκίμιος.

A word belonging to the Greek Bible which the Papyri are bringing again to life, after the exegetes had well-nigh strangled it. With reference to the passages James 1³ τὸ δοκίμιον ὑμῶν τῆς πίστεως κατεργάζεται ὑπομονήν, and 1 Pet. 1⁷ ἵνα τὸ δοκίμιον ὑμῶν τῆς πίστεως πολυτιμότερον χρυσίου τοῦ ἀπολλυμένου διὰ πυρὸς δὲ δοκιμαζομένου εὑρεθῇ εἰς ἔπαινον καὶ δόξαν καὶ τιμὴν ἐν ἀποκαλύψει Ἰησοῦ Χριστοῦ, it is commonly stated that τὸ δοκίμιον is equal to τὸ δοκιμεῖον, *means of testing*. This hypothesis is linguistically possible; the author certainly knows no reason why, in such case, the word is always accented δοκίμιον and not δοκιμῖον. But on material grounds there are grave objections to the hypothesis. Even the thorough-going defence of it in connection with the Petrine passage by E. Kühl¹ still leaves the present writer with the feeling that, so taken, the Apostle's thought is unnatural and indistinct, not to say unintelligible. And this also gives us the reason why most exegetes search for another meaning of the word, one which will in some degree suit the context; thus, *e.g.*, *Clavis*³, p. 106, decides for *exploratio* in James 1³, and for *verification* in 1 Pet. 1⁷, two meanings which the word never has anywhere else, and all but certainly cannot have. But the whole difficulty of the case was primarily brought about by the exegetes themselves, nearly all of whom misunderstood the word. Only Schott and Hofmann have fallen on the right view in their surmise (see Kühl, p. 88) that δοκίμιον is the neuter of an adjective.² On this Kühl observes, with a reference to Winer⁷, p. 220, that this interpretation is rendered void by the fact that δοκίμιον is not an adjective, but a genuine substantive, while Winer says "there is no adjective δοκίμιος". True, there is no δοκίμιος—that is, in the lexica; nor would Schott and Hofmann be able to find it. This want, however, is supplied by the Fayyûm Papyrus documents of the Archduke

---

¹ Meyer, xii.⁶ (1897), p. 87 ff.

² Tholuck also, in *Beiträge zur Spracherklärung des Neuen Testaments*, Halle, 1832, p. 45, makes this conjecture, with a reference to Wahl; but he has no example at his disposal.

Rainer's collection. In the pawn-ticket *PER.* xii. 6 *t.* (93 A.D.)
there are mentioned gold buckles of *the weight of* 7½ *minae of
good gold* (χρυσοῦ δοκιμίου); the marriage contract xxiv. 5 (136
A.D.) enumerates ornaments in the bride's dowry to the
value of 13 *quarters of good gold* (χρυσοῦ δοκιμείου *sic*) ; a fragment of the same contract, xxvi., reads in line 6 [χρυσ]ίου
[δοκ]ιμίου, and in line 9 [χρ]υ[σ]οῦ [δ]οκι[μ]είου *sic* ; similarly
the fragments of marriage contracts xxiii. 4 (reign of
Antoninus Pius) [χρυσίου] δοκειμείου *sic*, xxii. 5 (reign of
Antoninus Pius) [χρυ]σίου δο[κιμίου], and xxi. 12 (230 A.D.)
[χρυσοῦ] δοκιμίου. There can be no doubt about the meaning
of this δοκίμιος, and, in addition, we have the advantage of
possessing a Papyrus which gives information on the matter.
The marriage contract, *PER.* xxiv., is also preserved in a
copy, and this copy, *PER.* xxv., line 4, reads χρυσίου δοκίμου
instead of the χρυσοῦ δοκιμείου of the original. Now this
δοκίμου can hardly be a clerical error, but rather an easy
variant, as immaterial for the sense as χρυσίου for χρυσοῦ :
δοκίμιος has the meaning of δόκιμος *proved, acknowledged,*
which was used, precisely of metals, in the sense of *valid,
standard, genuine* (*e.g.,* LXX Gen. 23 16 ἀργυρίου δοκίμου,
similarly 1 Chron. 29 4, 2 Chron. 9 17 χρυσίῳ δοκίμῳ ; particulars in Cremer [8], p. 335 f.).

Hence, then, the adjective δοκίμιος, *proved, genuine,* must
be recognised, and may be adopted without misgiving in both
the New Testament passages.[1] τὸ δοκίμιον ὑμῶν τῆς πίστεως
is the exceedingly common classical construction of the substantival neuter of an adjective with genitive (often of an
abstract noun) following, which we find in the New Testament, especially in Paul.[2] An almost identical example is

---

[1] It is very highly probable that the Greek writer Oecumenius still
understood it as an adjective in these passages ; he interprets δοκίμιον τὸ
κεκριμένον λέγει, τὸ δεδοκιμασμένον, τὸ καθαρόν (Tischendorf in reference to James
1 3). The substitution, in some minuscules, of δόκιμος for δοκίμιος, in both the
New Testament passages (as in the Papyrus document *PER.* xxv. 4), likewise
supports the view that late Greek copyists understood the word. The formation of the word is plain : δοκίμιος comes from δόκιμος, as ἐλευθέριος from
ἐλεύθερος, and καθάριος from καθαρός.

[2] *Cf.* most recently Blass, *Gramm.*, p. 151 f. [Eng. Trans., p. 155.]

2 Cor. 8⁸ τὸ τῆς ὑμετέρας ἀγάπης γνήσιον.¹ We would render *whatever is genuine in your faith* in both passages. Luther's translation of the passage in James, viz., *euer Glaube, so er rechtschaffen ist* (*your faith, so it be upright*), must be pronounced altogether correct. And thus, too, all ambiguity disappears from the passage in Peter : *so that what is genuine in your faith may be found more precious than gold—which, in spite of its perishableness, is yet proved genuine by fire—unto praise and glory and honour at the revelation of Jesus Christ.* We would here avoid entering more particularly into the exegetical controversy : the proposed explanation must be its own justification.

But the tale of the ill-treatment of this word is not even yet fully told. The exegetes have disowned it also in the LXX ; it was suppressed by dint of taking two instances of the traditional δοκίμιον as identical. According to *Clavis* ³, p. 106, δοκίμιον = δοκιμεῖον LXX Prov. 27²¹ and Ps. 11 [Hebr. 12]⁷ with the meaning of *crucible ;* according to Kühl, it signifies here as always *means of testing.* Now it is certain that, in Prov. 27²¹ δοκιμιον ἀργυρίῳ καὶ χρυσῷ πύρωσις, we must take δοκιμῖον (or δοκίμιον ?) as a substantive; it does not, indeed, mean *crucible,* though that is the meaning of the original—just as little as πύρωσις means *furnace,* the original notwithstanding. The fact is rather that in the translation the sense of the original has been changed. As it stands the sentence can only be understood thus : *fire is the test for silver and gold;* only so does one catch the point of the apodosis. The case is quite different with Ps. 11 [12]⁷ τὰ λόγια κυρίου λόγια ἀγνὰ ἀργύριον πεπυρωμένον δοκιμιον τῇ γῇ κεκαθαρισμένον ἑπταπλασίως. The sense of the original of δοκιμιον τῇ γῇ is a matter of much controversy. Τὸ δοκίμιον corresponds עֲלִיל (*crucible ? workshop ?*) of which the etymology is obscure, and τῇ γῇ is a rendering of לָאָרֶץ, the grammatical relations of which are likewise uncertain. The solution of these difficulties is of no further consequence to our question ; in any case the sense has been again altered by the

¹ See p. 250, *sub* τὸ γνήσιον.

translators, for the Greek word can mean neither *crucible* nor *workshop*. We must therefore deal with the Greek sentence as we best can. If, with Kühl, we take δοκίμιον as a substantive equivalent to *means of testing* (which δοκιμῖον [or δοκίμιον?] can quite well mean), then the sentence runs: *The words of the Lord are pure words, silver purified by fire, a seven times refined means-of-testing for the earth* (or *for the land ?*). Such would, indeed, be the most obvious rendering,[1] but what is gained thereby? We get a tolerable meaning only by taking δοκίμιον adjectivally: *the words of the Lord are pure words, genuine silver, purified by fire, seven times refined, for the land.* Godly men cease, untruth and deceit are found on every side, a generation speaking great things has arisen: but Jahweh promises succour to the wretched, and, amidst the prevailing unfaithfulness, His words are the pure, tried defence of the land. Taken somewhat in this way, the sentence fits into the course of thought in the Greek psalm.

Finally, the texts of the LXX yield still further testimony to the existence of this adjective. In 1 Chron. 29[4], B[a b] gives the reading ἀργυρίου δοκιμίου instead of ἀργυρίου δοκίμου. The same confusion of δόκιμος and δοκίμιος, which we have already seen in the Papyri and the New Testament MSS., is shown in Zech. 11[13]: instead of δόκιμον, ℵ[c a vid] Q* (Marchalianus, 6th cent. A.D., Egypt) have δοκίμιον, Q[a] δοκίμειον.

ἐκτένεια, ἐκτενῶς.

The ethical sense *endurance* (2 Macc. 14[38], 3 Macc. 6[41], Judith 4[9], Cic. *ad Attic.* 10, 17, 1, Acts 26[7]) is also found in *IMAe.* 1032 [10] (Carpathus, 2nd cent. B.C.) τὰν πᾶσαν ἐκτένειαν καὶ κακοπαθίαν παρεχόμενος. In line [2] of the same Inscription ἐκτενῶς is used in a corresponding sense.

---

[1] τῇ γῇ could also be connected with the verb as an instrumental dative: but that would make the sentence more enigmatic than ever. We do not understand the suggestion of Cremer[8], p. 340, at the end of the article δοκίμιον.

ἔσθησις.

But few references for this word are given in connection
with Acts 1 ¹⁰, Luke 24 ⁴ A, etc.; cf. BU. 16 R ₁₂ (Fayyûm,
159-160 A.D.) χρω[μ]ένου ἐρεαῖς ἐσθήσεσι.¹

κακοπάθεια or κακοπαθία.

For this word in James 5 ¹⁰, usually written κακοπάθεια,
Clavis ³, p. 222, gives only the meaning vexatio, calamitas,
aerumna, and Beyschlag ² expressly rejects the meaning vexa-
tionum patientia. Cremer ⁸, p. 749, likewise enters the
passage under affliction, pains, misfortune, but this must be
an error, as he again records it three lines below under
the other meaning, bearing of affliction. The context supports this interpretation (though we cannot think it
impossible that James might have said: Take an example
from the prophets in affliction and patience). From the references given in Clavis we might judge that this sense of
the word could not be authenticated. But the passages
quoted by Cremer, 4 Macc. 9 ⁸ and Plut. Num. 3, 5, may be
supplemented by references from the Inscriptions. In IMAe.
1032 ₁₀ (Carpathus, 2nd cent. B.C.) τὰν πᾶσαν ἐκτένειαν καὶ
κακοπαθίαν παρεχόμενος, this meaning may be inferred from
the co-ordination of the word with ἐκτένεια; similarly Perg.
252 ₁₆ ₜ. (early Roman period, therefore after 133 B.C.) τῶν τε
ἐκκομι[δῶν] ἐπιμελείᾳ καὶ κακοπαθίᾳ διει[πὼν τὰ δέοντα
πᾶ]σαν ἐπιστροφὴν ἐποήσατ[ο] ˢⁱᶜ. Fränkel, indeed (p. 184),
translates the word here by pains, but the context permits
us to infer that not pains, in the passive sense of suffering, is
intended here, but the active taking pains. In support of
this "weakening of the concept," Fränkel further quotes
the Inscription in honour of the gymnasiarch Menas of
Sestos (Dittenberger, Sylloge 247), lines ₄ and ₂₃. W. Jerusalem ³ observes, in connection with this passage from the

---

¹ Corrected reading in the Supplement, p. 395.

² Meyer, xv. ⁵ (1888), p. 222.

³ Wiener Studien, i. (1879), p. 47.—Cf. also A. Wilhelm, GGA., 1898, p. 227:
"The κακοπαθία, with which the travelling of embassies, particularly over sea,
is usually associated, is prominently mentioned in numberless psephismata".

Inscription of Sestos (*ca.* 120 B.C.), that "of course" the word at first meant *suffering of misfortune*, but that, in the Inscription, it has the more general meaning of *exertion, endurance*, which meaning, he says, is also met with in contemporary Inscriptions, and is much more frequent in Polybius than the common one.

The objection may be made that these are in reality two different words with different meanings. But even granting that κακοπαθία is of different formation from κακοπάθεια,[1] there still remains the question whether the traditional κακοπαθείας may not be an itacistic variation of κακοπαθίας. The present writer would, with Westcott and Hort, decide for this alternative, and read κακοπαθίας (so B* and P).

κατάκριμα.

This rare word is authenticated (apart from Rom. 5 [16. 18], 8 [1]) only in Dion. Hal. 6, 61. All the less should the following passages be disregarded. In the deed of sale, *PER.* i. (Fayyûm, 83-84 A.D.), line 15 f., it is said of a piece of land that it is transferred to the purchaser καθαρὰ ἀπὸ παντὸς ὀφειλήματος ἀπὸ μὲν δημοσίων τελεσμάτων (16) πάντων καὶ [ἑτέρων εἰ]δῶν καὶ ἀρταβίων [2] καὶ ναυβίων καὶ ἀριθμητικῶν καὶ ἐπιβολῆς κώμης καὶ κατακριμάτων πάντων καὶ παντὸς εἴδους, similarly line 31 f. καθαρὰ ἀ[πὸ] δημοσίων τελεσμάτων καὶ ἐπι[γρ]αφῶν πασῶν καὶ ἀρταβίων καὶ ναυβίων καὶ ἀριθμητικοῦ (32) [καὶ ἐπιβ]ολῆς κ[ώμης καὶ κατακριμάτ]ων πάντων καὶ παντὸς εἴδους. Corresponding to this we have, in the deed of sale *PER.* clxxxviii. 14 f. (Fayyûm, 105-106 A.D.), καθαρὰ ἀπὸ μὲν δημοσίων τελεσμάτων πάντων καὶ ἐπιγραφῶν πασῶν (15) . . . . . . ἐπιβολῆς κώ[μ]ης καὶ [κατα]κ[ρι]μάτων πάντων καὶ π[αντ]ὸς εἴδους. It is obvious that in these passages κατακρίματα is used technically : some kind of burdens upon a piece of land must be meant. Wessely translates the first passage thus : *free of all debts, free of all arrears of public assessments of all kinds, of artabae-taxes, naubia-taxes, and taxes for the taking*

---

[1] Further particulars in Winer-Schmiedel, § 5, 13 c (p. 44 f.).
[2] Also in *BU.* 233 [11] to be thus read, not ἀρταβιωτ [. . .].

of evidence (? Evidenzhaltungssteuern), *of the additional payments of the village-communities—in short, of all* payments *of every kind ;* in line 32 of the same Papyrus he again renders [κατακριμάτ]ων by *taxes*. We doubt the accuracy of these renderings, though ourselves unable to interpret the word with certainty. We, nevertheless, conjecture that it signifies a burden ensuing from a judicial pronouncement —a servitude. One may perhaps render *legal burden*. We are of opinion that the meaning *poena condemnationem sequens*, which was accepted by earlier lexicographers, but which is now no longer taken into consideration by *Clavis* [3] and Cremer [8]—a meaning in accordance with the abovementioned usage—is particularly suitable in Rom. 8[1]; *cf.* Hesychius : κατάκριμα · κατάκρισις, καταδίκη.

μαρτυροῦμαι.

This word, especially the participle, is common in the Acts of the Apostles and other early Christian writings, as a designation of honour, *viz.*, *to be well reported of ;* similarly in *IMAe.* 832 15 (Rhodes, pre-Christian?) μαρτυρηθέντα καὶ στεφανωθέντα, said of a priest of Athena; 2 14 (Rhodes, 51 A.D.) καὶ μαρτυρηθέντων τῶν ἀνδρῶν, without doubt in the same sense. We find this attribute of honour also in Palmyra : in Waddington, 2606 a (second half of 3rd cent. A.D.), it is said of a caravan-conductor μαρτυρηθέντα ὑπὸ τῶν ἀρχεμπόρων.[1] Here we have the construction with ὑπό as in Acts 10[22], 16[2], 22[12]. So in an Inscription from Naples, *IGrSI.* 758 10 t. (second half of 1st cent. A.D.), μεμαρτυρημένον ὑφ' ἡμῶν διά τε τὴν τῶν τρόπων κοσμιότητα.

μετὰ καί.

With the late pleonastic καί after μετά in Phil 4[3][2] Blass [3] rightly compares σὺν καί in Clem. 1 Cor. 65[1]. In the Papyri we have found μετὰ καί only in *BU.* 412 6 t. (4th

---

Quotation from Mommsen, *Römische Geschichte*, v.[4], Berlin, 1894, p. 429.

[2] See p. 64, note 2.

[8] *Gr. des Neutest. Griechisch*, p. 257. [Eng. Trans., p. 263.]

cent. A.D.); σὺν καί is more frequent, *e.g.*, in the Fayyûm Papyri *BU.* 179 19 (reign of Antoninus Pius),[1] 515 17 (193 A.D.), 362 vi. 10 (215 A.D.).

ὀψώνιον.[2]

Neither *Clavis*[3] nor Thayer gives any authority earlier than Polybius († 122 B.C.) for the meaning *pay;* it is only when, guided by their reference, we consult Sturz, *De Dial. Mac.*, p. 187, that we find that, according to Phrynichus, the comedian Menander († 290 B.C.) had already used the word in this sense. Soon afterwards, in the agreement (preserved in an Inscription) of King Eumenes I. with his mercenaries, we find it used several times, *Perg.* 13 7. 13. 14 (soon after 263 B.C.)—always in the singular. Note in line 7 the combination ὀψώνιον λαμβάνειν as in 2 Cor. 11 8. The singular is used in the Papyri for *army pay, BU.* 69 8 (Fayyûm, 120 A.D.); for *wages* of the ὑδροφύλακες in 621 12 (Fayyûm, 2nd cent. A.D.) ; for *wages* of the watchmen of the vineyards in 14 v. 20 (Fayyûm, 255 A.D.); the plural of the *wages* of another workman 14 v. 7 ; the word is similarly used in the passage iii. 27, but it is abbreviated, so that one does not know whether it is singular or plural.

πάρεσις.

Cremer[8], p. 467, in reference to the meaning *remission* (important in respect of Rom. 3 [25]), observes that the word is so used only in Dion. Hal., *Antt. Rom.* 7, 37, where it means *remission of punishment.* It probably occurs in *BU.* 624 21 (Fayyûm, reign of Diocletian) in the sense of *remission of a debt* (*cf.* line 19 ἱερᾶς μὴ ἀμέλει ὀφιλῆ[ς] *sic*) ; but it can only be a temporary remission that is here spoken of. The diction being concise and full of technical terms, the meaning is not quite clear to us.

πατροπαράδοτος.

The few hitherto-known authorities for the word (in 1 Pet. 1 [18]) are to be expanded by *Perg.* 248 49 (135-134 B.C.):

---

[1] Improved reading in Supplement, p. 357.　　　[2] Above, p. 148.

Attalus writes in a letter to the council and people of Pergamus that his mother Stratonike has brought τὸν Δία τὸν Σαβάζιον πατροπαράδοτον [1] to Pergamus.

σμαράγδινος.

Apart from Rev. 4 [3], *Clavis* [3] gives no references at all. Thayer adds Lucian. In *PER*. xxvii. 8 (Fayyûm, 190 A.D.) the word is used to describe a woman's garment: *emerald-green*.

τήρησις.

As in Acts 4 [3], 5 [18], *imprisonment, ward*, also in *BU*. 388 iii. 7 (Fayyûm, 2nd-3rd cent. A.D.) ἐκέλευσεν Σμάραγδον καὶ Εὔκαιρον εἰς τὴν τήρησιν παραδοθῆναι.

τόπος.

With Acts 1 [25] λαβεῖν τὸν τόπον τῆς διακονίας ταύτης καὶ ἀποστολῆς Wendt [2] compares Sirach 12 [12]. In the latter passage it is one's *place* in life, generally, that is spoken of. A more significant example—referring as it does to a *place* within a definitely closed circle—is the technical use of the word in a dedication of the Pergamenian association, consisting of thirty-five or thirty-three members, of the ὑμνῳδοὶ θεοῦ Σεβαστοῦ καὶ θεᾶς ῾Ρώμης : Perg. 374 B 21 ff. (reign of Hadrian) τοῖς δὲ ἀν[α]παυομένοις εἰς λίβανον προχρήσει ὁ ἄρχων (δηνάρια) ιε′, ἃ ἀπολήψεται παρὰ τοῦ εἰς τὸν τόπον αὐτοῦ εἰσιόντος. [3] Fränkel, p. 266, translates: " The officer (the Eukosmos) shall advance, for incense for those deceased, 15 denarii, which he shall withhold from the one who enters the association in place of the departed ".

With τόπος as *sitting-place* Luke 14 [10], *cf. Perg.* 618 (date ?), where τόπος probably means *seat in a theatre;* Fränkel, p. 383, names the following as indubitable instances of this usage: *CIG*. 2421 = Lebas, ii. 2154 (Naxos); Lebas, 1724 e (Myrina), with a reference to Bohn-Schuchhardt, *Altertümer von Aegae*, p. 54, No. 7.

[1] Stratonike came originally from Cappadocia.
[2] Meyer, iii. 6/7 (1888), p. 52.
[3] Fränkel, p. 267, remarks on this that εἰσιέναι εἰς τὸν τόπον is used like εἰσιέναι εἰς ἀρχήν (*e.g.* Speech against Neaira, 72, Plutarch's *Praec. Ger. Reip.* 813 D). 'Αρχή is similarly used in Jude [6]; *cf.* LXX Gen. 40 [21].

IV.

AN EPIGRAPHIC MEMORIAL OF THE SEPTUAGINT.

. . . εἰ ἄραγε ψηλαφήσειαν αὐτὸν καὶ ευροιεν.

AN EPIGRAPHIC MEMORIAL OF THE SEPTUAGINT.

The Alexandrian translation of the Old Testament passed from the sphere of Jewish learning after Hellenistic Judaism had ceased to exist. Later on, the very existence of a Greek translation was completely forgotten.[1] It is therefore all the more interesting to follow the traces which reveal any direct or indirect effects which the Septuagint had upon the common people—their thoughts and their illusions.

The materials for a knowledge of the popular religious and ethical ideas of the Jews and Christians in the imperial period are more meagre than those which yield us the thoughts of the cultured and learned. But those materials, scanty though they be, have not as yet been fully worked. Scholars are usually more interested in the theologians of Tiberias, Alexandria, Antioch and Rome, than in such people as found their edification in the " Apocryphal " Legends, Gospels and Acts. But surely it is erroneous to suppose that we have a satisfactory knowledge of the history of religion when we have gained but a notion of the origin and development of dogma. The history of religion is the history of the religious feeling (*Religiosität*) not that of theology, and as truly as religion is older than theology,— as truly as religion has existed in every age outside of theology and in opposition to dogma, so imperious must grow the demand that we shall assign a place in the gallery of history to the monuments of popular piety. These are

---

[1] *Cf.* L. Dukes, *Literaturhistorische Mittheilungen über die ältesten hebräischen Exegeten, Grammatiker u. Lexikographen* (Ewald & Dukes, *Beiträge*, ii.), Stuttgart, 1844, p. 53; Schürer, ii., p. 700 ff. [Eng. Trans., ii., iii., p. 168 f.]; J. Hamburger, *Real-Encyclopädie für Bibel und Talmud*, ii., Leipzig, 1883, p. 1234.

necessarily few. For while theology, and the religion of theologians, have always been capable of asserting themselves, the religion of the people at large has not been concerned to raise memorials of itself. Thus it is not to be wondered at that the copious literature of theology should, so far as appearance goes, stifle the insignificant remains of the people's spontaneous expression of their religion,[1]—not to speak of the fact that much that was of value in the latter was intentionally destroyed. That which was extra-theological and extra-ecclesiastical was looked upon by the official theology as *a priori* questionable. Why, even at the present day, most of those productions of ancient popular religion come to us bearing the same stigma: we are accustomed to think of them as *Apocryphal, Heretical, Gnostic*, and as such to ignore them.

But those ideas, further, which we commonly designate as *Superstition*[2] seem to the author to deserve a place in the history of popular religion. The ordinary members of the community, townsman and peasant, soldier and slave, went on living a religious life of their own,[3] unaffected by the theological tendencies around them. We may very well doubt, indeed, whether that which moved their hearts was religion in the same sense as Prophecy or the Gospel, but their faith had received from the illustrious past the religious temper, at least, of ingenuous and unquestioning childhood. Their faith was not the faith of Isaiah or of the Son of Man; still, their "superstition" was not wholly forsaken of God. A devout soul will not be provoked by their follies, for throughout all their "heathenish" myth-forming and the natural hedonism of their religion there throbbed a yearning anticipation of the Divine.

The superstitions of the imperial period do not permit

[1] A similar relation subsists in kind between the materials of literary speech and of popular speech.

[2] J. Grimm, *Deutsche Mythologie*, ii.[3], Göttingen, 1854, p. 1060, says "Superstition formed in some ways a religion for the homes of the lower classes throughout".

[3] *Cf.* F. Piper, *Mythologie der christlichen Kunst, Erste Abth.*, Weimar, 1847, p. ix. f.

of being divided into the three classes: *Heathen, Jewish, Christian.* There is frequently no such clear distinction between the faith of the Heathen and the Jew and that of the Christian. Superstition is syncretic in character: this fact has been anew confirmed by the extensive recently-discovered remains of the Literature of Magic. And yet it is possible, with more or less precision, to assign certain fragments of these to one of the three departments named.

The literary memorial which is to be discussed below has been influenced in the most marked degree by the ideas of Greek Judaism, or, what is practically the same, of the Alexandrian Old Testament. After a few remarks about the circumstances of its discovery,[1] the text itself is given.

The tablet of lead upon which the Inscription is scratched comes from the large Necropolis of ancient Adrumetum, the capital of the region of Byzacium in the Roman province of Africa. The town lies on the coast to the south-east of Carthage. In connection with the French excavations which have been successfully carried on there for some time, the rolled-up tablet was incidentally found by a workman in the

---

[1] The author here follows the information which G. Maspero, the first editor of the Inscription, gave in the *Collections du Musée Alaoui, première série, 8ᵉ livraison*, Paris, 1890, p. 100 ff. A phototypic fac-simile of the tablet forms the frontispiece of BIBELSTUDIEN. Only after the original issue of the present work did the author learn of the sketch by Josef Zingerle in *Philologus*, liii. (1894), p. 344, which reproduces the text from *Revue archéologique, iii t.* xxi. (1893), p. 397 ff. (Reprint from *Collections du Musée Alaoui*, i., p. 100 ff.) The text has been discussed also by A. Hilgenfeld, *Berl. Philol. Wochenschrift*, xvi. (1896), p. 647 ff.; R. Wünsch, *CIA. Appendix* (1897), xvii. f.; and L. Blau, *Das altjüdische Zauberwesen* (1898), p. 96 ff. The tablet has been noticed (with observations by A. Dieterich) by F. Hiller von Gaertringen in the *Sitzungsberichte der Berliner Akademie der Wissenschaften*, 1898, p. 586. *Cf.* also Schürer, ³iii., p. 298 f. Individual textual conjectures and exegetic proposals are found in the various critiques of the BIBELSTUDIEN. The author hopes subsequently to take special advantage of the new exegetic material afforded by Hilgenfeld and Blau in particular. In the following he has corrected his former reading Δομιτιανὰν (line [6]) to Δομιτιανὴν, and (line [15]) ἵνα αὐτὴν to ἵν' αὐτὴν. Hilgenfeld's assertion (p. 648) that Δομιτιανὴν should be read throughout is erroneous.

18

June of 1890;[1] he noticed it only when a prong of his mattock
had pierced the roll.   This damaged the tablet in three places.[2]
There were also other three holes in the lead—probably
caused by a nail with which the roll had been perforated.
The tablet is thus damaged in six places, but the few letters
which are in each case destroyed permit, with one exception,
of being easily supplied.

We read the text thus [3] :—

'Ορκίζω σε, δαιμόνιον πνεῦμα τὸ ἐνθάδε κείμενον, τῷ ὀνό-
ματι τῷ ἁγίῳ Αωθ
Αβ[αω]θ τὸν θεὸν τοῦ Αβρααν καὶ τὸν Ιαω τὸν τοῦ
Ιακου, Ιαω

Line 2, Ιακου: M. corr. 'Ι(σ)άκου.

[1] In 1889 a *tabula devotionis* had been discovered in the Necropolis of
Adrumetum, and it was discussed by M. Bréal and G. Maspero in the fifth
instalment of the *Collections* (1890) just cited; it, too, contains a love-spell,
but is, apart from a few Divine names, free from biblical ideas and phrases.
A third tablet of Adrumetum, the publication of which was prospectively
announced on the cover of the eighth instalment, has not yet been issued.
Professor Maspero of Paris, Member of the Institute of France, had the great
kindness to inform the author (16th April, 1894) that the contents of this
tablet and similar unpublished pieces were likewise non-Jewish. In *CIL.*
viii., *Suppl.* i. (1891), *sub* Nos. 12504-12511, there have recently been brought
together some *tabulæ execrationum* discovered in Carthage, of which the
last affords some parallels to our tablet: see below.—*Cf.* now the copious
material collected by R. Wünsch in the *CIA. Appendix continens de-
fixionum tabellas in Attica regione repertas*, Berlin, 1897; also M. Siebourg,
Ein gnostisches Goldamulet aus Gellep, in *Bonner Jahrbücher*, Heft 103 (1898),
p. 123 ff.

[2] We imagine that these are the three holes upon the right margin
of the tablet.

[3] We have indicated the divergent readings of Maspero by M. The
numerous errors in accentuation which his text contains are not noted here.
Restorations are bracketed [ ], additions ( ). We have left unaccented the
Divine names and the other transcriptions, not knowing how these were
accented by the writer of the tablet and the author of his original text. To
furnish them with the "traditional" accents given in the editions of the
Greek Bible, so far as the names in question occur there, serves no purpose,
to say nothing of the fact that these "traditional" accents themselves cannot
be scientifically authenticated. *Cf.* Winer-Schmiedel, § 6, 8 *b* (p. 75 f.). [Eng.
Trans., p. 59.]

Αω[θ Αβ]αωθ θεὸν τοῦ Ισραμα· ἄκουσον τοῦ ὀνόματος
ἐντίμου
4 & 5 καὶ [φοβ]εροῦ καὶ μεγάλου καὶ ἄπελθε πρὸς τὸν Ο(ὐ)ρ-
βανὸν, ὃν ἔτεκ(ε)ν Οὐρβανὰ, καὶ ἄξον αὐτὸν πρὸς τὴν
6 Δομιτιανὴν, ἣν ἔτεκεν Κ[αν]δίδα,ͺ ἐρῶντα μαινόμενον
ἀγρυπνο[ῦν]-
τα ἐπὶ τῇ φιλίᾳ αὐτῆς καὶ ἐπιθυμίᾳ,καὶ δεόμενον αὐτῆς
ἐπανελθεῖν
εἰς τὴν οἰκίαν αὐτοῦ σύμβιο[ν] γενέσθαι. Ὁρκίζω σε τὸν
μέγαν θεὸν
τὸν αἰώνιον καὶ ἐπαιώνιον καὶ παντοκράτορα τὸν ὑπεράνω τῶν
10 ὑπεράνω θεῶν. Ὁρκίζω [σε] τὸν κτίσαντα τὸν οὐρανὸν
καὶ τὴν θά-
λασσαν. Ὁρκίζω σε τὸν διαχωρίσαντα τοὺς εὐσεβεῖς.
Ὁρκίζω σε
τὸν διαστήσαντα τὴν ῥάβδον ἐν τῇ θαλάσσῃ, ἀγαγεῖν καὶ
ζεῦξαι
[τὸ]ν Οὐρβανὸν, ὃν ἔτεκεν Οὐρβανὰ, πρὸς τὴν Δομιτιανὰν,
ἣν ἔτεκεν
[Καν]δίδα, ἐρῶντα βασανιζόμενον ἀγρυπνοῦντα ἐπὶ τῇ
ἐπιθυμίᾳ αὐ-
15 τῆς καὶ ἔρωτι, ἵνα αὐτὴν σύμβιον ἀπάγῃ εἰς τὴν οἰκίαν
ἑαυτοῦ. Ὁρκί-
ζω σε τὸν ποιήσαντα τὴν ἡμίονον μὴ τεκεῖν. Ὁρκίζω σε
τὸν διορίσαν-
τα τὸ [φῶς] ἀπὸ τοῦ σκότους. Ὁρκίζω σε τὸν συντρίβοντα
τὰς πέτρας.
Ὁρκίζ[ω σ]ε τὸν ἀπο(ρ)ρήξαντα τὰ ὄρη. Ὁρκίζω σε τὸν
συνστρέφοντα τὴν
γῆν ἐ[πὶ τ]ῶν θεμελίων αὐτῆς. Ὁρκίζω σε τὸ ἅγιον ὄνομα
ὃ οὐ λέγεται· ἐν
20 τῷ [. . .]ῳ [ὀ]νομάσω αὐτὸ καὶ οἱ δαίμονες ἐξεγερθῶσιν
ἔκθαμβοι καὶ περί-
φοβ[οι γεν]όμενοι, ἀγαγεῖν καὶ ζεῦξαι σύμβιον τὸν Οὐρβανὸν, ὃν ἔτεκεν

Line 3 and line 39, Ισραμα: M. corr. Ἰσραήλ.
Line 4, line 5 had to be commenced after μεγἀλου.
Line 20, τῷ[. . .]ῳ: M τῷ (ἀδύτ)ῳ.

Οὐρβανὰ, πρὸς τὴν Δομιτιανὰν, ἣν ἔτεκεν Κανδίδα, ἐρῶντα
καὶ δεόμε-

νον αὐτῆς, ἤδη ταχύ. ᾽Ορκίζω σε τὸν φωστῆρα καὶ ἄστρα
ἐν οὐρανῷ ποιή-

σαντα διὰ φωνῆς προστάγ[μ]ατος ὥστε φαίνειν πᾶσιν
ἀνθρώποις.

25　᾽Ορκίζω σε τὸν συνσείσαν[τ]α πᾶσαν τὴν οἰκουμένην καὶ
τὰ ὄρη

ἐκτραχηλίζοντα καὶ ἐκβρά[ζ]οντα τὸν ποιοῦντα ἔκτρομον
τὴν [γ]ῆ-

ν ἅπασ(αν καὶ) καινίζοντα πάντας τοὺς κατοικοῦντας. ᾽Ορ-
κίζω σε τὸν ποιή-

σαντα σημεῖα ἐν οὐρανῷ κ[αὶ] ἐπὶ γῆς καὶ θαλάσσης,
ἀγαγεῖν καὶ ζεῦξαι

σύμβιον τὸν Οὐρβανὸν, ὃν ἔ[τ]εκεν Οὐρβανὰ, πρὸς τὴν
Δομιτιανὰν, ἣν

30　ἔτεκεν Κανδίδα, ἐρῶντα αὐτῆς καὶ ἀγρυπνοῦντα ἐπὶ τῇ
ἐπιθυμίᾳ αὐ-

τῆς δεόμενον αὐτῆς καὶ ἐρωτῶντα αὐτήν, ἵνα ἐπανέλθῃ
εἰς τὴν οἰκίαν

[α]ὐτοῦ σύμβιος γενομένη. ᾽Ορκίζω σε τὸν θεὸν τὸν μέγαν
τὸν αἰώ-

[νι]ον καὶ παντοκράτορα, ὃν φοβεῖται ὄρη καὶ νάπαι καθ᾽
ὅλην [τ]ὴν οἰ-

κο[υ]μέ[ν]ην, δι᾽ ὃν ὁ λέων ἀφίησιν τὸ ἅρπαγμα καὶ τὰ
ὄρη τρέμει

35　κα[ὶ ἡ γῆ] καὶ ἡ θάλασσα, ἕκαστος ἰδάλλεται ὃν ἔχει
φόβος τοῦ Κυρίου

α[ἰωνίου] ἀθανάτου παντεφόπτου μισοπονήρου ἐπισταμένου τὰ

[γενόμεν]α ἀγαθὰ καὶ κακὰ καὶ κατὰ θάλασσαν καὶ πο-
ταμοὺς καὶ τὰ ὄρη

κα[ὶ τὴν γ]ῆν, Αωθ Αβαωθ τὸν θεὸν τοῦ Αβρααν καὶ
τὸν [Ι]αω τὸν τοῦ Ιακου,

Ια[ω] Αωθ Αβαωθ θεὸν τοῦ Ισραμα· ἄξον ζεῦξον τὸν
Οὐρβανὸν, ὃν

Line 27, καὶ before καινίζοντα had fallen out by hemigraphy.

Line 33, ὃν: M. οὔ.

Line 35, ἕκαστος (in place of the ἕκαστον of the original) ἰδάλλετα.: M.
(ὃν) ἕκαστος (ε)ἰδάλλεται.

40　ἔτεκεν Οὐρβα(νὰ), πρὸς τὴν Δομιτιανὰν, ἣν ἔτεκεν Καν-
　　δίδα, ἐρῶντα

　　μαι[ν]όμενον βασανιζόμενον ἐπὶ τῇ φιλίᾳ καὶ ἔρωτι καὶ
　　ἐπιθυμίᾳ

　　τῆς Δομιτιανῆς, ἣν ἔτεκεν Κανδίδα, ζεῦξον αὐτοὺς γάμῳ
　　καὶ

　　ἔρωτι συμβιοῦντας ὅλῳ τῷ τῆς ζωῆς αὐτῶν χρόνῳ· ποίη-
　　σον αὐ-

　　τὸν ὡς δοῦλον αὐτῇ ἐρῶντα ὑποτετάχθέναι, μηδεμίαν ἄλλη[ν]

45　γυναῖκα μήτε παρθένον ἐπιθυμοῦντα, μόνην δὲ τὴν Δο-
　　μιτια[νὰν],

　　ἣν ἔτεκεν Κανδίδα, σύμβ[ι]ον ἔχειν ὅλῳ τ[ῷ] τῆς [ζωῆς
　　αὐτῶν χρόνῳ],

　　ἤδη ἤδη ταχὺ ταχύ.

Line 44, ἄλλη[ν]: M. μήτε.

Keeping up the formal peculiarities of the text, we may, perhaps, translate it as follows :—

"I adjure thee, demonic spirit, who dost rest here, with the sacred names Aoth Abaoth, by the God of Abraan and the Jao of Jaku, the Jao Aoth Abaoth, the God of Israma : hearken to the glorious and fearful
4 & 5 and great name, and hasten to Urbanus, whom Urbana bore, and bring him to Domitiana, whom Candida bore, so that he, loving, frantic, sleepless with love of her and desire, may beg her to return to his house and become his wife. I adjure thee by the great God, the
10 eternal and more than eternal and almighty, who is exalted above the exalted Gods. I adjure thee by Him who created the heaven and the sea.. I adjure thee by him who separates the devout ones. I adjure thee by him who divided his staff in the sea [sic], that thou bring Urbanus, whom Urbana bore, and unite him with Domitiana, whom Candida bore, so that he, loving, tormented, sleepless with desire of her and with love, may take her
15 home to his house as his wife. I adjure thee by him who caused the mule not to bear. I adjure thee by him who divided the light from the darkness. I adjure

thee by him who crusheth the rocks. I adjure thee by
him who parted the mountains. I adjure thee by him
who holdeth the earth upon her foundations. I adjure
20   thee by the sacred Name which is not uttered; in the
[— —] I will mention it and the demons will be startled,
terrified and full of horror, that thou bring Urbanus,
whom Urbana bore, and unite him as husband with
Domitiana, whom Candida bore, and that he loving
may beseech her; at once! quick! I adjure thee by
him who set a lamp and stars in the heavens by the
command of his voice so that they might lighten all
25   men. I adjure thee by him who shook the whole world,
and causeth the mountains to fall and rise, who causeth
the whole earth to quake, and all her inhabitants to
return. I adjure thee by him who made signs in the
heaven and upon the earth and upon the sea, that thou
bring Urbanus, whom Urbana bore, and unite him as
30   husband with Domitiana, whom Candida bore, so
that he, loving her, and sleepless with desire of her,
beg her and beseech her to return to his house as his
wife. I adjure thee by the great God, the eternal and
almighty, whom the mountains fear and the valleys in
35   all the world, through whom the lion parts with the
spoil, and the mountains tremble and the earth and the
sea, (through whom) every one becomes wise who is
possessed with the fear of the Lord, the eternal, the
immortal, the all-seeing, who hateth evil, who knoweth
what good and what evil happeneth in the sea and the
rivers and the mountains and the earth, Aoth Abaoth;
by the God of Abraan and the Jao of Jaku, the
Jao Aoth Abaoth, the God of Israma, bring and unite
40   Urbanus, whom Urbana bore, with Domitiana, whom
Candida bore,—loving, frantic, tormented with love and
affection and desire for Domitiana, whom Candida bore;
unite them in marriage and as spouses in love for the
whole time of their life. So make it that he, loving,
45   shall obey her like a slave, and desire no other wife or
maiden, but have Domitiana alone, whom Candida

bore, as his spouse for the whole time of their life, at once, at once! quick, quick!"

EXPLANATION.

The tablet, as is shown not only by its place of origin (the Necropolis of Adrumetum belongs to the second and third centuries, A.D.; the part in which the tablet was found is fixed in the third), but also by the character of the lettering, is to be assigned to the third century,[1] that is—to determine it by a date in the history of the Greek Bible—about the time of Origen.

Maspero includes it among the Imprecation-tablets (*Devotions- oder Defixionstafeln*) not infrequently found in ancient tombs.[2] A leaden tablet, rolled up like a letter, was placed in the tomb with the dead, in order, as it were, to let it reach the residence of the deities of the underworld; to their vengeance was delivered the enemy whose destruction was desired.[3] This tablet, however, contains no execrations against an enemy, but is a love-spell[4] dressed in the form of an energetic adjuration of a demon, by means of which a certain Domitiana desires to make sure of the possession of her Urbanus. The technical details of the spell have no direct significance for our subject; we are interested only in the formulæ by which the demon is adjured. It is upon these, therefore, that the greatest stress will be laid in the following detailed explanation.

We may at once take for granted that these formulæ were not composed by Domitiana herself. She copied them, or had them copied, from one of the many current books of Magic, and in doing so had her own name and that of the

[1] Maspero, p. 101.

[2] *Cf.* upon these A. Dieterich most recently, Fleckeisen's *Jahrbb. Suppl.* xvi., p. 788 ff. ; as regards the literature *cf.* also *CIL.* viii., *Suppl.* i., p. 1288, and specially Wünsch, *CIA. Appendix* (1897).

[3] *Cf.* M. Bréal, in the fifth instalment of the already-cited *Collections* (1890), p. 58.

[4] On this species of Magic *cf.* the instructive citations of E. Kuhnert, *Feuerzauber, Rhein. Museum für Philologie, N. F.*, vol. xlix. (1894), p. 37 ff.

person loved inserted at the respective places. To conclude
from the biblical nature of the formulæ she used, that she
must have been a Jewess, or even a Christian,[1] would be a
precarious inference; it seems to the author more probable that
she and Urbanus, to judge from their names perhaps slaves or
emancipated[2] persons, were "heathens".[3] Quite ingenuously
the love-sick girl applied the spell, which her adviser asserted
to be of use in love-troubles—just because it so stood, black on
white, in the "Books". On this assumption the historical
value of the formulæ is increased, for the formulæ thus employed in the third century must have been extracted by the
writer of the book in question at a certainly much earlier
date[4] from the Alexandrian Old Testament. In the Magic
books now in Paris, Leiden and London, which were in the
main composed before the third century, we find quite a
multitude of similar adjurations compiled from biblical
materials, and the task of subjecting these to a critical sur-
vey is well worth while.[5] It would thus, for the reasons
indicated, be a mistake, as the author thinks, to add this
tablet to the proofs of the presence of Jews westwards of

[1] Maspero, p. 107 f.   [2] *Ibid.*, p. 107.

[3] This is directly supported by the fact that several of the best-known
Bible names in the tablet are corrupt; they have been incorrectly copied.
Cf. the Explanation.

[4] *Cf.* p. 323.

[5] C. Wessely, *On the spread of Jewish-Christian religious ideas among
the Egyptians*, in *The Expositor*, third series, vol. iv. (London, 1886), No.
xxi. (incorrectly xiii. on the part), pp. 194-204. Further in A. Dieterich,
Abraxas, p. 136 ff.; Blau, p. 112 ff.; Schürer,[3] iii., p. 298 ff. A small collection of Hellenistic-Jewish invocations of God, which might be made
on the basis of the Magic Papyri and Inscriptions, would be, in consideration
of the relatively early period of their composition, certainly not without
interest as regards the LXX-Text. Reference may also be made here to
the biblical passages found in the Inscriptions. The author is unaware
whether these have been treated of collectively from the standpoint of textual
criticism. They are also instructive for the history of the way in which the
Bible has been used. In very few cases will they be found to have been
derived from direct biblical readings.—Beginnings of the task here indicated
have been made by E. Böhl, *Theol. Studien u. Kritiken*, 1881, p. 692 ff., and
E. Nestle, *ibid.*, 1883, p. 153 f. Materials from the Inscriptions have recently
been largely added to.

Cyrenaica, a collection of which has been made by Schürer[1] so far as regards the imperial period.

In detail, the following observations must be made :—

Line 1 f.   It is the δαιμόνιον πνεῦμα of the tomb in which or upon which the spell was laid that is addressed. That the δαιμόνια stay beside the grave is an idea of post-biblical Judaism : these demons of the tomb help men in the practice of Magic.[2]   It is in the Papyri a frequently given direction, to make sure of the assistance of a spirit who resides in the grave of a murdered person or of one who has in any other way perished unfortunately.[3]—ὁρκίζω τῷ ὀνόματι τῷ ἁγίῳ: cf. 1 (3) Esd. 1[48], ὁρκισθεὶς τῷ ὀνόματι κυρίου; for τὸ ὄνομα τὸ ἅγιον, exceedingly frequent in "biblical" Greek, specially in Lev., Pss. and Ezek., particular references are unnecessary.—Aωθ : a Divine name in Magic, not infrequent in the Papyri; in the *Clavis Melitonis*[4] it is "explained" as *gloriosus*.   As in *Pap. Lond.* xlvi. 134,[5] so also here it stands in connection with AβαωΘ, likewise a Magical Divine name. —τὸν θεὸν τοῦ Aβρααν: ὁρκίζειν τινά = *to adjure by any one*, as in Mark 5[7], Acts 19[13].   *The God of Abraham, etc.*, is the solemn biblical designation of God.   We thought it well to leave the form Aβρααν in the text, as it is significant for the nationality of the writer of the tablet : a Jew would hardly have written it so.   Domitiana—or the obliging magician—did not know the word.   The writer of *Pap. Lugd.*

---

[1] ii., p. 504 (= [3]iii., p. 26). [Eng. Trans., ii., ii., p. 231, note 48.]

[2] Hamburger, ii., p. 283.   We may compare the idea of the Gospels, that demons reside in lonely and desert regions (Matt. 12[43]); the ἄνθρωπος ἐν πνεύματι ἀκαθάρτῳ had his dwelling among the tombs (Mark 5[3]).   In Baruch 4[35], devastated cities are already recognised as dwelling-places of demons.

[3] Maspero, p. 105.   It was believed that the soul of such a person had to hover about the grave so long as he should have lived had not his life come to an untimely end (Maspero, *ibid.*).   With reference to the notion as a whole cf. E. Rohde, *Psyche, Seelencult und Unsterblichkeitsglaube der Griechen*, Freiburg in Baden and Leipzig, 1894, p. 373 f. (= [2]ii., p. 410 f.); also Kuhnert, p. 49.

[4] In J. B. Pitra, *Spicilegium Solesmense*, iii., Paris. 1855, p. 305.

[5] Kenyon, p. 69.

J 384, ix. 7 [1] has made a similar corruption where he, in the
midst of a long series of Magical Divine names, writes
Αβρααν, τὸν Ισακ, τὸν Ιακκωβι; so also Codex B (Birch)
has Αβρααν in Luke 3 [34]. The interchanging of μ and ν at
the end of Semitic words is to be frequently seen elsewhere;
see below, p. 310 f.—τὸν Ιαω τὸν τοῦ Ιακου: on Ιαω see
below, p. 324; observe the article here. Ιακου was likewise
left as it was; probably it is a corruption of Ισακου; [2] even
Josephus Græcises the simple transcription, as with most
proper names; Ισακ or Ισαακ he gives as Ἴσακος.

Line 3 f.   τοῦ Ισραμα: clearly a corruption of Ισραηλ,
arising from a copyist's error; the Λ might easily become
Λ. The use of the solemn designation *the God of Abraham,
of Isaac and of Jacob* is exceedingly common in the Magical
formulæ. [3] These names, according to Origen, had to be left
untranslated in the adjurations if the *power* of the incantation
was not to be lost. [4]—ἄκουσον τοῦ ὀνόματος ἐντίμου
καὶ φοβεροῦ καὶ μεγάλου: LXX Deut. 28 [58], φοβεῖσθαι
τὸ ὄνομα τὸ ἔντιμον τὸ θαυμαστὸν τοῦτο (*cf.* also Ps. 71 [72][14],
ὄνομα ἔντιμον said of a human name); Ps. 110 [111][9], φοβερὸν

----

[1] A. Dieterich, Fleckeisen's *Jahrbb. Suppl.* xvi., p. 810; Leemans, ii.,
p. 31.

[2] The form might also be a corruption of Ιακουβ, *Pap. Lond.* cxxi. 649
(see below, p. 324), and *Pap. Par. Bibl. nat.* 2224 (Wessely, i., p. 100); similarly
in a leaden tablet from Carthage published by A. L. Delattre, *Bulletin de
correspondance hellénique*, xii. (1888), p. 300 = *CIL.* viii., *Suppl.* i., No. 12511.
—But the other assumption is supported by the following Ισραμα (= Ισραηλ
= Ιακωβ).

[3] *Cf.*, for instance, the Gem found in ancient Cyrenaica—Baudissin,
Studien, i., p. 193.   Further particulars, especially also patristic authorities,
in R. Heim, *Incantamenta magica Graeca Latina;* Fleckeisen's *Jahrbb. Suppl.*
xix. (1893), p. 522 ff.

[4] *Contra Celsum*, v. 45 (Lomm., xix., p. 250 f.): καὶ ἐὰν μὲν ὁ καλῶν ᾖ ὁ
ὁρκῶν ὀνομάζῃ θεὸν Ἀβραὰμ καὶ θεὸν Ἰσαὰκ καὶ θεὸν Ἰακὼβ τάδε τινὰ ποιῆσαι ἂν ἤτοι
διὰ τὴν τούτων φύσιν ἢ καὶ δύναμιν αὐτῶν καὶ δαιμόνων νικωμένων καὶ ὑποταττομένων
τῷ λέγοντι ταῦτα. Ἐὰν δὲ λέγῃ · ὁ θεὸς πατρὸς ἐκλεκτοῦ τῆς ἠχοῦς καὶ ὁ θεὸς τοῦ
γέλωτος καὶ ὁ θεὸς τοῦ πτερνιστοῦ οὕτως οὐδὲν ποιεῖ τὸ ὀνομαζόμενον, ὡς οὐδ' ἄλλο
τι τῶν μηδεμίαν δύναμιν ἐχόντων. Cf. *ibid.*, i. 22, and iv. 33, and also G,
Anrich, *Das antike Mysterienwesen in seinem Einfluss auf das Christentum.*
Göttingen, 1894, p. 96.

τὸ ὄνομα αὐτοῦ, similarly Ps. 98 [99]³; τὸ ὄνομα τὸ μέγα of the name of God, Ps. 98 [99]³, Ezek. 36²³, cf. Ps. 75 [76]² and Is. 33²¹; the combination μέγας καὶ φοβερός is very frequently applied to God in the LXX: Deut. 10¹⁷, 1 Chron. 16²⁵, Neh. 1⁵, 4¹⁴, Ps. 46 [47]³, 88 [89]⁸, 95 [96]⁴, Sirach 43²⁹.

Lines 4-8. The persons named, as has been said, were probably slaves or had been emancipated. An Οὐρβανός is found also in Rom. 16⁹; he was a Christian of Ephesus,[1] and is distinguished by Paul with the title of honour συνεργός.—The consistent annexation of the name of the person's mother is stereotyped in the Magic formulæ, and manifests itself up to a late period.[2] The directions found in the Magic Papyri exhibit this pattern in innumerable examples; the construction is such that the particular person's name requires only to be inserted instead of the provisional ὁ δεῖνα, ὃν ἔτεκεν ἡ δεῖνα.—ἀγρυπνέω ἐπί: cf. LXX Prov. 8³⁴, Job 21³².—σύμβιος: as to the usage of this word, especially in Egyptian Greek, attention should be paid to the collection of W. Brunet de Presle,[3] which may be extended by many passages in the Berlin Papyrus documents now in course of publication. The word is common among the Christians later on.

Line 8 f. τὸν μέγαν θεὸν τὸν αἰώνιον: LXX Is. 26⁴, ὁ θεὸς ὁ μέγας ὁ αἰώνιος; cf. Is. 40²⁸, Sus. ⁴².—ἐπαιώνιον: LXX Exod. 15¹⁸, κύριος βασιλεύων τὸν αἰῶνα καὶ ἐπ᾽ αἰῶνα καὶ ἔτι.—παντοκράτορα, very frequent in LXX.—τὸν ὑπεράνω τῶν ὑπεράνω θεῶν: cf. LXX Ezek. 10¹⁹, καὶ δόξα θεοῦ Ἰσραὴλ ἦν ἐπ᾽ αὐτῶν (the cherubim) ὑπεράνω,

---

[1] If Rom. 16 is [or belongs to] a letter to Ephesus.

[2] Particulars in Kuhnert, p. 41, note 7. With regard to the later Jewish usage, cf. Schwab, *Coupes à inscriptions magiques* in the *Proceedings of the Society of Biblical Archæology*, xiii. (1890-91), p. 585 f., and J. Wohlstein, *Über einige aramäische Inschriften auf Thongefässen des kgl. Museums zu Berlin*, in the *Zeitschrift für Assyriologie*, viii. (1893), p. 331, and ix. (1894) p. 19 f.

[3] *Notices et extraits des manuscrits de la bibliothèque impériale*, vol. xviii. pt. 2, Paris, 1865, p. 425.

similarly 11 [22] ; and with the idea, φοβερός ἐστιν ἐπὶ πάντας τοὺς θεούς, Ps. 95 [96][4].[1]

Line 10 f.   τὸν κτίσαντα τὸν οὐρανὸν καὶ τὴν θάλασσαν; an echo of Gen. 1[1], not in expression,[2] but in sense, like LXX Gen. 14[19, 22], 1 [3] Esd. 6[13], Bel[5], cf. Rev. 10[6], and with this LXX Ps. 145 [146][6]. The collocation *Heaven and sea* instead of *Heaven and earth* is surprising in this connection, but it is not foreign to the O.T. An exhaustive collection of the many variants—echoes of Gen. 1[1]— for *Creator of the heavens and the earth* in Judæo-Hellenistic and early Christian literature which have become formulaic, would be an important contribution to the history of the text of the " Apostolic " Symbol.

Line 11.   τὸν διαχωρίσαντα τοὺς εὐσεβεῖς can only mean, *he who separates the devout ones*, *i.e.*, from the godless ; διαχωρίζω = *to separate from* is common in the LXX. The passage is an allusion to Sir. 36 [33][11 ff.] ἐν πλήθει ἐπιστήμης κύριος διεχώρισεν αὐτούς (men) : so we have the contrast ἀπέναντι εὐσεβοῦς ἁμαρτωλός (in ver. [14]).

Line 12.   τὸν διαστήσαντα τὴν ῥάβδον ἐν τῇ θαλάσσῃ, literally, *he who divides his staff in the sea.* This is, of course, meaningless; the first writer of the incantation, without doubt, wrote inversely : τὸν διαστήσαντα τὴν θάλασσαν ἐν τῇ ῥάβδῳ or τῇ ῥάβδῳ, *who divided the sea with his staff*, an allusion in sense to LXX Exod. 14[15 f.]: εἶπε δὲ κύριος πρὸς Μωϋσῆν· ... καὶ σὺ ἔπαρον τῇ ῥάβδῳ σου καὶ ἔκτεινον τὴν χεῖρά σου ἐπὶ τὴν θάλασσαν καὶ ῥῆξον αὐτήν, with the difference that in the Bible it is Moses who lifts the staff—though of course at God's command. In regard to form its similarity with Theodotion Ps. 73 [74][13]:[3] σὺ (God) διέστησας ἐν τῇ

---

[1] With regard to the whole expression, *cf.* the passage of the aforementioned leaden tablet from Carthage in *Bull. de corr. hell.*, xii., 302 = *CIL.* viii., *Suppl.* i., No. 12511 : ἐξορκίζω ὑμᾶς κατὰ τοῦ ἐπάνω τοῦ οὐρανοῦ θεοῦ τοῦ καθημένου ἐπὶ τῶν χερουβι, ὁ διορίσας τὴν γῆν καὶ χωρίσας τὴν θάλασσαν, Ιαω κτλ. The nominatives are illustrative of the formal rigidity of these expressions.

[2] Aquila alone has ἔκτισεν (F. Field, *Origenis Hexaplorum quae supersunt 2 tomi, Oxonii*, 1875, i., p. 7).

[3] Field, ii., p. 217.

δυνάμει σου τὴν θάλασσαν, with which should be compared LXX Exod. 15 ⁸: καὶ διὰ πνεύματος τοῦ θυμοῦ σου διέστη τὸ ὕδωρ . . . ἐπάγη τὰ κύματα τῆς θαλάσσης. The miracle at the Red Sea, so frequently celebrated in the Psalms and elsewhere, is also alluded to in other Magical formulæ.[1] See under ἐν, above, Art. ii., upon the possible ἐν τῇ ῥάβδῳ.

Line 16. τὸν ποιήσαντα τὴν ἡμίονον μὴ τεκεῖν, a most peculiar designation of God. It does not occur, as such, in the Old Testament, but the underlying idea of God's *providentia specialissima* for the animals is very similarly expressed in the sublime address of Jahweh to the doubting Job (Job 38 ff.) ; *cf.*, in particular, 39 ¹⁻³ : *Knowest thou the time when the wild goats of the rock bring forth ? Or canst thou mark when the hinds do calve ? Canst thou number the months that they fulfil, or knowest thou the time when they bring forth ? They bow themselves, they bring forth their young, they cast out their sorrows.* It is God who directs all this. Just as He gives young to the wild goats and the hinds, so, the present passage would say, He has made the mule to be barren. The barrenness of the mule is often mentioned in the Mishna ;[2] it was manifestly a fact of great interest in the Jewish Philosophy of Nature, as also in Greek and Latin authors :[3] Plin. *Nat. Hist.* viii. 173 : *observatum ex duobus diversis generibus nata tertii generis fieri et neutri parentium esse similia, eaque ipsa quae sunt ita nata non gignere in omni animalium genere, idcirco mulas non parere.* When Zopyrus was besieging Babylon he received, according to Herod. iii. 153, the oracle ἐπεάνπερ ἡμίονοι τέκωσιν, τότε τὸ τεῖχος ἁλώσεσθαι. The *partus* of a mule was reckoned a *prodigium* : Cic. *de Div.* ii. 22 ₄₉, 28 ₆₁, Liv. xxxvii. 3 ₃, Juv. xiii. 64, Sueton. *Galba*, 4, and this explains the Roman proverb *cum mula peperit, i.e., never.* Then the fact played a great part in incantations. Gargilius Martialis

---

[1] *Cf.* A. Dieterich, *Abraxas*, p. 139 f.

[2] Hamburger, i.³ (1892), p. 785.

[3] Heim, 493 f. The passages which follow, to which the author's notice was directed by A. Dieterich, are taken from Heim. *Cf.* also *Centuria illustrium quaestionum . . . a Joh. Jac. Hermanno, Herbornensi, Herbornae Nassoviorum*, 1615, *decas septima, quaestio quinta.*

(third cent. A.D.) in *de cura boum* § 19 (ed. Schuch)[1] hands
down the following healing charm: *nec lapis lanam fert, nec
lumbricus oculos habet, nec mula parit utriculum;* similarly
Marcellus (fifth cent. A.D.), *De Medicam.* viii. 191 (ed. Helm-
reich):[2] *nec mula parit nec lapis lanam fert nec huic morbo
caput crescat aut si creverit tabescat,* and a *Codex Vossianus* ed.
Piechotta *Anecd. lat.* clxx. :[3] " *quod mula non parit*" et exspues,
"*nec cantharus aquam bibit*" et exspues, "*nec palumba dentes
habet*" et exspues, "*sic mihi dentes non doleant*" et expues.
Finally, reference must be made to a passage in the Leiden
copy of the *Codex Corbeiensis* of Vegetius,[4] which gives the
formula: *focus alget, aqua sitit, cibaria esurit, mula parit, tasca
masca venas omnes.* But what comes nearest to our passage
is a sentence preserved in a poem of the *Codex Vindobonensis,*
93 :[5] *herbula Proserpinacia, Horci regis filia, quomodo clausisti
mulæ partum, sic claudas et undam sanguinis huius,* and in a
still more instructive form in the *Codex Bonnensis,* 218 (66 a):[6]
*herbula Proserpinatia, Horci regis filia, adiuro te per tuas virtutes,
ut quomodo clausisti partum mulae, claudas undas sanguinis huius.*
Strange as at first sight the affirmation thus made of God
may appear in connection with the others, we now see that
in an incantation it is least of all strange. The Jewish compiler of our text borrowed it from pagan sources, probably
unconsciously but perhaps intentionally using a biblical
phrase—and, indeed, the intention did not directly oppose
the biblical range of thought.

Line 16 f. τὸν διορίσαντα τὸ φῶς ἀπὸ τοῦ σκότους:
cf. LXX Gen. 1⁴, καὶ διεχώρισεν ὁ θεὸς ἀνὰ μέσον τοῦ φωτὸς
καὶ ἀνὰ μέσον τοῦ σκότους—similarly Gen. 1¹⁸. The compiler
quotes freely: διορίζειν, frequent elsewhere in the LXX, also
with ἀπό, does not stand in any of the Greek translations of
this passage. It is significant that he has avoided the repeated
"between," a Hebraism taken over by the LXX.

---

[1] Heim, 493 f.   [2] *Ibid.*   [3] *Ibid.*
[4] In M. Ihm, *Incantamenta magica, Rh. Mus. f. Phil.,* N. F., xlviii.
(1893), p. 635.
[5] Heim, pp. 488, 547.   [6] *Ibid.,* p. 554.

Line 17. τὸν συντρίβοντα τὰς πέτρας: an echo
in form of LXX 1 Kings 19¹¹, πνεῦμα μέγα . . συντρῖβον
πέτρας ἐνώπιον κυρίου: cf. LXX Nah. 1⁶, καὶ αἱ πέτραι διε-
θρύβησαν ἀπ᾽ αὐτοῦ.

Line 18. τὸν ἀπορρήξαντα τὰ ὄρη: cf. LXX Ps.
77 [78]¹⁵ διέρρηξε πέτραν ἐν ἐρήμῳ, similarly Ps. 104 [105]⁴¹;
parallels to the thought are easily found.

Line 18 f. τὸν συνστρέφοντα τὴν γῆν ἐπὶ τῶν
θεμελίων αὐτῆς: συστρέφω, current in the LXX, though
not in this connection; τὰ θεμέλια τῆς γῆς is likewise
frequent. With regard to the sense, cf. LXX Prov. 8²⁹
ἰσχυρὰ ἐποίει τὰ θεμέλια τῆς γῆς, and the common phrase
ἐθεμελίωσε τὴν γῆν.

Line 19 ff. ὁρκίζω σε τὸ ἅγιον ὄνομα ὃ οὐ
λέγεται·: It is possible to doubt this punctuation. Maspero writes ὃ οὐ λέγεται ἐν τῷ ἀδύτῳ, but if the reading ἀδύτῳ
is correct, then, with his punctuation, the thought would be
in direct opposition to the Jewish view, for the Temple was just
the one place in which the name of God could be pronounced;
Philo, *De Vit. Mos.* iii. 11 (M., p. 152), says . . ὀνόματος ὃ
μόνοις τοῖς ὦτα καὶ γλῶτταν σοφίᾳ κεκαθαρμένοις θέμις ἀκούειν
καὶ λέγειν ἐν ἁγίοις, ἄλλῳ δὲ οὐδενὶ τὸ παράπαν οὐδαμοῦ. The
Mischna, *Tamid*, vii. 2,¹ has "In the Temple the name of
God is pronounced as it is written; in the land [elsewhere]
another title is substituted". We consider it absolutely
impossible that any one having any kind of sympathy with
Judaism whatever could assert that the holy name was
not pronounced in the Temple. If the word read by Maspero
as ἀδύτῳ can be made out at all—which to us, judging
at least from the fac-simile, appears impossible—then, if it
is to be read after ὃ οὐ λέγεται, it must be a general term of
place such as κόσμῳ or λαῷ; if, again, it is to be connected
with the following ὀνομάσω αὐτό, then ἐν τῷ ἀδύτῳ were
meaningless, or at least very singular. Of which Temple
could the Jewish compiler be thinking? Can it be that he

¹ Hamburger, i.³, p. 53; Schürer, ii., p. 381 (= ³ii., p. 458). [Eng.
Trans., ii., ii., p. 82, note 143.]

wrote before the destruction of the Temple?[1] We would
therefore propose to consider ὁ οὐ λέγεται as a clause by
itself: it expresses the well-known Jewish idea that the
name of God is an ὄνομα ἄρρητον,—see LXX Lev. 24[16]
ὀνομάζων δὲ τὸ ὄνομα κυρίου θανάτῳ θανατούσθω; Josephus,
Antt. ii. 12₄: καὶ ὁ θεὸς αὐτῷ σημαίνει τὴν ἑαυτοῦ προσηγορίαν
οὐ πρότερον εἰς ἀνθρώπους παρελθοῦσαν, περὶ ἧς οὔ μοι θεμιτὸν
εἰπεῖν.[2]——ἐν τῷ [. . .]ῳ ὀνομάσω αὐτὸ καὶ οἱ δαίμονες
ἐξεγερθῶσιν ἔκθαμβοι καὶ περίφοβοι γενόμενοι.
How the lacuna after ἐν τῷ is to be filled up the present
writer does not know, and he will make no conjectures; thus
much only is probable, viz., that what stood there was a
designation of place or time. The magician utters the
severest possible threat against the demon; he will, in order
to win him over, pronounce the unutterable Name of God,
the very sound of which fills the demons with shudder-
ing and dread. That demons and spirits are controlled by
the mention of sacred names has remained to the present
day one of the most important ideas in magic.[3] We have
no direct example of this in the LXX, but we can point to
James 2[19] as being valid for biblical times, καὶ τὰ δαιμόνια
πιστεύουσιν καὶ φρίσσουσιν, which presupposes the same
fearful impression upon the demons of the thought of God.
With this is to be compared Pap. Lond. xlvi. 80t.[4] (fourth cent.
A.D.), where the Demon is adjured κατὰ τῶν φρικτῶν ὀνομά-
των, just as Josephus, Bell. Jud. v. 10₃, speaks of the φρικτὸν
ὄνομα τοῦ θεοῦ. The overwhelming effect of the Divine name
upon the Demons was a very familiar idea in post-biblical
Judaism.[5]

[1] Moreover, ἄδυτον is very infrequent in "biblical" literature; it is found
only in LXX 2 Chron. 33[14], Cod. A.

[2] Cf. Hamburger, i.[3], p. 52 ff., with reference to the point as viewed by
post-biblical Judaism.

[3] And not in magic only!

[4] Kenyon, p. 68; Wessely, i., p. 129. More definitely still in Pap.
Lugd. J 384, iv. 11f. (Fleck. Jbb. Suppl. xvi., p. 800; Leemans, ii., p. 17):
μέλλω τὸ μέγα ὄνομα λέγειν Αωθ (or Θωθ), ὃν . . . πᾶς δαίμων φρίσσει.

[5] Cf., e.g., Hamburger, ii., pp. 283 and 75; also J. A. Eisenmenger,
Entdecktes Judenthum, 1700, i., p. 165; the present author cites this work

Line 23.　ἤδη ταχύ, cf. line 47, ἤδη ἤδη ταχὺ ταχύ:
a very frequent concluding formula in the incantations,[1] which
is still seen, e.g., on Coptic amulets of the 5th-6th and
11th centuries;[2] it is also to be restored, of course, at the
end of the previously-cited Inscription from Carthage.[3]
ταχύ for ταχέως is very common in the LXX.

Line 23 ff.　τὸν φωστῆρα καὶ ἄστρα ἐν οὐρανῷ
ποιήσαντα: LXX Gen. 1¹⁶ ᶠ·, καὶ ἐποίησεν ὁ θεὸς|τοὺς δύο
φωστῆρας τοὺς μεγάλους . . . καὶ τοὺς ἀστέρας.　The single
φωστήρ mentioned in the Tablet, since it is associated with
the stars, is probably the moon; the moon is also named
φωστήρ by Aquila and Symmachus, Ps. 73 [74]¹⁶·[4]—διὰ
φωνῆς προστάγματος αὐτοῦ: the acts of creation take
place at the command of God—LXX Ps. 32 [33]⁹, ὅτι
αὐτὸς εἶπε καὶ ἐγενήθησαν, αὐτὸς ἐνετείλατο καὶ ἐκτίσθησαν;
in respect of form should be compared the not infrequent
phrases of the LXX, διὰ φωνῆς κυρίου and διὰ προστάγματος
κυρίου.　Observe the so-called "Hebraising" periphrasis[5] of
the preposition διά by διὰ φωνῆς, which a Greek might feel
to be a pleonasm, but which is not altogether un-Greek.
—ὥστε φαίνειν πᾶσιν ἀνθρώποις: LXX Gen. 1¹⁷ καὶ

according to the copy in his possession, which was ostensibly *printed in
the year after the birth of Christ 1700*, but as it announces itself as *Des* ᶦⁿ
*bey 40. Jahr von der Judenschafft mit Arrest bestrickt gewesene, nun-
mehro aber Durch Autorität eines Hohen Reichs-Vicariats relaxirte Johann
Andreä Eisenmengers . . . Entdecktes Judenthum*, it could manifestly have
been printed at the earliest in 1740. The explanation probably is that, in
the copies of the edition of 1700 (cf. C. Siegfried in the *Allg. deutschen Bio-
graphie*, v. [1877], p. 772 ff.), the interdict on which was cancelled about 1740,
the original title-page was supplanted by the present misleading one.

[1] Cf. Wessely's Index *sub* ἤδη.

[2] J. Krall, *Koptische Amulete*, in *Mittheilungen aus der Sammlung der
Papyrus Erzherzog Rainer V.* Vienna, 1892, pp. 118, 121.

[3] Delattre, in *Bulletin de correspondance hellénique*, xii. (1888), p. 302,
takes from the unmistakeable ΗΔΗΗΔΗΤΑΧΥΤΑ the extraordinary reading
"ἤδη, ἤδη, ταῦτα (?)".

[4] Field, ii., p. 218.

[5] Cf. A. Buttmann, *Grammatik des neutestamentlichen Sprachgebrauchs*,
Berlin, 1859, pp. 78, 158, 162, 273 f.　As to the questionableness of commonly
asserting such periphrases to be "Hebraising," see above II., *sub* κατά.

ἔθετο αὐτοὺς ὁ θεὸς ἐν τῷ στερεώματι τοῦ οὐρανοῦ ὥστε φαίνειν ἐπὶ τῆς γῆς.

Line 25 f. τὸν συνσείσαντα πᾶσαν τὴν οἰκου-μένην : LXX Ps. 59 [60]⁴, συνέσεισας τὴν γῆν. For πᾶσαν τὴν οἰκουμένην, cf. LXX Is. 13⁵.—καὶ τὰ ὄρη ἐκτραχηλί-ζοντα καὶ ἐκβράζοντα:¹ a repetition of the thought in line 18, but verbally independent.

Line 26 f. τὸν ποιοῦντα ἔκτρομον τὴν γῆν ἅπασ(αν): cf. LXX Ps. 103 [104]³² ὁ ἐπιβλέπων ἐπὶ τὴν γῆν καὶ ποιῶν αὐτὴν τρέμειν; ἔκτρομος does not seem to have been retained anywhere else, the LXX using ἔντρομος in the same sense, Ps. 17 [18]⁸ and 76 [77]¹⁹.

Line 27. (καὶ) καινίζοντα πάντας τοὺς κατοι-κοῦντας: the author follows Maspero in adding the καί. We may reject the idea that καινίζοντα has an ethical refer-ence in the sense of the πνεῦμα καινόν of Ezek. 11¹⁹, cf. Ps. 50 [51]¹², or of the καρδία καινή of Ezek. 36²⁶; we must rather take it as expressing the idea of the preservation of the race by the ceaseless upspringing of new generations. The compiler may have had a confused recollection of phrases like ἐπέβλεψεν ἐπὶ πάντας τοὺς κατοικοῦντας τὴν γῆν, LXX Ps. 32 [33]¹⁴, and κύριος ὁ θεὸς ... καινιεῖ σε ἐν τῇ ἀγαπήσει αὐτοῦ, Zeph. 3¹⁷; cf. Ps. 102 [103]⁵, ἀνακαινι-σθήσεται ὡς ἀετοῦ ἡ νεότης σου. In Wisdom 7²⁷, τὰ πάντα καινίζει is predicated of the divine σοφία.

Line 27 f. τὸν ποιήσαντα σημεῖα ἐν οὐρανῷ καὶ ἐπὶ γῆς καὶ θαλάσσης: see Dan. 6²⁷ καὶ ποιεῖ σημεῖα καὶ τέρατα ἐν τῷ οὐρανῷ καὶ ἐπὶ τῆς γῆς, cf. LXX Joel 2³⁰.

Line 31. ἐρωτῶντα: here, as often in Paul, Synopt., Acts, John, in the sense of beg, beseech; not "an application of the word which was manifestly first made through the influence of the Hebrew שאל"² (which in that case must

---

¹ ἐκβράζω, LXX Neh. 13²⁸, 2 Macc. 1¹², 5⁸ (Cod. A).

² H. Cremer, Biblisch-theologisches Wörterbuch der Neutestamentlichen Gräcität,⁷ Gotha, 1893, p. 393 (= ⁸ [1895], p. 415).

surely have appeared first of all in the LXX), but popular Greek.[1]

Line 33. ὃν φοβεῖται ὄρη καὶ νάπαι: instead of the unmistakable ὄν Maspero writes οὗ. A specialising of the idea that the earth also has a "fear of God": cf. LXX Ps. 32 [33][8], φοβηθήτω τὸν κύριον πᾶσα ἡ γῆ, and Ps. 66 [67][8], φοβηθήτωσαν αὐτὸν πάντα τὰ πέρατα τῆς γῆς. For the combination of ὄρη and νάπαι cf. LXX Is. 40[12], Ezek. 6[3], 36[6].

Line 34. δι᾽ ὃν ὁ λέων ἀφίησιν τὸ ἅρπαγμα: the fact stated in this connection vividly recalls τὸν ποιήσαντα τὴν ἡμίονον μὴ τεκεῖν in line 16. It is surprising that it should be said that God causes the lion to abandon his prey,[2] whereas the biblical idea is just that God supplies the lion's food, Job 38[39]. One might suppose an allusion to Dan. 6[27], ὅστις ἐξείλατο τὸν Δανιὴλ ἐκ χειρὸς τῶν λεόντων, and similar passages, the more so as a little before, in line 27 f., there was a strong resemblance to the first half of the same verse; but this may be considered as negatived by ἅρπαγμα. We shall not err in considering the statement to be an expression of God's omnipotence, of His complete dominion over nature: God is even able to make possible that which is against nature, viz., that the lion shall relinquish his prey. We may be reminded by this of the prophetic pictures of the Messianic future in Is. 11[6], καὶ μοσχάριον καὶ ταῦρος καὶ λέων ἅμα βοσκηθήσονται καὶ παιδίον μικρὸν ἄξει αὐτούς, and Is. 65[25] = 11[7], καὶ λέων ὡς βοῦς φάγεται ἄχυρα, in which it is likewise affirmed that the lion may change his nature, if God so wills it. The clause has been freely compiled from biblical materials.—καὶ τὰ ὄρη τρέμει: LXX Jer. 4[24] εἶδον τὰ ὄρη καὶ ἦν τρέμοντα.

Line 35. ἕκαστος ἰδάλλεται ὃν ἔχει φόβος τοῦ Κυρίου: perhaps this is the most difficult passage in the Inscription. ἰδάλλομαι (εἰδάλλομαι) or ἰνδάλλομαι means to seem, appear, become visible, show oneself, also to resemble. The

---

[1] U. von Wilamowitz-Moellendorff in Guil. Schmidt's *De Flavii Iosephi elocutione observationes criticae*, Fleck. *Jbb. Suppl.* xx. (1894), p. 516.

[2] ἅρπαγμα is used for the lion's prey in LXX Ezek. 22[25]; cf. 19[3. 6].

word does not occur in the LXX, but ἴνδαλμα, the noun, is
found in Jer. 27 [50][39], probably in the sense of *ghost*, in
Wisd. 17[3] for *image*, which meanings are easily obtained
from the verb. The first appearance of the verb in biblico-
ecclesiastical literature, so far as the author knows, is in
Clement of Rome, 1 Cor. 23[2], διὸ μὴ διψυχῶμεν μηδὲ ἰνδαλ-
λέσθω ἡ ψυχὴ ἡμῶν ἐπὶ ταῖς ʽπερβαλλούσαις καὶ ἐνδόξοις
δωρεαῖς αὐτοῦ (God), where either it has the meaning *to
seem, imagine oneself*, somewhat like φυσιοῦσθαι, or it is, as
Bryennios, following others, has recently again proposed, a
synonym of the verbs ἰλιγγιᾶν, *to be confused*, and ἐνδοιάζειν,
to waver.[1] Now ἔκαστον ἰδάλλεται, as the passage runs in the
original, does not give sense: Maspero conjectures ὃν ἔκα-
στος εἰδάλλεται and translates *à qui chacun devient sembl-
able*, which appears to us to be grammatically impossible.
In regard to the reading which we propose, which may recommend itself by the insignificance of the textual change,
we would refer to the explanation of the verb which
is given by Hesychius: ἰνδάλλεται· ὁμοιοῦται, φαίνεται,
δοκεῖ, στοχάζεται, ἰσοῦται, σοφίζεται,[2] with which is to be
compared the note of Suidas: εἰδαλίμας· συνετάς. Taking
then ἰδάλλεται = σοφίζεται,[3] we get the familiar biblical
thought that the *Fear of God* gives men *Wisdom*, as in
LXX Ps. 110 [111][10] = Prov. 1[7], 9[10] ἀρχὴ σοφίας φόβος
κυρίου, Prov. 22[4] γενεὰ σοφίας φόβος κυρίου; cf. Ps. 18
[19][8. 10] ἡ μαρτυρία κυρίου πιστὴ σοφίζουσα νήπια . . . . ὁ φόβος
κυρίου ἁγνὸς διαμένων εἰς αἰῶνα αἰῶνος. The only possible
objection to this explanation is that the clause has no connection with the previous one; and certainly a καὶ or the
repetition of the δι᾿ ὃν were desirable—only it would be
equally required with any other reading. The writer of
the tablet seems not to have understood the statement.—

---

[1] Further particulars in *Patrum Apostolicorum opera recc.* O. de Geb-
hardt, A. Harnack, Th. Zahn, fasc. i., part. i.[2], Leipzig, 1876, p. 42.

[2] σοφίζομαι *sapiens fio, sapio*, often in LXX, *e.g.*, 1 Kings 4[27 [31]]; specially
frequent in Sir.

[3] The *vox media* ἰνδάλλομαι would then stand here *sensu bono*, as in
Clem. Rom. 1 Cor. 23[2] *sensu malo*.

With regard to ὃν ἔχει φόβος τοῦ κυρίου (cf. LXX Job
31 ²³ φόβος γὰρ κυρίου συνέσχε με), reference should be made
to the equivalent (in profane Greek likewise common) use
of ἔχειν, LXX Job 21⁶, Is. 13⁸, Mark 16⁸. Examples of
φόβος τοῦ κυρίου would be superfluous.

Line 36. ἀθανάτου: Sir. 51⁹ ⁽¹³⁾ Cod. A has καὶ ἀπὸ
ἀθανάτου ῥύσεως ἐδεήθην, which probably means *and to the
Immortal One did I pray for deliverance;* cf. 1 Tim. 6¹⁶, ὁ μόνος
ἔχων ἀθανασίαν. The thought is a Greek one; this attribute
of God, in the present connection (cf. line 35), recalls the sublime Hellenistic-Jewish thought that the knowledge of God,
the possession of the divine σοφία and δικαιοσύνη, impart
immortality : Wisd. 15³ εἰδέναι σου τὸ κράτος ῥίζα ἀθανασίας,
8¹⁷ ἔστιν ἀθανασία ἐν συγγενείᾳ σοφίας, cf. ver. ¹³, ἔξω δι᾽
αὐτὴν ἀθανασίαν, 1¹⁵ δικαιοσύνη γὰρ ἀθανασία ἐστίν.¹—παντε-
φόπτου:² Add. Esth. 5¹ τὸν πάντων ἐπόπτην θεόν; 3 Macc.
2²¹ ὁ πάντων ἐπόπτης θεός; 2 Macc. 7³⁵ (cf. 3³⁹) τοῦ παντο-
κράτορος ἐπόπτου θεοῦ; cf. LXX Job 34²⁴ ὁ γὰρ κύριος
πάντας (Cod. A, τὰ πάντα) ἐφορᾷ, similarly 2 Macc. 12²² and
15².—μισοπονήρου: the idea is common in the O.T.; ³ in
regard to the word cf. μισοπονηρέω, 2 Macc. 4⁴⁹ and 8⁴;
μισοπονηρία, 2 Macc. 3¹.

Line 36 ff. ἐπισταμένου κτλ.: a well-known biblical
idea, here developed independently with the assistance of
biblical expressions.

Line 43. συμβιοῦντας: Sir. 13⁵ has the word.

Line 45. ἐπιθυμοῦντα with the Accusative as not
infrequently in LXX; cf., *e.g.,* Exod. 20¹⁷, οὐκ ἐπιθυμήσεις
τὴν γυναῖκα τοῦ πλησίον σου.

Looking again at the Inscription, we find, in the first
place, confirmation of the supposition that the writer of the

---

¹ *Cf.* also Aquila Ps. 47 [48]¹⁵ and the observations of Field, ii., p. 169,
thereon.
² *Re* the vulgar φ *cf.* Winer-Schmiedel, § 5, 27e (p. 59 ff.): ἐφόπτας is
also found in *Pap. Par. Bibl. nat.* ₁₃₅₃ (Wessely, i., p. 78).
³ *Cf.* also LXX Ps. 96 [97]¹⁰ οἱ ἀγαπῶντες τὸν κύριον μισεῖτε πονηρόν.

tablet, whether male or female, and the original author of the text cannot have been the same individual. No one apparently so familiar with even the deeper thoughts of the Greek Bible could fall into such childish errors in the most everyday matters, such as the names of the patriarchs and other things. It is in all probability most correct to suppose that the tablet (with the exception of such parts as referred to the particular case) was copied from a book of Magic, and that even there the original text was already corrupt. If the tablet was itself written in the third century, and if between it and the compiler of the original text there was already a considerable period, in which corrupt copies were produced and circulated, then the second century A.D. will probably form a *terminus ad quem* for the *date of its composition ;* nevertheless there is nothing to prevent our assigning to the original text a still earlier date.

As the *locality* of the original composition we may assume Egypt, perhaps Alexandria, not only from the general character of the text, but also by reason of the Egyptian origin of texts which are cognate with it.

The *author* was a Greek Jew : [1] this follows incontrovertibly, as it seems to us, from the formal character of the text. If we had in the incantation a succession of verbal citations from the Septuagint, the hypothesis of a Jewish author were certainly the most natural, but we should then have to reckon also with the presumption that some " heathen," convinced of the magic power of the alien God, may have taken the *sayings* from the mysterious pages of the holy and not always intelligible *Book* of this same God, very much in the same way as passages at large from Homer [2] were written down for magical purposes, and as to this day amulets are made from biblical sayings. [3] Really

---

[1] A. Hilgenfeld in *Berl. Philol. Wochenschrift* xvi. (1896), p. 647 ff., considers that the author was a follower of the Samaritan Simon Magus.

[2] *Cf.* with reference to "Homeromancy," especially *Pap. Lond.* cxxi. (third century A.D.), and the remarks upon this of Kenyon, p. 83 f.

[3] A. Wuttke, *Der deutsche Volksaberglaube der Gegenwart*, 2nd edition, thoroughly revised, Berlin, 1869, p. 321 f.

verbal quotations, however, such as could be copied mechanically, are almost entirely absent from our text, in spite of
its extreme dependence in substance and form upon the
Greek Old Testament. We have here an instructive example of the reproduction of biblical passages from memory
which played such a great part in quotations and allusions
in the early Christian writings. The compiler of our text
certainly did not consult his Greek Bible as he set down one
biblical attribute of God after another ; the words flowed
from his pen without any consideration on his part of what
might be their particular origin, or any thought of checking
the letters in a scrupulous bibliolatry. Only a man who
lived and moved in the Bible, and, indeed, in the Greek
Bible, could write as he wrote. And if here and there something got mixed with his writing which has no authority in
the Septuagint, then even that speaks not against, but in
favour of, our view. For the theological conception of the
Canon has never been a favourite with popular religion,—we
might almost say, indeed, with religion in general. In every
age the religious instinct has shown an indifference in respect to the Canon,—unconscious, unexpressed, but none the
less effective—which has violated it both by narrowing it and
extending it. How many words of the canonical Bible have
never yet been able to effect what *Holy* Scripture should !
How much that is extra-canonical has filled whole generations with solace and gladness and religious enthusiasm !
Just as the Christians of New Testament times not infrequently quoted as *scripture* words for which one should have
vainly sought in the Canon (assuming that even then an
exact demarcation had been made, or was known), so also
does this text from Adrumetum, with all its obligations to
the Bible, manifest an ingenuous independence with regard
to the Canon.

In respect of form, the following facts also merit attention. *The text is almost wholly free from those grammatical
peculiarities of the Septuagint* which are usually spoken
of as *Hebraisms* — a term easily misunderstood. This is a
proof of the fact, for which there is other evidence as

well,[1] that the syntactic "influence" of the Alexandrian translation was less powerful by far than the lexical. The spirit
of the Greek language was, in the imperial period, sufficiently
accommodating where the enlarging of its stock of terms
was concerned; the good old words were becoming worn
out, and gropings were being made towards new ones and
towards the stores of the popular language—as if internal
deterioration could be again made good by means of external
enlargement. But notwithstanding all this it had a sense of
reserve quite sufficient to ward off the claims of a logic which
was repugnant to its nature. The alleged "Jewish-Greek,"
of which the Alexandrian translation of the Old Testament is
supposed to be the most prominent memorial, never existed
as a living dialect at all. Surely no one would seriously affirm
that the clumsy barbarisms of the Aramæan who tried to make
himself understood in the Greek tongue were prescribed by
the rules of a "Jewish-Greek" grammar. It may be, indeed,
that certain peculiarities, particularly with regard to the
order of words, are frequently repeated, but one has no right
to search after the rules of syntax of a "Semitic Greek" on
the basis of these peculiarities, any more than one should
have in trying to put together a syntax of "English High-
German" from the similar idioms of a German-speaking
Englishman. We need not be led astray by the observed
fact that Greek translations of Semitic originals manifest a
more or less definite persistence of Semitisms; for this persistence is not the product of a dialect which arose and
developed in the Ghettos of Alexandria and Rome, but the
disguised conformity to rule of the Semitic original, which
was often plastered over rather than translated. How comes
it that the syntax of the Jew Philo and the Benjamite Paul
stands so distinctly apart from that of such Greek translations? Just because, though they had grown up in the
Law, and meditated upon it day and night, they were yet
Alexandrian and Tarsian respectively, and as such fitted
their words naturally together, just as people spoke in Egypt

---

[1] *Cf.* the author's sketch entitled *Die neutestamentliche Formel* "*in
Christo Jesu*" *untersucht*, Marburg, 1892, p. 66 f.

and Asia Minor, and not in the manner of the clumsy pedan-
try [1] of the study, submitting line after line to the power of
an alien spirit.   The translators of the Old Testament were
Hellenists as well as were Philo and Paul, but they clothed
themselves in a strait-jacket—in the idea perhaps that such
holy labour demanded the putting on of a priestly garment.
Their work gained a success such as has fallen to the lot of
but few books: it became one of the "great powers" of history.
But although Greek Judaism and Christianity entered into,
and lived in, the sphere of its ideas, yet their faith and their
language remained so uninjured that no one thought of the
disguised Hebrew as being sacred, least of all as worthy of
imitation,[2]—though, of course, there was but little reflection
on the matter.

Then the Tablet from Adrumetum manifests a peculiarity, well known in the literature of Hellenistic Judaism,
which, we think, ought also to be considered as one of
form.   This is the *heaping up of attributes of God*, which
appears to have been a favourite custom, especially in
prayers.[3]   It is a characteristic of certain heathen prayers ;
it was believed that the gods were honoured, and that the
bestowal of their favours was influenced,[4] by the enumera-

---

[1] We would point out that this judgment upon the LXX refers only
to its syntax.   But even in this respect the investigation of Egyptian
and vernacular Greek will, as it advances, reveal that many things that
have hitherto been considered as Semitisms are in reality Alexandrianisms
or popular idioms.   With regard to the vocabulary the translators have
achieved fair results, and have not seldom treated their original with
absolute freedom.   This matter has been more thoroughly treated in Articles
II. and III. of the present work.

[2] The Synoptic Gospels, for instance, naturally occupy a special
position, in so far as their constituent parts go back in some way to
Aramaic sources.   But the syntactic parallels to the LXX which they show
are not so much an "after-effect" of that book as a consequence of the
similarity of their respective originals.

[3] Grimm, *HApAT*. iv. (1857), p. 45.

[4] Grimm, *ibid*.   The ὑμνῳδία κρυπτή of Hermes Trismegistos (given by
A. Dieterich in *Abraxas*, p. 67), for example, affords information on this point,
though, of course, it is very markedly pervaded by biblical elements.

tion of their attributes. We think it probable that this
notion also influenced the form of Judæo-Greek prayers.[1]
At all events we hear in them the expression of the same
naïve tendency which Grimm unjustifiably reproaches as "a
misunderstanding of and lack of the true spirit of prayer".
Good words were given to God—something must be given:
His divine self-importance, as it were, was appealed to. It
is children that flatter thus. With regard to this characteristic in prayer, unmistakably present also in our text,
compare the prayer of the Three Men, then 3 Macc. 2 ² ᶠᶠ.
and 6 ² ᶠᶠ., but specially the following passages:—

2 Macc. 1 ²⁴ ᶠ.: κύριε κύριε ὁ θεὸς ὁ πάντων κτίστης ὁ
φοβερὸς καὶ ἰσχυρὸς καὶ δίκαιος καὶ ἐλεήμων, ὁ μόνος βασιλεὺς
καὶ χρηστὸς ὁ μόνος χορηγὸς ὁ μόνος δίκαιος καὶ παντοκράτωρ
καὶ αἰώνιος, ὁ διασώζων τὸν Ἰσραὴλ ἐκ παντὸς κακοῦ, ὁ ποιήσας
τοὺς πατέρας ἐκλεκτοὺς καὶ ἁγιάσας αὐτούς.

Prayer of Manasses (in O. F. Fritzsche, *Libri apocr. V.
T. graece*, p. 92) ¹⁻⁴: κύριε παντοκράτωρ ὁ θεὸς τῶν πατέρων
ἡμῶν τοῦ Ἀβραὰμ καὶ Ἰσαὰκ καὶ Ἰακὼβ καὶ τοῦ σπέρματος
αὐτῶν τοῦ δικαίου, ὁ ποιήσας τὸν οὐρανὸν καὶ τὴν γῆν σὺν παντὶ
τῷ κόσμῳ αὐτῶν, ὁ πεδήσας τὴν θάλασσαν τῷ λόγῳ τοῦ προσ-
τάγματός σου, ὁ κλείσας τὴν ἄβυσσον καὶ σφραγισάμενος αὐτὴν
τῷ φοβερῷ καὶ ἐνδόξῳ ὀνόματί σου, ὃν πάντα φρίσσει καὶ τρέμει
ἀπὸ προσώπου δυνάμεώς σου.

The agreement, especially of the latter passage, with the
tablet of Adrumetum is so striking that we should have
to suppose that our compiler used the Prayer of Manasses,
unless the case was that both were working with the same
materials in the same framework of a customary form. That
this form came in course of time to be of great influence
liturgically, and that it can still be perceived in the monotony
of many a service-book prayer, can only be indicated here.
It is doubtless a partial cause of the fact that the word
Litanei, in our customary speech, has gained an unpleasant
secondary signification. [*Litanei* = litany + jeremiad.]

The peculiarity just treated of was described as a formal
one. For even if its origin points, psychologically, to a

---

[1] Observe, however, the form seen already in certain Psalms.

temper of mind not entirely alien to religion, yet the employment of it, where the religious motive has given place to the
liturgical, the unconstrained feeling of the true worshipper
to the literary interest of the prayer-book writer, is in general
purely ritualistic, that is, formal.   But the attributes of God
which are found in the text from Adrumetum are of deep
interest even in substance, when considered in reference to
the choice which the compiler has made.   It is true that
they are here used as the vehicle of an incantation, but
how different is their simplicity and intelligibility from the
meaningless chaos of most other *incantamenta !* The context
in which they stand must not cause us to ignore their religious value.   If we put aside the adjuration of the demon
for the trivial ends of a sickly affection, we are enabled to
gain a notion of how the unknown author thought about
God.   The suspicion that he was an impostor and that he
intentionally employed the biblical expressions as hocus-
pocus is perhaps not to be flatly denied ; but there is nothing
to justify it, and to assert, without further consideration, that
the literary representatives of magic were swindlers, would
be to misapprehend the tremendous force with which the
popular mind in all ages has been ruled by the " superstitious " notion that the possession of supernatural powers
may be secured through religion.   Our compiler, just because
of the relative simplicity of his formulæ, has the right to be
taken in earnest.   What strikes us most of all in these are
the thoughts which establish the omnipotence of God.   The
God, through Whom he adjures the demon, is for him the
creator, the preserver and the governor of nature in its
widest sense : He has, of course, the power to crush the
miserable spirit of the tomb.   But besides this conception
of God, which impresses the senses more strongly than
the conscience, and upon which the poetry of biblical and
post-biblical Judaism long continued to nourish itself,[1] this
unknown man has also extracted the best of what was

---

[1] For a somewhat more remote application of this thought *cf.* J.
Bernays, *Die heraklitischen Briefe,* Berlin, 1869, p. 29.   The magic Papyri
yield a multitude of examples of the idea.

best in the Jewish faith, *viz.*, the ethical idea of the God of
prophecy, Who separates the pious from the transgressors
because He hates evil, and the "fear" of Whom is the
beginning of wisdom.

Thus the tablet of Adrumetum is a memorial of the
Alexandrian Old Testament. Not only does it reveal what
a potent formal influence the Greek Bible, and especially
the praise-book thereof, exercised upon the classes who
lived outside of the official protection of the Synagogue and
the Church, and who thus elude the gaze of history, but it
lets us also surmise that the eternal thoughts of the Old
Testament had not wholly lost their germinative power
even where, long after and in an obscure place, they had
seemingly fallen among thorns.

NOTES ON SOME BIBLICAL PERSONS AND NAMES.

τὸν ἥλιον αὐτοῦ ἀνατέλλει ἐπὶ πονηροὺς καὶ ἀγαθοὺς καὶ βρέχει ἐπὶ δικαίους καὶ ἀδίκους.

NOTES ON SOME BIBLICAL PERSONS AND NAMES.

1. HELIODORUS.

The Second Book of Maccabees has a wonderful story to tell of how King Seleucus IV. Philopator made an unsuccessful attempt to plunder the temple-treasury in Jerusalem. A certain Simon, who had occasion to revenge himself upon Onias the high-priest, had gone hurriedly to Apollonius, the Syrian governor of Cœlesyria and Phœnicia, and had contrived to impress him with the most marvellous ideas of the temple property in Jerusalem. The king, having been informed of the sacred store, thought it well to send his minister Heliodorus to Jerusalem, with orders to bring back the gold with him. Heliodorus was the very man for such a mission. Having reached Jerusalem, neither the expostulations of the high priest nor the lamentations of the people were able to dissuade him. In the extremity of their distress recourse was had to prayer. And just as the heartless official and his minions were actually preparing to pillage the treasury, "there appeared unto them a horse with a terrible rider upon him, and adorned with a very fair covering, and he ran fiercely, and smote at Heliodorus with his fore-feet; and it seemed that he that sat upon the horse had complete harness of gold. Moreover, two other young men appeared before him, notable in strength, excellent in beauty, and comely in apparel; who stood by him on either side, and scourged him continually, and gave him many sore stripes. And Heliodorus fell suddenly to the ground and was compassed with great darkness; but they that were with him took him up, and put him into a litter and carried him forth." A sacrifice offered by the high-

priest saved the half-dead man, and then the two young
men, apparelled as before, appeared to him again, and told
him that he owed his life to Onias.   Then Heliodorus, being
asked by the king after his return, who might be the proper
person to send on the same errand to Jerusalem, replied:
"If thou hast any enemy or adversary to thy government,
send him thither, and thou shalt receive him well scourged,
if he escape with his life : for in that place without doubt
there is an especial power of God".

The historical foundations of this tale in 2 Macc. 3,
which is certainly better known to-day through Raphael's
picture than through its original narrator, are not so obvious
as its pious aim.   Grimm [1] is inclined to allow it a kernel of
history ; up to verse 23 the story does not contain a single
feature which might not have been literally true.   Owing
to the financial difficulties occasioned by the conclusion of
peace with Rome, temple-robbings seem to have become,
to some extent, the order of the day with the Seleucidae.
Grimm therefore accepts the historicity of the attempt to
plunder the temple, but leaves undecided the actual nature
of the event, thus ornamented by tradition, by which the
project of Heliodorus was baffled.   The author is not in a
position to decide this question, though, indeed, the answer
given by Grimm seems to him to be in the main correct.[2]
But in any case the observation of Schürer,[3] *viz.*, that the
book as a whole (or its source, Jason of Cyrene) is not seldom
very well-informed in the matter of details, is confirmed in
the present passage.

The book undoubtedly says what is correct of the hero
of the story, Heliodorus,[4] in describing him as first minister

[1] *HApAT.* iv. (1857), p. 77.

[2] The author, however, finds, even previous to verse 23, features which
are to be explained by the "edifying tendency" of the book.

[3] Schürer, ii., p. 740 (= [3]iii., p. 360).   [Eng. Trans., ii., ii., p. 211 f.]

[4] According to the "fourth" Book of Maccabees, which uses this narrative for purposes of edification, it was not Heliodorus, but Apollonius, who
tried to plunder the Temple.   J. Freudenthal, in *Die Flav. Joseph. beigelegte
Schrift Ueber die Herrsch. der Vernunft*, p. 85 f., is inclined to reject both
reports as suspicious, but to consider that of 4 Macc. to be the better of the

of the Syrian king. It is indeed true that this assertion is
not vouched for in ancient literature; for Appian, *Syr.*, p.
45 (Mendelssohn, i., p. 416) makes mention of only one
Heliodorus as τινὸς τῶν περὶ τὴν αὐλήν of Seleucus. But
even if this note makes it more than "probable"[1] that it
refers to the same man as is alluded to in the Second Book
of Maccabees, yet, if there were no further proof of the
identity, it would be necessary to reckon seriously with the
possibility that the author of that book, in accordance with
his general purpose, transformed some mere court-official
into the first minister of the king of Syria, in order to make
still more impressive the miracle of his punishment and his
repentance. But this very detail, suspicious in itself, can be
corroborated by two Inscriptions from Delos, made known by
Th. Homolle, which may be given here:—

I.[2] Ἡλιόδωρον Αἰσχύλου Ἀντ[ιοχέα]
τὸν σύντροφον[3] τοῦ βασιλέως Σ[ελεύκου]
Φιλοπάτορος καὶ ἐπὶ τῶν πρα[γμάτων]
τεταγμένον οἱ ἐν Λα[οδικείᾳ?]
τῇ ἐν Φοινίκῃ ἐγδοχεῖς καὶ να[ύκληροι?]
εὐνοίας ἕνεκεν καὶ φιλοστο[ργίας]
[τ]ῆς εἰς τὸν βασιλέα καὶ εὐεργ[εσίας]
τῆς εἰς αὐτοὺς
Ἀπόλλωνι.

The Inscription stands upon the base of a statue no
longer extant: its purport is that some Phœnician ship-
masters dedicated the statue of Heliodorus, out of gratitude

two: it "reports simply and without ornament that which is told in 2 Macc.
with distorted exaggeration". The present writer cannot agree with this
opinion; what Freudenthal calls in the one case "simple and without
ornament" and in the other "distorted exaggeration," should only, in view
of the wholly distinct purposes of the two books, be characterised by the
formal antitheses *concise* and *detailed* respectively. The hybrid form, *Apollo-
doros*, of which L. Flathe speaks in his *Geschichte Macedoniens*, ii., Leipzig,
1834, p. 601, was in all probability formed from the Apollonius of 4 and
the Heliodorus of 2 Macc. (Freudenthal, p. 84).

[1] Grimm, p. 69.

[2] *Bulletin de correspondance hellénique*, i. (1877), p. 285.

[3] On this, see p. 310 f. below.

for his kindness, and on account of his being well-affected towards the king, to the Delian Apollo.

II.[1] Ἡλιόδωρον Αἰσχύλου τὸν σ[ύντροφον βασιλέως]
Σελεύκου τεταγμένον δὲ κ[αὶ ἐπὶ τῶν πραγμάτων]
καὶ τὴν συγγένειαν αὐτο[ῦ] . . . .
Ἀρτεμίδωρος Ἡρακλείδου τῶν . . . .
ἀρετῆς ἕνεκεν καὶ δικα[ιοσύνης . . . . . . ἧς ἔχων]
διατελεῖ εἴς τε τὸν βασιλέα κ[αὶ] . . . . . .
φιλίας δὲ καὶ εὐεργεσίας τ[ῆς εἰς ἑαυτὸν ἀνέθηκεν]
Ἀπόλλωνι Ἀ[ρτέμιδι Λητοῖ].

This Inscription also is found on the base of a statue; its contents quite resemble those of No. 1; in line 3 συγγένειαν, with some supplementary participle, will signify the same title which is already known to us as συγγενής.[2]

Homolle's conjecture that this Heliodorus is identical with the one mentioned in 2 Maccabees, and by Appian, seems to us to be fully established;[3] note how accurately 2 Macc. 3[7] also introduces him as Ἡλιόδωρον τὸν ἐπὶ τῶν πραγμάτων. This title, which is current elsewhere in the Books of Maccabees (1 Macc. 3[32], 2 Macc. 10[11], 13[2.23], 3 Macc. 7[1]) is proved by other writings to have belonged to Syria,[4] as also to Pergamus.[5] In Polybius and Josephus it is applied to the *viceroy, the representative of the* absent *king*, similarly in 1 Macc. 3[32], 2 Macc. 13[23]; in 2 Macc. 3[7] it has the further meaning of *chancellor of the kingdom, first minister*,[6] similarly 10[11], 13[2], 3 Macc. 7[1].

The first Inscription, moreover, confirms the reading πραγμάτων which is given by most MSS. in 2 Macc. 3[7].

---

[1] *Bull. de corr. hell.*, iii. (1879), p. 364.   [2] See p. 159 above.

[3] In that case the Inscriptions must certainly have been written before 175 B.C.; for in that year Heliodorus carried out his φιλοστοργία εἰς τὸν βασιλέα, which is here extolled, in a strange way, *viz.*, by murdering the king.

[4] Fränkel, *Altertümer von Pergamon*, viii. 1, p. 110, cites Polyb. v. 41 and Joseph. *Antt.* xii. 7₂.

[5] Inscriptions Nos. 172-176 (first half of 2nd cent. B.C.) in Fränkel, p. 108 f.

[6] This interpretation, proposed by Grimm, p. 69, is maintained also by Fränkel, p. 110.

Codices 19, 44, 71, etc., which substitute χρημάτων for πραγμάτων in this passage,[1] have obviously been so influenced by the contents of the narrative as to turn the *chancellor* into a *chancellor of the exchequer;* for such must have been the sense of the title given by them, *viz.,* τὸν ἐπὶ τῶν χρημάτων. As for Syncellus (8th cent. A.D.), *Chronogr.,* p. 529 7 (Bonn edition), who likewise describes Heliodorus as ὁ ἐπὶ τῶν χρημάτων, he is probably dependent on these codices.[2]

Evidence from the Inscriptions has extended our knowledge thus far : Heliodorus came originally from Antioch,[3] and was the son of a certain Aischylos.   In the lofty position of first minister of King Seleucus IV. Philopator, to whose familiar circle (σύντροφοι) he had certainly belonged previously, he earned good repute in connection with the shipping trade, and was in consequence the recipient of frequent honours.

The marble statue of Heliodorus was prepared for Phœnician merchants by the ancient sculptors, and the pious gift was dedicated to the Delian Apollo ; some narrator of late pre-Christian times, full of faith in the written word, made him the central figure of a richly-coloured picture, and the fate of the temple-robber became a theme for edification, not unmixed with pious horror ; fifteen hundred years afterwards Raphael's *Stanza d'Eliodoro* transformed this naïve exultation in the penalty paid by the godless man into the lofty though unhistorical idea that the Church of the Vatican is ever triumphant.

2. BARNABAS.[4]

The writer of the Acts of the Apostles reports, 4 [36], that there was given to the Cyprian Ἰωσήφ the surname Βαρναβας ἀπὸ τῶν ἀποστόλων, ὅ ἐστιν μεθερμηνευόμενον υἱὸς παρα-

---

[1] This variation is found here only.

[2] Against Freudenthal, p. 86, who attributes the alteration to Syncellus.

[3] *I.e.,* if the restoration in No. I. be correct, as the author holds to be very probable.

[4] See p. 187 f. above.

κλήσεως. Now even if it be true that "the Apostles" so
named him, yet it is improbable that they were the first to
coin the name, which rather appears to be an ancient one.
The derivation given by the writer of the early history of
Christianity is clear only as regards its first part : βαρ is of
course the Aramaic בַּר, *son*, so frequently found in Semitic
names. In regard to ναβας, however, the second element in
the name, it is not evident which Semitic word has been
translated παράκλησις in the Apostolic text. The usual
conjecture is נְבוּאָה. But this signifies a *prophecy*, and is
accordingly rendered quite accurately in LXX 2 Es. [Ezra]
6 [14], Neh. 6 [12], 2 Chron. 15 [8] by προφητεία, and in 2
Chron. 9 [29] by λόγοι. A. Klostermann [1] therefore proposes
the Aramaic נֶחְדָא, *pacification*, *consolation ;* but we doubt
whether this will explain the transcription ναβας. It
would seem better, even were the etymology given in Acts
more intelligible than it is, to leave it out of account as a
basis of explanation, [2] since we are at once assailed by the
suspicion that we have here, as in many other passages, a
folk-etymology *ex post facto.* We must rather try to understand the name from itself ; and, as we believe, two possible
explanations of the -ναβας, which is alone in question, lie
open to us.

In the Greek Bible, *Nun*, the father of Joshua, is called
Ναυη. Whatever be the explanation of this form, whether
or not it is actually to be understood, as has been supposed,
as a corruption [3] of ΝΑΤΝ into ΝΑΤΗ, does not signify.
The only important matter is that, for Ναυη, there also
occur the variants Ναβη or Ναβι. Whether this Ναυη—

---

[1] *Probleme im Aposteltexte neu erörtert*, Gotha, 1883, p. 8 ff.

[2] Even Jerome, *Liber interpretationis Hebraicorum nominum*, 67 [23] f.
(*Onomastica sacra* Pauli de Lagarde *studio et sumptibus alterum edita*, Göttingen, 1887, p. 100), has not straightway adopted the etymology given in Acts ;
he gives three interpretations : *Barnabas filius prophetae uel filius uenientis
aut* (*ut plerique putant*) *filius consolationis.*

[3] The author fails to understand how Nun should have originally been
transcribed Ναυν. It seems to him more probable that the LXX read נֶחְדָ,
or that Ναυη (or Ναβη) or Ναβι was in actual use as a personal name, and that
they substituted it for *Nun.*

$Na\beta\eta$—$Na\beta\iota$ was already in use as a personal name
(= *prophet*) in the time of the LXX cannot be ascertained;
certainly, however, it had later on become known as such to
the Jews through the Greek Bible. We might, then, possibly
find this name in the -$\nu a\beta a\varsigma$: $Ba\rho\nu a\beta a\varsigma$ would be a $Ba\rho\nu a\beta\eta$
or $Ba\rho\nu a\beta\iota$ with a Greek termination—*son of a prophet*.

But the author thinks it a more promising theory to
connect $Ba\rho\nu a\beta a\varsigma$ with the recently-discovered Semitic name
$Ba\rho\nu\epsilon\beta o\hat{\upsilon}\varsigma$. An Inscription[1] found in Islahie, the ancient
Nicopolis, in Northern Syria, which is assigned, probably on
account of the written character, to the 3rd or 4th century
A.D., runs as follows:—

$Ba\rho\nu\epsilon\beta o\hat{\upsilon}\nu$ $\tau\grave{o}\nu$ $\kappa a\grave{\iota}$[2] '$A\pi o\lambda\lambda\iota\nu\acute{a}\rho\iota o\nu$ $\Sigma a\mu\mu a\nu\hat{a}$ $a\vartheta\theta a\acute{\iota}\rho\epsilon\tau o\nu$
$\delta\eta\mu\iota o\upsilon\rho\gamma\grave{o}\nu$ $\kappa a\grave{\iota}$ $\gamma\upsilon\mu\nu a\sigma\acute{\iota}a\rho\chi o\nu$ $\phi\acute{\iota}\lambda[o\iota]$.

The editors explain the name quite correctly as *son of
Nebo*.[3] Their conjecture can be further confirmed, particularly by Symmachus, who in Is. 46[1] renders נְבוֹ, *Nebo*,
by $N\epsilon\beta o\hat{\upsilon}\varsigma$, while the LXX, Aquila and Theodotion tran-
scribe it by $Na\beta\acute{\omega}$.[4] $Ba\rho\nu\epsilon\beta o\hat{\upsilon}\varsigma$ is one of the many personal
names which have *Nebo* as a constituent part, and, as a
theophoric name, will be relatively old. The hypothesis of
the affinity, or of the original identity, of $Ba\rho\nu a\beta a\varsigma$ and
$Ba\rho\nu\epsilon\beta o\hat{\upsilon}\varsigma$ is further borne out by the well-known fact that
in the transcription of other names compounded with *Nebo*
the E-sound of the word is sometimes replaced by a,[5] *e.g.*,
Nebuchadnezzar = (LXX) $Na\beta o\upsilon\chi o\delta o\nu o\sigma o\rho$ = (Berosus and
Josephus) $Na\beta o\upsilon\chi o\delta o\nu\acute{o}\sigma o\rho o\varsigma$ = (Strabo) $Na\beta o\kappa o\delta\rho\acute{o}\sigma o\rho o\varsigma$;

---

[1] K. Humann and O. Puchstein, *Reisen in Kleinasien und Nordsyrien*,
Textband, Berlin, 1890, p. 398. A much older Inscription has already been
cited, p. 188 above.

[2] For this $\tau\grave{o}\nu$ $\kappa a\acute{\iota}$ see below, p. 313 f.

[3] '$A\pi o\lambda\lambda\iota\nu\acute{a}\rho\iota o\varsigma$ is (*cf.* '$A\pi o\lambda\lambda\acute{\omega}\nu\iota o\varsigma$ = '$I\omega\nu\acute{a}\theta a\varsigma$, p. 149 *ante, sub* $\pi a\rho\epsilon\pi\acute{\iota}\delta\eta\mu o\varsigma$)
an imitation of the theophoric $Ba\rho\nu\epsilon\beta o\hat{\upsilon}\varsigma$; but one need not on that account
have recourse to any such religious-historical equation as Nebo = *Apollo*, as
the editors suggest.

[4] Field, ii., p. 522.

[5] The A-sound is also found in the Babylonian and Assyrian primary
forms. It is not impossible that the name $Na\beta\eta$, discussed above, if not
coined by the LXX, may be connected in origin with *Nebo*.

and *Nebuzaradan* 2 Kings 25 ^{8} = (LXX) Ναβουζαρδαν. It is therefore highly probable that the form Βαρναβοῦς might occur instead of Βαρνεβοῦς. The former appears to us to be the original form of the name Βαρναβᾶς.[1] The termination -οῦς must, in that case, have developed into -ᾶς, but this is no extraordinary phenomenon in view of the arbitrariness with which Semitic names were Graecised ; perhaps the Jews intentionally substituted the very common Greek name-ending -ας for -ους in order to remove from the name its suspiciously pagan appearance : the mutilation of Gentile theophoric names was looked upon by the Jews as an actual religious duty,[2] on the authority of Deut. 7 ^{26} and 12 ^{3}. We indeed see this duty discharged in another personal name formed with *Nebo* : the name *Abed Nego* [3] in the Book of Daniel is most probably an intentional defacement of *Abed Nebo, servant of Nebo.* Thus did the later Graeco-Jewish Βαρναβᾶς arise from the ancient Semitic Βαρνεβοῦς or Βαρναβοῦς. It then became the part of popular etymology to give a religious interpretation to the name thus defaced from motives of piety. The very difficulty of establishing which Semitic word was believed to correspond to -ναβας bears out the hypothesis enunciated above.

3. MANAËN.

In 1 Macc. 1 ^{6}, according to the common reading, mention is made of παῖδες σύντροφοι ἀπὸ νεότητος of Alexander the Great, and, in 2 Macc. 9 ^{29}, of a certain Philippos as σύντροφος of King Antiochus IV. Epiphanes; similarly, in Acts 13 ^{1}, the esteemed Antiochian Christian Manaën [4]

---

[1] In that case this accentuation would commend itself as preferable to the "traditional" Βαρνάβας.—Blass, *Gramm. des neutest. Griechisch*, p. 123, also writes Βαρναβᾶς; on p. 31, Βαρνάβας. [Eng. Trans., pp. 125 and 31.]

[2] Winer-Schmiedel, § 5, 27 *a*, note 56 (p. 58). Many similar cases are given there.

[3] LXX, Ἀβδεναγώ. Note the rendering of the *E*-sound by α here also.

[4] His name is Μαναήν; that is, of course, מְנַחֵם. The Alexandrinus likewise transcribes Menachēm in LXX 2 Kings 15 ^{16} ff. by Μαναήν, while the other Codices have Μαναήμ. The termination -ην gave the foreign name a

is distinguished by the attribute Ἡρώδου τοῦ τετραάρχου
σύντροφος.

In the first passage, however, we have good authority
(Alexandrinus, Sinaiticus, etc.) for συνέκτροφοι, a word not
found elsewhere, "but which, precisely on that account,
may have been displaced by συντρ.";[1] the addition of ἀπὸ
νεότητος seems to us to give additional support to the
assumption that συνέκτροφοι was the original form.[2] Accordingly O. F. Fritzsche, in his edition, has also decided
for συνέκτροφοι. The meaning of the word is unquestionably
one reared along with another in the proper sense.[3]

The case is different with the σύντροφος of the other
two passages. The commentaries give, in connection with
Acts 13[1], the alternative meanings *foster-brother* and *companion in education;*[4] but the former explanation is forthwith
rendered void by the frequent occurrence (to be established
presently) of the expression in connection with a king's
name, if we but think what strange inferences would
follow from it! We should have to assume, for instance,
that in the most diverse localities, and at times most widely
apart, the newly-born crown-princes had very frequently
to be entrusted to the care of healthy citizens, and, further,
that the son of the plebeian nurse was still alive when

kind of Greek look: pet names in -ην are occasionally used by the Greeks
(A. Fick, *Die Griechischen Personennamen nach ihrer Bildung erklärt*, 2nd
ed. by F. Bechtel and A. Fick, Göttingen, 1894, p. 28). It will hardly be
necessary in this case to assume the arbitrary interchange of μ and ν which
occurs not infrequently in the transcription of Semitic proper names (*cf.* on
this point, Winer-Schmiedel, § 5, 27 *g*, and note 63 [p. 61]).

[1] Grimm, *HApAT.* iii. (1853), p. 6.

[2] The word appears to be confirmed also by the Syriac versions,
Grimm, *ibid.*, p. 7.

[3] It cannot be urged against this that the view thus obtained does not
correspond with the historical circumstances (*i.e.* the παῖδες among whom
Alexander divided his empire could hardly be all his συνέκτροφοι in the proper
sense); but the writer of Macc. certainly held this opinion. The variant
σύντροφοι may perhaps be explained by the attempt of some thoughtful
copyist to get rid of the historical discrepancy; σύντροφοι in the technical
sense presently to be determined was more accurate: the thoughtless thinker
of course allowed the ἀπὸ νεότητος to stand.

[4] H. Holtzmann, *H.C.* i.[2] (1892), p. 371.

his *conlactaneus* ascended the throne of his father. The interpretation *companion in education* is better : one might in this connection compare the *play-mates* of the Dauphin, who were, as a matter of course, taken from the best families, and of whom, later on, one or another continued, so far as consistent with the reverence that "doth hedge a king," to be the intimate friend of the prince, now come to man's estate. But this hypothesis is likewise too special; σύντροφος τοῦ βασιλέως is a court title, which is of course to be explained by the fundamental meaning of the word, but in the usage of which this fundamental meaning had disappeared, having given place to the general meaning of *intimate friend.* The case is on all fours with that of the title of king's *relative.*[1] σύντροφος τοῦ βασιλέως is established as regards Pergamus by Polybius, xxxii. 25 10 ; further by the Pergamenian Inscriptions, Nos. 179 3, 224 2, 248 6 and 28,[2] all of pre-Roman times (before 133 B.C.). "It appears to have been in general use throughout the Hellenistic kingdoms."[3] In regard to Macedonia, Fränkel cites Polyb. v. 9 4 ; for Pontus, he refers to the Inscription, *Bulletin de correspondance hellénique,* vii. (1883), p. 355 ; for Egypt, to the observations of Lumbroso.[4] But the Inscription of Delos (first half of 2nd cent. B.C.) given above,[5] in which the title is established for Syria also, is the most instructive of all in connection with the passage in Acts; Heliodorus, probably an Antiochian likewise, is there invested with the honorary title σύντροφος τοῦ βασιλέως Σελεύκου Φιλοπάτορος. And in the same way it was allowable to speak of Manaën as the *intimate friend* of Herod Antipas; nothing further is implied by the technical term, and any inference drawn from it regarding the antecedents of the man, or regarding any tender relationship between his mother and the infant Herod, would be very precarious. In the context of the narrative the attribute, when understood in this sense, is of course still more honourable for Manaën and the church at Antioch than would be the case according to the traditional interpretation.

---

[1] *Cf.* p. 159 above, *sub* συγγενής.   [2] Fränkel, pp. 111, 129, 164 ff.
[3] Fränkel, p. 111 f.   [4] *Recherches,* p. 207 ff.   [5] P. 305.

4. SAULUS PAULUS.

In Acts 13⁹ the words $\Sigma a\hat{u}\lambda o\varsigma$ $\dot{o}$ $\kappa a\grave{\iota}$ $\Pi a\hat{u}\lambda o\varsigma$ are quite abruptly introduced to designate the Apostle who has always hitherto been spoken of as $\Sigma a\hat{u}\lambda o\varsigma$, and from this place onwards in the book the name $\Pi a\hat{u}\lambda o\varsigma$ is always used. The passage has given rise to the most extraordinary conjectures; it has even been asserted that the narrator meant the $\dot{o}$ $\kappa a\grave{\iota}$ $\Pi a\hat{u}\lambda o\varsigma$ to indicate that the change of name had some sort of connection with the conversion of the Proconsul Sergius Paulus described immediately before. It must not be forgotten, in investigating the point, that it is not said that the Apostle made the change; it is the narrator who does so: by means of the $\dot{o}$ $\kappa a\acute{\iota}$ he makes the transition from the previously-used $\Sigma a\hat{u}\lambda o\varsigma$ to the $\Pi a\hat{u}\lambda o\varsigma$ to which he henceforth keeps.

We have never yet seen the fact recorded in connection with this passage[1] that the *elliptically-used $\kappa a\acute{\iota}$ with double names* is an exceedingly common usage in N. T. times. W. Schmid,[2] in his studies on Atticism (of great importance for the history of the language of the Greek Bible), has recently shown from the Papyri and Inscriptions how widespread this usage was in all quarters; he names an Inscription of Antiochus Epiphanes as his first authority. " As *qui et* is similarly used in Latin in the case of familiar designations . . . , we might suspect a Latinism, had the

---

[1] Winer-Lünemann, § 18, 1 (p. 102), refers only to quite late writings. On the other hand, the painstaking Wetstein had already in 1752 annotated the passage "Inscriptiones"! That means more for his time than dozens of other "observations" by the industrious and open-eyed exegetes of last (18th) century.

[2] *Der Atticismus*, iii. (1893), p. 338.—His authorities are to be supplemented by the Inscription of Mylasa in Caria, Waddington, iii. 2, No. 361 (imperial period), by a multitude of examples from Lycian Inscriptions,—see the lists of the Gerontes of Sidyma in O. Benndorf and G. Niemann, *Reisen in Lykien und Karien*, Vienna, 1884, p. 73 ff. (time of Commodus)—likewise by many passages from the Egyptian documents in the Royal Museum at Berlin, *e.g.*, Nos. 39; 141²; 200; 277²; 281. In the *Pap. Berol.* 6815 (*BU.* ii., p. 43, No. 30) we even find Μάρκου ᾿Αντωνίου Διοσκόρου ὁ καὶ Πτολεμαίου, an evidence of the fixedness and formulaic currency of this ὁ καί.

Antiochus Inscription not made it more likely that the Latin
usage is really a Graecism." [1]

W. Schmid seems to think that certain passages from
Ælianus and Achilles Tatius are the earliest instances of this
construction in the literature. But even in the literature
the usage, most likely derived from the popular speech, can
be shown to go much farther back. We find the reading
Ἄλκιμος ὁ καὶ Ἰάκιμος in 1 Macc. 7 [5. 12. 20 ff.], 9 [54 ff.], 2 Macc.
14 [3], at least in Codd. 64, 93, 19 (also 62 in the last passage).
But even should this reading not be the original, yet we
need not be at a loss for literary authorities; a relatively
large number are supplied by Josephus.[2] The Jewish historian, in giving double names, employs not only the fuller
forms of expression, such as Σίμων ὁ καὶ δίκαιος ἐπικληθείς
(Antt. xii. 2 4), Ἄλκιμος ὁ καὶ Ἰάκιμος κληθείς (Antt. xii. 9 7),
Ἰωάννην τὸν καὶ Γαδδὶν λεγόμενον (Antt. xiii. 1 2), Διόδοτος ὁ
καὶ Τρύφων ἐπικληθείς (Antt. xiii. 5 1), Σελήνη ἡ καὶ Κλεο-
πάτρα καλουμένη (Antt. xiii. 16 4), Ἀντίοχος ὁ καὶ Διόνυσος
ἐπικληθείς (Bell. Jud. i. 4 7), but he often simply connects the
two names by ὁ καί: Ἰανναῖον τὸν καὶ Ἀλέξανδρον (Antt. xiii.
12 1),[3] Ἰώσηπος ὁ καὶ Καϊάφας (Antt. xviii. 2 2),[3] Κλεόδημος ὁ
καὶ Μάλχος (Antt. i. 15), Ἄρκη ἡ καὶ Ἐκδείπους (Antt. v. 1 22),
Ἰούδας ὁ καὶ Μακκαβαῖος (Antt. xii. 6 4), Πακόρῳ τῷ καὶ πρε-
σβυτέρῳ (Antt. xx. 3 3).

When Acts 13 [9] is placed in this philological context, we
see that it cannot mean "Saul who was *henceforth* also called
Paul"; an ancient reader could only have taken it to mean
"Saul who was *also* called Paul".[4] Had the writer of Acts
intended to say that Paul had adopted the Graecised Roman
name in honour of the Proconsul, or even that he now
adopted it for the first time, he would have selected a
different expression. The ὁ καί admits of no other supposition than that he was called *Saulos Paulos* before he came to

[1] W. Schmid, *Der Atticismus*, iii. (1893), p. 838.

[2] Guil. Schmidt, *De Flav. Ios. Elocutione*, Fleck. *Jahrbb. Suppl.* xx.
(1.. .), p. 355 f.

[3] For the text see Guil. Schmidt, p. 355.

[4] *Cf.* H. H. Wendt, Meyer, iii. 6/7 (1888), p. 284.

Cyprus; he had, like many natives of Asia Minor, many
Jews and Egyptians of his age, a double name. We know
not when he received the non-Semitic name in addition to
the Semitic one. It will hardly be demanded that we should
specify the particular circumstance which formed the occasion of his receiving the surname *Paulos*. The regulations
of Roman Law about the bearing of names cannot in this
question be taken into consideration. If in Asia Minor or on
the Nile any obscure individual felt that, in adopting a non-
barbaric surname, he was simply adapting himself to the
times, it is unlikely that the authorities would trouble themselves about the matter. The choice of such Græco-Roman
second names was usually determined by the innocent freedom of popular taste. But we can sometimes see that such
names as were more or less similar in sound to the native
name must have been specially preferred.[1] In regard to
Jewish names this is the case with, *e.g.*, Ἰάκιμ—Ἄλκιμος
(Joseph. *Antt.* xii. 9 7), Ἰησοῦς ὁ λεγόμενος Ἰοῦστος (Col. 4 11),
Ἰωσὴφ . . . ὃς ἐπεκλήθη Ἰοῦστος (Acts 1 23);[2] of Egyptian
names, we have noticed Σαταβοῦς ὁ καὶ Σάτυρος (*Pap.
Berol.* 7080, Col. 2, Fayyûm, 2nd cent. A.D.).[3] Thus, too, in

---

[1] Winer-Schmiedel, § 16, 9 (p. 143).

[2] We must not confuse these cases, in which non-Jewish names of
similar sound *were attached* to the Jewish, with those in which non-Jewish
names of similar sound were *substituted for* the Jewish; those who had
adopted new names bore these alone in their intercourse with strangers.
Thus the name Ἰάσων, common among Jews, is a substitute for Ἰησοῦς; the
Apostle Symeon (Peter) is usually called Σίμων, not because (as *Clavis*³, p.
400, still maintains) this word is a transcription of שִׁמְעוֹן, but because it
resembles Συμεών, the actual transcription of the Hebrew name (so, of Peter,
Acts 15 14, 2 Pet. 1 1). Σίμων is a good Greek name (Fick-Bechtel, p. 251);
thus, too, the Vulgate substitutes *Cleophas* (= Κλεοφᾶς, Fick-Bechtel, p. 20
and foot of p. 164; not to be confounded with Κλεοπᾶς in Luke 24 18, Fick-
Bechtel, middle of p. 164) for the (probably) Semitic name Κλωπα(ς? Accent?
[John 19 25]; the author does not know what authority *Clavis*³, p. 244, has
for saying that the Semitic form of Κλωπα(ς?) is חַלְפָּא, still less how P.
Feine, *Der Jakobusbrief*, Eisenach, 1893, p. 16, can maintain that it is "elsewhere recognised" that Κλωπᾶς is Greek, and = Κλεοπᾶς); similarly Σιλουανός
seems to be a substitute for the Semitic Σίλας.

[3] *BU.* ix., p. 274, No. 277 ².

the case of the Tarsian Σαούλ,[1] when he received a non-Semitic second name (we do not know the exact time, but it must have been before Acts 13[9]) the choice of Παῦλος may have been determined by nothing more than the fact that Παῦλος had a sound somewhat similar to the name made venerable by association with his fellow-tribesman of old.[2]

So far as we know, there has hitherto been no evidence to show that the name Παῦλος was adopted by any other Jew; it is therefore of interest that the recently-published Papyrus fragments relating to the Jewish war of Trajan[3] several times mention an Alexandrian Jew called Παῦλος,[4] who seems to have been the leader of a deputation which negotiated with the emperor. The question why the narrator calls the Apostle Σαῦλος previous to Acts 13[9], and Παῦλος afterwards, has nothing to do with the science of names, or with the history of Paul; it is altogether a question of literary history. The most satisfactory solution

---

[1] The frequently-noted circumstance that in the accounts of Paul's conversion, Acts 9[4.17], 22[7.13], 26[14], he is addressed by Jesus and Ananias as Σαούλ may be explained by the historian's sense of liturgical rhythm;—compare the way in which he puts the name Συμεών (for Peter, whom he elsewhere calls Σίμων and Πέτρος) in the mouth of James in a solemn speech, 15[14]. Similarly, the early Christians did not Graecise, e.g., the venerable name of the patriarch Jacob: Ἰακώβ had a "biblical," Ἰάκωβος a modern, sound. In the same way Paul appears to have made a distinction between the ancient theocratic form Ἱερουσαλήμ and the modern political name Ἱεροσόλυμα: when he uses the former, there is ever a solemn emphasis upon the word, especially noticeable in Gal. 4[26.25] (cf. Hebr. 12[22], Rev. 3[12], 21[2.10]); but also as the dwelling-place of the saints, Jerusalem is more to him than a mere geographical term: hence in 1 Cor. 16[3], Rom. 15[25 ff.], he lovingly and reverently marks a distinction by writing Ἱερουσαλήμ; lastly, in Rom. 15[19] this form again best suits the subject, viz., an enthusiastic retrospect of the diffusion of the gospel. We must also bear in mind that the Gospels preserve many of our Lord's sayings in Aramaic; see p. 76 above. The assertion of A. Buttmann, Gramm. des neutest. Sprachgebr., p. 6, that, when Paul is addressed, the "popular" (??—for the readers of the Greek Book of Acts?) form Σαούλ is regularly employed, is contradicted by Acts 26[24], 27[24].

[2] Cf. Acts 13[21], and also Rom. 11[1] and Phil. 3[5].

[3] See p. 68 above.

[4] The name, indeed, is mutilated in almost all the passages, so that the restoration Σαῦλος would also be possible, but in Col. vii. of the edition of Wilcken, Hermes, xxvii. (1892), p. 470, Παῦλος can be distinctly made out.

so far (unless we are willing to go back to a difference in the sources) is the supposition[1] that the historian uses the one or the other name according to the field of his hero's labours; from chap. 13[1] the Jewish disciple Σαῦλος is an apostle to the whole world: it is high time, then, that he should be presented to the Greeks under a name about which there was nothing barbaric, and which, even before this, was really his own.

Σαῦλος ὁ καὶ Παῦλος: only as such perhaps did many of his brethren of the same race understand him; from his own confessions we know that he was rather a Παῦλος ὁ καὶ Σαῦλος—a man who laboured for the future and for humanity, though as a son of Benjamin and a contemporary of the Cæsars. Christians in later times would often have fain called him Saul only; but on this account it is the name Paul alone which in history is graven above the narrow gate at which Augustine and Luther entered in.[2]

---

[1] The following phenomenon is perhaps instructive on this point. In several passages of Acts mention is made of a Ἰωάννης ὁ ἐπικαλούμενος Μάρκος, either by this double name or by his Jewish name Ἰωάννης; in 13[13] it is particularly evident that Ἰωάννης has been used purposely: the man had forsaken the Apostle Paul and had returned to Jerusalem. Quite different]~ in 15[39]; he now goes with Barnabas to Cyprus, and this is the only passage in Acts where the Greek name Μάρκος, standing alone, is applied to him. This may, of course, be purely accidental.

[2] With this should be compared Professor W. M. Ramsay's brilliant section on the same subject, *St. Paul the Traveller and the Roman Citizen*[2], London, 1896, pp. 81-88.—Tr.

VI.

GREEK TRANSCRIPTIONS OF THE TETRAGRAMMATON.

καὶ φοβηθήσονται τὰ ἔθνη τὸ ὄνομά σου κύριε.

GREEK TRANSCRIPTIONS OF THE TETRA-GRAMMATON.

In a notice of Professor W. Dindorf's edition of Clement, Professor P. de Lagarde[1] reproaches the editor, in reference to the passage *Strom.* v. 6 34 (Dindorf, iii. p. 27 25), with having "no idea whatever of the deep significance of his author's words, or of the great attention which he must pay to them in this very passage". Dindorf reads there the form 'Ιαού as τὸ τετράγραμμον ὄνομα τὸ μυστικόν. But in various manuscripts and in the Turin Catena to the Pentateuch[2] we find the variants 'Ià οὐαί or 'Ià οὐέ.[3] Lagarde holds that the latter reading "might have been unhesitatingly set in the text; in theological books nowadays nothing is a matter of course". The reading 'Ιαουέ certainly appears to be the original; the ε was subsequently left out because, naturally enough, the name designated as the Tetragrammaton must have no more than four letters.[4]

The form 'Ιαουέ is one of the most important Greek transcriptions of the Tetragrammaton usually referred to in seeking to ascertain the original pronunciation. F. Dietrich in a letter of February, 1866,[5] to Franz Delitzsch, makes the following collection of these transcriptions:—

---

[1] *GGA.* 1870, part 21, p. 801 ff. *Cf. Symmikta*, i., Göttingen, 1877, p. 14 f.

[2] *Cf.* upon this E. W. Hengstenberg, *Die Authentie des Pentateuchs*, i., Berlin, 1836, p. 226 f.

[3] With reference to the itacistic variation of the termination, *cf.* the quite similar variants of the termination of the transcription Εἰμαλκουαί 1 Macc. 11 39. 'Ιμαλκουέ, Σινμαλκουή, etc., and on these C. L. W. Grimm, *HApAT.* iii., Leipzig, 1853, p. 177.

[4] Hengstenberg, p. 227.

[5] *ZAW.* iii. (1883), p. 298.

	יְהוָֹה	יְהוּ	יָהּ
Cent. 2. Irenaeus	—	Ιαοθ (?) [1]	—
„ 2-3. Clement	(Ιαουε) [2]	Ιαου	—
„ 3. Origen	—	Ιαω (Ιαω Ια)	Ια—IAH
„ 4. Jerome	—	*Jaho*	—
„ — Epiphanius	Ιαβε	—	Ια
„ 5. Theodoret	Ιαβε	Ιαω	Αϊα (*cod. Aug.*
(Sam.)			Ια)
„ 7. Isidore	—	—	*Ja. Ja.*

It is an important fact that nearly all the transcriptions which have thus come down from the Christian Fathers are likewise substantiated by "heathen" sources. In the recently-discovered Egyptian Magic Papyri there is a whole series of passages which—even if in part they are not to be conceived of as transcriptions of the Tetragrammaton—merit our attention in this connection. As early as 1876 W. W. Graf Baudissin,[3] in his investigation of the form 'Ιάω, had referred to passages relating to it in the Magic Papyri in Leiden[4] and Berlin.[5] Since that time the edition of the Leiden Papyri by C. Leemans,[6] and that of the Paris and London Papyri by C. Wessely,[7] the new edition of the Leiden Papyri by A. Dieterich,[8] the latest publications of the British

---

[1] Wrongly questioned by F. Dietrich; *cf.* p. 327 below.

[2] F. Dietrich reads Ιαου.

[3] *Studien zur semitischen Religionsgeschichte*, Heft i., Leipzig, 1876, **p.** 197 ff.

[4] At that time there were only the preliminary notes of C. J. C. Reuvens: *Lettres à M. Letronne sur les papyrus bilingues et grecs . . . du musée d'antiquités de l'université de Leide*, Leiden, 1830.

[5] Edited by G. Parthey, *AAB.*, 1865, *philol. und histor. Abhh.*, 109 ff.

[6] In his publication, *Papyri Graeci musei antiquarii publici Lugduni-Batavi*, vol. ii., Leiden, 1885.

[7] *DAW. philos.-histor. Classe*, xxxvi. (1888), 2 Abt. p. 27 ff. and xlii. (1893), 2 Abt. p. 1 ff.

[8] *Papyrus magica musei Lugdunensis Batavi*, Fleckeisen's *Jahrbb. Suppl.* xvi. (1888), p. 749 ff. (= the edition of Papyrus J 384 of Leiden). Dieterich, *Abraxas, Studien zur Religions-Geschichte des späteren Altertums*, Leipzig, 1891, p. 167 ff. (=edition of Papyrus J 395 of Leiden). The author has to thank his colleague and friend the editor (now in Giessen) for divers information and stimulating opposition.

Museum,[1] and other works, have rendered still more possible the knowledge of this strange literature, and an investigation of these would be worth the trouble, both for the historian of Christianity [2] and for the Semitic philologist.[3]

The Papyri in their extant form were written about the end of the third and beginning of the fourth century A.D. ; their composition may be dated some hundred years before —in the time of Tertullian.[4] But there would be no risk of error in supposing that many elements in this literature belong to a still earlier period. It is even probable, in view of the obstinate persistence of the forms of popular belief and superstition, that, e.g., the books of the Jewish exorcists at Ephesus, which, according to Acts 19 [19], were committed to the flames in consequence of the appearance of the Apostle Paul, had essentially the same contents as the Magic Papyri from Egypt which we now possess.[5]

In the formulæ of incantation and adjuration found in this literature an important part is played by the Divine names. Every possible and impossible designation of deities,

---

[1] F. G. Kenyon, *Greek Papyri in the British Museum*, London, 1893, p. 62 ff.

[2] *Cf.* A. Jülicher, *ZKG.* xiv. (1893), p. 149.

[3] *Cf.* E. Schürer, *Geschichte des jüdischen Volkes im Zeitalter Jesu Christi*, 3 [3], Leipzig (1898), p. 294 ff., and especially L. Blau, *Das altjüdische Zauberwesen (Jahresbericht der Landes-Rabbinerschule in Budapest, 1897-98)*, Budapest, 1898.

[4] Wessely, i., p. 36 ff. Though A. Harnack, *Geschichte der altchristlichen Litteratur bis Eusebius*, i., Leipzig, 1893, p. ix., maintains that the age of the Magic Literature is as yet quite undetermined, this must so far be limited as that at least a *terminus ad quem* can be established on palæographical and internal grounds for a not inconsiderable part of this literature.

[5] The Book of Acts—if we may insert this observation here—manifests in this passage an acquaintance with the terminology of magic. Thus the expression τὰ περίεργα, used in 19 [19], is a *terminus technicus* for *magic* ; *cf.*, in addition to the examples given by Wetstein, *ad loc.*, *Pap. Lugd.*, J 384, xii. 19 and 21, περιεργία and περιεργάζομαι (Fleck. *Jahrbb. Suppl.* xvi., p. 816 : *cf.* Leemans, ii., p. 73). So also πρᾶξις, 19 [18], a *terminus technicus* for a particular *spell*, of which the indexes of Parthey, Wessely and Kenyon afford numerous examples. The ordinary translation *artifice* (Ränke) obliterates the peculiar meaning of the word in this connection. [English A.V. and R.V. *deeds* even more completely].

Greek, Egyptian and Semitic, is found in profuse variety, just as, in general, this whole class of literature is characterised by a peculiar syncretism of Greek, Egyptian and Semitic ideas.

But what interests us at present are the forms which can in any way be considered to be transcriptions of the Tetragrammaton. For the forms which are handed down by the Fathers, in part still questioned, are all verified by the Papyri, with the sole possible exception of Clement's *Ιαουε*.

Ιαω.

To the examples given by Baudissin there is to be added such a large number from the Papyri since deciphered, that a detailed enumeration is unnecessary.[1] The palindromic form *ιαωαι*[2] is also frequently found, and, still more frequently, forms that seem to the author to be combinations of it, such as *αρβαθιαω*.[1] The divine name *Ιαω* became so familiar that it even underwent declension : *εἰμὶ θεὸς θεῶν ἁπάντων ιαων σαβαωθ αδωναι α[βραξ]ας* (*Pap. Lugd.* J 384, iii. 1).[3]

Ια.

Likewise not infrequent. Without claiming exhaustiveness we cite the following :—

ὁ ἐπὶ τῆς ἀνάγκης τεταγμένος ιακουβ ια ιαω σαβαωθ αδωναι [α]βρασαξ (*Pap. Lond.* cxxi. 648, 649),[4] with which compare the gem-inscription *ια ια ιαω αδωναι σαβαωθ*,[5] the combinations *ιαηλ* (*Pap. Lond.* xlvi. 56,[6] *Pap. Paris. Bibl. nat.*

---

[1] *Cf.* the indexes of Leemans, Wessely and Kenyon.

[2] In the form *ιαοαι* in *Pap. Par. Bibl. nat.* 996 (Wessely, i., p. 69). It is to be regretted that the editor does not give the library number of this Papyrus.

[3] Fleck. *Jahrbb. Suppl.* xvi., p. 798 ; Leemans, ii., p. 15. K. Buresch, ΑΠΟΛΛΩΝ ΚΛΑΡΙΟΣ, *Untersuchungen zum Orakelwesen des späteren Altertums*, Leipzig, 1889, p. 52, unnecessarily brackets the *ν* of *ιαων*.

[4] Kenyon, p. 105 ; Wessely, ii., p. 44. We do not give Wessely's numbering of the lines, which is different from Kenyon's. In line 327 of the same Papyrus we are not quite certain whether *ια* is meant for a Divine name or not.

[5] U. F. Kopp, *Palaeographia critica*, iv., Mannheim, 1829, p. 226.

[6] Kenyon, p. 67 ; Wessely, i., p. 128.

961 and 3033[1]), and ιαωλ (*Pap. Paris. Louvre* 2391 151),[2] as also a whole mass of other combinations.

Ιαωια : [3]

(read) ἐπὶ τοῦ μετώπου ἴαωϊα (*Pap. Paris. Bibl. nat.* 3257).[4]

Ιαη

occurs more frequently; in particular, in the significant passage :—

ὁρκίζω σε κατὰ τοῦ θεοῦ τῶν ʽΕβραίων ʼΙησοῦ· ιαβα· ιαη· αβραωθ· αϊα· θωθ· ελε· ελω· αηω· εου· ιιβαεχ· αβαρμας· ἴαβα ραου· αβελβελ· λωνα· αβρα· μαροια· βρακιων (*Pap. Paris. Bibl. nat.* 3019 ff.; [5] again, in the same Papyrus, 1222 ff. [6] κύριε ιαω αιη ιωη ωιη ωιη ιη αιωαι αιουω αηω ηαι ιεω ηνω αηι αω αωα αεηι νω αευ ιαη ει·. One might surmise that the form ιαη in the latter passage should be assigned to the other meaningless permutations of the vowels.[7] But against this is to be set the fact that the form is authenticated as a Divine name by Origen, that in this passage it stands at the end of the series (the ει of the Papyrus should likely be accented εἶ), and thus seems to correspond to the well-known form ιαω at the beginning. Nevertheless, too great stress should not be laid upon the occurrence, in similar vowel-series, of purely vocalic transcriptions of the Tetragrammaton.

Further, in the same Papyrus, 1564[8] and 1986[9]; also in *Pap. Lond.* xlvi. 23.[10]

---

[1] Wessely, i., pp. 68 and 121.   [2] *Ibid.*, p. 144.

[3] Combined from Ιαω and Ια (*cf.* Baudissin, p. 183 f., and F. Dietrich, p. 294).

[4] Wessely, i., 126.

[5] *Ibid.*, p. 120. This passage, so far as regards the history of religion, is one of the most interesting : Jesus is named as the *God of the Hebrews ;* observe the Divine names combined with αβ (in reference to αβελβελ, *cf.* Baudissin, p. 25, the name of the King of Berytus ʼΑβέλβαλος); on αϊα and ἴαβα see below, pp. 326 and 333 f. ; with reference to θωθ (Egyptian deity) in the Papyri, *cf.* A. Dieterich, *Abraxas*, p. 70.

[6] *Ibid.*, p. 75.   [7] *Cf.* upon these, p. 329 below.

[8] Wessely, i., p. 84.   [9] *Ibid.*, p. 94.

[10] Kenyon, p. 66 ; Wessely, i., p. 127.

This form is also found in W. Fröhner's[1] issue of the bronze tablet in the Museum at Avignon : the last two lines should not be read καὶ σὺ συνέργει 'Αβρασάξ ιλη 'Ιαώ, as Fröhner reads them, but καὶ σὺ συνέργει αβρασαξ ι α η[2] ιαω. The reverse combination ιαω ιαη is found in a leaden tablet from Carthage, CIL. viii. Suppl. i., No. 12509.

We may, finally, at least refer to the passage ὅτι δισύλλαβος εἶ α η (Pap. Paris. Bibl. nat. 944).[3] According to A. Dieterich,[4] αη is " simply a mystical Divine name," and " it is possible that it should be read αω ". We consider this alteration quite unnecessary. Either αη is an indistinct reminiscence of our ιαη, or else we must definitely conclude that the ι of ιαη coming after ει has fallen out by hemigraphy.[5]

Aïa.

Theodoret's form A ï a, for which the Augsburg Codex and the ed. princ. of Picus read Ia,[6] is found not only in the above-cited passage, Pap. Par. Bibl. nat. 3019 ff., but also in Pap. Lugd. J 395, xvii. 31,[7] as—a fact of special interest— the correction of the αιρα which originally stood in the MS.

Jaoth.

The Latin codices of Irenæus yield the form Jaoth.[8] Irenæus distinguishes one pronunciation with a long, and another with a short, o (ii. 35 3, Massuet : Jaωth, extensa cum aspiratione novissima syllaba, mensuram praefinitam manifestat ; cum autem per o graecam corripitur ut puta Jaoth, eum qui dat fugam malorum significat).

---

[1] Philologus, Suppl. v. (1889), p. 44 f.

[2] That is, A instead of Λ; tacitly corrected by Wessely, Wiener Studien, viii. (1886), p. 182.

[3] Wessely, i., p. 68.   [4] Abraxas, p. 97.

[5] The ι of ιαη must, in that case, on account of the metre and the δισύλλαβος, be pronounced as a consonant (cf. on this point, Kühner-Blass, Ausführliche Grammatik der griechischen Sprache, i[3]. 1, Hanover, 1890, p. 50).

[6] Hengstenberg, p. 227 ; F. Dietrich, p. 287.

[7] A. Dieterich, Abr., p. 196 ; Leemans, ii., p. 141.

[8] Cf., in particular, Baudissin, p. 194 f.

F. Dietrich has erroneously questioned this form.[1]   The following should be added to the citations given by Baudissin :—

> *Pap. Lond.* xlvi. 142 ($\iota a \omega \tau$),[2]
>
> „   „   xlvi. 479 ($\iota a \omega \theta$),[3]
>
> *Pap. Par. Bibl. nat.* 3263 ($\iota a \omega \theta$),[4]
>
> *Pap. Lugd.* J 395, xxi. 14 ($a \beta \rho a \tau \iota a \omega \theta$),[5]
>
> *Pap. Lond.* xlvi. 56 ($a \rho \beta a \theta \iota a \omega \theta$),[6]
>
> *Pap. Berol.* 2 125 ($a \mu \beta \rho \iota \theta \iota a \omega \theta$).[7]

With reference to the agglutination of a *T*-sound to $\iota a \omega$, *cf.* the literature cited by Baudissin.[8]   The Papyri yield a large number of examples of similar forms in -$\omega \theta$.   Similar forms with Greek terminations (*e.g.*, $\Phi a \rho a \omega \theta \eta s$), in Josephus and others.[9]

$Iaoue$.

Regarding Clement's form $Iaoue$, the author calls attention to the following passages :—

$\theta \epsilon \grave{o} s$ $\theta \epsilon \tilde{\omega} \nu$, $\dot{o}$ $\kappa \acute{u} \rho \iota o s$ $\tau \tilde{\omega} \nu$ $\pi \nu \epsilon \upsilon \mu \acute{a} \tau \omega \nu$[10] $\dot{o}$ $\dot{a} \pi \lambda \acute{a} \nu \eta \tau o s$ $a \grave{\iota} \grave{\omega} \nu$ $\iota a \omega o \upsilon \eta \iota$, $\epsilon \grave{\iota} \sigma \acute{a} \kappa o \upsilon \sigma \acute{o} \nu$ $\mu o \upsilon$ $\tau \tilde{\eta} s$ $\phi \omega \nu \tilde{\eta} s \cdot$ $\dot{\epsilon} \pi \iota \kappa a \lambda o \tilde{u} \mu a \acute{\iota}$ $\sigma \epsilon$ $\tau \grave{o} \nu$ $\delta \upsilon \nu \acute{a} \sigma \tau \eta \nu$ $\tau \tilde{\omega} \nu$ $\theta \epsilon \tilde{\omega} \nu$, $\dot{u} \psi \iota \beta \rho \epsilon \mu \acute{e} \tau a$ $Z \epsilon \tilde{u}$, $Z \epsilon \tilde{u}$ $\tau \acute{u} \rho a \nu \nu \epsilon$, $a \delta a \iota \nu a \iota$ ^{sic} $\kappa \acute{u} \rho \iota \epsilon$ $\iota a \omega o \upsilon \eta \epsilon \cdot$ $\dot{\epsilon} \gamma \acute{\omega}$ $\epsilon \grave{\iota} \mu \iota$ $\dot{o}$ $\dot{\epsilon} \pi \iota \kappa a \lambda o \acute{u} \mu \epsilon \nu \acute{o} s$ $\sigma \epsilon$ $\sigma \upsilon \rho \iota \sigma \tau \grave{\iota}$ $\theta \epsilon \grave{o} \nu$ $\mu \acute{e} \gamma a \nu$ $\zeta a a \lambda a \eta \rho \iota \phi \phi o \upsilon$ $\kappa a \grave{\iota}$ $\sigma \grave{u}$ $\mu \grave{\eta}$ $\pi a \rho a \kappa o \acute{u} \sigma \eta s$ $\tau \tilde{\eta} s$ $\phi \omega \nu \tilde{\eta} s$ $\dot{\epsilon} \beta \rho a \ddot{\iota} \sigma \tau \grave{\iota}$ $a \beta \lambda a \nu a \theta a \nu a \lambda \beta a$ $a \beta \rho a \sigma \iota \lambda \omega a \cdot$ $\dot{\epsilon} \gamma \acute{\omega}$ $\gamma \acute{a} \rho$ $\epsilon \grave{\iota} \mu \iota$ $\sigma \iota \lambda \theta a \chi \omega o \upsilon \chi$ $\lambda a \iota \lambda a \mu$ $\beta a a \sigma a \lambda \omega \theta$ $\iota a \omega$ $\iota \epsilon \omega$ $\nu \epsilon \beta o \upsilon \theta$ $\sigma a \beta \iota o \theta a \rho \beta \omega \theta$ $a \rho \beta a \theta \iota a \omega$ $\iota a \omega \theta$ σa-$\beta a \omega \theta$ $\pi a \tau o \upsilon \rho \eta$ $\zeta a \gamma o \upsilon \rho \eta$ $\beta a \rho o \upsilon \chi$ $a \delta \omega \nu a \iota$ $\epsilon \lambda \omega a \iota$ $\iota a \beta \rho a a \mu$ $\beta a \rho$-$\beta a \rho a \nu \omega$ $\nu a \upsilon \sigma \iota \phi$ $\dot{u} \psi \eta \lambda \acute{o} \phi \rho o \nu \epsilon$ . . . (*Pap. Lond.* xlvi. 466-482).[11]

---

[1] P. 294.   [2] Kenyon, p. 69 ; Wessely, i., p. 130.

[3] Kenyon, p. 80 ; Wessely, i., p. 139.   [4] Wessely, i., p. 126.

[5] A. Dieterich, *Abr.*, p. 201.   [6] Kenyon, p. 67 ; Wessely, i., p. 128.

[7] Parthey, p. 154.   We begin the word with *a*, and affix the θ to the previous word ; *cf.* Kenyon, p. 111, line 849, $a \mu \beta \rho \iota \theta \eta \rho a$.

[8] P. 195.

[9] *Cf.*, for example, the $\Phi a \rho \epsilon \theta \acute{\omega} \theta \eta s$ of Artapanus (Eusebius, *Praep. ev.* ix. 18), and, upon this, J. Freudenthal, *Hellenistische Studien*, Heft 1 and 2, Breslau, 1875, p. 169.

[10] With this expression, also common in the Book of Enoch, compare LXX Num. 16 22, 27 16.

[11] Kenyon, p. 80 ; Wessely, i., 139.   We have given the passage *in extenso* because it is particularly instructive in respect to the Syncretism of this literature.

ἀκουσάτω μοι ˢⁱᶜ πᾶσα γλῶσσα καὶ πᾶσα φωνή, ὅτι ἐγώ
εἰμι περταω [μηχ χαχ] μνηχ σακμηφ ιαωουεη ωηω ωηω ιεουωηι
ηιαηα [corrupt] ιηωυοει¹ . . . (Pap. Lugd. J 384, vi. 12-14).²

σὺ εἶ ὁ ἀγαθοδαίμων ὁ γεννῶν ἀγαθὰ καὶ τροφῶν τὴν
οἰκουμένην, σοῦ δὲ τὸ ἀένναον κομαστήριον, ἐν ᾧ καθίδρυταί
σου τὸ ἑπταγράμματον ὄνομα πρὸς τὴν ἁρμονίαν τῶν ζ΄ φθόγ-
γων ἐχόντων φωνὰς πρὸς τὰ κη΄ φῶτα τῆς σελήνης, σαραφαρα
αραφ αια βρααρμαραφα αβρααχ περταωμηχ ακμηχ ιαωουεη
ιαωουε ειου αηω εηου ιαω . . . (Pap. Lugd. J 395, xvii. 25-32).³

ὅτι προσείλημμαι τὴν δύναμιν τοῦ Ἀβραὰμ Ἰσὰκ καὶ τοῦ
Ἰακὼβ καὶ τοῦ μεγάλου θεοῦ δαίμονος ιαω αβλαναθαναλβα
σιαβραθιλαω λαμψτηρ ιηι ωω. θεέ, ποίησον, κύριε, περταωμηχ
χαχ μηχ ιαωουηε ιαωουηε ιεοναηω εηουιαω (Pap. Lugd., J
395, xviii., 21-26).⁴

It might appear at first sight very natural to assume that
these forms are related to Clement's Ιαουε. In consideration of the great freedom with which the Hebrew vowels
were transcribed in Greek, it need not seem strange that
the E-sound at the end of words is rendered by ηι, ηε and εη
in the Papyri; in point of fact the strengthening or length-
ening of the ε by the addition of η would give a more distinct
rendering of the הֶ than the bare ε of Clement. The coming
of ω before ου is the only strange feature. Still, even this
peculiarity might be explained by the preference for Ιαω, the
most popular transcription, which it was desired should have
a place also here.

For these reasons Kenyon maintains that the form
Ιαωουηε is actually the Divine name, and, indeed, that it is
an expansion of the form Ιαω.⁵

Notwithstanding, we must not trust entirely to plausi-

---

¹ Considered by A. Dieterich to be a palindrome of the ιεουωηι.

² A. Dieterich, Fleck. Jahrbb. Suppl. xvi., p. 804; Leemans, ii., p. 23.

³ A. Dieterich, Abr., p. 195 f.; Leemans, ii., p. 141 f.

⁴ A. Dieterich, Abr., p. 197; Leemans, ii., p. 145.

⁵ P. 63: "The exact pronunciation of that name . . was preserved a
profound secret, but several approximations were made to it; among which
the commonest is the word Ιαω . ., which was sometimes expanded, so as
to employ all the vowels, into Ιαωουηε".

bility. We must first of all investigate whether the said
forms do not belong to the manifold permutations of the
seven vowels,[1] which are all but universally considered to be
capricious and meaningless, mocking every possible attempt
at explanation, and which can therefore, now less than ever,
yield a basis for etymological conjectures.

An instructive collection of these permutations and combinations of the seven vowels for magical purposes is found
in Wessely's treatise, *Ephesia Grammata*.[2] That writer elsewhere[3] passes judgment upon them as follows : " other
[names] again appear to have no special meaning, for, just
as magical formulæ are formed from the seven vowels αεηιουω
and their permutations and combinations . . ., so in all
probability there were magic formulæ formed from the
consonants also, now Hebraising, now Egyptianising, now
Græcising, and without any definite meaning ". We are
unable to decide whether this assertion concerning the
consonantal formulæ is correct. But certainly when the
chaos of the vocalic formations is surveyed, the possibility
of accounting for the great majority of the cases may be
doubted.[4] If, then, it were established that the forms cited
above should also be assigned to this class, they could, of
course, no longer be mentioned in the present discussion.
We should otherwise repeat the mistake of old J. M. Gesner,[5]
who believed that he had discovered the Divine name
Jehovah in the vowel series *IEHΩOYA*.

But in the present instance the matter is somewhat
different, and the conjecture of Kenyon cannot be summarily rejected. To begin with, the form ιαωουηε or ιαωουηι,

---

[1] *Cf.* on this point Baudissin, p. 245 ff.; Parthey, p. 116 f.; A. Dieterich,
Abr., p. 22 f.

[2] The 12th *Jahresb. über das K. K. Franz-Josephs-Gymn. in Wien*, 1886.

[3] *Wiener Studien*, viii. (1886), p. 183.

[4] Let one example suffice: *Pap. Lugd.* J 395, xx. 1 ff. (A. Dieterich,
Abr., p. 200; Leemans, i., p. 149 f.): ἐπικαλοῦμαί σε ιυενο ωαεηιαω αεηαιεηαη
ιουαευη ιεουαηωηι ωηιιαη ιωουηαυη υηα ιωιωαι ιωαι ωη εε ου ιωι αω τὸ μέγα ὄνομα.

[5] *De laude dei per septem vocales* in the *Commentationes Soc. Reg. Scient.
Gotting.*, i. (1751), p. 245 ff.

in the first passage quoted, does not stand among other vowel-series ; on the contrary, it is enclosed on both sides by a number of indubitable Divine names. Further, the same form with insignificant modifications is found in various passages of various Papyri; from this we may conclude that it is at least no merely hap-hazard, accidental form. Finally, its similarity with Clement's *Iaove* is to be noted.

At the same time, wider conclusions should not be drawn from these forms—none, in particular, as to the true pronunciation of the Tetragrammaton : for the fact that in three of the quoted passages the form in question is followed by vocalic combinations in part meaningless, constitutes an objection that is at all events possible.

The value of the vocalic transcriptions of the Tetragrammaton for the determination of its true pronunciation appears to us, by reason of the diffuse and capricious usage of the vowels which we find throughout the Magic Literature, to be at most very small. The very great uncertainty of the traditional texts must also be urged as an objection to its being so employed. Nowhere could copyists' errors[1] be more easily made, nowhere are errors in reading by editors more possible, than in these texts. Let any one but attempt to copy half a page of such magic formulæ for himself : the eye will be continually losing its way because there is no fixed point amidst the confusion of meaningless vowels by which it can right itself.

Iaβε.

It is thus all the more valuable a fact that the important consonantal transcription of the Tetragram, *Iaβε*, given by Epiphanius and Theodoret, is attested likewise by the Magic Literature, both directly and indirectly. The author has found it four times in the collocation *ιαβε ζεβυθ* :—

ἐξορκίζω ὑμᾶς τὸ ἅγιον ὄνομ[α
ερηκισθαρηαραραραχαραραηφθισ . . . . .

---

[1] *Cf.* Wessely, ii., p. 42, on the "frivolity" (*Leichtfertigkeit*) with which the copyists treated the magic formulæ. The state of the text generally with regard to Semitic names in Greek manuscripts, biblical and extra-biblical, is instructive.

ιαω ιαβε ζεβυθ λαναβισαφλαν . . . .

εκτιπαμμουποφδηντιναξο

ὁ τῶν ὅλων βασιλεὺς εξεγέρθητι

(leaden tablet of cent. 2 or 3 from a Cumæan tomb, *CIG.* iii., No. 5858 *b*). J. Franz[1] has correctly explained this form : *habes in ea formula* ΙΑΩ *Judaicum satis notum illud ex monumentis Abraxeis, deinde* ΙΑΒΕ, *quo nomine Samaritanos summum numen invocasse refert Theodoretus Quaest. in Exod.* xv. On ζεβυθ see below. Wessely[2] conjectures that Ιαω ΣΑΒΑωΘ appears in the third line. But ζεβυθ is vouched for by the two following passages which give the same magic precept as a precept, which is actually put in practice in the Cumæan tablet :—

On a tablet of tin shall be written before sunrise among other words the λόγος ει . . . σιφθη′ ιαβε ζεβυθ (*Pap. Lond.* cxxi. 419),[3]

On a chalice one shall write besides other words ερη-κισιθφη λόγον ιαβε ζεβυθ (*Pap. Par. Bibl. nat.* 2000),[4]

Similarly ἐπικαλοῦμαί σου . . τῷ μεγάλῳ σου ὀνόματι . . . . ερηκισιθφη αραραχαρ αρα ηφθισικηρε ιαβε ζεβυθ ϊωβυθιε (*Pap. Par. Bibl. nat.* 1784 ff.).[5]

How are we to explain the form ζεβυθ[6] which thus occurs four times in union with ιαβε? F. Lenormant[7] maintains that it is the names *Beelzebuth* and *Jao* which are found on the tablet. He reads ιαὼ ιᾶ βεζεβὺθ θλαναβὶ σαφλαν. . . .[8] Leaving aside the fact that the form *Beelzebuth* can be no-

---

[1] *CIG.* iii., p. 757.　　[2] *Wiener Studien,* viii. (1886), p. 182.

[3] Kenyon, p. 98 ; Wessely, ii., p. 34.　　[4] Wessely, i., p. 95.

[5] *Ibid.,* p. 89. This passage renders it possible to restore the text of the Inscription *CIG.* iii., No. 5858 *b*, and of the quotation from *Pap. Lond.* cxxi. 419, with certainty ; observe the palindrome ερηκισιθφη αραραχ, etc.

[6] *Cf.* also κύριε αρχανδαρα φωταζα πυριφωτα ζαβυθ . . . (*Pap. Par. Bibl. nat.* 631-632; Wessely, i., p. 60).

[7] *De tabulis devotionis plumbeis Alexandrinis, Rhein. Mus. für Philologie, N. F.,* ix. (1854), p. 375.

[8] *Ibid.,* p. 374.

where authenticated,[1] it is very precarious to see it in the
βεζεβυθ of the Inscription. The mere absence of the λ,
indeed, would not be decisive [2] against Lenormant's idea, but
certainly the υ, which cannot be read as u,[3] is decisive, and
above all the great improbability of the assumption that the
names of God and the Devil stand thus closely together.
We consider it to be much less objectionable to explain [4]
ζεβυθ as a corruption of צְבָאֹות, and to see in ιαβε ζεβυθ
the familiar יְהֹוָה צְבָאֹות.

With reference to this identification, the author's colleague, Herr P. Behnke, Pastor and Repetent at Marburg, has
kindly given him the following additional information:— [5]

"υ = Heb. ō is frequently found. The examples, however, in which this vowel-correspondence appears before ρ
should not be taken into account (מֹר = μύῤῥα, צֹר = Τύρος,
תָּבֹור = Ἰταβύριον, Ἀταβύριον, כֹּורֶשׁ = Κῦρος, כִּנֹּור = κινύρα.
In מֹר, צֹר, כֹּורֶשׁ, תָּבֹור [?] the ō is a lengthened ŭ, and the
ordinary transcription of Sem. ŭ is υ. But a difference

---

[1] The French scholar's assertion is only to be explained by the fact
that the form of Satan's name is, in French, Belzébuth or Belsébuth. We
have not been able to ascertain when this form can be first vouched for,
or how it is to be explained. Should we find in the variant belzebud of
(Vulgate) Codex mm, Matt. 10 [25] (Tischendorf), authority for saying that the
T-sound has supplanted the original ending b or l in later Latin, and so in
French also? What form is found in the "Romance" Bibles?

[2] Cod. B., occasionally also א, of the N. T. yield the form βεεζεβουλ;
cf. on this Winer-Schmiedel, § 5, 31 (p. 65).

[3] Viva-voce information by W. Schulze. Cf. Winer-Schmiedel, § 5, 21 b
(p. 51), on κολλούριον.

[4] Cf. Franz, p. 757. Franz, in his explanation of the syllable βυθ,
recalls the βυθός of the Valentinians. It is more correct to point to the
frequently occurring (Egyptian?) termination in -υθ—the β is got from
ζεβαωθ. Cf. the name of deities and months θωυθ, the formations βιεννυθ
(Kopp, iv., p. 158), μεννυθυθ ιαω (Pap. Lond. cxxi. 820; Kenyon, p. 110;
Wessely, ii., p. 49), ιωβυθιε (Pap. Par. Bibl. nat. 1799; Wessely, i., p. 89).
Cf. on Egyptian female names in -υθ, A. Boeckh, AAB., hist.-phil. Klasse,
1820-1821, p. 19.

[5] Cf. also H. Lewy, Die semitischen Fremdwörter im Griechischen,
Berlin, 1895, pp. 38, 42 f., 225.

appears in כִּנּוֹר, which goes back to an original *kannār;* here therefore the *v* corresponds to an *ō* which has been derived from *ā*, as would be the case with *-vθ* = רוֹת). But it seems to me to be of greater consequence that the Phœnician pronunciation of Heb. *ō* (and *ŏ*) is *y*. Thus we have in the *Poenulus* of Plautus (*ed.* Ritschl) [*chyl* = כֹּל = *kull*], מוֹצָאִי (= *maūṣāi*) given as *mysehi;* אוֹת (*sign*, original form *āth*) as *yth*, זֹאת as *syth.* Moreover, Movers (*Phöniz.,* ii., 1, p. 110) has identified Berytos with בְּאֵרוֹת, and Lagarde (*Mitteil.,* i., p. 226) has acknowledged the identification. It is thus quite possible that צְבָאוֹת could have become ζεβυθ in the mouth of a Phœnician juggler. Still, the omission of the *ā* before *ōth* in the pronunciation remains a difficulty."

Perhaps *Iaβε* is also contained in the word σεριαβε-βωθ (*Pap. Lond.* xlvi. 8)[1]; but the text is uncertain and the composition of the word doubtful.

Reference must finally be made to a number of forms, in respect of which the author is again unable to allow himself a certain conclusion, but which appear to him to be *corruptions of the form ιαβε,* and therefore in any case to merit our attention:—

ιαβοε, *Pap. Lond.* xlvi. 63 ;[2]

ιαβα[3] is frequently found: ὁρκίζω σε κατὰ τοῦ θεοῦ τῶν Ἑβραίων Ἰησοῦ· ιαβα· ιαη· .... αβαρμας· ἴαβα ραου. αβελβελ ... (*Pap. Par. Bibl. nat.* 3019 ff.),[4] ἐπικαλοῦμαί σε τὸν μέγαν ἐν οὐρανῷ .... βαθαβαθι· ιατμων· αλει· ιαβα θαβαωθ[5] σαβαωθ· αδωναι ὁ θεὸς ὁ μέγας ορσενοφρη (*Pap. Par.*

---

[1] Kenyon, p. 65 ; Wessely, i., p. 127.

[2] Kenyon, p. 67 ; Wessely, p. 128.

[3] F. Dietrich, p. 282: "The principal thing is, however, that the pronunciation *Jahavá* has no historic authority whatever. If Theodoret had intended to signify that, while יהוה was pronounced 'Ιαβέ by the Samaritans, the Jews pronounced this full form of the name with *a* at the end, then he would have written 'Ιουδαῖοι δὲ 'Ιαβά, which is warranted by none of the variants." But "historic authority" for this form has now been shown as above.

[4] Wessely, i., p. 120.

[5] With the form θαβαωθ cf. ταβαωθ, *Pap. Par. Bibl. nat.* 1413 (Wessely,

Bibl. nat. 1621 ff.),[1] ὑμᾶς ἐξορκίζω κατὰ τοῦ ἴαω καὶ τοῦ σαβαωθ καὶ αδωναι ...... βαλιαβα (*Pap. Par. Bibl. nat.* 1484 ff.),[2] ιαβα εδδ ιαω (a gem-inscription)[3] ;

ιαβαωθ[4] : ιαωθ ιαβαωθ (*Pap. Par. Bibl. nat.* 3263),[5] διὰ τὸ μέγα ἔνδοξον ὄνομα αβρααμ εμεινααεουβαωθ βαιθωβ εσια ιαβαωθ (*Pap. Lond.* cxxi. 314 f.)[6] ;

ιαβας: σὺ εἶ ιαβας σὺ εἶ ιαπως (*Pap. Lond.* xlvi. 104).[7] A. Dieterich[8] thinks it superfluous "to seek a 'Ιάβης or similar name" in this; it is but "mystical play-work set down at random". But the supposition that ιαβας and ιαπως are not mere capricious forms, but rather corrupt Græcisings of Ιαβε, is supported by the context of the whole passage, which belongs to those that are most strongly permeated by Jewish conceptions.

There may also be mentioned another series of forms, chiefly verbal combinations, in which this transcription appears, in part at least, to be contained. We mention only the examples: ιαβω (*Geoponica*, ed. Niclas, ii., 42 5) ;[9] ιαβουνη (*Pap. Lond.* xlvi. 340) ;[10] the names of angels βαθιαβηλ and αβραθιαβρι (*Pap. Lond.* cxxi. 906 f.) ;[11] further, ιαβουχ and ιαβωχ (*Pap. Par. Bibl. nat.* 2204).[12]

Even putting aside the last-quoted series of forms, we consider it to have nevertheless been made plain that Ιαβε must have enjoyed an extraordinary popularity in the Magic Literature. Now this may appear strange if we remember the observation given by the Fathers that it was the *Samaritan* pronunciation of the Tetragram: how did it get to Egypt and the land of the Cumæan Sybil? The question,

---

i., p. 80), *Pap. Lond.* xlvi. 62, 63, in which the form ιαβοε follows (Kenyon, p. 67; Wessely, i., p. 128), *Pap. Lugd.* J 384, iii. 7 (Fleck. *Jahrbb. Suppl.*, xvi., p. 798; Leemans, ii., p. 15).

[1] Wessely, i., p. 85.   [2] *Ibid.*, p. 82.

[3] Kopp, iv., p. 159 f.   [4] *Cf.* above on ιαωθ.

[5] Wessely, i., p. 126.   [6] Kenyon, p. 94; Wessely, ii., p. 31.

[7] Kenyon, p. 68; Wessely, i., p. 129.   [8] *Abr.*, p. 68.

[9] In R. Heim's *Incantamenta magica Graeca Latina;* Fleck., *Jahrbb Suppl.* xix. (1893), 523.

[10] Kenyon, p. 76, *cf.* the note to line 357; Wessely, i., pp. 135, 136.

[11] Kenyon, p. 113; Wessely, ii., p. 52.   [12] Wessely, i., p. 100.

however, does not appear to the writer to be unanswerable. We must not of course so conceive of the dissemination of the form as if it had been consciously employed, in such various localities, as the true name of the Mighty God of the Jews ; the writer of the Cumæan tablet simply copied it along with other enigmatic and, of course, unintelligible magic formulæ from one of the numerous books of Magic, all of which, very probably—to judge from those still extant—point to Egypt as their native region. But Egypt was just the country which, because of the ethnological conditions, was most ready to transfer Jewish conceptions into its Magic. One may therefore not unjustifiably suppose that here especially the Tetragrammaton was used by the magicians as a particularly efficacious *Name* in its correct pronunciation, which was, of course, still known to the Jews, though they shrank from using it, up to and into the Christian era. Thus we have been using the *Iaβε* not necessarily for the purpose of indicating the specifically *Samaritan* pronunciation as such, but rather as an evidence for the correct pronunciation. But we consider it quite possible to account for the occurrence of *Iaβε* in Egyptian Papyri by " Samaritan " influence. Besides the Jews proper [1] there were also Samaritans in Egypt. " Ptolemy I. Lagi in his conquest of Palestine had taken with him many prisoners-of-war not only from Judæa and Jerusalem but also ' from Samaria and those who dwelt in Mount Gerizim,' and settled them in Egypt [Joseph. *Antt.* xii. 1]. In the time of Ptolemy VI. Philometor, the Jews and Samaritans are reported to have taken their dispute concerning the true centre of worship (Jerusalem or Gerizim) to the judgment-seat of the king [Joseph. *Antt.* xiii. 3 4]." [2] Some Papyri of the Ptolemaic period confirm the relatively early residence of Samaritans in Egypt. As early as the time of the second Ptolemy we find (*Pap. Flind Petr.* ii. iv.

---

[1] *Cf.* on the Jewish *diaspora* in Egypt, Hugo Willrich, *Juden und Griechen vor der makkabäischen Erhebung*, Göttingen, 1895, p. 126 ff. ; and, against Willrich, Schürer, *ThLZ.* xxi. (1896), p. 35. *Cf.* also Wilcken, *Berl. Philol. Wochenschrift*, xvi. (1896), p. 1492 ff.

[2] E. Schürer, *Geschichte des jüdischen Volkes im Zeitalter Jesu Christi*, ii., Leipzig, 1886, p. 502 (= ³iii., p. 24). [Eng. Trans., ii., ii., p. 230.]

11)¹ mention of a place *Samaria* in the Fayyûm, and two inhabitants of this Samaria, Θεόφιλος and Πυῤῥίας,² are named in *Pap. Flind. Petr.* ii. xxviii.³ Even more important, in this connection, than such general information, is a passage in the supposed letter of Hadrian to Servianus, in which it is said that the Samaritans in Egypt, together with the Jews and Christians dwelling in that country, are all *Astrologers, Aruspices and Quacksalvers*.⁴ This is of course an exaggeration; but still the remark, even if the letter is spurious, is direct evidence of the fact that magic and its allied arts were common among the Egyptian Samaritans. We may also refer here to Acts viii.: Simon the *magian* was altogether successful among the Samaritans : " *to him they all gave heed, from the least to the greatest, saying, This man is that power of God which is called Great* ".⁵ As the Divine name played a great part in the adjurations, we may conclude that the Samaritan magicians used it too—naturally in the form familiar to them. From them it was transferred, along with other Palestinian matter, to the Magic Literature, and thus it is explained why we should find it in a remote region, scratched by some one unknown, full of superstitious dread, upon the lead of the minatory magical tablet.

¹ In J. P. Mahaffy, *The Flinders Petrie Papyri*, ii., Dublin, 1893 [14]. The paging of the text is always given in brackets [ ] in Mahaffy. Vol. i. was published in Dublin, 1891.

² Mahaffy, ii. [97], conjectures that these are translations of *Eldad* and *Esau*. With this he makes the further conjecture that the name Θεόφιλος, common in the imperial period, occurs here for the first time. But the name is found earlier, and Mahaffy's question whether it is perhaps a "Jewish invention" must be answered in the negative.—The author has made further observations on *Samaria* in the Fayyûm in *ThLZ.* xxi. (1896), p. 611.

³ Mahaffy, ii. [87] ff.

⁴ Vopisc., *vita Saturnini, c.* 8 ₁ (*Scriptores historiae Augustae, ed.* Peter, *vol.* ii., p. 225): *nemo illic archisynagogus Judaeorum, nemo Samarites, nemo Christianorum presbyter non mathematicus, non haruspex, non aliptes.* Schürer refers to this passage, ii., p. 502 (= ³iii., p. 24). [Eng. Trans., II., ii., p. 230.] *Cf.* also c. 7 ₄.

⁵ Compare with the expression ἡ δύναμις τοῦ θεοῦ ἡ καλουμένη μεγάλη, *Pap. Par. Bibl. nat.* 1275 ff. (Wessely, i., 76), ἐπικαλοῦμαί σε τὴν μεγίστην δύναμιν τὴν ἐν τῷ οὐρανῷ (ἄλλοι: τὴν ἐν τῇ ἄρκτῳ) ὑπὸ κυρίου θεοῦ τεταγμένην. See also Harnack, *Bruchstücke des Evangeliums und der Apokalypse des Petrus* (*TU* ix. 2), 2 Aufl., Leipzig, 1893, p. 65 f.

VII.

SPICILEGIUM

ἵνα μή τι ἀπόληται.

1. THE CHRONOLOGICAL STATEMENT IN THE PROLOGUE TO JESUS SIRACH.

Ἐν γὰρ τῷ ὀγδόῳ καὶ τριακοστῷ ἔτει ἐπὶ τοῦ Ἐνεργέτου βασιλέως παραγενηθεὶς εἰς Αἴγυπτον καὶ συγχρονίσας εὗρον οὐ μικρᾶς παιδείας ἀφόμοιον : of this chronological statement of the grandson of the son of Sirach, which is of the highest importance not only as regards the date of the book itself, but also, on account of the other contents of the prologue, for the history of the Old Testament canon, various interpretations are given.[1] If it be "a matter of course" that the writer of the Prologue wishes to indicate, not the year of his own life, but the thirty-eighth year of King Euergetes,[2] no doubt can exist as to the year in which the writer came to Egypt; of the two Ptolemies who bore the surname of *Euergetes*, the reign of the second only, Ptolemy VII. Physcon, extended to thirty-eight years, and hence the date given in the Prologue would signify the year 132 B.C. But when we find a writer like L. Hug preferring the other interpretation,[3] we cannot but feel that there must be a difficulty somewhere. The chief support of those who interpret the date as the year of the prologue-writer's age, and, at the same time, the chief difficulty of the other interpretation, lie in the ἐπί which stands between the number and the name of the king. "*La préposition ἐπί paraît ici tout à fait superflue, puisque toujours le mot ἔτους est suivi d'un génitif direct. On ne dit jamais ἔτους πρώτου, δευτέρου . . . ἐπὶ τινός, en parlant d'un roi, mais bien ἔτους . . . τινός ou τῆς βασιλείας τινός. Cette locution serait donc sans exemple*" : the difficulty in question may be formulated in these words of

---

[1] See O. F. Fritzsche, *HApAT*. v. (1859), p. xiii. ff.

[2] Schürer, ii., p. 595 (= [3]iii., p. 159). [Eng. Trans., ii., iii., p. 26.]

[3] *Cf. HApAT*. v. (1859), p. xv.

Letronne,[1] written in reference to a passage in the Inscription of Rosetta to be noticed presently.

The difficulty, nevertheless, can be removed. But certainly not by simply referring, as does O. F. Fritzsche,[2] to the passages LXX Hagg. 1[1], 2[1], Zech. 1[7], 7[1], 1 Macc. 13[42], 14[27], to which may be added LXX Zech. 1[1], for, all these passages being translations of Semitic originals, the ἐπί *might* be a mere imitation of לְ, and would thus yield nothing decisive for the idiom of the Prologue to Sirach, which was in Greek from the first. The following passages seem to the present writer to be of much greater force. In an Inscription from the Acropolis,[3] as old as the 3rd cent. B.C., we find in line 24 f. the words ἱερεὺς γενόμενος ἐν τῷ ἐπὶ Λυσιάδου ἄρχοντος ἐνιαυτῷ. Still more significant for the passage in Sirach are the following parallels of Egyptian origin. The Inscription of the Rosetta Stone (27th March, 196 B.C.), line 16,[4] runs thus: προσέταξεν [Ptolemy V. Epiphanes] δὲ καὶ περὶ τῶν ἱερέων, ὅπως μηθὲν πλεῖον διδῶσιν εἰς τὸ τελεστικὸν οὗ ἐτάσσοντο ἕως τοῦ πρώτου ἔτους ἐπὶ τοῦ πατρὸς αὐτοῦ [Ptolemy IV. Philopator]. Though Letronne, in view of the alleged want of precedent for this usage of ἐπί,[5] tries a different interpretation, he is yet forced to acknowledge that, if we translate the concluding words by *until the first year* [*of the reign*] *of his father*, the whole sentence is made to fit most appropriately into the context;[6] the priests, who are hardly inclined to speak of the merits of Epiphanes for nothing, would be again but manifesting their ability to do obeisance to him, and, at the same time, to extol the memory of his father. Had Letronne known the example

---

[1] *Recueil*, i. (1842), p. 277.   [2] P. xiii.

[3] *Bulletin de corr. hell.*, i. (1877), p. 36 f.

[4] In Letronne, *Recueil*, i., p. 246 = *CIG.* iii., No. 4697. Lumbroso, *Recherches*, p. xxi., has already referred to this.

[5] See his words as cited above. J. Franz, in *CIG.* iii., p. 338, agrees with Letronne, and refers to line 29 of the Inscription. But the present writer is again unable to see how the words occurring there, viz., ἕως τοῦ ὀγδόου ἔτους, can signify the years of the priests' service.

[6] The author thinks that the explanation given by Letronne (*year of their priesthood*) is somewhat forced.

from the Prologue to Sirach, perhaps he would have decided
for this way of taking ἐπί, which so admirably suits the
context. The two passages mutually support one another.
But the usage of ἐπί is further confirmed by other passages
of Egyptian origin. In *Pap. Par.* 15 [1] (120 B.C.) two αἰγύπ-
τιαι συγγραφαί are mentioned, which are dated as follows:
μιᾶς μὲν γεγοννίας [τοῦ ΙΗ' ἔτους παχ]ὼν ἐπὶ τοῦ Φιλομήτορος, *the one of Pachon* (Egyptian month) *of the* 18*th*
year (*of the reign*) *of Philometor;* ἑτέρας δὲ γεγονυίας τοῦ ΛΕ'
μεσορὴ ἐπὶ τοῦ αὐτοῦ βασιλέως, *the other of Mesore* [Egyptian
month] (*of the year*) 35 (*of the reign*) *of the same king.* Finally,
Pap. Par. 5 [2] begins thus: βασιλευόντων Κλεοπάτρας καὶ
Πτολεμαίου θεῶν Φιλομητόρων Σωτήρων ἔτους Δ' ἐφ' ἱερέως
βασιλέως Πτολεμαίου θεοῦ Φιλομήτορος Σωτῆρος Ἀλεξάνδρου
καὶ θεῶν Σωτήρων, κτλ. If the interpretation advocated by
Brunet against Brugsch,[3] *viz., under King Ptolemy* . . . . , *the
priest of Alexander* [the Great] *and of the gods* be correct,
then this passage also must be taken into consideration.

The pleonastic ἐπί of the Prologue to Sirach is thus supported by several authorities of about the same date and
place. Hence also, in the light of this result, the passages
from the Greek Bible, cited above, acquire a new significance. The pleonastic ἐπί found in these is not to be
explained by that excessive scrupulosity of the translators
which manifests itself elsewhere ; in point of fact, their
desire to translate literally was assisted by a peculiar idiom
of their locality, and hence we have a translation which
is at once literal and accurate.

2. THE SUPPOSED EDICT OF PTOLEMY IV. PHILO-
PATOR AGAINST THE EGYPTIAN JEWS.

In 3 Macc. 3 [11 ff.] is quoted a decree of Ptolemy IV.
Philopator against the Egyptian Jews, according to which a
reward is promised to every one who informs against a Jew.
In our editions the Greek text of verse [28] runs thus : μηνύειν

---

[1] *Notices*, xviii. 2, p. 220 f.   [2] *Ibid.*, p. 130.

[3] *Ibid.*, p. 153. Brugsch translates thus: *under the priest of* " *the* " *king
Ptolemy.* . . .

δὲ τὸν βουλόμενον ἐφ᾿ ᾧ τὴν οὐσίαν τοῦ ἐμπίπτοντος ὑπὸ τὴν εὔθυναν λήψεται καὶ ἐκ τοῦ βασιλικοῦ ἀργυρίου δραχμὰς δισχιλίας καὶ τῆς ἐλευθερίας τεύξεται καὶ στεφανωθήσεται. Grimm [1] explains the ungrammatical (*constructionslos*) accusative at the beginning of the verse as an anacoluthon,—as if the writer had in his mind some such construction as εἰς τὴν ἐλευθερίαν ἀφαιρησόμεθα. In that case we translate as follows: *him, however, who is willing to inform against a Jew—he shall receive, in addition to the property of him upon whom the punishment falls, two thousand silver drachmae from the royal treasury, shall obtain his freedom, and shall be crowned with a garland.* A most extraordinary proclamation,—extraordinary even for the third Book of Maccabees, which is by no means wanting in extraordinary things. "It cannot but seem strange that slaves only are invited to become informers, and that this fact is announced quite indirectly, and, what is more, only at the end of the statement." [2] But even this invitation, which, in the circumstances related in the book, is by no means impossible, does not appear so strange to the present writer as the proffered reward, which, in consideration of the great ease with which an information might be lodged against any individual Jew among so many,[3] is hardly less than horrifying: not so much, indeed, the monetary reward, as the declaration that the slave who acted as informer was to receive not only his freedom, but also the honour which was the special prerogative of distinguished men, *viz.*, the being crowned with a garland. The passage thus awakes suspicion of its being corrupt, and, as a matter of fact, the Alexandrinus, as well as other manuscripts, omits τεύξεται καὶ, and reads thus: καὶ τῆς ἐλευθερίας στεφανωθήσεται. But nothing is really gained thereby, for this reading, as such, gives no sense—though, indeed, its very unintelligibility makes it probable that it represents the older, though already corrupt, form of the

---

[1] *HApAT.* iv. (1857), p. 249.   [2] Grimm, *ibid.*

[3] According to 4 [20], the number of the Jews was so enormous that, when their names were being entered in the lists before their execution, pens and papyrus ran short!

text, by which the received reading can be explained as
being an attempt to make the statement more plausible.
Hence Grimm gives it the preference, and "cannot hesitate
for a moment" to accept the emendation of Grotius, *viz.*,
καὶ τοῖς Ἐλευθερίοις στεφανωθήσεται, *i.e.*, *and he shall be
crowned at the feast of the Eleutheria.* The alteration is
certainly not extensive, and the conjecture has at all events
the advantage of explaining away the invitation to the
slaves, which seems so offensive to its proposer. Nevertheless, O. F. Fritzsche[1] hesitates to accept it, and, as we
think, not without good reason. We know nothing of
any feast of the Eleutheria as a custom in Egypt under
the Ptolemies, and it is extremely precarious to take refuge
in a conjecture which, by introducing an entirely new
historical consideration, would give the text such a very
special meaning.

The author believes that the following facts from
Egyptian sources contribute something towards the elucidation of the verse.

In the first place, for the supposed "construction-less"
accusative μηνύειν δὲ τὸν βουλόμενον, reference might have
been made to the similar, apparently absolute, infinitive at
the end of the edict of Ptolemy II. Philadelphus which is
given in the Epistle of Aristeas (*ed.* M. Schmidt), p. 17 f.,
viz., τὸν δὲ βουλόμενον προσαγγέλλειν περὶ τῶν ἀπειθησάντων
ἐπὶ τοῦ φανέντος ἐνόχου τὴν κυρίαν ἕξειν (p. 18 τ.) ; as a matter
of fact, ἕξειν depends upon the technical διειλήφαμεν of the
previous sentence. Similarly we might construe the μηνύειν
δὲ τὸν βουλόμενον with the διειλήφαμεν of verse[26]. We
cannot but perceive that there is on the whole a certain
similarity between the official formulæ of the two edicts,
and it seems very natural to suppose that, even if both
are spurious, yet in form they fully represent the official
style of the Ptolemaic period. In fact, a comparison of
this Maccabean passage with *Pap. Par.* 10[2] (145 B.C.)—a

---

[1] In a critical note upon the text of the passage in his edition of the
Old Testament Apocrypha.

[2] *Notices*, xviii. 2, p. 178 f.

warrant for the apprehension of two runaway slaves—raises
the supposition to a certainty. The warrant first gives an
exact description of each fugitive, and then sets forth a
reward for their recapture, or for information concerning
their whereabouts. When we place the two passages in
parallel columns as below, we see at once the remarkable
similarity between the formulæ employed in each; be it
noted that the Maccabean passage has been correctly
punctuated.

<table>
<tr><td>3 Macc. 3 28.</td><td>Pap. Par. 10.</td></tr>
<tr><td>μηνύειν δὲ τὸν βου-
λόμενον, ἐφ᾽ ᾧ τὴν οὐσίαν
τοῦ ἐμπίπτοντος ὑπὸ τὴν εὔ-
θυναν λήψεται καὶ ἐκ τοῦ
βασιλικοῦ ἀργυρίου δραχμὰς
δισχιλίας [Codd. 19, 64, 93,
Syr. : τρισχιλίας].</td><td>τοῦτον ὃς ἂν ἀναγάγῃ
λήψεται χαλκοῦ τάλαντα
δύο τρισχιλίας (δραχμάς).
..... μηνύειν δὲ τὸν βου-
λόμενον τοῖς παρὰ τοῦ στρα-
τηγοῦ.</td></tr>
</table>

In reference to the absolute μηνύειν δὲ τὸν βουλόμενον
of the Papyrus, the French editor[1] remarks that the infinitive does duty for the imperative, as in similar formulæ
generally. It would perhaps be more accurate, especially
as the imperative infinitive is itself to be explained as a
breviloquence, to make the infinitive depend upon a verb
of command which the edict tacitly presupposes.[2] We must,
in any case, reject the hypothesis of an anacoluthon in the
Maccabean passage; it would destroy the impression given by
the peculiarly official style of the edict. The words μηνύειν
δὲ τὸν βουλόμενον are a complete sentence in themselves:
he shall inform, who so desires. Hence the comparison in-
stituted above is not without interest for the criticism of

---

[1] *Notices*, xviii. 2, p. 203.

[2] *Cf.* διειλήφαμεν in the other two edicts. The official language of the
Ptolemaic period may depend here also (*ante*, p. 104 ff.) on the usage of
Greek jurisprudence. The identical usage of the infinitive is found in an
Inscription on a building in Tegea (*ca.* 3rd cent. B.C., Arcadian dialect), line
24ᵗ. : ἰμφαῖνεν δὲ τὸμ βολόμενον ἐπὶ τοῖ ἡμίσσοι τᾶς ζαμίαν (edited by P. Cauer;
see p. 114, note 2, above). These examples of the absolute infinitive in
edicts might be largely supplemented from Inscriptions.

the third Book of Maccabees ; while, conversely, it may be
maintained that the Ptolemaic edicts in Jewish-Alexandrian
literature, even if they were each and all spurious, and were
without value as sources for the facts, are yet of great
historical importance, in so far, that is,[1] as they faithfully
represent the forms of official intercourse.

What, then, shall we say of the "extraordinary" proclamation at the end of v. [28]? There is no necessity whatever that we should connect the passage itself (according to
the ordinary reading) with *slaves;* the present writer is
surprised that Grimm did not perceive the much more
obvious explanation, *viz.,* that the invitation is really
directed to the Jews. The edict threatened their freedom
and their lives, as may not only be inferred from the circumstances of the case, but as is also confirmed by the expression
of their feelings once the danger had been happily averted :
they felt that they were ἀσινεῖς, ἐλεύθεροι, ὑπερχαρεῖς.[2]
Hence when those who appeared as king's evidence against
their proscribed brethren were thereby promised the freedom
which was otherwise in danger, the bargain was an exceedingly tempting one. It is, finally, quite unnecessary to speak
of a *crowning* of the informer. Assuming that the reading of
the Alexandrinus, καὶ τῆς ἐλευθερίας στεφανωθήσεται, is the
older—though itself a corrupt—form of the text, the author
would propose to make a trivial alteration, and read καὶ τῇ
ἐλευθερίᾳ στεφανωθήσεται.[3] The verb στεφανόω has not
infrequently the general meaning *reward,*[4] and this is what
it means here.

[1] To say nothing of their value as indicating the wishes and ideas of
the writers of them.

[2] 3 Macc. 7 [20].

[3] In τῇ ἐλευθερίᾳ στεφανωθήσεται, ἐλευθερίας might very easily arise from
dittography, and this error, again, might result in τῆς ἐλευθερίας.

[4] Brunet de Presle, *Notices,* xviii. 2, p. 308; he refers, *inter alia,* to
Polyb. xiii. 9 5, ἐστεφάνωσαν τὸν Ἀντίοχον πεντακοσίοις ἀργυρίου ταλάντοις, and to
the use of στεφάνιον for *reward* in *Pap. Par.* 42 (153 B.C.); on this *cf.* the
Thesaurus, and Lumbroso, *Recherches,* p. 285.—In reference to the whole
subject see now E. Ziebarth, *Popularklagen mit Delatorenprämien nach
griechischem Recht,* in *Hermes,* xxxii. (1897), pp. 609-628.

3. THE "LARGE LETTERS" AND THE "MARKS OF JESUS" IN GAL. 6.

Paul began his preaching of the gospel to the Galatians in most promising circumstances; they received the invalid traveller as a messenger of God, yea, as if it had been the Saviour himself who sank down upon their threshold under the burden of the cross. Whereas others might have turned from Paul with loathing, they came to him, aye, and would have given away their eyes if by so doing they could have helped him. And then with childlike piety they gazed upon the majestic Form which the stranger pictured to them. Ever afterwards they were his children; and like a father's, indeed, are the thoughts which, across land and sea, bind him to the far-off churches of Galatia. True, he knows that they had forsaken their native idols with the zeal of the newly-awakened, but he also knows that they had not followed up this advance by full realisation of the sacred fellowship in which the majesty of the living Christ ever anew assumes human form. The confession regarding his own life in Christ, which Paul, on the very eve of his martyrdom, made to his dearest friends, had been confirmed in his own mind by the painful yet joyful experience of his long apostolic labours among the churches: *Not as though I had already attained!* So then, as he left these infant churches in Asia Minor, his heart, full of love and gratitude, would yet have some foreboding of the dangers which their isolation might bring about; we cannot imagine that he was one to think, with the blind affection of a father, that the newly-awakened had no further need of tutors and governors. Nay, but rather that, as he prayed to the Father on their behalf, his remembrance of them would be all the more fervent.

With their good-natured Gallic flightiness of disposition, these young Christians, left to themselves, succumbed to the wiles of their tempters. Paul was compelled to recognise that here too, the wicked enemy, who was always sowing tares among his wheat, did not labour in vain. In their

simple-hearted ignorance the Galatians had allowed themselves to be bewitched by the word of the Law, and, in
course of time, their idea of the man whom they had once
honoured as their father in Christ became somewhat distorted in the light which streamed from national and
theological animosity.

How shall we figure to ourselves the feelings of the
Apostle as the news of this reached his ears ? If we would
understand not only the words, but, so to speak, also the
spirit, of the Letter to the Galatians, we must, above
all, endeavour to bring home to our minds the movements
of this marvellous human soul. The keen biting polemic
of the missive gives us to know exactly how Paul judged
of the legal particularism of his opponents; it was the
salutary indignation of the reformer that guided his pen
here. But we dare not assume that he meted out the
same measure to the tempted as to their tempters. The
bitter incisiveness with which he speaks of these churches
does not proceed from the self-willed sullenness of the mis-
interpreted benefactor who is pleased to pose as a martyr:
it is rather the lament of the father who, in the unfilial
conduct of his son, sees but the evil which the wrong-doer
brings upon himself. The harsh and formal speech of the
first page or two of the letter is that of the παιδαγωγὸς εἰς
Χριστόν. But he speaks thus only incidentally ; once he
has risen above the warfare of embittering words to the
praise of the faith in Christ which may again be theirs,
the warm feelings of the old intimacy will no longer be
subdued, and the man who a moment before had feared
that his labour among these foolish ones had been in vain,
changes his tone and speaks as if he were addressing the
Philippians or his friend Philemon.

As in his other letters, so in this does Paul add to the
words he had dictated to his amanuensis a postscript in his
own handwriting. More attention ought to be paid to the
concluding words of the letters generally; they are of the
highest importance if we are ever to understand the Apostle.
The conclusion of the Letter to the Galatians is certainly a

very remarkable one.   Once again, in short and clear antitheses, the Law and Christ are set over against each other;
and, moreover, the fact that it is only his opponents whom
he now treats severely, fully consorts with the mood of
reconciliation with the church, to which, in course of writing,
he had been brought.   The letter does not close with com-
plaints against the Galatians ; and in view of the occasion
of the letter, this must be taken as signifying very much the
same as what can be observed in the conclusion of other
letters called forth by opposition, *viz.*, the express indication
of the cordiality that subsisted between the writer and the
readers.   Paul has again attained to perfect peace—so far,
at least, as concerns his Galatian brethren ; and we are of
opinion that in this placid frame of mind lies the explanation
of the much-discussed words at the beginning of the autograph conclusion : *See with how large letters I write unto you
with mine own hand.*   The true mode of interpreting these
words is to take them as a piece of amiable irony, from which
the readers might clearly realise that it was no rigorous
pedagogue that was addressing them.   The amanuensis,
whose swift pen was scarcely able to record the eloquent
flow of Paul's dictation upon the coarse papyrus leaves, had
a minute commonplace handwriting.   Between his fluent
hand and that of Paul there was a pronounced difference [1]—
not only in the Letter to the Galatians.   Surely it is hardly
quite accurate to say that Paul used large letters in the
present isolated instance for the purpose of marking the
importance of the words to follow.   The *large letters* naturally
suggest that the explanation rather lies in the formal and
external matter of caligraphy, and the fact that Paul calls
special attention to them can only be explained, as we
think, on the theory indicated above.   *Large letters* are
calculated to make an impression on children ; and it is as
his own dear foolish children that he treats the Galatians,
playfully trusting that surely the large letters will touch
their hearts.   When Paul condescended to speak in such a

---

[1] See the remarks of Mahaffy, i., p. 48.

way, the Galatians knew that the last shadows of castigatory
sternness had died from his countenance. The real sternness of the letter was by no means obliterated thereby ; but
the feeling of coolness that might have remained behind was
now happily wiped away by Paul's thrice-welcome good-
natured irony, and the readers were now all the more ready
to receive the final message that still lay on his heart.

The closing words present no difficulty in themselves.
It is only the last sentence but one[1]—one of the strangest
utterances of Paul—which is somewhat enigmatical. *Τοῦ*
λοιποῦ[2] *κόπους μοι μηδεὶς παρεχέτω · ἐγὼ γὰρ τὰ στίγματα*
τοῦ Ἰησοῦ ἐν τῷ σώματί μου βαστάζω, henceforth let no man
trouble me, for I bear in my body (R.V. *branded on my body*) *the*
marks of Jesus. Two questions arise here: first, what does
Paul mean by the *marks of Jesus ?* and, secondly, to what
extent does he base the warning, that no one shall trouble
him, upon his *bearing* of these marks ?

" *στίγματα* . . are signs, usually letters of the alphabet
(Lev. 19[28]), which were made upon the body (especially on
the forehead and the hands) by branding or puncturing,—
on slaves as a symbol of their masters, on soldiers as a
symbol of their leaders, on criminals as a symbol of their
crime, and also, among some oriental peoples, as a symbol
of the deity they served (3 Macc. 2[29], . .)."[3] Hence an
ancient reader would know perfectly well what these *stig-
mata* were, but the very variety of their possible application
renders less evident the special reference in the case before
us. In any case, it seems to us quite evident that Paul is
speaking metaphorically; is alluding, in fact, to the scars
of the wounds he had received in his apostolic labours,[4]
and not to actual, artificially-produced *στίγματα.* Sieffert[5]
decides in favour of the hypothesis that Paul's intention
was to describe himself as the *slave* of Christ; but in that
case, how can the *γάρ* possibly be explained? We feel,
in fact, that the *γάρ* is of itself sufficient to invalidate
the hypothesis. Had Paul said the exact contrary; had

---

[1] Gal. 6[17].   [2] For *τοῦ λοιποῦ cf.* W. Schmid, *Der Atticismus*, iii., p. 135.
[3] F. Sieffert, Meyer, vii.[7] (1886), p. 375.   [4] 2 Cor. 11.   [5] P. 376.

he said, for instance, *Henceforth go on troubling me as you
will*,[1]—then the γάρ would have admirably fitted the context; that is, Paul might have gone on [to say, with
proud resignation, *I am accustomed to that*, for *I am naught
but a despised slave of Jesus Christ.*

No one will seriously contend that Paul wished to compare himself with a branded criminal; and the reference to
the tattooing of soldiers would seem equally far-fetched.
The γάρ speaks against the latter explanation quite as
forcibly as against the hypothesis of slave-marks; for the
miles christianus does not quench the fiery darts of the Evil
One by striking a treaty, but by going forth to active warfare,
armed with the shield of faith.

The explanation of Wetstein [2] still seems to us to
be the best; according to this, Paul means *sacred signs*,
in virtue of which he is declared to be one consecrated to
Christ, one therefore whom no Christian dare molest. But
Wetstein, too, fails adequately to show the causal relation
between the two clauses, and as little does he justify
the unquestionably strange periphrasis here used to express
metaphorically the idea of belonging to Christ.[3]

Provisionally accepting, however, this theory of the
στίγματα, we might represent the causal relation somewhat
as follows: Anyone who bears the marks of Jesus is His
disciple, and, as such, is under His protection; hence anyone who offends against Paul lays himself open to the
punishment of a stronger Power. We should thus be led to
look upon the στίγματα as sacred *protective-marks*, and to
interpret our passage in connection with certain lines of
thought to which B. Stade has recently called attention.[4]
Already in the Old Testament, according to him, we find not

---

[1] *Cf.* J. J. Wetstein, *Novum Testamentum Graecum*, ii., Amsterdam,
1752, p. 238 f. : " *Notae enim serviles potius invitabant aliorum contumeliam* ".

[2] P. 238 : " *Sacras notas intelligit Paulus; se sacrum esse, cui ideo nemo
eorum, qui Christum amant, molestus esse debeat, profitetur* ".

[3] Besides, Paul does not speak of the marks of *Christ* at all; he uses
the name *Jesus*, otherwise rare in his writings.

[4] *Beiträge zur Pentateuchkritik*, *ZAW.* xiv. (1894), p. 250 ff.

a few indications of such protective-marks.   He explains
the mark of Cain as such, but, even apart from this,
reference may be made to Is. 44 ^{51} and Ezek. 9; ^{2} in the
latter passage we read that, before the angels bring ruin
upon Jerusalem and destroy its inhabitants, one of them
sets a mark upon the forehead of all those who mourn for
the abominations practised in the city; these are spared by
the destroying angels.^{3} In Lev. 19 $^{27\,f.}$,^{4} 21 $^{5\,f.}$, Deut. 14 $^{1\,f.}$,
there is likewise implied an acquaintance with sacred signs
by which the bearer indicates that he belongs to a certain
deity : were the Israelites to permit of the sign of another
god among them, they would thereby rupture their special
relation to Jahweh as being His people.   Circumcision, too,
may be looked upon as a mark of Jahweh.^{5} The following
passages, belonging to a later time, may be mentioned : ^{6}
Psal. Sol. 15 ^{8} ὅτι τὸ σημεῖον τοῦ θεοῦ ἐπὶ δικαίους εἰς
σωτηρίαν, cf. v. ^{10}, where it is said of the ποιοῦντες ἀνομίαν
that they have τὸ σημεῖον τῆς ἀπωλείας ἐπὶ τοῦ μετώπου
αὐτῶν; according to 3 Macc. 2 ^{29} the Alexandrian Jews were
compelled by Ptolemy IV. Philopator to have branded upon
them an ivy leaf, the sign of Dionysos, the king himself
being similarly marked ; ^{7} Philo, de Monarchia (M.), p. 220 f.,
reproaches the Jewish apostates for allowing themselves to
be branded with the signs of idols made with hands (ἔνιοι δὲ
τοσαύτῃ κέχρηνται μανίας ὑπερβολῇ, ὥστ' . . . ἵενται πρὸς
δουλείαν τῶν χειροκμήτων γράμμασιν αὐτὴν ὁμολογοῦντες . . . .
ἐν τοῖς σώμασι καταστίζοντες αὐτὴν σιδήρῳ πεπυρωμένῳ
πρὸς ἀνεξάλειπτον διαμονήν · οὐδὲ γὰρ χρόνῳ ταῦτα ἀμαυροῦν-

---

^{1} καὶ ἕτερος ἐπιγράψει χειρὶ αὐτοῦ· τοῦ θεοῦ εἰμι ; see the remarks upon 1
Kings 20 ^{35} ff., and Zech. 13 ^{6} in Stade, p. 313, also p. 314 ff.

^{2} Stade, p. 301.

^{3} Stade also draws attention to the protective-marks of the Passover
night; as these, however, were not made upon the body, they come less into
consideration here.   But note that in Exod. 13 $^{9.\ 16}$ the feast of the Passover
is compared to a sign upon the hand and upon the forehead.

^{4} Note that the LXX has γράμματα στικτά here.

^{5} Gen. 17 ^{11}, Rom. 4 ^{11} ; cf. on this point Stade, p. 308.

^{6} Cf., most recently, Stade, pp. 301, 303 ff.

^{7} Etymologicum Magnum, sub Γάλλος.

ται) ; and similarly the worshippers of the beast in Revelation bear the name or the number of the beast as a χάραγμα on the forehead or on the right hand,[1] while the faithful are marked with the name of the Lamb and of the living God.[2] Finally—a fact which is specially instructive in regard to the significance of *protective-marks* in Greek Judaism—the *Thephillin*, prayer-fillets, were regarded as *protective-marks*, and were designated φυλακτήρια, the technical term for *amulets*. These various data are sufficient, in our opinion, to justify us in supposing that the Apostle might quite easily characterise his scars metaphorically as *protective-marks*.[3]

In confirmation of this supposition we feel that we must draw attention to a certain Papyrus passage, which seems to grow in significance the longer we contemplate it, and which, moreover, may even merit the attention of those who cannot at once accept the conclusions here drawn from it, as we think, with some degree of justification.

It is found in the bilingual (Demotic and Greek) Papyrus J. 383 (Papyrus Anastasy 65) of the Leiden Museum. C. J. C. Reuvens[4] was the first to call attention to it, assigning it to the first half of the 3rd cent. A.D.[5] Then it was published in fac-simile[6] and discussed[7] by C.

---

[1] Rev. 13 16f., 14 9 ff., 16 2, 19 20, 20 4. See *ante*, p. 240 ff.

[2] Rev. 14 1, 7 2 ff., 9 4. On the meaning of *signs* in the Christian Church, see the suggestions of Stade, p. 304 ff.

[3] We think it probable that the expression forms an antithesis to the previously mentioned *circumcision* (*cf.* Rom. 4 11 σημεῖον περιτομῆς), and that emphasis is to be laid upon τοῦ Ἰησοῦ.

[4] *Lettres à M. Letronne . . . sur les papyrus bilingues et grecs . . . du musée d'antiquités de l'université de Leide*, Leiden, 1830, i., pp. 3 ff., 36 ff. In the *Atlas* belonging to this work, Table A, some words from the passage under discussion are given in fac-simile.

[5] *Appendice* (to the work just cited), p. 151.

[6] *Papyrus égyptien démotique à transcriptions grecques du musée d'antiquités des Pays-Bas à Leide* (*description raisonnée*, J. 383), Leiden, 1839. Our passage is found in Table IV., col. VIII.; in the tables the Papyrus is signed A. [= Anastasy ?] No. 65.

[7] *Monumens égyptiens du musée d'antiquités des Pays-Bas à Leide*, Leiden, 1839.

Leemans, the director of the museum, who has lately again [1]
indicated his agreement with Reuvens' date. H. Brugsch [2]
has expressly emphasised the great importance of the
Papyrus for the study of the Demotic, and has made most
exhaustive use of it in his Demotic Grammar. [3] He follows
Reuvens and Leemans in describing it as *Gnostic*—a term
that may either mean much or little. The passage in
question has been recently discussed more or less elaborately
by E. Revillout, [4] G. Maspero [5] and C. Wessely. [6]

It is found in the Demotic text of this "Gnostic"
Papyrus, [7] which belongs to that literature of magic which
has been handed down to us in extensive fragments, and
recently brought to light. To judge from the fac-similes,
its decipherment is quite easy—so far, at least, as it affects
us here. First of all, the text, as we read it, is given, the
various readings of Reuvens (Rs), Leemans (L), Brugsch
(B), Maspero (M), Revillout (Rt) and Wessely (W) being
also indicated.

It is introduced by a sentence in the Demotic which
Revillout translates as follows : " *Pour parvenir à être aimé de
quelqu'un qui lutte contre toi et ne veut pas te parler* (*dire*) : "

---

[1] *Papyri graeci musei antiquarii publici Lugduni-Batavi*, ii., Leiden,
1885, p. 5.

[2] *Über das ägyptische Museum zu Leyden*, in the *Zeitschr. der Deutschen
morgenländischen Gesellschaft*, vi. (1852), p. 250 f.

[3] *Grammaire démotique*, Berlin, 1855. A fac-simile of our passage is
found on Table IX. of that book, a transcription on p. 202.

[4] *Les arts égyptiens*, in the *Revue égyptologique*, i. (1880), p. 164 ; *cf.* the
same author's discussion of the Papyrus, *ibid.*, ii. (1881-1882), p. 10 ff. His
book. *Le Roman de Setna*, Paris, 1877, was not accessible to the present
writer.

[5] *Collections du Musée Alaoui*, première série, 5ᵉ livraison, Paris, 1890,
p. 66 f. ; see the same author's discussion of the Papyrus in his *Études
démotiques*, in the *Recueil de travaux relatifs à la philologie et à l'archéologie
égyptiennes et assyriennes*, i. (1870), p. 19 ff. A study by Birch mentioned
there is unknown to the present writer. Our passage is found on p. 30 f.

[6] *Mittheilungen aus der Sammlung der Papyrus Erzherzog Rainer*, v.
(Vienna, 1892), p. 13 f.

[7] This Papyrus contains another and longer Greek incantation, most
recently read and discussed by Revillout, *Rev. ég.*, i. (1880), p. 165 f.

In the original the spell occupies three and a half lines. A rent runs down the Papyrus column, nearly in the middle; the number of the missing letters is indicated in the transcript by dots, the ends of the original lines by |.

ΜΗΜΕΔΙΩΚΕΟΔΕ ΑΝΟΧ
ΠΑΠΙΠΕΤ . . ΜΕΤΟΥΒΑΝΕΣ
ΒΑΣΤΑΖΩ ΤΗΝΤΑΦΗΝ
ΤΟΤΟΣΙΡΕΩΣΚΑΙΥΠΑΓΩ
5 *ΚΑΤΑ . . ΗΣΑΙΑΥΤΗΝΕ Σ*
ΑΒΙΔΟΣ|ΚΑΤΑΣΤΗΣΑΙΕΙΣ
ΤΑΣΤΑΣΚΑΙΚΑΤΑΘΕΣΘΑΙ
ΕΙΣ . . . ΧΑΣΕΑΝΜΟΙΟΔ
ΚΟΠΟΥΣ|ΠΑΡΑΣΧΗ ΠΡΟΣ
10 *ΡΕΨΩΑΥΤΗΝΑΥΤΩ|*

2 παπιπετ . . : Rs. παπιπε . . ., L. παπιπετ . , B. παπιπετ(ου), M. Papipetu, Rt. Παπεπιτου, W. παπιπετου | 4 οσιρεως: W. οσιριος [!] | 5 κατα . . ησαι: Rs. πατα(στη)σαι, L. κατα . . ησαι, B. M. Rt. καταστησαι, W. κατα[στη]σαι | ε s : Rs. B. M. Rt. εις, L. ε.s | 7 ταστας: Rs. τας τας, B. τας ταφας, W. τας τας sic | 8 . . . χας: Rs. (μ)αχας, L. . αχας, M. αλχας, W. . . αχας | Δ : B. M. Rt. interpret as δεινα, W. δ(ε)ι(να) | 9 ρεψω : B. M. Rt. τρεψω, W. φερω |

The editors differ from one another principally in their reproduction (or restoration) of the non-Greek words in the text. As these are irrelevant to our present purpose, we shall not further pursue the subject, feeling constrained to follow Maspero in reading thus :—

Μή με δίωκε ὅδε· ανοχ
παπιπετ[ου] μετουβανες·
βαστάζω τὴν ταφὴν
τοῦ Ὀσίρεως καὶ ὑπάγω
5 κατα[στ]ῆσαι αὐτὴν ε(ἰ)ς
Ἄβιδος, καταστῆσαι εἰς
ταστας καὶ καταθέσθαι
εἰς [αλ]χας· ἐάν μοι ὁ δεῖνα
κόπους παράσχῃ, προσ-
10 (τ)ρέψω αὐτὴν αὐτῷ.

In the Papyrus a Demotic rendering of the incantation follows the Greek text,—not literal, indeed, but showing,

few variations.   This Demotic version is thus rendered by
Revillout : [1]

"*Ne me persécute pas, une telle !—Je suis Papipetou Metou-
banès, je porte le sépulcre d'Osiris, je vais le transporter à Abydos; je
le ferai reposer dans les Alkah.   Si une telle me résiste aujourd'hui,
je le renverserai.—Dire sept fois.*"

We perceive at once that we have here a formula of
adjuration.   The following notes will help towards an understanding of the Greek text.

Line 1. The commentators take $avo\chi$ to be the Coptic
anok (cf. אָנֹכִי) *I am*.   In the Greek books of magic we very
frequently find similar instances of the $\dot{\epsilon}\gamma\dot{\omega} \, \epsilon \iota \mu \iota$ followed by
the divine name, by which the adjurer identifies himself with
the particular deity in order to invest his *spell* with special
efficacy, and to strike the demon with terror.

L. 2.   We have not as yet discovered any satisfactory
etymological explanation of the words $\pi a \pi \iota \pi \varepsilon \tau o \upsilon \, \mu \epsilon \tau o \upsilon \beta a \nu \epsilon \varsigma$;
Reuvens and Leemans give nothing more than conjectures.
It is sufficient for our purpose to remember that such foreign
words play a very great part in adjurations.   Even if they
had originally any meaning at all, it is yet unlikely that those
who used the formula ever knew it; the more mysterious
the words of their *spell* sounded, the more efficacious did
they deem it.

L. 3.   The editors translate $\tau \dot{\eta} \nu \, \tau a \phi \dot{\eta} \nu \, \tau o \hat{\upsilon} \, {}^{\prime} O \sigma \dot{\iota} \rho \epsilon \omega \varsigma$ as
the coffin, or *the mummy, of Osiris*. $\tau a \phi \dot{\eta}$ in this sense is of
frequent occurrence in the Papyri and elsewhere.[2]   By this
$\tau a \phi \dot{\eta} \, \tau o \hat{\upsilon} \, {}^{\prime} O \sigma \dot{\iota} \rho \epsilon \omega \varsigma$ we must understand a model of the coffin
or of the mummy of Osiris used as an amulet.   The *efficacy*

---

[1] *Cf.* also the translation of Brugsch, *Gramm. dém.*, p. 202.

[2] *Notices*, xviii. 2, pp. 234, 435 f.   Wessely, *Mitth. Rainer*, v., p. 14,
explains that "$\tau a \phi \dot{\eta}$ here means *mummy*, as we learn in particular from the
language of the wooden tablets which were employed in the conveyance of
mummies as labels of recognition".   See also Leemans, *Monumens*, p. 8.—
C. Schmidt, *Ein altchristliches Mumienetikett* in the *Zeitschr. für die
ägyptische Sprache und Alterthumskunde*, xxxii. (1894), p. 55, says, "I am
of opinion that in Roman times $\tau a \phi \dot{\eta}$ was understood as the 'mummy' only".

of this amulet is explained by the Osiris myth.[1]   The Osiris
of Graeco-Roman times was the god of the dead.   His
corpse, dismembered by Typhon, was again put together
with the greatest difficulty by Isis; and it was ever afterwards the most cherished task of Isis, Nephthys, Horus,
Anubis and Hermes, deities friendly to Osiris, to guard his
tomb, and to prevent the wicked Typhon from repeating
his mutilation of the divine body.   The magicians took
advantage of this conflict among the gods in order to make
sure of the assistance of those who were friendly to Osiris.
They strove to get possession of the sacred coffin; they
carried it about with them—at least *in effigie,* as an amulet—
and they threatened to demolish it if their desires were
not fulfilled.   Thus, according to Jamblichus,[2] the threats
*to destroy the heavens, to reveal the mysteries of Isis, to divulge
the ineffable secret hidden in the depths, to stay the sacred sun-
barge, to gratify Typhon by scattering the limbs of Osiris* belong
to the βιαστικαὶ ἀπειλαί of the Egyptian magicians.   The
adjuration under notice is an *efficacious minatory formula* of
this kind.   It is directed to a demon, who is believed to
be the cause of the difficulties which, it is hoped, will be
eluded by its means ;[3] the possession of the ταφὴ τοῦ Ὀσίρεως
cannot but impress him, being a guarantee for the support
of the most powerful deities, seeing that it was to their own
best interests to be favourable to the possessor of the im-
perilled mummy.   A quite similar menace, made by some
" obscure gentleman," is found in a recently-published
tabula devotionis[4] from Adrumetum : *if not, I shall go down
to the holy places of Osiris, and break his corpse in pieces, and
throw it into the river to be borne away.*[5]

---

[1] In reference to what follows, see Maspero, *Coll. Al.*, p. 66.

[2] *De mysteriis,* 6 5 (ed. G. Parthey, Berol., 1857, p. 245 f.) : ἢ γὰρ τὸν
οὐρανὸν προσαράξειν ἢ τὰ κρυπτὰ τῆς Ἴσιδος ἐκφανεῖν ἢ τὸ ἐν ἀβύσσῳ ἀπόρρητον [for
this we find, 6 7, p. 248, τὰ ἐν Ἀβύδῳ ἀπόρρητα ; cf. l. 6 of our formula] δείξειν
ἢ στήσειν τὴν βάριν, ἢ τὰ μέλη τοῦ Ὀσίριδος διασκεδάσειν τῷ Τυφῶνι.

[3] Reuvens, i., p. 41.   [4] See p. 279.

[5] *Collections du Musée Alaoui,* prem. série, 5ᵉ livraison (1890), p. 60 :
Si minus, descendo in adytus Osyris et dissolvam τὴν ταφὴν *et mittam, ut a
flumine feratur.*   See Maspero's explanatory notes.

L. 6. Ἄβιδος is the Egyptian Abydos. The town is of great importance in the history of Osiris. It was looked upon as the burial-place of the god, and its mysteries are spoken of by several ancient writers.[1] The assertion of the *bearer* of the amulet, *viz.*, that he is about to convey the mummy of Osiris to Abydos, seems to us to signify that he wishes, by means of an act which exercises a secret influence upon the friends of Osiris, to be all the more assured of their favour, and all the more dangerous to the demon.

L. 7 and 8. ταστας and αλχας are the Greek transcriptions of two Egyptian words which are rendered by Maspero[2] as *les retraites* and *les demeures éternelles* respectively. They help us to obtain a clearer understanding of the preceding lines : the user of the spell, in thus reverently entombing the body which Typhon had abused, lays the most powerful deities under the highest obligation to himself.

L. 8. ὁ δεῖνα is represented in the original by the abbreviation *Δ*, which is frequently used in the Papyri in the same way ; when the formula prescribed in the book of magic was actually used against some troublesome person, this person's name was substituted for the ὁ δεῖνα, just as the name of the demon who was the cause of the κόποι took the place of the ὅδε in line 1. (U. von Wilamowitz-Moellendorff informs the author by letter that he reads ὁ δε(ῖνα) also in line 1 (not ὅδε), for which there is much to be said).

L. 9. προσ(τ)ρέψω : the Papyrus distinctly shows προσρέψω, *i.e.*, the future of προσρέπω, *to incline towards*, intransitive : here it would be transitive, for which usage there is no authority.[3] Hence προστρέψω [4] would seem the preferable reading. But the question is of no importance for the sense of the concluding sentence ; in either case, the adjurer threatens to *use* his efficacious amulet *against* the troubler.

---

[1] *E.g.*, Epiphanius, *Adv. Haer.*, iii. 2, p. 1093 D (Dindorf, vol. iii., p 571). See Reuvens, p. 41 ff. and Leemans, *Monumens*, p. 9.

[2] *Coll. Al.*, p. 67.   [3] Leemans, *Monumens*, p. 9.

[4] Leemans, *ibid.*, suggests προσρίψω.

The spell may accordingly be translated as follows:—

Persecute me not, thou there!—I am PAPIPETOU METU-BANES; I carry the corpse of Osiris and I go to convey it to Abydos, to convey it to its resting-place, and to place it in the everlasting chambers. Should any one trouble me, I shall use it against him.

Now, differ as we may as to the meaning of the individual details of this *spell*, and, in particular, as to the allusions to Egyptian mythology, it is, after all, only the essential meaning which concerns us here, and this meaning the author holds to be established: the βαστάζειν of a particular amulet associated with a god acts as a *charm* against the κόπους παρέχειν on the part of an adversary.

Starting from this point, let us now seek to understand the enigmatical words of the Apostle. One can hardly resist the impression that the obscure metaphor all at once becomes more intelligible: *Let no man venture κόπους παρέχειν for me, for in the βαστάζειν of the marks of Jesus I possess a talisman against all such things.* In this way the sense of the γάρ, in particular, becomes perfectly clear. The words are not directed against the Judaisers, but to the Galatians, and, moreover, it seems probable that we must explain the threat by the same temper of mind[1] to which we attributed the sportive phrase about the *large letters*. Just as the Apostle, with kindly menace, could ask the Corinthians, *Shall I come unto you with the rod?*[2] so here, too, he smilingly holds up his finger and says to his naughty but well-beloved children: Do be sensible, do not imagine that you can hurt me—I am protected by a *charm*.

We must confess that we do not feel that Paul, by this mixture of earnest and amiable jest, lays himself open to the charge of trifling. Only by a total misapprehension of

[1] We would not, however, attach any special importance to this. The explanation given above is quite justifiable, even if Paul was speaking wholly in earnest.

[2] 1 Cor. 4 [21]; see p. 119 f.

the actual letter-like character of his writings as they have come down to us, could we expect that he should in them assume the severe manner of the *doctor gentium*, who, caught up into the third heaven, proclaims to mankind and to the ages what eye hath never seen. Paul is no bloodless and shadowy figure of a saint, but a man, a man of the olden time. One in whose letters utterance is found for the raptured glow of faith and for a sensitive and circumspect love, for bitter feelings of scorn and relentless irony—why should the winning kindliness of the jest be deemed alien to him? He wishes to bring back the Galatians to the true way, but perhaps feels that he, in treating as τέλειοι those who are but νήπιοι, has overshot the mark. So he withdraws, though as regards the manner rather than the matter of his charges; and who that has ever loved the Apostle could find fault? Paul has taken care, in this passage, that his words shall have no hackneyed ring; he does not use general terms about the purposelessness of the attacks made on him, but intimates that what *preserves* him are the protective-marks of Jesus. Jesus guards him; Jesus restrains the troublers; Jesus will say to them: τί αὐτῷ κόπους παρέχετε; καλὸν ἔργον ἠργάσατο ἐν ἐμοί.

We cannot, of course, go so far as to maintain that Paul makes conscious allusion to the incantation of the Papyrus; but it is not improbable that it, or one similar to it, was known to him, even were it not the case that he composed the Letter to the Galatians in the city of magicians and sorcerers. The Papyrus dates from the time of Tertullian; the incantation itself may be much older.[1] The same Papyrus furnishes us with another incantation,[2] manifestly pervaded by Jewish ideas,—another proof of the supposition that the Apostle may have been acquainted with such forms of expression. Moreover, we learn even from Christian sources that Paul on more than one

---

[1] See p. 323.

[2] It begins thus: ἐπικαλοῦμαί σε τὸν ἐν τῷ κενέῳ πνεύματι δεινὸν ἀόρατον παντοκράτορα θεὸν θεῶν φθοροποιὸν καὶ ἐρημοποιόν (*Revue égyptologique*, i., p. 168).

occasion came into contact with magicians,[1] while he himself warns the Galatians against φαρμακεία,[2] and reproaches them for having suffered themselves to be *bewitched*:[3] all these things but serve as evidence for the fact that the sphere, from which, haply, some light has been thrown upon the obscure phrase about the marks of Jesus, was in no wise outwith the circle of ideas in which the writer moved.[4]   Be it at least conceded that our contention should not be met by æsthetic or religious objections. We would not maintain, of course, that the figure used by Paul can be fitted into the formulas of dogmatic Christology; but in its context it forms a perfectly definite and forcible metaphor. And as for the possible religious objection, that Paul was not the man to apply terms originating in the darkest "heathenism" to facts distinctively Christian, it is a fair counter-plea to ask whether it is an unchristian mode of speech, at the present day, to use the verb *charm* (*feien*) in a similar connection, or to extol the Cross as one's *Talisman*. In the same manner does Paul speak of the wounds which he had received in his apostolic work—and which in 2 Cor. 4[10] he describes as the νέκρωσις τοῦ Ἰησοῦ—as the marks of Jesus, which protected him as by a charm.

4. A NOTE TO THE LITERARY HISTORY OF SECOND PETER.

Graven upon the stones of a locality where we should not expect it, we find a piece of evidence which, in any treatment of the Second Epistle of Peter, deserves the highest consideration. The beginning of this early Christian booklet has many points in common with a decree of the inhabitants of Stratonicea in Caria in honour of Zeus Panhemerios and of Hekate, which, dating from the early imperial period, has been preserved in an Inscription. This Inscription has already, in our investigation of the word

[1] Acts 13 and 19.   [2] Gal. 5[20].   [3] Gal. 3[1].

[4] The peculiarly emphatic ἐγώ, too, recalls the emphasis of certain incantations ; see p. 355 with reference to *anok*.

ἀρετή, been laid under contribution,[1] and it will once again engage our attention.[2] We begin here by giving the two texts in parallel columns, duly marking the cognate elements in each ; be it observed that it is not only the unquestionable similarities in expression and meaning which are thus emphasised, but also certain—for the present let us call them mechanical—assonances between the two texts, the calling of attention to which will be justified as we proceed. In order to understand the Inscription, which, omitting the introductory formula, we give in the original orthography, let it be borne in mind that the infinitive σεσῶσθαι depends upon an antecedent εἰπόντος.

Decree of Stratonicea.

... τὴν πόλιν ἄνωθεν τῇ τῶν προεστώτων αὐτῆς μεγίστων θεῶν [προνοίᾳ Διὸς Π]ανημε-
[ρίου καὶ Ἑ]κάτης ἐκ πολλῶν **καὶ μεγάλων καὶ συνεχῶν** κινδύνων σεσῶσθαι, ὧν καὶ τὰ ἱερὰ ἄσυλα **καὶ** ἱκέται καὶ ἡ ἱερὰ σύνκλητος δόγματι Σε-
[βαστοῦ Καίσαρος ἐπὶ]τῆς τῶν κυρίων Ῥωμαίων αἰωνίου ἀρχῆς ἐποιήσαντο προφανεῖς ἐναργείας· καλῶς δὲ ἔχι πᾶσαν σπουδὴν ἰσφέρεσθαι ἰς τὴν πρὸς [αὐτοὺς εὐσέβ]ειαν καὶ μηδένα καιρὸν παραλιπῖν τοῦ εὐσεβεῖν καὶ λιτανεύιν αὐτούς· καθίδρυται δὲ ἀγάλματα ἐν τῷ σεβαστῷ βουλευτηρίῳ τῶν προειρημένω[ν θεῶν ἐπιφαν]εστάτας παρέχοντα τῆς θείας δυνάμεως ἀρετάς, δι' ἃς

2 Pet. 1 [3 ff.]

ὡς τὰ πάντα ἡμῖν τῆς θείας δυνάμεως αὐτοῦ τὰ πρὸς ζωὴν καὶ εὐσέβειαν δεδωρημένης διὰ τῆς ἐπιγνώσεως τοῦ καλέσαντος ἡμᾶς ἰδίᾳ δόξῃ καὶ ἀρετῇ, δι' ὧν τὰ τίμια ἡμῖν καὶ μέγιστα ἐπαγγέλματα δεδώρηται, ἵνα διὰ τούτων γένησθε θείας κοινωνοὶ φύσεως ἀποφυγόντες τῆς ἐν τῷ κόσμῳ ἐν ἐπιθυμίᾳ φθορᾶς, καὶ αὐτὸ τοῦτο δὲ σπουδὴν πᾶσαν παρεισενέγκαντες ἐπιχορηγήσατε ἐν τῇ πίστει ὑμῶν τὴν ἀρετὴν ἐν δὲ τῇ ἀρετῇ τὴν γνῶσιν ἐν δὲ τῇ γνώσει τὴν ἐγκράτειαν ἐν δὲ τῇ ἐγκρατείᾳ τήν ὑπομονὴν ἐν δὲ τῇ ὑπομονῇ τὴν εὐσέβειαν ἐν δὲ τῇ εὐσεβείᾳ τὴν φιλαδελφίαν ἐν δὲ τῇ φιλαδελφίᾳ τὴν ἀγάπην.

---

[1] See p. 95 ff. The Inscription is given in *CIG.* ii., No. 2715 *a*, *b* = Waddington, iii. 2, Nos. 519-520 (p. 142).
[2] P. 370.

καὶ τὸ σύνπαν πλῆθος θύει τε
καὶ ἐπιθυμιᾷ καὶ εὔχεται καὶ
εὐχαριστεῖ ἀ[εὶ τοῖσ]δε τοῖς
οὕτως ἐπιφανεστάτοις θεοῖς
κἀκ τῆς δι᾽ ὑμνῳδίας προσόδου
καὶ θρησκείας εὐσεβεῖν αὐτοὺς[εἴθισται]· ἔδοξε τῇ βουλῇ
κτλ.

. . . . . (V. 11) : οὕτως γὰρ
πλουσίως ἐπιχορηγηθήσεται
ὑμῖν ἡ εἴσοδος εἰς τὴν αἰώνιον
βασιλείαν τοῦ κυρίου ἡμῶν καὶ
σωτῆρος Ἰησοῦ Χριστοῦ.

Let us allow these parallels to speak for themselves,
wholly ignoring the feelings of unpleasantness or, it may
be, of wonder which they may wake in the breasts of some.
The most important feature is manifestly this : that both
texts contain the expression ἡ θεία δύναμις,[1] and in the same
case to boot. Now this is no trite expression ; its occurrence
in the Inscription could not be ignored, even if there were
no further point of similarity with the Epistle. But the fact
that this solemn periphrasis of the term *God* is in both
passages connected with the word ἀρετή, and further, that
it occurs in an altogether peculiar and unfamiliar sense,
lends a peculiar intrinsic importance to the external similarity. Suppose for a moment that the τῆς θείας δυνάμεως
ἀρετάς of the decree occurred somewhere in the LXX ; there
would not, in that case, be the shadow of a doubt that the
Epistle had quoted it—dismembered, it might be—or at
all events had alluded to it. Nor can this analogy be set
aside by the objection that the use, by the author of the
Epistle, of an out-of-the-way Inscription, in a manner corresponding to that of biblical quotation, is inconceivable—for
we have as yet said nothing as to our idea of the relation
between the two texts ; the objection, in any case, would
be a pure *petitio principii* But further : it is an especially
significant, though apparently trivial, circumstance, that in
both texts a relative sentence beginning with διά follows
the ἀρετάς (or ἀρετῇ) ; if on other grounds it seems probable
that the Inscription and the Epistle are so related that either

---

[1] In 2 Pet. 1 ³ the genitive τῆς θείας δυνάμεως is of course the subject of
the middle verb δεδωρημένης.

presupposes a knowledge of the other, then we should have here the recurrence of a phenomenon often observed in parallel or internally-dependent texts, *viz.*, that consciously or unconsciously the dependent text has been so framed, by means of a slight alteration,[1] as to obliterate the traces of its origin.

We are of opinion that the parallels already indicated are sufficiently evident. Should further instances be made out, these will naturally gain a much stronger evidential value from their connection with what has been already pointed out. There is nothing remarkable in the mere fact that the Inscription contains this or that word which occurs in the Epistle. But what *is* significant, is that the same definite number of what are, in part, very characteristic expressions, is found in each of the two texts; and it is this which renders improbable the hypothesis of mere accident. Little value as we would place upon individual cases of similarity, yet in their totality these strike us as very forcible. Hence the connection also brings out the full importance of the parallels ἡ αἰώνιος βασιλεία τοῦ κυρίου and ἡ τῶν κυρίων αἰώνιος ἀρχή, an importance which appears still more decided, when we compare these parallels with, *e.g.*, those (by no means so striking) given by H. von Soden[2] in connection with the Epistle *ad loc.*, *viz.*, Heb. 12²⁸ βασιλεία ἀσάλευτος, and 2 Tim. 4¹⁸ βασιλεία ἐπουράνιος. In both of these passages the only real parallel is the word βασιλεία; but it was surely unnecessary to seek references for that.[3] The outstanding feature of the phrase in the Epistle is the term αἰώνιος, applied to *kingdom ;*[4] hence, even if the Inscription joins this term with what is only a synonym of βασιλεία, the force of

---

[1] Note that the cases following διά are different.

[2] *HC.* iii. 2² (1892), p. 199.

[3] A real biblical parallel is LXX Dan. 3³³.

[4] αἰώνιος, of which the Inscriptions contain many examples, is, in titles and solemn forms of expression, nearly similar in meaning to the Latin *perpetuus ;* ἀίδιος, in similar connections, appears to be a synonym. References in *Bull. de corr. hell.*, xii. (1888), p. 196 f. Hence, when we find the word in the Bible, we should not allow the presuppositions concerning an alleged biblical Greek to induce us to interpret it mechanically in every case,

our parallel is in no way lessened. Observe, moreover,
κυρίων ‖ κυρίου. Then, again, the likeness of πᾶσαν σπουδὴν
εἰσφέρεσθαι in the Inscription to σπουδὴν πᾶσαν παρεισενέγκαντες in the Epistle, cannot fail to strike the eye. Even at
some risk of repetition, we cannot help remarking that this
expression would not of itself prove anything, for it is common in later Greek. It is only by a false method of procedure that M. Krenkel[1] reckons it among the assonances
which are thought to prove an alleged indebtedness to
Josephus on the part of the author of the Second Epistle of
Peter. But in the present case the phrase, connected as it is
with the other parallels, has a force at least equivalent to
that ascribed to the shorter σπουδὴν πᾶσαν[2] in connection
with our Epistle's numerous unquestionable plagiarisms from
the Epistle of Jude.[3] The same will hold good, with more
or less force, of the εὐσέβεια. The statistics of the word in
the biblical writings—if we may, for once, isolate the
concept " biblical Greek "—are very remarkable. Relatively
seldom,[4] on the whole, as it occurs there, it is yet quite
frequently found in the Pastoral Epistles and the Second
Epistle of Peter ; while the Acts of the Apostles also uses
εὐσέβεια, εὐσεβεῖν and εὐσεβής.[5] Now these words occur
frequently in the Inscriptions of Asia Minor : they appear to
have been familiar terms in the religious language of the
imperial period.

The more external resemblances between the two texts
have also been indicated ; for, if the hypothesis of relationship be valid, they cannot but prove to be of interest. In
connection with this very Epistle of Peter it has been
demonstrated that the writer of it not seldom depends upon
his assiduously-used model, the Epistle of Jude, in quite an

---

[1] *Josephus und Lukas*, Leipzig, 1894, p. 350. Krenkel refers to Josephus, *Antt.* xx. 9₂; a more acute glance into Wetstein would have made him
more cautious.

[2] *Cf.* Jude³.				[3] See *e.g.*, Jülicher, *Einleitung in das N.T.*, p. 151.

[4] The same may be said of the adjective and the verb. The "Fourth
Book of Maccabees" forms an exception.

[5] These words are not found elsewhere in the New Testament.

external way. " Some peculiar expression, the purpose of
which is made plain only by the context in Jude, is retained,
or an expression is fabricated from reminiscences of the
purely local connection in that book. In 2 Pet. 2 [13], the
leading word συνευωχούμενοι is taken from Jude v. [12], and
yet its concrete relationship to the love-feasts has been allowed
to fall out, so that it is only the sound of the words which
influences the choice of the essentially different expressions
(ἀπάταις [1] instead of ἀγάπαις, σπίλοι instead of σπιλάδες)." [2]
Now, precisely as in regard to the formal assonances in the
very instructive example just given, viz. :—

Jude v. [12] :	2 Pet. 2 [13] :
οὗτοί εἰσιν οἱ ἐν ταῖς ἀγά-	σπίλοι [3] καὶ μῶμοι ἐντρυ-
παις ὑμῶν σπιλάδες, συνευω-	φῶντες ἐν ταῖς ἀπάταις αὐ-
χούμενοι ἀφόβως	τῶν συνευωχούμενοι ὑμῖν,

so might we perhaps judge of the instance ἀγάλματα—
ἐπαγγέλματα in the Decree and the Epistle respectively—
although the author would advance the point with all due
reserve. Shall we count it more probable that the επιθυμια
of the one text has exercised an outward influence on the
syntactically and lexically different επιθυμια of the other?
Once more, the use of the superlative μέγιστος in both passages cannot be ignored,—though, at first sight, such a statement may seem strange ; but its cogency will be more readily
perceived when it is remembered that the superlative of
μέγας occurs nowhere else in " the " New Testament. [4]

---

[1] [But see Revisers' text.—TR.].

[2] B. Weiss, *Lehrbuch der Einleitung in das N.T.*, Berlin, 1886, p. 439.

[3] For the accentuation see Winer-Schmiedel, § 6, 3 *b* (p. 68).

[4] Further, in the whole range of "biblical" Greek (apart from 2nd, 3rd
and 4th Maccabees), μέγιστος occurs elsewhere (if we may depend upon
Tromm) only in Job 26 [3] and 31 [28] ; moreover, the Alexandrinus reads μεγάλη
for μεγίστη in the latter passage. μέγιστος seems to be very rare also in the
Papyri of the Ptolemaic period. According to the indexes we have only the
idiomatic phrase ὃ ἐμοὶ μέγιστον ἔσται, in *Pap. Flind. Petr.*, ii., xiii. (19), *ca.*
255 B.C. (Mahaffy, ii. [45]), and τῆς μεγίστης θεᾶς "Ηρας, *Pap. Par.*, 15, 120
B.C. (*Notices*, xviii. 2, p. 219), as a solemn designation, most probably a
fixed form of expression, similar to that in our Inscription.

Is it possible to hold that the similarities in the two texts are merely accidental? We have again and again pondered this question, but have always come to the conclusion that it must be answered in the negative. Doubtless, the deciding of such questions always implies a certain inner susceptibility, and is thus subjective. But here, as we judge, there are objective grounds to proceed upon. We would endeavour, therefore, to define more precisely the very general impression made by the two texts, by saying that they must be inter-related in some way.

Now the Decree of Stratonicea is undoubtedly older than the Second Epistle of Peter. From its contents, we might infer its date to be previous to 22 A.D.; from its form, somewhat later. But even if the Inscription were of later date than the Epistle, it would be an improbable hypothesis that the former was in its contents dependent upon the latter. The dependence must rather be, if the relationship is granted, on the side of the Epistle. Hence the general statement made above may be specialised thus far: the beginning of the Second Epistle of Peter must be in some way dependent upon forms of expression occurring in the Decree of Stratonicea.

We speak of the *forms of expression* of the Decree. For it is not urgently necessary to assert a dependence upon the Decree itself. Of course, it is certainly possible that the writer of the Epistle may have read the Inscription. Assuredly Paul is not the only Christian of the century of the New Testament who read "heathen" inscriptions, and reflected thereon. The inscriptions, official and private, found in the streets and market-places, in temples and upon tombs, would be the only reading of the great majority of people who could read. Of what we call classical literature, the greater number would hardly ever read anything at all. The heads of the Christian brotherhoods who were versed in literature were influenced, in respect of their range both of words and thoughts, by their sacred books, but manifestly also by the forms of expression common in their locality. The present writer would count the expressions

before us, found in the Inscription of Stratonicea, as belonging to the solemn forms of the official liturgical language of
Asia Minor.　From the nature of the case it seems certain
that they were not used for the first time in this Decree in
honour of Zeus Panhemerios and Hekate.　Conceivable
though it be that the author of the Second Epistle of Peter
had adopted them directly from the Carian Inscription,[1] yet
we would confine ourselves to the more cautious conjecture
that the author of the Epistle, like the author of the Decree
before him, simply availed himself of the familiar forms and
formulæ of religious emotion.[2]　The mosaic-like character
of the writer's work, specially evident in his relation to the
Epistle of Jude, is illustrated once more by the facts just
adduced.

Should our conjecture hold good—particularly, of course,
if a direct dependence upon the Decree of Stratonicea could
be made probable—we should have a new factor for the
solution of the problem as to the origin of the Epistle.
Certainly the hypothesis of an Egyptian origin, which has
gained great favour in recent years, is not confirmed by the
local colouring, which belongs to Asia Minor; we would,
however, refrain meanwhile from categorically asserting
that it originated in Asia Minor,[3] as we have not yet mastered

---

[1] The above-discussed series of purely formal assonances might be put
forward as supporting this.

[2] How such formulæ were used, spontaneously, so to speak, in the
writings of other representatives of the new Faith, may be seen, *e.g.*, in the
relationship between certain Pauline passages and the solemn words made
known to us by an Inscription of Halicarnassus of the early imperial period :
see C. T. Newton, *A History of Discoveries at Halicarnassus, Cnidus and
Branchidae*, ii. 2, London, 1863, p. 695.—*Cf.* also W. M. Ramsay, *The Greek
of the Early Church and the Pagan Ritual*, in the *Expository Times*, vol. x.,
p. 9 ff.—A similar instance from ancient times has been noted by R. Kittel in
ZAW. xviii. (1898), p. 149 ff. : Isaiah 45 [1] ff. shows dependence upon the court-
phraseology made known to us by the clay-cylinders of Cyrus.

[3] The theory becomes still more probable when we compare the above
conjecture with what Th. Zahn, *Geschichte des Neutestamentl. Kanons*, i. 1,
Erlangen, 1888, p. 312 ff., says about the locality in which the Epistle "was
first circulated, and gained the esteem of the church"; but see A. Harnack,
Das N.T. um das Jahr 200, Freiburg i. B., 1889, p. 85 f.

the lexical relations of the Epistle. It would at least be
necessary to inquire how far its peculiar vocabulary has
points of contact with that of literary sources (of the imperial period) from Egypt,[1] or Asia Minor,[2] including those
of the Papyri and the Inscriptions.

5. WHITE ROBES AND PALMS.

"After these things I saw, and behold, a great multitude, which no man could number, out of every nation,
and of all tribes and peoples and tongues, standing before
the throne and before the Lamb, arrayed in white robes,
and palms in their hands ; and they cry with a great voice,
saying, Salvation unto our God which sitteth on the throne,
and unto the Lamb." So does the early Christian seer
depict those who have been made perfect, who have come
out of the great tribulation, and now serve God day and
night in His temple. Few Bible passages have taken such
hold of the everyday Christian consciousness, few have been
inscribed so hopefully on the impassive tombstone, as these
chaste verses from the mysterious final pages of the Holy
Book. So deeply have they entered into the sphere of
religious ideas, that, generally speaking, we are not struck
by the thought, how eloquent of ancient days is the colouring of the artist who created the picture. The inner
beauty of the thought keeps in abeyance any impression
which its form might suggest ; the captivated spirit even

---

[1] Of course, such expressions as may probably seem to be derived from
the Alexandrian translation of the O.T. would not prove anything regarding
the hypothetical Egyptian origin of the Epistle.

[2] So far as we are able, from a general knowledge of a portion of
the Inscriptions of Asia Minor, to judge, the lexical relations of the Epistle
do, indeed, point to Asia Minor or Syria. He gives but one example here,
which he would likewise attribute to the fixed phraseology of solemn speech.
In 2 Pet. 1⁴ we find the peculiar phrase, ἵνα . . γένησθε θείας κοινωνοὶ φύσεως ;
with this compare a passage from a religious Inscription of King Antiochus I.
of Kommagene (middle of 1st cent. B.C. ; discovered at Selik), viz., πᾶσιν ὅσοι
φύσεως κοινωνοῦντες ἀνθρω[πί]νης (in Humann and Puchstein's Reisen in Kleinasien und Nordsyrien, Textband, p. 371). The resemblance had already struck
the editors of the Inscription. The Kommagenian Inscriptions, moreover,
afford other materials for the history of the language of early Christianity.

of the modern man readily and unconstrainedly accepts the unaccustomed scenery, which yet has its proper place only under the eternal blue of the eastern sky, or in the serene halls of an ancient temple. The pious Christian of the times of decadence did not depict things to come in the forms of the pitiful present; he saw them rather in the crystal mirror of the authoritative past.

The exegetes of Rev. 7 [9 ff.] have striven, in widely divergent ways, to explain the peculiar colouring of this celestial scenery. How does it come about that the adornment of the blessed choir of the saints before the throne of God should be portrayed exactly as it is? The explanation of the *individual* elements provides no difficulty.[1] The *white robes*, of course, according to the bold symbolism of the text itself, are connected with the cleansing power of the blood of the Lamb (v. [14]); and, even without this special reference, they have already a distinct and well-known sense (see 6 [11]). Again, the expression *palms in their hands* is familiar to the reader of the Bible as a sign of festive joy. Attempts have been made to supply a more definite background for this latter feature, now from Jewish, now from Hellenic, ideas. On the one hand, the *palms* have been looked upon as suggesting a comparison of the heavenly glory with the Feast of Tabernacles; on the other, they have been taken as an allusion to the palm-twigs bestowed upon the victor in the Greek games.

We would not deny that such explanations, so far as concerns the details of a picture which is not after all so difficult to grasp, are quite adequate. But they do not elucidate the scene *in its entirety*. How did the writer come to bring together precisely these two features? And how comes it that both are assigned to the *choir* of the blessed, which, in alternate song with the angels, raises a hallelujah to the Most High? If we knew of no historical circumstance which might suggest an answer to these questions, we might naturally enough infer that the writer of the Apocalypse had himself composed his picture from

[1] For what follows *cf.* F. Düsterdieck, Meyer, xvi. [4] (1887), p. 289.

diverse elements. But we are of opinion that there are good grounds for the supposition that the portrayer of the πανήγυρις ἐπουράνιος had availed himself of the scenery of a religious ceremony with which he was familiar.

In the Inscription of Stratonicea in Caria (already mentioned several times), belonging to the beginning of the imperial period,[1] the inhabitants of the city, out of gratitude to Zeus Panhemerios and Hekate, resolve that, in honour of these deities, thirty boys of noble parentage, under the leadership of the παιδονόμος and the παιδοφύλακες, shall daily sing a prescribed *hymnus* in the bouleuterion—*clothed in white and crowned with a twig, likewise holding a twig in their hands.* This custom would hardly be inaugurated by the piety of the people of Stratonicea; such choirs of sacred singers, similarly accoutred, were, without doubt, also to be seen elsewhere in the Greek districts of Asia Minor.

Here, then, in all probability, we have the model by which the writer of the Apocalypse was consciously or unconsciously guided; and those belonging to Asia Minor who read his book—a book full of the local colour of that region —would grasp his imagery with special facility. What they beheld in heaven was something that had, by association with their native soil, become familiar and dear to them— a choir of pious singers in festive attire; and if they had an ear to hear what the Spirit said to the churches, they could also, of course, surmise that in this instance what came from holy lips was a new song.

---

[1] See pp. 96 f. and 360 ff. The passage runs: ... λευχιμονοῦντας καὶ ἐστεφανωμένους θαλλοῦ ἔχοντας δὲ μετὰ χῖρας [for this construction of μετά, which is found elsewhere in the idiom μετὰ χεῖρας ἔχειν (W. Schmid, *Der Atticismus*, iii., p. 285), *cf.* the variant of LXX Gen. 43 [21], τίς ἐνέβαλεν ἡμῖν μετὰ χεῖρας τὸ ἀργύριον, Codd. 31 and 83, Field, i., p. 61] ὁμοίως θαλλοὺς οἵτινες συνπαρόν[των κα]ὶ κιθαριστοῦ καὶ κήρυκος ᾄσονται ὕμνον. The original orthography has been retained. On the fact *cf.* the remark of the scholiast upon Theocr. *Id.* ii. 12, quoted by the editor, Waddington, iii. 2, p. 143: οἱ παλαιοὶ τὴν Ἑκάτην τρίμορφον ἔγραφον χρυσεοσάνδαλον καὶ λευχείμονα καὶ μήκωνας ταῖν χεροῖν ἔχουσαν καὶ λαμπάδας ἡμμένας.

THE END.

I.

INDEX OF GREEK WORDS AND PHRASES.

(371)

-οῦς, 188.
ὀφειλή, 221.
ὀφείλω, 191.
ὀφείλω ἀμαρτίαν, 225
ὀφίλατε, 191.
ὔφιλεν, 191.
ὀψώνιον, 148, 266.
ὀψώνιον λαμβάνω, 266.

π for ⅃ (?), 189.
(παδώσω), 192.
παντεπόπτης, 293.
παντεφόπτης, 293.
παντοκράτωρ, 283.
παπίπετον, 355.
παραγενάμενος, 191.
παράδεισος, 148 f.
παράδετε, 192.
παραίτιος ἀγαθῶν, 253.
παρακατατίθομαι, 193.
παράκλησις, 308.
παραλογεία, 143.
παραλογεύω, 143.
παρεπιδημέω, 149.
παρεπίδημος, 149.
πάρεσις, 266.
παρέχομαι ἐμαυτόν, 254.
παρίστημι θυσίαν, 254.
πάροικος, 227 f.
Παρταρᾶς, 188 f.
παστοφορίον, 149 f.
πατροπαράδοτος, 266.
Παῦλος, 316.
πεῖν, 182 f.
περιδέξιον, 150.
τὰ περίεργα, 323.
περιεργάζομαι, 323.
περιεργία, 323.
περιπατεῖν ἀξίως, 194.
περίστασις, 150.
περιτέμνω, 151 f.
περιτομή, 152.
ἀπὸ πέρυσι, 221.
πῆχυς, 153 f.
πῖν, 183.
πίνω, 182 f.
πίστις, 79.
πλῆθος, 232 f.
πλήρωμα, 110.
ποτισμός, 154.
πρᾶγμα, 233.
πρᾶγμα ἔχω πρός τινα, 233.
πράκτωρ, 154.
πρᾶξις, 323.
πρεσβύτεροι, οἱ, 154 f., 233 f.
πρεσβύτεροι ἱερεῖς, 154 f., 233 f.
πρεσβύτερος, 154 f., 233 f.
πρεσβυτικόν, 156.
κατὰ τὰ προγεγραμμένα, 250.
προγέγραπται, 250.
προεγαμοῦσαν, 191.
πρόθεσις, 157.
πρόθεσις ἄρτων, 157.
μετὰ πάσης προθυμίας, 254.
προσευχή, 222.

προσρέπω, 357.
προσρίπτω, 357.
προστίθεσθαι, 67.
προστρέπω, 357.
προφήτης, 235 f.
πταίω, 68.
πυρράκης, 157.
Πυρρίας, 336.

σ interchanging with ζ, 185.
-σαν for -ν, 191.
Σαούλ, 316.
Σαῦλος ὁ καὶ Παῦλος, 313 f.
Σεβ., 218.
Σεβαστή, 218 f.
σεριαβεβωθ, 333.
Σιλας, 315.
Σιλουανός, 315.
Σίμων, 315, 316.
Σινμαλκουή, 321.
σιτομετρέω, 158.
σιτομετρία [?], 158.
σιτομέτριον, 158.
σιφωνολογεία, 219.
σκεοφυλακα [?], 158.
σκευοφυλάκιον, 158.
σκευοφύλαξ, 158.
σμαράγδινος, 267.
Σμύρνα, 185.
Σμυρναῖος, 185.
σουδάριον, 223.
σοφίζομαι, 292.
σπείρας, 186.
σπείρης, 186.
σπουδὴν εἰσφέρομαι, 364.
σπυρίδιον, 158.
σπυρίς, 158, 185.
στάσις, 158 f.
στεφάνιον, 345.
στεφανόω, 345.
στήλωμα, 159.
στήλωσις, 159.
στίγματα, 349 f.
στρατεία, 181 f.
στρατία, 181 f.
συγγενής, 159.
σύμβιος, 283.
συμβιόω, 293.
συμβούλιον, 238.
Συμεών, 316.
ἐκ συμφώνου, 255.
σὺν καί, 265.
συνέδριον τῶν πρεσβυτέρων, 156.
συνέκτροφος, 310.
συνέσχαν, 191.
συνέχω, 160.
συνσείω, 290.
συντρίβω, 287.
σύντροφος, 305, 310 f.
σύντροφος τοῦ βασιλέως, 311 f.
συστρέφω, 287.
σφραγίζω, 238 f.
σφουρίδιον, 185.
σφυρίς, 158, 185.
σφυρίτιν, 185.

σῶμα, 160.
σωματοφύλαξ, 98.
σωτήρ, 83.

τ for ⊓, 189.
ταβαωθ, 333.
ταμεῖον, 182 f.
ταμιεῖον, 182 f.
-ταρα, 189.
Ταραθ, 189.
ταστας, 357.
ταφή, 355 f.
ταχύ, 289.
τέκνα ἀπωλείας, 163, 165.
τέκνα τοῦ διαβόλου, 163.
τέκνα τῆς ἐπαγγελίας, 163
τέκνα κατάρας, 164.
τέκνα ὀργῆς, 164.
τέκνα πορνείας, 165.
τέκνα τῆς σοφίας, 163.
τέκνα ὑπακοῆς, 163.
τέκνα φωτός, 163.
τέκνον, 161 f.
τέτευχα, 190.
τήρησις, 267.
τιθέω, 192 f.
τίθημι, 192.
τιθῶ, 192.
τίθω, 192.
τόπος, 267.
τυγχάνω, 190.
Τύρος, 332.
οὐχ ὁ τυχών, 255.

υ = Heb. ō, 332.
-υθ, 332.
υἱοθεσία, 239.
καθ' υἱοθεσίαν, 239.
υἱοὶ τοῦ αἰῶνος τούτου, 163
υἱοὶ τῆς ἀναστάσεως, 163.
υἱοὶ τῆς ἀπειθείας, 163.
υἱοὶ ἀποικίας, 165.
υἱοὶ τῆς βασιλείας, 162.
υἱοὶ βροντῆς, 162.
υἱοὶ τῆς διαθήκης, 163.
υἱοὶ δυνάμεως, 165.
υἱοὶ ἡμέρας, 163.
υἱοὶ θεοῦ, 73.
υἱοὶ τοῦ νυμφῶνος, 162.
υἱοὶ παρανόμων, 165.
υἱοὶ τοῦ πονηροῦ, 162.
υἱοὶ τῶν προφητῶν, 163.
υἱοὶ τοῦ φωτός, 163.
υἱός, 161 f.
υἱὸς ἀνομίας, 165.
υἱὸς τῆς ἀπωλείας, 163.
υἱὸς Ἀφροδισιέων, 166.
υἱὸς γεένης, 162.
υἱὸς τῆς γερουσίας, 165.
υἱὸς τοῦ δήμου, 165.
υἱὸς διαβόλου, 163.
υἱὸς εἰρήνης, 163.
υἱὸς θανάτου, 165.
υἱὸς θεοῦ, 73, 83, 131, 166 f.
υἱὸς παρακλήσεως, 163, 307 f.
υἱὸς τῆς πόλεως, 165.
υἱὸς τῆς ὑπερηφανίας, 165.

II.

INDEX OF SUBJECTS.

[1] On the same characteristic in Christian liturgies, see F. Probst, *Liturgie des vierten Jahrhunderts und deren Reform*, Münster i. W., 1893, p. 344 ff.

III.

INDEX OF TEXTS.

GENESIS.

Reference	Page
1^1	284
1^4	286
$1^{16\,f.}$	289
1^{17}	289
1^{18}	286
$2^{8\,ff.}$	148
$6^{16\,[15]}$	128
$14^{19\cdot 22}$	284
17^{11}	153, 351
17^{12}	152
18^{17}	168
22^{17}	207
23^4	149
23^{11}	164
23^{16}	260
25^{25}	157
32^{10}	120
34^{29}	160
36^6	160
36^{24}	160
40^{21}	267
41^1	258
43^{21}	370
45^5	258
47^{12}	158
47^{18}	123
$50^{2\,f.}$	120

EXODUS.

Reference	Page
4^{26}	152
$5^{6\cdot 10\cdot 14\cdot 15\cdot 19}$	112
$13^{9\cdot 16}$	351
$14^{15\,f.}$	284
15^8	285
15^{18}	283
17^5	120
20^{17}	293
21^{20}	120
$25^{16\,[17]}$	125 f.
$25^{20\,[21]}$	128
25^{30}	157
26^{34}	127
30^{25}	125
31^{10}	141
35^{22}	150
37^6	125, 127
38^5	127
39^1	141
$39^{41\,[19]}$	141

LEVITICUS.

Reference	Page
2^{11}	135 f.
4^{18}	123
$13^{41\cdot 42\cdot 43}$	88
16^{14}	127
19^{23}	151
$19^{27\,f.}$	351
19^{28}	349
19^{36}	116
21^4	106
$21^{5\,f.}$	351
24^{16}	288
25^{10}	101, 138
$25^{10\cdot 11\cdot 12\cdot 13\cdot 15\cdot}$	100 f.
25^{23}	106, 229
25^{30}	106
27	101

NUMBERS.

Reference	Page
$4^{12\cdot 26}$	141
7^5	141
14^{27}	110
14^{28}	205
16^{22}	327
23^{19}	199
27^{16}	327
31^{50}	150
$33^{27\,f.}$	189
36^{11}	164

DEUTERONOMY.

Reference	Page
1^{16}	230
1^{31}	199
4^{12}	114
7^{26}	310
10^{16}	151
10^{17}	283
12^3	310
12^{32}	114
$14^{1\,f.}$	351
15^2	123
25^2	165
25^{15}	116
26^{14}	136 f.
27^{26}	248
28^{58}	282
30^6	151

JOSHUA.

Reference	Page
5^{12}	136

JUDGES.

Reference	Page
5^{10}	160
5^{14}	110, 112
19^{10}	160
19^{22}	165

1 SAMUEL.

Reference	Page
$4^{2\cdot 3}$	68
$16^{12}, 17^{42}$	157
17^{22}	158
17^{43}	120
20^{13}	90
20^{31}	165
21^6	157
28^2	98

2 SAMUEL.

Reference	Page
2^7	165
7^{14}	120
$12^5, 13^{28}$	165
22^3	91
22^{16}	98
23^{21}	120

1 KINGS.

Reference	Page
$4^{27\,[31]}$	292
$7^{2\cdot 38}$	153
19^{11}	287
20^{35}	163
$20^{35\,ff.}$	351

2 KINGS.

Reference	Page
$2^{3\cdot 5\cdot 7}$	163
$15^{16\,ff.}$	310
18^{14}	102
$24^{18\,f.}, 25^{19}$	110 f.
25^8	310

1 CHRONICLES.

Reference	Page
5^{10}	139
$9^{26\cdot 33}$	150
11^{23}	120
16^{25}	283
18^{17}	115
28^2	158
28^9	190
28^{11}	127
29^4	260, 262